SIMPSON

IMPRINT IN HUMANITIES

The humanities endowment
by Sharon Hanley Simpson and
Barclay Simpson honors

MURIEL CARTER HANLEY

whose intellect and sensitivity
have enriched the many lives
that she has touched.

The publisher and the University of California Press Foundation gratefully acknowledge the generous support of the Simpson Imprint in Humanities.

Their Own Best Creations

FEMINIST MEDIA HISTORIES

Shelley Stamp, Series Editor

Their Own Best Creations

Women Writers in Postwar Television

Annie Berke

UNIVERSITY OF CALIFORNIA PRESS

University of California Press
Oakland, California

© 2022 by Annie Berke

Library of Congress Cataloging-in-Publication Data

Names: Berke, Annie, 1985– author.
Title: Their own best creations : women writers in postwar
   television / Annie Berke.
Other titles: Feminist media histories (Series) ; 1.
Description: Oakland, California : University of California Press,
   [2022] | Series: Feminist media histories ; 1 | Includes bibliographical
   references and index.
Identifiers: LCCN 2021033062 (print) | LCCN 2021033063 (ebook) |
   ISBN 9780520300781 (cloth) | ISBN 9780520300798 (paperback) |
   ISBN 9780520972025 (epub)
Subjects: LCSH: Kallen, Lucille. | Berg, Gertrude, 1899–1966. | Lynch,
   Peg, 1916–2015. | Phillips, Irna, 1901–1973. | Women television
   writers—United States—Biography. | Television and women—United
   States—History. | Television editors. | BISAC: PERFORMING ARTS /
   Television / History & Criticism | HISTORY / Women
Classification: LCC PN1992.4.A2 B467 2022 (print) |
   LCC PN1992.4.A2 (ebook) | DDC 812/.025099287—dc23
LC record available at https://lccn.loc.gov/2021033062
LC ebook record available at https://lccn.loc.gov/2021033063

Manufactured in the United States of America

30 29 28 27 26 25 24 23 22
10 9 8 7 6 5 4 3 2 1

To my family

Contents

Illustrations

Acknowledgments

The last ten years, I have had countless imaginary coffee dates with the women writers of postwar television, and always, I have been confronted with the same two questions: Why does a woman write, and why does she stop? In the case of the women of *Their Own Best Creations*, they divided their time between their personal and professional responsibilities while striving to distinguish themselves in an intense, ever-changing job market. That is why, first, I want to thank the subjects of this book for their determination, their humor, and their ingenuity: it has been a responsibility and a privilege to tell their stories as best as I know how. Being able to speak with writer Peg Lynch, her daughter, Astrid King, and Marian Cockrell's daughter, Amanda Cockrell, were some of the greatest pleasures in this process. It was an honor to meet and spend time with Ms. Lynch in particular, her warmth and generosity coming through in person as much as it came through in her shows.

Time and again, for the women of *Their Own Best Creations*, it was their communities of peers, supervisors, friends, and family who made the work possible, and such has been the case for me. This project began at Yale as my doctoral dissertation, so I want to give special thanks to my mentors, Charles Musser and J. D. Connor. Charlie instilled in me the historian's responsibility to track changing time, and J. D. taught me how to read social forms into cultural objects, and both have been invaluable in the growth of this manuscript and my own thinking as a scholar. More thanks go to my dissertation committee: Laura Wexler,

Jane Gaines, and Ronald Gregg, whose insights inspired me to rejoice in what was working in the project and gave me the confidence to work on what wasn't. Much appreciation also goes to Dudley Andrew, Mary Lui, Joanne Meyerowitz, and Katie Trumpener, for their unofficial mentorship, both administrative and intellectual, as well as one-woman department "fixers" Katherine Germano, Victorine Shepard, and Susan Shand. I am deeply indebted to Hollins University for supporting the project while I was on faculty and to my colleagues there, who shaped my thinking as a teacher, writer, and higher education professional. These include Rebekah Chappell, Amy Gerber-Stroh, Julie Pfeiffer, Lanie Presswood, Darla Schumm, and Elise Schweitzer. Michelle De Groot, you have been my book-writing brother-in-arms, and I couldn't have asked for a better one. I am grateful to my students at both Hollins and Yale for being sharp and curious, inviting me to keep rediscovering why I love this particular kind of hard work.

Thanks go to my friends and colleagues who encouraged me throughout this process—Taylor Arnold, Jenna Beatrice, Jordan Brower, Maya Cantu, Marc Francis, Jessica Hertz, Erin Kilpatrick, Najwa Mayer, Devin McGeehan-Muchmore, Yahel Matalon, Mihaela Mihailova, Tessa Paneth-Pollak, Teresa Pham-Carsillo, and Lauren Tilton. My colleagues in television studies, including Phoebe Bronstein, Catherine Martin, and Molly Schneider, as well as members of the SCMS Comedy scholarly interest group, have all motivated me with their exciting and important work. As for those who read drafts and offered constructive feedback, what can I say to Claudia Calhoun, Joshua Glick, Maggie Hennefeld, Nicholas Miller, and Masha Shpolberg? You did more than track changes in my prose—as needed, you proofread my spirit. Gratitude is due to Jon Kraszewski, Suzanne Leonard, Erin Hill, Christina Lane, Elana Levine, and John Mark Ockerbloom for their valuable guidance and support from the book's beginnings into its final stretch. I also want to thank my fellow writers and editors at the *Los Angeles Review of Books*, especially Boris Drayluk, whose work has inspired me to consider why the humanities matter, both within and outside the academy. Though I started this project almost a decade prior to my time at *LARB*, I know this book in its final incarnation would not be the same without these collaborations.

I want to acknowledge the archive professionals who have sustained my project and made the work possible, in particular Joanne Lammers, formerly of the Writers' Guild Foundation, Hilary Swett of the Writers' Guild, Mark Quigley at UCLA, Nicolette A. Dobrowolski at the Gertrude Berg Papers, and Linda Long and Elizabeth Peterson at the Peg Lynch

Papers for making the research process easy. Grants from the Popular Culture Association–American Culture Association, the John Morton Blum Fellowship for Graduate Research in American History and Culture, the Beinecke Library, the University of Wisconsin–Madison Library, Yale's Department of American Studies, and Hollins University all helped to pay for my research travel and made these trips possible.

To Raina Polivka and Shelley Stamp: thank you for helping me see my project anew and in fresh, important ways. You have both been my champions through this endeavor, and I cannot thank you enough. My anonymous readers provided their expertise and offered crucial guidance for strengthening the work, so thanks to them as well.

And to my family: this book is for my grandmothers who loved their families and their work, and to my grandfathers, who were their wives' partners in all things. This is for my in-laws, for the workspaces they set up in their homes over too many holiday and summer breaks. This is for my parents, who have never counted me out, for Aunt Judy and her unflagging cheerleading, and to all three for the hours of childcare that made my revisions possible. "*The book*," as we have referred to it for so long, could not have happened without you. Finally, this is for my Swiss-Army knife of a husband, who is my editor, my best friend, and my home. And, last but never least, to our own Best Creation.

Introduction

On September 15, 1952, *I Love Lucy* (CBS, 1951–1957) aired "Job Switching" for the first time. In this episode, Lucy Ricardo (Lucille Ball) and Ethel Mertz (Vivian Vance) and their respective husbands, Ricky (Desi Arnaz) and Fred (William Frawley), disagree on whether men or women have it harder. In order to test their theories, the wives go to work, while the husbands take over the responsibilities at home. Lucy and Ethel get jobs at a candy factory, where their task is to wrap the bonbons traveling down a conveyor belt (Figure 1). When the belt speeds up, the women cannot keep up with their duties and hide the chocolates in their blouses, hats, and mouths. They are presented as incapable buffoons, the comedy a clear backlash against the capable "Rosie the Riveter" figure central to the war effort a decade earlier.[1] The writing is literally on the wall: the sign behind them says "Danger," while the door on the right side of the screen reads "Kitchen": when a woman leaves the home, the results can only be disastrous. This danger is averted, however, with the episode's conclusion, the gendered distribution of labor happily restored—the women at home and the men back at work.

Though the comedy upholds a return to order by episode's end, the assembly line sequence contains multiple and, at times, contradictory meanings. Many interpretations of this famous scene have focused on performance. Two women performers simultaneously embedded in and resisting the "machinery" of collaborative labor through failure speaks

FIGURE 1. Lucy (Lucille Ball) and Ethel (Vivian Vance) struggle to keep up with the pace of their work in "Job Switching," *I Love Lucy.* © 1952 CBS Television.

to Patricia Mellencamp's point that "if Lucy's plots for ambition and fame *narratively* failed, with the result that she was held, often gratefully, to domesticity, *performatively* they succeeded."[2] The joke may be on Lucy and Ethel, but never on Lucille Ball or Vivian Vance, who triumphantly ape failure and, in the process, make fun of (and with) a dumb, automated machine. Sianne Ngai echoes this sentiment by asking rhetorically: "Although Lucy Ricardo's efforts to break into showbiz by way of multiple odd jobs never succeed, do not these failures testify constantly to the virtuosity of the professional actress Lucille Ball?"[3] Through her impeccable execution of Lucy Ricardo the klutz, Lucille Ball establishes herself as a comic virtuoso. The specter of Charles Chaplin's Tramp from *Modern Times* (1936) looms, but the work-weary Everyman is replaced by a contemporary Everywoman whose work is never done. In performing this homage to Chaplin, Ball inducts herself into a distinguished comic lineage.

But the Tramp is not the only invisible figure haunting the comedy: there is also the aforementioned Madelyn Pugh, *I Love Lucy*'s woman staff writer, who worked alongside writing partner Bob Carroll and producer Jess Oppenheimer. With Pugh at its interpretative heart, this assembly-line slapstick can also be understood as an industry artifact: that of the woman writer rushing to get the words typed in time. The relentlessly fast-paced production schedule was a hallmark of television writing in the network era (1952–1980s), writer Dorothy Foote (*My Three Sons*) remarking that, "One learns quickly that time is of the essence."[4] As Norman Lear (*All in the Family, One Day at a Time*) would recall his early career: "We were all last minute writers," while writer Horton Foote (*The Philco Television Playhouse, The United States Steel Hour*) moved on to stage and film writing, because television writing "would be death. You'd be churning things out, week after week after week. You're just bound to go crazy."[5] And as *I Love Lucy*'s Madelyn Pugh details in her memoir, she and Carroll hoped the show would be interrupted by news coverage "so [they] could get a week ahead because no one did reruns in those days."[6] She describes breaking into their office and working through holidays in the desperate effort to keep up.

This stringent set of professional expectations and constraints are only compounded for women balancing work and family. Pugh cracks wise about a different episode in which Lucy "likes having a career, but finds it keeps her from spending time with her son so she quits," adding, dryly, "I wonder where that idea came from."[7] Pugh quit the entertainment business for a short time to stay home with her children, but she returned to Ball's employ, having missed her work too much to stay away. Lucy Ricardo's desire to work, her containment to the home, and the meta-escape through Ball's comic stardom coincide with Pugh's personal narrative and her authorial perspective. The scene internalizes the tensions of Pugh's own choices: it takes a woman's desire to work outside the home, puts it through the conservative ideological "machine" of the self-contained sitcom, and pops out an ending in which Lucy and Ethel do what Pugh and Ball did not, namely return to the kitchen.[8]

Pugh is just one of the many women who wrote during the earliest days of commercial television, contributing to the formation of television as both an industry and an art form. Women worked as freelance or staff writers and story editors, and some even created and managed their own shows decades before the advent of the term "showrunner," defined by Michael Z. Newman and Elana Levine as "potentially an *auteur*: an artist of unique vision whose experiences and personality are expressed through storytelling craft, and whose presence in cultural discourses functions to produce authority for" the medium.[9] In these different capacities, women writers, writer-producers, and story department professionals forged key genres for the small screen: comedy-variety, family serial, daytime soap, suspense anthology. Postwar women television writers between the years 1949 to 1963 navigated an industry that sought to capitalize on female viewership while keeping executive power largely in men's hands. These women, including, but not restricted to, Lucille Kallen, Selma Diamond, Gertrude Berg, Peg Lynch, Joan Harrison, Charlotte Armstrong, and Irna Phillips, were, by and large, white, middle-class, and educated. Through modes of communication and self-fashioning, women television writers often forged public personas that downplayed issues of craft or artistry in favor of traditionally feminine virtues such as collegiality, emotionality, and competence when caring for others. Their statements on marriage and family ranged from the glowing to the sharply critical. Those writers who were married with children explained how their experiences made them ideally equipped to write for the new domestic medium of television; those who were single mourned or mocked their unmarried state, suggesting that their loss could be television's gain. By speaking regularly and publicly about their male collaborators—husbands, cowriters, industry allies—women writers could show how well they played with others, particularly when those others were men.[10]

Women writers' stories often followed the misadventures of full-time homemakers. However, as we see from the candy assembly line sequence in *I Love Lucy*, the housewife character can be both the stay-at-home matriarch and the creative professional in disguise. This interpretative doubleness serves as a testament to the *scripted lives* women television writers led: writing scripts about marriage and motherhood that obliquely addressed their shared professional travails, while crafting public personas that drew on dominant cultural idioms of white, middle-class femininity. Women writers' creative work and their personal personas were intertwined, mutually sustaining narratives, carefully packaged for the benefit of dubious industry executives and a general viewing public.

The best-known women writers in television reconciled cultural contradictions in their public lives: speaking confidently but modestly, being forceful yet gentle, and making holding down the full-time jobs of writer, wife, and mother look easy and intuitive. Many writers lived out loud and in line with the genres they innovated, leaning into their roles as nervy goofballs, tireless wives and mothers, heartsick spinsters, and unflappable ice blondes.[11] As *All My Children* creator Agnes Nixon described her protégée, soap opera pioneer Irna Phillips (chapter 4), Phillips was "her own best creation," weaving the story of her personal tragedies and triumphs as a kind of real-life soap.[12] Often, women writers' scripts document the strain of performing postwar femininity more directly than their interviews or publicity materials might permit. In his theorization of production culture, John Thornton Caldwell asserts that "although critics seldom acknowledge film/video workers as theorists or ethnographers, these workers do in fact produce 'self-ethnographic' accounts and daily deploy . . . *critical industrial practices.*"[13] By rereading women writers' scripts as "self-ethnographic," a common set of professional objectives and narrative themes emerges across writer, series, and genre, the complicated, often ambivalent, gender politics of early television and of postwar culture on full display.

This study stands at the intersection of television studies and media industry studies, leveraging the latter to produce new readings of both famous and lesser-known programs of the period. Commercial television underwent a series of important shifts over the course of its first ten years, most notably the gradual move from New York to Los Angeles and the shift from mostly live broadcasts to pre-filmed content.[14] With these changes came even bigger changes in genre, aesthetic, and the talent pool from which the industry drew. The scripted lives of women writers in postwar television come into focus when viewed through the lens of these industry changes and the understanding that the ground was always shifting beneath writers' feet. Timothy Havens, Amanda D. Lotz, and Serra Tinic compare the movements of institutions and individuals by calling them, respectively, corporate *strategies* and subjects' *tactics*. Individual tactics are "the ways in which cultural workers seek to negotiate, and at times perhaps subvert, the constraints imposed by institutional interests."[15] The media object internalizes this tension between strategy and tactic, pointing to the many voices and interests that shape the politics of television programming. Many postwar television histories frame the period through the lens of the corporate need to sell homogeneity and ivory soap. Accounts that emphasize institutional strategies can miss how women writers tactically made space in their scripts to argue for their own relevance to the television industry, ventriloquizing their arguments through fictionalized characters and premises.

The primary platform from which writers could make their cases was growing fast. Television set ownership increased quickly over the course of the decade, the medium became what Anna McCarthy calls a "citizen machine," a force with the power to sustain—but also to potentially undermine—dominant ideologies.[16] Under 1 percent of American residences had televisions in 1946 and only 9 percent in 1950. But by 1955, special deals, financing, and access to personal credit made television ownership accessible to a large swath of middle-class America, and the number climbed to 65 percent of American residences in 1955 and 88 percent in 1960.[17] Lynn Spigel explains that in the years following World War II, "consumer spending rose by 60 percent ... most significant[ly] ... in household furnishings and consumer appliances, which increased by 240 percent. In this land of plenty, television would become one of the most sought-after products."[18] These statistics speak to television's growing audience and, with it, the growing centrality of the medium in everyday life.

Sponsors pursued women viewer-consumers in particular, not only by sponsoring soap operas and talk shows in the daytime hours, but also through putting money into prime-time programming. Revlon bankrolled the popular game show, *The $64,000 Question* (CBS, 1955–1958), spending a "whopping 25 percent of its retail sales on advertising and promotion" with the express purpose of cornering the female demographic.[19] Meanwhile, a Purex-sponsored daytime special on sexual frigidity was so popular that women audiences demanded it be rebroadcast in the evening for men to watch too.[20] Just as the home was treated as the woman's domain, so too was the television, Spigel describing how "illustrations and advertisements in women's magazines ... suggested ways for women to control their husband's sexual desires through television" and that "television ... was shown to contain men's pleasure by circumscribing it within the confines of domestic space and placing it under the auspices of women."[21] Women viewers were treated as the keepers of the set and were thus valued by sponsors and networks alike. The tastes and preferences of women were paramount, whether that meant agencies sponsoring women's preferred genres or networks finding a prominent place to air women's favorite stars.

The increasing visibility of television's homegrown personalities, largely imported from film and radio, contributed to the popular curiosity around how television shows were made and what was happening behind the scenes.[22] This interest extended beyond the fandoms of individual performers to include attention to writers and producers with profiles and interviews published in publications ranging from industry trade paper *Variety* to Norman Rockwell's magazine of choice, the *Saturday Evening Post*. As television became more entrenched in the middle-class home, so too did the figure of the writer—and the woman television writer specifically—took root in the American imagination. The woman television writer deliberately labored in public view, so any viewer who watched the end credits of a favorite series, watched interview programs, or read fan magazines would know she was there.

How does the presence of the woman writer on television change how Americans might have understood or processed what they were watching? The meanings of television series and programs are neither singular nor overdetermined. Horace Newcomb and Paul M. Hirsch, in their essay on television as a cultural forum, write that "ritual and the arts offer a metalanguage," and that television specifically "present[s] a multiplicity of meanings . . . focus[ing] on our most prevalent concerns, our deepest dilemmas."[23] The inherent polysemy of television stems from the multiple authors and constructive forces that, to quote Stuart Hall, "encode" meaning into their scripts; audiences "decode" these meanings using their own contexts, feelings, and sets of knowledge.[24] And one possibility that Lynn Spigel offers to this decoding process is one of "women us[ing] TV to invert sexist hierarchies" and empowering themselves through their viewing and their stewardship of the set.[25] Exploring the place of women writers' scripted lives in their broader cultural contexts reveals how shows demanded to be read at the time and how they need to be understood now: as precursors of second-wave feminist rhetoric and identity.

So, while the personal was not yet political for women writers in postwar television, the personal *was* professional—both for the writers themselves and for the characters they created. Women writing across genre used their shows and celebrity to showcase the challenges of all forms of women's work: in the home, behind the typewriter, and within the television industry. They advocated for their own careers—and, by extension, for the value of women's labor more broadly—through a critique of the postwar cult of domesticity. Elaine Tyler May describes gender roles in Cold War suburbia as widespread "domestic containment," a nation-wide policy in which the woman's patriotic duty is to manage the home while raising their children to be model citizens.[26] Allison McCracken, in her work on radio thrillers, explores the mechanisms of these cultural pressures:

> Government propaganda, psychiatric discourses, and the media suggested that women who did not want to leave the work world to occupy their proper roles within the family were a threat to society generally. . . . Men and women who did not perform these roles were seen as deviant, immature, homosexual, psychotic.[27]

But although white women were being told to report home for duty, many declined to answer the call. Between the years 1950 and 1963, the percentage of women working outside the home jumped from 18.3 million to 24.7 million, and by 1962, more than 60 percent of those women were married.[28] So, even as television narratives seemed to suggest that white, middle-class women had uniformly returned to the home, this was not only a myth, but some of the mythmakers were themselves working women.

The public-facing woman television writer highlights the truth of this historical moment: that a number of women remained in the postwar workforce by choice, not out of necessity, and that white, middle-class women were not just consumers of media but makers as well. As *Lucy*'s "girl writer" Pugh explains: "I mean, no one actually wanted to hire women in 1944, but what else was there? I believe there was some theory going around that women were just filling in until all the men came home from the war and then things would go back like they used to be. Surprise!"[29] Joanne Meyerowitz explores this fissure between lived experience and media representation in the 1994 anthology *Not June Cleaver: Women and Gender in Postwar America, 1945–1960*, a title that directly confronts the extent to which television representation shapes contemporary reckonings with the past. In her introduction, Meyerowitz explains how "the postwar story is a romance steeped in nostalgic longings for an allegedly simpler . . . time . . . [but] many women were not white middle-class, married, and suburban; and many white middle-class, married, and suburban women were neither wholly domestic nor quiescent."[30] The fictional archetype of the exemplary housewife can thus index the "multidimensional complexity" and ideological oppositions of postwar femininity, particularly when she has been coauthored or cocreated by professional women.[31] For example, *Leave It to Beaver* (CBS, ABC, 1957–1963), the sitcom in which June Cleaver features so prominently, had a number of women writers, including Katherine Albert and Mathilde Ferro, both of whose husbands also wrote on the show.

The stories women television writers told tweaked and even lampooned the cultural ideal of the happy homemaker. Lucy and Ethel may have made a mess of their job at the factory, but meanwhile, at home, Ricky and Fred were botching their baking so royally that the grotesque loaf actually breaks down the oven's door. (Like the women, away at work, this bread resists its own domestic containment.) And as Gothic and suspense dramas revealed the home as a site of claustrophobia and danger, soaps thematized the tightness of the domestic space—and of daytime television budgets—as indicative of broader family and societal strains. Even when attempting to mask the sexism of American life, these genres inadvertently exposed the misogyny threaded throughout postwar mass culture. Movies and television internalized these contradictions and manufactured new ones: Were women innocent beach-loving teens or corrupt femmes fatales? Was a mother's love essential to the health of the free world, or was her smothering, emasculating affection a threat to the global order?

Women writers' television scripts confronted the no-win situation many women found themselves in—desperately needed but constantly criticized, busy yet bored—and took further aim at rampant consumerism, women's diminished political autonomy, and stringent beauty ideals. In her history of consumer culture in the twentieth century, Lizabeth Cohen examines how women held active roles in unions and consumer protection movements throughout the 1930s and '40s, but that, in the postwar period, "the gendering of the 'consumer'. . . shifted from women to couples"; this new and "persistent male presence on what often is assumed to be purely female terrain" amounted to women's demotion across both the public and private spheres.[32] The rise of consumer spending and the decline in financial independence for middle-class women coincided with an increasing reliance on kitchen technologies. Mass culture encouraged women to take their newly freed-up time to lose weight, fix their hair, and turn themselves into desirable commodities, all in the eternal quest to keep up with the Joneses. As Elizabeth M. Matelski details in her work on the postwar female ideal, the "renewed emphasis on domesticity required a rededication to cosmetic standards," amounting to a rise in breast-augmentation surgeries and severe "reducing" diet regimens.[33] Women writers for television circled these issues in their scripts without explicitly crossing into the territory of "political" or "radical," and they crafted similar public personas that balanced the progressive and the traditional, the professional and the domestic.

Thus, even as both husbands and wives felt oppressed by what Barbara Ehrenreich calls the masculine "breadwinner ethic," female-authored scripts dismantled the dream of the domestic ideal and, in the process, argued for women writers' value to the television industry.[34] Women's scripts explore the struggles of balancing professional and familial responsibilities; of playing dumb and hiding one's savvy; and of accruing power and agency without giving offense. Not only did women writers thus narrativize the struggles of working women in their scripts, but they also offered hopeful, even liberating, visions of egalitarian marriages, scripted stories of supportive, if challenging, relationships between female characters, and staged moments in which women are recognized for their hard work and sacrifice.

While some women undermined the cult of domesticity by writing about rebellious, misfit housewives, others wrote of proficient matriarchs whose skills and insights overlap with those of the competent television professional. Women like Irna Phillips, Gertrude Berg, and Peg Lynch (chapters 3 and 4) posited themselves as managers of domestic matters and virtuosic nurturers, and their fictional characters were much the same. With respect and care, they portrayed the complexities of women's lives and work, both in their scripts and through their public personas as wives, mothers, and writers. By equating the maintenance of marriage and family with the running of a television show, women writers could discuss the creativity, ingenuity, and discipline required of television writers without sounding intimidating or careerist themselves.

The challenge set before the woman writer, then, was analogous to that of the middle-class housewife being expected to cook "creative[ly] . . . in very structured, controlled ways . . . while accounting for family members' tastes [and] . . . balancing very real budget and time limitations."[35] Being creative but structured, assessing the needs of others, and keeping to a budget and a timeline: all these skills describe the ideal postwar homemaker but equally apply to the aspiring television professional. To that end, women television writers articulated what Jessica Weiss calls the "mid-twentieth-century . . . maternalism," an ideology based on "women's nurturing, which women employed outside of the home as well as within it."[36] These stereotypically feminine strengths and qualities did not condemn a woman's professional aspirations—quite the contrary, by their own account. Television required both a mother's love and her organizational prowess.

By making this claim, women writers, together with their fictional on-screen proxies, revised what Lynn Spigel calls the "spatial hierarchies" of the masculinized public sphere and the femininized private home.[37] Television, much like its forerunner, radio, troubled the distinction between the public and the private, bringing scripted entertainments both light and melodramatic, as well as news, lifestyle programming, and quiz shows into the American home. Radio serials in particular focused on the minor goings-on of family life, composed of what Spigel calls "incidents . . . as they might be told when neighbors visit," allowing housewives to listen while doing their housework.[38] But unlike radio, television added a visual track, the story no longer living in the imagination of the listener but unfolding on-screen. Television writers, directors, and art directors worked together to establish the domestic space for the small screen, but as any *Good Housekeeping* reader knew all too well, the private sphere had long been a matter of public scrutiny and prying eyes.

The postwar homemaker and the media industry professional became discursively linked, as white, middle-class women demonstrated their capacity for professional work through their management of the home. As Kathleen McHugh writes, while the home has historically been "constructed as a place of autonomy and individuality in contradistinction to the workplace . . . it was necessarily reliant on externally produced goods, methods and technologies."[39] In this way, women who wrote and produced shows about the domestic arena proved the complementarity of public and private forms of work, asserting that the home was best understood as a place where women exercised their creative abilities. Women writers further suggested that they had a lot to gain from working in television, but television had just as much to gain from them.

In these ways, women television writers—as generators of texts and cultural texts themselves—sowed the seeds for second-wave feminism. In her literary biography of Betty Friedan's 1963 bestselling manifesto, *The Feminine Mystique*, Stephanie Coontz emphasizes Friedan's "forceful analysis of consumerism . . . [her] defense of meaningful, socially responsible work—paid or unpaid—as a central part of women's identity . . . [and how men and women can] share happier relationships at home" if both husband and wife are satisfied in their work.[40] However, in both their scripts and public personas, women writers addressed these same topics, if in less polemical, more genre-inflected ways. So, while Friedan's writings were shaped by the leftist politics of her youth, *The Feminine Mystique* is equally indebted to popular representations and the work of women television writers.[41] Friedan might not have agreed, having deemed what she called the "housewife-writer" a hypocrite who feigned frustrations and promoted retrograde gender roles in her work:

"Laugh," the Housewife Writers tell the real housewife, "if you are feeling desperate, empty, bored, trapped in the bed making, chauffeuring and dishwashing details. Isn't it funny? We're all in the same trap." Do real housewives then dissipate in laughter their dreams and their sense of desperation? Do they think their frustrated abilities and their limited lives are a joke? Shirley Jackson makes the beds, loves and laughs at her son—and writes another book. Jean Kerr's plays are produced on Broadway. The joke is not on them.[42]

But what if the joke was not on the women watching at home but the sponsors footing the bill? It was housewife-writers for television, after all, who very publicly infiltrated the industry and built careers, even as they earned their keep writing about stay-at-home wives and mothers.

One such instance of this infiltration is the skillful eliding of Donna Reed the movie star and Donna Stone the ideal housewife in *The Donna Reed Show* (ABC, 1958–1966). Though "Donna Reed" today has come to mean "happy homemaker without a hair out of place," Reed was in fact a film actress best known for her roles in *It's a Wonderful Life* (1946) and *From Here to Eternity* (1953), which is how audiences at the time would have seen her. Reed's reinvention as "Donna Stone" was a shift in part scripted by a team of writers that included both men and women writers. Women writers for *The Donna Reed Show* included Helen Levitt, blacklisted and writing under the pseudonym "Helen August," and Barbara Avedon. Avedon went on to cocreate the female cop show *Cagney and Lacey* (CBS, 1982–1986) and, during her tenure with Reed, wrote an episode in which Donna entertains a possible writing career.[43] By dismissing the tactics of women writers in this cultural moment, Friedan neglects the productive contradictions that television's housewife-writers occupied and performed, not to mention the possibilities they presented to women at home.

Women writers' treatment of domesticity primed a suburban reading public for *The Feminine Mystique* and its discussions of female empowerment and self-actualization. To McHugh's point, the "stultifying environment of domesticity [of the 1950s] . . . gave rise to what would be feminism and the reorientation in American culture of white bourgeois women."[44] And just as Friedan's book is written for middle-class American housewives, so too was postwar women's writing steeped in an exclusionary language of choice and creative autonomy, directed to fellow women with options. Women of color, women without high school or college degrees, and those lacking other class and financial privileges rarely saw themselves on-screen and did not have the freedom to write their own scripted lives. This problem is in no small part a product of television's capitalist motives. The feminism on American television was, for many decades, what Bonnie J. Dow calls "lifestyle feminism," referring to the emphasis on class and stylishness in *The Mary Tyler Moore Show* (CBS, 1970–1977), a sitcom that relied on its own coterie of women writers.[45] But rather than treat second-wave feminism as a countercultural movement that got co-opted by commercial interests, we must consider how postwar television popularized major feminist tenets nearly a decade before the publication of *The Feminist Mystique*. Maybe the second wave was not so much a movement that sold out as one made to be marketed.

All these industrial, cultural, and historical forces together rendered the woman television writer not only possible but necessary, both to television's growth as a commercial medium and to an evolving set of cultural and gender norms. The woman writing for television in this period serves as an occasion for theorizing the relationship between production culture (industry workings and lived experiences) and cultural production (media texts), as well as how a writer's persona bridges these distinctions in establishing a publicly visible scripted life. While the television industry was not immune to the wider cultural sexisms of the period, the imperative to reach and retain female viewers meant that shows, networks, and agencies had to make room for women's voices and perspectives. The irony was that women television writers' visibility and agency would decrease just as second-wave feminism entered the mainstream. This was a product of numerous institutional changes, including the industry's move to Hollywood, shifts in favored and prioritized genres, and the growing anonymity of the "hack" television writer. Meanwhile, however, to make a career in television, the woman television writer needed to navigate all of these systems, professional, personal, and ideological, even when their demands proved wildly contradictory. And even then, there was no guarantee.

Every work of writing, whether a television script from 1951 or the book you are reading right now, is a product of decisions: what to put in and what to leave out, what terms to use, and how to speak to an imagined audience. In laying out my focus and arc, I need to go beyond asking whether there were women writers in television (there were) and if we need to revisit their lives and works, particularly in conjunction with one another (we do), and speak to how I have set up the parameters of this study. The book's title, *Their Own Best Creations*, reveals my investment in looking at these women writers' scripted lives, their personas and creative output, as formative presences in postwar femininity, as precursors to second-wave feminism's emphasis on professionalism and self-actualization, and as exemplars of how feminist media historiography holds the power to rewrite dominant cultural and institutional histories. But the subtitle—*Women Writers in Postwar Television*—demarcates the "who" and "when" of this account. "Postwar," for these purposes, includes the years 1949–1963, but many of the writers in this study had careers that predate the advent of commercial television or worked on shows that exceed this decade-long scope. And in establishing the category of "woman writer," I include any female-identifying professional who authored scripts or worked with story materials as an editor, analyst, or producer. All their work contributed to television's voice and continuity, even as some of their input is not fully under-stood or acknowledged. Women wrote for all kinds of television—top-ten Nielsen-ranked programs but also one-night specials, mid-season replacements, and sponsored programming—and in all kinds of ways. Revealing this history of women's authorial participation forges a broader, more varied portrait of what commercial television looked and sounded like in its earliest years.

Throughout this volume, I use the terms *postwar television* and *early television* interchangeably. Numerous television scholars refer to 1950s television as "early," but the descriptor also has feminist historiographic implications in the area of film studies. In her work on slapstick come-diennes in early cinema, Maggie Hennefeld writes that "to group three decades of women's film history under the term 'early' helps to make clear the specifically feminist stakes of how temporal metaphors animate categories of film periodization . . . [and] reinforces its connotations of social latency."[46] "Earliness" as a temporal metaphor, then, applies to formal and narrative experimentation, but also speaks to the makeup of the industry's labor force. In many but not all respects, the "early" film and television industries allowed for more female participation, due in part to the work itself being higher risk and lower status. Often, an era of media history ceases to be "early" once the most marginalized talent (women television writers and Black radio professionals being two such examples) have disappeared. This pattern clashes with a broader cul-tural fallacy of liberalism and perpetual progress: things must be better for women *now*, because it was worse *before*.[47]

To that end, in determining an endpoint for this history, I chose the year 1963 for two reasons. The first is that 1963 is a crucial turning point in popular feminist thought as the publication year of *The Femi-nine Mystique*. Secondly, it is the midpoint of the run of *The Dick Van Dyke Show* (NBC, 1961–1966), a sitcom that prominently features a woman television writer character but was scripted by a male writing staff. Sally Rogers was inspired by real-life writer Selma Diamond, pro-jecting a 1950s past into a 1960s present, but concealed the many real women writers whose careers faltered with television's postwar move-ments and priority shifts.[48] Importantly, the advent and popularization of second-wave feminism may have changed on-screen representation, but this did not translate to a more inclusive television industry overall.

While many television writers suffered diminished status and autonomy with the industry's move from New York to Los Angeles, the exception being hyphenate talent like writer-producers or writer-performers, those writers who remained accrued greater financial and professional stability. The woman television writer early in the 1950s might have leaned into the perceived strengths of the female professional, but, moving into the 1960s, a willingness to listen, nurture, even mother her coworkers was no longer needed or even desired. The television industry became a playground for so-called "hacks" and authors-for-hire who were flexible, versatile, and glad to have their scripts rewritten by like-minded hustlers. In other words, this was work for an unsentimental man, not a wife and mother eager to share her voice and vision with her extended family of fans. Television was no longer expected to look or feel homemade, and all the business-savvy and shrewdness women showrunners had suppressed in their public lives had become essential.

Her Own Best Creations tells the stories of two cohorts of women: those who thrived in the era of live, New York programming, which commenced in 1949, and those who more successfully navigated the changing demands of the television industry as it transitioned to Los Angeles in the latter half of the 1950s. The decline of the Hollywood studio system and the rise of independent production precipitated many of these changes, though the move from east to west, from live to prerecorded, was a gradual one. Erik Barnouw explains how "by the end of 1957 more than a hundred series of television films—telefilms—were on the air or in production. Almost all were Hollywood products, and most were of the episodic-series type."[49] And two years later, in 1959, as much as 80 percent of network television, excluding daytime, was coming from Hollywood.[50] Christopher Anderson explains that this assembly-line mentality stemmed from the realization within the industry that "the only way to make a profit in television was to produce a high volume of programming as inexpensively as possible."[51] Scholarship on secretaries and female administrators employed in the Hollywood studio system has begun to remedy this mid-century historiographic gap, but *Their Own Best Creations* is the first work to reckon with the collective impact women writers of all kinds had on television from its beginnings.[52]

Chapter 1, "Craftsmen and Work Wives: The Gendering of Television Writing," explores how television writing emerged as a desirable profession that both men and women tried to claim for their own. Similar debates transpired in the beginnings of film and radio, in which experts, professionals, and pundits discussed women's proper place in a new culture industry. What particular skills and strengths did women have to bring to this new career path, the job description of which was still being determined? Film and radio historiographies offer revealing

CRACKReplace

parallels that indicate how women are permitted to enter the ranks and why they are sidelined when industries become increasingly capitalized. By putting these accounts in conversations with the specific tropes of postwar gender politics, this study informs our understanding of how men and women writers for television explained their work in gendered terms. Women writers' depictions of the American career girl anticipate second-wave feminist discussions of personal fulfillment through professional autonomy, the danger of misogynistic institutions, and the strain that comes with trying to "have it all."

Subsequent chapters integrate writerly personas with bodies of work, demonstrating how these two intersect and sustain one another in the context of women writers' scripted lives. Chapter 2, "'A Sea of Male Interests': *Your Show of Shows* and the Comedy of Female Mischief" centers on the life and times of comedy writer Lucille Kallen and her place in the "boys' club" of *Your Show of Shows* (NBC, 1950–1954). The writers' room has long served as a microcosm for the industry's mechanisms of inclusion and exclusion, and Kallen stages this drama using some very well-known players, including Sid Caesar, Carl Reiner, and Mel Brooks. Kallen's reflections on making herself heard amid the chaos of collaboration, as well as her creative rapport with performer Imogene Coca, serve as testaments to the professional possibilities and limitations of being a woman writer in postwar television.

Chapters 3 and 4 focus on how female writer-personalities adapted their voices to the new medium of television and to the postwar moment. "Gertrude Berg, Peg Lynch, and the 'Small Situation' of the Stay-at-Home Showrunner" and "'What Girl Shouldn't?' The Many Children of Irna Phillips" look at how all three women cultivated public personas that reconciled the professional and the domestic, the managerial and the maternal. Together, these writers engineered television genres from their roots in radio, where they had worked previously, rescripting women's "chatter" as emotional labor and elevating the domestic space to a site of female self-expression. Berg, Lynch, and Phillips successfully maintained varying levels of creative, even productional, control over their shows—*The Goldbergs* (CBS, 1949–1956) for Berg, *Ethel & Albert* (NBC, ABC, CBS, 1953–1956) for Lynch, and a host of daytime television serials including *These Are My Children* (NBC, 1949) and *Guiding Light* (CBS, 1952–2009) for Phillips. But each woman contended with how that executive authority might mark her as driven or overly calculating and found ways to avoid or reframe conversations of craft and money, while all enjoyed conspicuous collaborations with male directors and producers.

Chapter 5, "'Knowing All the Plots': Presenting the Woman Television Story Editor," provides the occasion to witness television's institutional transitions and the effect they had on women writers. As the television industry became increasingly bi-coastal and was absorbed into Hollywood, there came, with these shifts, new standards of storytelling, production, and labor practices. The amount of television was large and growing ever more unwieldy between the anthology dramas of New York and the generic series of Los Angeles. Women story editors were needed to perform—often uncredited—editorial work, maintaining continuity for series and networks while working closely with screenwriters to strengthen individual scripts. By exploring the authorial role that women story editors played in television, on-screen representations of male-female partnerships become traces of these obscure professional collaborations, with all the emotional and intellectual investments they entailed.

Finally, chapter 6, "'A Girl's Gotta Live': The Literate Heroines of the Suspense Anthology Drama," looks at Hollywood's colonization of the television industry and the evolving modes of gendered authorship this shift demanded. Although the anthology drama was not a hallmark of 1960s television, there were a few notable exceptions, including *The Twilight Zone* (CBS, 1959–1964) and *Alfred Hitchcock Presents* (CBS, NBC, 1955–1962). And while film director-*auteur* Hitchcock lent his brand and expertise to the series, it was producer Joan Harrison, along with writers such as Marian Cockrell and Charlotte Armstrong, who did the daily work of combining elements of gothic literature, film noir, and the radio thriller into a new television aesthetic. In the process, these women invented themselves as "literate heroines" similar to the ones they wrote about: ones who knew how to mobilize and manipulate genre conventions to survive a hostile environment.

Women writers' scripted lives are an industry constant that help scholars and practitioners better analyze our contemporary understandings of television authorship. Though "the 1950s" have become cultural shorthand for a more sexist time, this study illustrates how many opportunities were available to a small but vocal subset of women writers who knew how to play the part. The creative afterlives of these writers and of postwar television are as relevant as ever, the shortcomings of second-wave feminism, together with the increasing pressure for gender parity in entertainment, being the subjects of many journalistic exposés, angry internet arguments, and institutional efforts within Hollywood. The women of this study in many ways set the terms for second-wave feminist thinking through the rendering and repetition of stories about women like them, white women who wanted to work and aspired to egalitarian partnerships with men, both professionally and personally.

Today, the television industry is under pressure, both within its ranks and by a socially engaged public, to do better. This means soliciting and retaining a diverse community of screenwriters, television showrunners, and content creators that transcends the male/female binary to include writers of color, of different class and educational backgrounds, gender identities, sexualities, and abilities. But, even as studios and networks have commenced these efforts, the scripted life for the television writer, especially those from marginalized groups, still informs television narrative and its extra-textual publicity machine. So, while evolving notions of progress in film and television might not map onto the historical study of a bygone era, important continuities exist. Hennefeld considers how "feminist histories reveal the social impasses and intellectual challenges of the historical moments in which they are written," and this particular feminist history—that is to say, the one you are reading right now—is centered on an industry past that resembles the present in urgent ways.[53] The contemporary television mediascape is also in the midst of institutional, technological, and even legal change, and any movement toward industry reform is tied up with industry statements of good intentions and bad faith, leaks, scandals, and public relations damage control. Now, as then, we can look to writers' scripts and storylines as powerful disclosures of how industry gender politics work and why they matter.

CHAPTER I

Craftsmen and Work Wives

The Gendering of Television Writing

In 1956, *Variety* published two letters a week apart. The first was from a woman who wrote that "Television needs new writers!" and implored that "the placard 'For Men Only' [be] taken away from the door of all tv script departments."[1] A woman television agent named Blanche Gaines contested these claims, and her letter was promptly printed in response. As Gaines saw it, "there is no prejudice against women writers in TV—if they come up with a good story," implying there were simply more talented men in the pool.[2] These letters encapsulate television's long-running debates around who should write for the medium, what stories are needed, and to what extent the industry is accountable to the public. But they also gesture to how the role of the television writer was invented and reinvented over the course of the postwar moment, roughly the first dozen years of commercial television (1949–1963). And in detailing their own writerly processes to the public—what inspired them? how and why did they write?—men and women writers typically explained their work in gendered terms, fighting this battle in writers' rooms and private office spaces, in fan magazines, and through speeches and dialogues between their characters.

Male television writers often described their work as that of the sensible, self-employed craftsman, individualistic without being eccentric, creative without being artsy. Together, these men constituted a fraternity of "lone wolves," as Jon Kraszewski calls them, hashing out dialogue in writers' rooms or commiserating over coffees at a deli.[3] And in line with these professional demands and public personas, writers like Reginald Rose ("Twelve Angry Men") and Paddy Chayefsky ("Marty") wrote stories of American Everymen whose humble jobs and vernacular speech belied hidden reserves of wisdom and soul. Women writers could not explain their work or themselves in the same terms, excluded, as they were, from such masculinist rhetoric. Many instead described the job of television writing as requiring a woman's touch or perspective, with all the administrative, creative, and emotional intelligence that entailed. Accordingly, the scripts they wrote for television centered on female characters seeking professional satisfaction, establishing a contented romantic and family life, or struggling to achieve both. Men and women writers framed the same job in opposing ways, and, in the process, made different arguments for television's future as an industry and a storytelling medium.

The gendering of the television writer reflected and revised dominant ideals around men's and women's work at mid-century. But these debates were built on prior discussions around what Liz Clarke calls the emotional and administrative dimensions of "creative labor."[4] To understand the woman writer in early television, we must first meet her forerunners in silent film and radio and examine how female authorship had been touted, dismissed, and incorporated in media forms past. Feminist histories of film and radio consistently illustrate how women have functioned as vital personnel at moments of media transition, instability, and informality. But the matter of who can be called a "professional"—and whose expertise is most valued—is inflected by race, class, and political affiliation, as well as gender.

Discussions of television authorship in the postwar period drew on what men and women were perceived as best suited to do, not only in creative work but also within interpersonal relationships. In many ways, industry culture reiterated the dominant gender ideals of the day, ones in which men were active providers, women passive nurturers.[5] Men and women writers themselves drew on this shared cultural shorthand when explaining their work to the public, though some scripts and shows exposed, even inadvertently, the shortcomings of this stark gender binary. And women writers' comparatively modest rhetoric around writing, sometimes tender-hearted, other times pragmatic, has had rippling effects on the historiography of the medium and the period. Men outnumbered women in the staffing of television writers' rooms, and this inequity was compounded by how many women writers downplayed their own accomplishments and interventions. What are the first steps toward building an archive that spotlights women's contributions, knowing that so much of the history is already lost?

THE WOMAN IN THE MACHINE: GENDER AND THE MEDIA INDUSTRIES

It is impossible to tell the story of women writers in television without considering patterns of work that characterized the culture industries in the first half of the twentieth century. Gatekeeping plays a prominent role in the histories of film and broadcasting, in particular considering when women are permitted to join, how they might rise in the ranks of a new commercial art form, and why that might change. The openness that characterizes the "early" periods of these commercial art forms allows women—largely, white, middle-class, and educated ones—to participate in greater numbers and with more creative input. This is in part because the demand of jobs has not yet surpassed the supply, allowing otherwise marginalized workers increased, if still limited, access and opportunity.[6]

White women benefited from early media industries' institutional flexibility and formal experimentation, both in terms of job availability and the possibility of advancement. In her study of Hollywood laborers at mid-century, Erin Hill defines institutional "informality" as comprised of "less formal, more holistic early work systems in which women moved fluidly between different work sectors (presenting a kind of unintended or latent) feminism."[7] In Hill's context of studio Hollywood, these "informal" or "soft systems" allowed women to participate at all levels of film production, "continually co-constructing" the rules—and their roles—"as they go."[8] Informality, then, produced a temporarily inclusive industry, because women had not yet been relegated to areas of "woman's work": they could get in, rise up the ranks, and, in an early film context, run their own production companies. The freedoms afforded to women professionals in periods of transition and institutional invention read as exhibits of "latent feminism," women striving for equality and mobility at work.

This same sense of openness and informality shapes the history of women's participation in radio. Donna Halper writes about how radio stations were initially open to female managers in the 1920s, because women ran the best music schools and had the broadest network of contacts; women were also able, on and off, to work as announcers, personalities, and even station owners, making early radio a moment in which "there were few rules and stations felt free to innovate."[9] Likewise, Michele Hilmes's account of the American radio industry connects institutional informality with aesthetic possibility: "Early flexibility gave way to institutionalized rigidity that worked to contain and repress radio's potentially disruptive aspects ... [including] radio's capacity to blur the basic distinctions of gender identity and its potential for allowing the private voices of women access to the public airwaves."[10] Hilmes's account explores how a more progressive industry results in more daring gender representation, while she and Allison McCracken both write about the power of the "disembodied" female voice to occupy a position of political authority, to blur the strict male-female binary, and even to gesture to queer forms of performance.[11] But the possibilities for subversive entertainment on a massive scale did not end with radio. Postwar television's "transgressive" gender messaging may be more subtle or stifled, but it is still there, encoded in visuality and through the scripted life of the woman writer.[12]

Women writers' public personas bridged industry-specific understandings of women's work with cultural conceptions of women's innate strengths and abilities. Giuliana Muscio demonstrates how fan coverage of women scenario writers stressed their glamor and feminine allure over their "intelligence, or efficiency, presenting them as mothers and wives, not as the independent creatures they often were."[13] This image of the charming ingenue at work, her manicured fingernails clicking at the typewriter keys, was just as Hill describes her: an archetype collectively authored by the woman writer, the public relations teams out of the studios, numerous journalists' coverage, and even fan communications.[14] The very notion of "women's work" is ever in flux, the dynamic product of tensions between "the system—the structures that produced gendered understandings of labor—and the individual—the experiences of workers themselves and how they negotiated, resisted, and otherwise cocreated their professional identities."[15]

The persona of the female writer-professional has thus always been rife with oppositions and contradictions. In her analysis of the coverage of women screenwriters in the 1910s and '20s, Anne Morey tracks the "divide between [the] 'wild' and [the] 'domestic'"; while women photoplaywrights were treated as "representatives of a new order of femininity that had many masculine attributes (such as logic, a taste for action, vigor, and a capacity to visualize)," they were also thought to render more psychologically driven storytelling and to establish a "homelike scenario department" to the benefit of all.[16] Elinor Glyn and Lois Weber, two celebrity writer-personalities with their respectively "wild" and "domestic" personas, speak to these industry conceptions of femininity and creativity. While the famously cosmopolitan and often risqué figure of Elinor Glyn (*It*) "circulated as a brand . . . her persona, as much as her fictions . . ." through her glamour and savvy, Weber presented a more respectable middle-class alternative.[17]

Weber, who worked alongside her husband on films such as *Where Are My Children?* (1916) and *Shoes* (1916), made films explicitly dissuading white, Protestant women from falling into sinful behaviors, providing stern, maternal guidance, updated from eighteenth-century sentimental seduction narratives, Victorian novels, and the occasional eugenicist pamphlet. Weber's scripted life drew heavily on themes and elements of the domestic, the familial, and even the handmade, implying that a strong moral fiber was just one strength that women might bring to the otherwise questionable popular entertainment of moviegoing. Shelley Stamp notes how Weber's films engaged with tropes of "quality filmmaking" without losing the archetypal woman's touch, Weber always "foreground[ing] her distinctly feminine mode of authorship [within the films themselves], epitomized by the handwritten signature 'Yours Sincerely, Lois Weber,' inscribed at the outset of *Hypocrites* (1915)."[18] The film, through its aesthetic and form of address, internalizes the homespun wisdom of its middle-class matriarch-*auteur*, a tactic that women show creators and writers in postwar television would also deploy (chapters 3 and 4).

But while informality within the culture industries had distinct benefits for women in film, radio, and, later, television, it came with its drawbacks. Women encountered less institutional discrimination or fewer obstacles at first, but as the institutions grew and changed, so did their ability to get these jobs or keep them. As Mark Cooper writes, the dominant historiographic model of Hollywood history in the 1910s and 1920s is that of going "from cottage industry to corporation," the formalization of the industry resulting in its masculinization of its workforce.[19] Mark Cooper revises this idea with his study of the women directors of Universal Studios in the 1910s. He demonstrates how industry interests converged with ideological pressures in removing the material supports on which women professionals had previously relied. As the studio system became increasingly entrenched and systematized, "the institution [of Universal] structured a version of home and particular sorts of careers as incompatible."[20] Studio executives achieved this shift, first, by eliminating homes from the studio lot, so women could not easily move from home to the office and back again. This presented a logistical challenge to women balancing work obligations and child-rearing and broadcast to any woman interested in the job that it would not accommodate wives and mothers. Second, Universal produced and circulated films in which "a stridently idealized home [was] a central goal," meaning that women made the very movies and promoted the very values that later enshrined them as unemployable.[21] The latter claim is a variation on the "no good deed goes unpunished" arguments from Jane Gaines and Erin Hill, whose histories reveal how women made film so successful and lucrative in the early decades that it prompted men to take over the industry almost entirely by the sound era.[22]

As the film and broadcasting industries grew, female professionals were increasingly called on to perform those collaborative forms of institutional women's work that offer long hours but little in the way of credit. In the case of the Hollywood studio system, from the late 1920s into the 1930s, women took on key roles in feminized professionals such as casting, costume design, and script work. In terms of the latter example, the work women did managing scripts and story properties is not typically treated as "authorial," which is a gap in the history that I will begin to address in chapter 5.[23] Hill writes of how, in studio Hollywood, "female clerical workers, the studios' primary paper workers, were marginalized in their potential to succeed beyond the typewriter."[24] And while women personalities thrived in radio throughout its heyday, women also inhabited influential, but less lauded, positions of administrative and network maintenance. In her study of the female labor force that peopled NBC's Information Department, Catherine Martin describes their labor as that of "network spokes(women), an authoritative role typically associated with male expertise."[25] Though their work was "discussed in ambivalent and feminized terms," a running tally of the concrete and creative contributions women administrators gave to radio can never be fully understood.[26] (Martin gives the example of women in the information department writing letters to fans and listeners, only to have their letters signed by male executives.)

Institutional flexibility and a desire to court female audiences initially garnered women more visible or high-status jobs, including as writers, but the specter of propriety—and, most likely, disguised self-interest, paired with ingrained misogyny—got them replaced by men. Sometimes the compromises they made along the way backfired, the gendered abdication of ambition or literary craft rendering women's writerly work invisible or illegible. Being a secretary in a network or at a studio sometimes drew on women's authorial or editorial abilities, and historians are only beginning to grasp the nature of the work these women did by studying their reports, memos, intradepartmental correspondence, and other forms of internal communications.[27]

The arcs of women's roles in film and radio provide crucial context for the history of women writers in postwar television. Women television writers, like those for radio and film, sought to craft public personas that explained their work and value to the industry. The resulting public cachet, together with the openness of television's early years, made women writers a necessary ingredient in building the profession and establishing an audience of female viewer-consumers. Over the course of the 1950s, the power and place of women television writers diminished. For television, this was in large part due to the industry's move to Los Angeles, the changing priorities of the industry, and shifting audience tastes.[28] Cooper's formulation of women being the engineers of their own destruction at Universal Studios is not precisely what happened in television. More accurately, television went in a direction where only some women could follow. Further, with the exception of the hyphenate writer-producer, the television writer of the 1960s became an anonymous professional, a hired hand rather than a public face. As a result, the figure of the woman television writer no longer circulated as a fixture of popular interest or an occasion for conversations around working women or gendered authorship. Nevertheless, in television's nascent period, the issue of who was best suited to be a professional writer was still being worked through, both in the writers' room and in the public square.

PROFESSIONALIZATION AND THE POSTWAR TELEVISION WRITER

The professionalization of television writing and the gendering of the job were entangled processes. Writers looking to break into television had at their disposal a host of organizations through which to seek professional support, mentorship, and even bargaining power. The Screen Writers' Guild, as well as its precursor, the Television Writers' Association (TWA), both ran courses open to trained writers and amateurs alike.[29] The Central Broadcasting System (CBS) and the National Broadcasting Company (NBC) also established their own training programs.[30] The CBS program, which began in 1955, was run through the network's business affairs department, while the NBC Comedy Writing

Program, launched in the same year, functioned as an apprenticeship program. Both NBC and CBS sought to professionalize the aspiring writer and bolster the power of the networks in competition with increasingly powerful talent agencies.[31] For women specifically, the nonprofit American Women in Radio and Television (AWRT), founded in 1950, connected professionals across specialties and fields of expertise, including costume designers, public relations executives, and, of course, writers. These institutions together produced not only a standardization of the job description and the craft of writing but a community of professionals that included some and excluded others.

What was at stake for the woman television writer with the entrenchment of the "professional"? As anthology drama writer and story editor Lois Jacoby wrote in 1958, "Although television devours material at an alarming rate, it is a field for professionals and not for enthusiastic amateurs."[32] Jacoby had herself worked her way up the television ranks, and she emphasized the need to educate oneself in the industry standards, noting that "networks are interested in the work of college students who are taking courses in television writing for credit."[33] Her perspective diverges from that of writer Robert Dozier, who, reminiscing about his writer buddies ("a whole bunch of guys") at a local "saloon," claimed: "If you wrote something halfway passable you could sell it."[34] For women, occupying a professional persona could be a protective credential, one that would hopefully compensate for being excluded from the homosocial bonds of a boys' club. But even as gendered language suggested how men and women experienced the job differently, the mantle of "professional" remained limited to applicants of some means, with access to training or education. For example, Gertrude Berg (chapter 3), who wrote and played a working-class Jewish matriarch on *The Goldbergs*, had actually studied playwriting at Columbia.[35]

Professionalization, then, was not simply a matter of writerly craft and expertise; it was also a matter of establishing an agreeable, homogeneous labor force, working in line with sponsors, networks, and governmental agencies. The lack of a Black presence in postwar television writers' rooms is evidence of how talent from Black radio was excluded in the transition to television and how disinterested sponsors were in speaking to Black audiences.[36] Black writer-producer Richard Durham (*Destination Freedom*) is a representative instance of commercial television reaping the work of Black radio without conferring any of the rewards to its visionaries. With *Here Comes Tomorrow*, Durham created the first Black radio soap, with an entirely Black cast and storylines that confronted inequality and prejudice.[37] Network television did not hold the same promise for Durham. In 1950, he brought a lawsuit against NBC for $250,000 in damages, for violation of the author's copyright and ownership of *Destination Freedom*. The suit took six years to be resolved in favor of Durham, who in subsequent decades would concentrate his energies on political activism and working in public television.[38]

Commercially driven network television was more comfortable putting Black talent in front of the camera than behind it. The corporate-liberal leadership of the television networks aimed to perform inclusivity without courting controversy. To that end, in 1955, NBC launched a network-wide "Integration without Identification" policy, in which Black actors were cast in nonspeaking roles. The network envisioned this initiative as a compromise between casting Black actors as offensive stereotypes and not casting them at all.[39] A 1950 article for *Variety*, titled "Negro Talent Coming into Own on TV, without Use of Stereotypes," sought to promote a flattering image of Black representation on television, but notes "only a few Negros have been able to crack the technical side" and makes no mention of writers; it cites *Amos 'n' Andy* (CBS, 1951–1953) and *Beulah* (ABC, 1950–1953) as two nuanced renderings of Black life, despite the protests these shows had garnered from the NAACP and other civil rights groups.[40]

Being politically amenable or, at least, politely agnostic, was another prerequisite for the professional television writer. Any writer perceived as outside of or hostile to white, middle-class capitalist ideology was potentially excluded from the ranks, with the leadership of organizations like its Television Writers of America coming under especial scrutiny for their political affiliations.[41] Carol Stabile describes anti-communist incursions on broadcasting content during this era as part of a "repressive war over popular culture that accompanied the new medium . . . [of television,]" adding that the "images that appeared on television after 1950 . . . were products of suppression, fear, and, eventually, self-censorship."[42] White writers with leftist politics and ones with ties to the Communist Party met with their own challenges when seeking out work in television, the 1950 hearings of the House Un-American Activities Committee mobilizing wider fears of communist messaging in the mass media. But because television needed more material at a quicker rate, sympathetic performers and producers, like actress Donna Reed and *Alfred Hitchcock Presents* producer Joan Harrison (chapter 6), were able to quietly hire blacklisted writers working under pen names.

Married couple Joan and Adrian Scott were one such pair, writing under the pseudonym "Joanne Court." The Scotts' work on *Lassie* allowed them to write scripts in line with their "recognizab[ly] . . . progressive" politics, their work "evoking the lost world of the New Deal rather than the shimmering consumerist settings of the 1950s."[43] As Joan Scott would later recount, "We did a lot of *Lassies*. . . . I fronted for [Adrian] on the TV show from 1955 on until 1961. I wrote some and he wrote some, but they were all under my pen name—Joanne Court. I got to be known as 'the woman who writes like a man.'"[44] Even writing under pseudonyms, the Scotts' successes in television were circumscribed. Adrian Scott was unable to sell his network television script on the struggles of a working-class woman named Ellie, who delivered such gutsy rejoinders as "The government better get wise! . . . It's hard work being wife and mother! If they don't know that in Washington, someone oughta tell 'em!"[45]

Blacklisted performers were under great pressure, but, unlike writers, actors could not work incognito. The release of *Red Channels* in 1950, a pamphlet that listed entertainment professionals with alleged ties to the Communist Party, stalled and destroyed numerous careers, including that of Philip Loeb, who played Jake Goldberg on *The Goldbergs* (CBS, NBC, DuMont, 1949–1957). The show's writer, executive producer, and star, Gertrude Berg, came to Loeb's defense but fired him when pressure from the sponsor grew too intense. The show did not air from June 1951 to February 1952, and Berg paid Loeb's salary out of pocket for two years. Still, Loeb was unable to make a living and committed suicide three years later in 1955.[46] Loeb's career was a cautionary tale for anyone in television who had attended a meeting of the Communist Party or identified as a fellow traveler. Berg was a very cautious entertainment personality, strategically evacuating her writing and her own persona of leftist resonances. For Berg, this is what it meant to be a "professional": being inoffensive, accommodating, and careful. Men and women writers had different approaches to the problem of creating the "television professional" and angling its definition to their own advantage.

CRAFTSMEN AND PROFESSIONALS: THE MASCULINIZATION OF TELEVISION WRITING

Television writing became a white, male profession not only through internal, executive decision-making but also through the evolution of public opinions and understandings of the industry. Anne Morey writes

that "American writing . . . [as] an indicator of masculinity was something of a truism around the turn of the century," and the idea that writing
was men's work persisted into the postwar moment.[47] This long-standing
preconception coincided with the renaissance of the cult of domesticity,
as well as a new cultural narrative: that of discontented, middle-class
masculinity and the plight of the unhappy organization man. The television writer's search for invigorating, meaningful employment cannot
be separated from the story of manhood in the 1950s. Television writing offered the white, middle-class man—from the college graduate to
the military veteran—the opportunity to make a decent living without
resorting to soul-crushing office work or donning the proverbial gray
flannel suit. Andrew Hoberek argues that the "Professional-Managerial
Class" of the postwar period was plagued by widespread "skepticism
about organization as such and nostalgia for the putative economy of
the property-owning old middle class."[48] The "salaried mental workers"
of the PMC conducted their work "within institutions: foundations,
museums, government, the media, and . . . higher education," ultimately
"finding themselves in the position of organization men par excellence,
their employment symbolizing the ultimate degradation of creative mental labor within the white-collar workplace."[49]

Cultural artifacts articulating and satirizing this phenomenon abound
—from books including Sloan Wilson's *The Man in the Gray Flannel
Suit* (1955) and David Riesman's *The Lonely Crowd* (1950) to Hollywood films such as Billy Wilder's *The Apartment* (1960) and *How to
Succeed in Business without Really Trying* (1967, based on the 1952
satire). Organization men labored under immense professional and personal pressure, and men like Jack Kerouac and Hugh Hefner presented
them with appealing lifestyle alternatives. Through these figures, they
could imaginatively escape into a world of glamour, sex without obligations, and freedom from familial responsibility.[50]

But what about the man who sought both professional autonomy
and familial harmony? A typically second-wave feminist sentiment, true
enough, but what existed for the man who dreamed of "having it all"?
The writer-for-hire—not an artist or a poet, but an average Joe with
drive—offered a third way, situated between the white-picket prison
and the Playboy mansion. The tantalizing possibility of the maverick
author figure is exemplified by Mickey Spillane's postwar private investigator character, Mike Hammer. Hammer debuted as the protagonist
of Spillane's 1947 novel, *I, the Jury*, and went on to appear in a series
of novels and film adaptations. Hoberek analyzes the figure of Hammer

as a "fantasy of entrepreneurial agency in a white-collar world," and, in the process, elaborates an important theory of postwar authorship:

> Fundamental here is the way in which *postwar fiction equates the agency of characters with the agency of authors*. . . . Because authors themselves perform mental labor, the question of agency cannot be constrained within the horizon of content, but leaks into the form of literary work understood as the material embodiment of the author's own mental labor.[51]

Hammer becomes an imaginative stand-in for the self-determining author into whom the reader can project himself. Writers are not organization men, as, even as they contend with the publishing market and its demands, their work still remains their own. He cultivates a "form of professionalism designed to protect [his] own authority as much from the public as from the institutions of corporate capitalism."[52] The writer is not so different from the private investigator, then, moving through the world responsible only to the truth—*his* truth. Like the self-employed, autonomous figure of Mike Hammer, the television writer can take on an enterprising role in his career, maintaining his livelihood through freelance work without compromising his creative vision or surrendering his will to a boss.

The television writer unwilling to write trash for pay—the creative equivalent of the organization man's office job—strove to adapt his work across media platforms and generate multiple revenue streams in the process. As Jon Kraszewski notes, anthology drama writers invented themselves in the mold of the postwar "new entrepreneur": the "lone-wolf figure who gains power and defines his identity by moving between a number of institutions."[53] These television authors, who included Rod Serling, Reginald Rose and Paddy Chayefsky, "strongly identified as industry workers, not as secluded Romantic artists," and subsequently made their fortunes by adapting their work across media and having their teleplays published or adapted into films.[54] This enabled television writers, Kraszewski explains, to "transform themselves from working-class scribes who labored constantly into wealthy dramatists who needed to write much less."[55] These writers' presence across media industries helped convert them into public personalities, garnering industry clout and fame in addition to job security and a reliable paycheck. The screenwriter-as-craftsman idiom, however, was not new: it began in the days of early cinema and circulated widely throughout the postwar period, including in television writing guidebooks.[56] In her 1952 book *The TV Writer's Guide*, author Margaret R. Weiss

advises the aspiring television writer to pursue "free-lance opportunities . . . [that] offer the new TV writer his chance to build a reputation
as a competent, reliable craftsman."[57] But, setting aside Weiss herself, it
was largely men, not women, who benefitted from this rhetoric of the
craftsman, which suggests expertise and skill are more important than
emotion, sensitivity, and female intuition.

This gendered formulation is most plainly illustrated in a 1953
spread for *Variety*, "Consider the Case of the TV Writer," which features brief statements from working television writers and constructs
a vision of the television writer as young, white, ambitious, and male.
It includes the writers Horton Foote, Sumner Locke Elliott, William
Kendall Clarke, Robert Alan Aurthur, and Thomas W. Phipps. Phipps,
who wrote for *Goodyear Playhouse* (NBC, 1951–1957) and *The Philco
Television Playhouse* (NBC, 1948–1955), touts the rewards of working
within the medium's institutional boundaries.[58] Clarke (*Philco Television Playhouse, Robert Montgomery Presents*) forges a similar claim,
averring that "the writer will be assured he is at least abreast of his
medium, for as a worker, as a craftsman, and perhaps even as an artist,
he actually will have come of age."[59]

But Paddy Chayefsky's essay most succinctly synthesizes the contradictions and challenges of writing in postwar television. For Chayefsky,
writing for the network and the sponsor is part of the job, but a true
lone wolf talent never surrenders his art to commercial imperatives. He
criticizes the dismissiveness of his compatriots who "approach . . . each
assignment like a plumber who is about to fit two pipes together . . .
talk[ing] in terms of package and royalties"; for them, television is not
an art form but purely "a business, a trade, a racket."[60] Chayefsky offers
instead the model of the "craftsman," as someone that reconciles the
practical with the romantic, fit for a man with both ambition and heart,
smart without being an egghead, emotional without being a woman.
He defends television's aesthetic merits, concluding that although the
"atmosphere of pseudo-professionalism . . . is pretty confining to the
serious writer . . . there is a lot of reward to be gotten out of television
writing."[61] Such discussions of the television writer as a craftsman with
talent and vision marked the authorial workforce as one in need of
masculine voices.

"Marty" (NBC, May 24, 1953), Chayefsky's best-known teleplay,
aired on *The Philco Television Playhouse* in the same year as his *Variety*
essay.[62] A story about a humble butcher seeking love and fulfillment,
"Marty" demands to be read through Chayefsky's philosophy of the

FIGURE 2. The story of "Marty" is pictured as both a book and a show, the image emphasizing the literariness of the television drama.

FIGURE 3. The transition from book to meat signals how Chayefsky's intellectual labor is transformed into something material and manly in "Marty."

television writer as craftsman. This organizing motif emerges as early as the opening credits, pictured below, which includes the title and author configured in the style of a novel's cover (Figure 2). Immediately, the teleplay is established as a literary object and an authored text, as opposed to a long-form advertisement or a product of the mass media assembly line. After the volume is paged through, offering the names of the show's cast and crew, the narrative begins with a close-up on Marty's hands cutting into what looks to be a side of beef (Figure 3). Dissolving from the image of a book to that of a meat slab, with its white-fat planes like the pages of a tome, links the blue-collar work of butchery with the "carving" out of story. Rather than positioning writing as an effeminized, frivolous occupation, Chayefsky and director Delbert Mann present writing and text-making as hands-on man's work, something productive and tangible. The butcher trafficked in the real and the messy—blood, bone, and heart—and so too did the television writer, albeit metaphorically.

Marty's friends would make terrible writers, because they lack any sensitivity to the beauty and poignancy of real life. Ignorant and crass, they classify women as either dishes or dogs, and their immature understandings of the world are shaped by—of all things—Mickey Spillane novels. One friend tells another that Spillane's protagonist, presumably Mike Hammer, "knows how to handle women," because he is always either spurning or killing them. In response, his friend can only affirm, "That Mickey Spillane, he sure can write!" Spillane's formulaic genre writing, obsessed as it is with sex and brutishness, taps into and has even formed readers' callow, cruel fantasies. Chayefsky's commitment to writing tender, warm-blooded realism is in direct opposition to the hard-boiled worlds of Spillane and Hammer. So, while Hoberek suggests how the Mike Hammer character stands in for the free and independent subject, in Chayefsky's telling, Hammer and Spillane are false prophets for the white, American man. Marty is an author in Chayefsky's image, as he embraces honest work, plain language, and genuine emotion. He knows to prize a real-life schoolteacher over an imaginary hot-to-trot heiress, because he sees beauty where others cannot. The writer's ideological commitments to craft and television realism dovetail with the sensitively wrought, working-class character of Marty, who in turn becomes a mouthpiece for the cause of (male) television writers everywhere.

As television was coming of age, so was television writing, a job that offered the freethinking white-collar worker the opportunity to support a family on the fruits of his creative labor. But this logic did not apply to women writers. White, middle-class women were supposed to raise families, not provide for them—even if, in reality, many did both. Women writers had to prove that their own female perspectives were not a mere novelty for television but a necessity. Commenting on the term "girl writer," Lucille Kallen (chapter 2) griped that the descriptor "'girl' put you—fondly—in your place."[63] In response to such patronizing language, many "girl writers" made forceful cases for their own importance in television by forging distinctly female-coded ways to rise in the ranks of television writing. For women, this often involved a promise to nurture the infant form of television, not to mention all the men who wrote for it.

"THE WOMAN'S TOUCH": TELEVISION WRITING AS WOMEN'S WORK

In 1955, comedy writing duo Carol Honig and Lois Balk were hired to write for the popular comedy-variety program *The Steve Allen Show* (NBC, ABC, 1956–1964). To a modern reader, the press coverage of Honig and Balk is predictably diminishing, with its detailed descriptions of the women's looks—their eye and hair color, as well as their petite statures ("both 5 feet, 5 inches, shoeless")—and an accompanying image of Honig and Balk sitting "at their hot little typewriters."[64] But even as these features objectified the two writers, they provided compelling details of the women's biographies and allowed Honig and Balk to articulate their training and craft to a general readership. Having graduated from Barnard College in New York City, the pair began writing genre fiction with titles such as "Confessions of a Teen-Age Alcoholic" and "Tamed, the Story of a Wild Girl."[65] Honig and Balk moved into writing for television, because, as they explain, it was "the greatest challenge we could think of. . . . [It] is the newest form of writing."[66] But, as one profile of Honig and Balk notes, the show's star promoted the women to staff writers because "it [was] cheaper to hire them permanently—or until they get married, at any rate."[67] The very qualities that made the woman television writer useful to postwar television—wit, pedigree, and charm—made her marriage material.[68] A white-collar man might want a smart and elegant wife with some education and all the class privilege that entails, one capable of accomplishing a great deal on her own but who only wants those things for him. But what if college and the work world made her *too* smart, too capable? What would that do to Steve Allen's payroll sheet, and what would it do to middle-class American men on the marriage market?

The challenge for the woman television writer was positioning herself and her work within these interlocking conversations about women's abilities, ambitions, and responsibilities. A woman's commitment to her education and her career could potentially undermine her responsibilities to husband and family. According to Lynn Peril, various cultural camps of magazine writers, pundits, and popular experts argued about whether college women were more or less prepared to take on their roles as keepers of the hearth. Peril explains how, "in the mid-twentieth century, it was as if all roads led to homemaking, no matter how circuitous the path."[69] Jobs in the fields of nursing, teaching, and social work were treated as training for the work of a stay-at-home partner and caregiver, so a woman could practice the management of her future family on strangers and their children. A college education was nearly essential for a woman to join the professional ranks, but it could come at a grave cost to her personal life and the nation's stability. The freedoms and intellectual stimulation that came with a college education could make a women careerist, and those with too much drive might become mannish and thus unmarriageable. These ideas circulated even as, in reality, many married women worked outside the home, and, as television writers, women held positions of creative authority and autonomy and existed as beloved public figures. Some women writers had husbands and children, while others remained "married to their work." But regardless of the choices they made privately, each woman writer had to address the question posed by the industry and the public alike: "What has television to gain by letting women write for it?"

Since the early days of radio, women writers were thought best equipped to capture the psychology and speech of the female consumer. Broadcasting and advertising companies directly solicited women writers, college graduates in particular, to address and appeal to those female consumers who looked, sounded, and shopped like them. At the J. Walter Thompson Agency (JWT), codirector Helen Lansdowne Resor "belie[ved] that women advertising executives were best qualified to reach this audience [of female consumers, which] was reflected in the organizational structure of JWT."[70] And as CBS Radio vice president John Karol told an audience full of women at the 1956 meeting of the Advertising Association of the West: "In virtually every product category, you are the goal. . . . You are the reason for almost every product innovation and every ad in print on the air. You are the subject of endless research."[71] William G. Werner, a high-ranking executive at Procter & Gamble, suggested that ads directed at women should possess the kind of "warmth," "excitedness," and "vigor" to which women were accustomed, not to mention plenty of "superlatives," asking "What then is wrong with talking to women in advertising in the sort of language they know best?"[72]

But it is one thing to know the language and another to harness it, the latter requiring a professional level of training and skill. In 1955, Grey Advertising ran an all-female panel, featuring a vice president, copy supervisor, television commercial writer, and art director, geared to an audience of college-educated women. According to reporting from *Broadcasting, Telecasting*, the executives explained that because

> women buy 80% of all products it is important to have the woman's touch in advertising. . . . At Grey there is a key woman executive in each department. . . . Still, one must be prepared with proper schooling and work interest to be able to make her way as a woman in advertising.[73]

Here, feminine intuition meets craft, rendering the ideal writer not only a woman but one with a particular set of abilities and references. By hailing college-educated women as budding creative professionals, agencies not only solicited writing talent but also established a rapport with the female consumers in the audience. Just as screenwriting correspondence courses like the Palmer Photoplay Corporation sought, as Anne Morey explains, to "create a 'better' audience—more engaged, more informed, more invested in Hollywood," so too did these agency-sponsored events function as public outreach for the brand and for broadcasting more generally.[74]

But regardless of whether she worked on a daytime soap, a sketch comedy program, or a sponsored special, the white, middle-class woman writer did not have the craftsman-entrepreneur or the beleaguered-breadwinner idioms available to her. Each woman had to find a way to frame her professional ambitions and her approach to their work in line with what the public would accept and understand. Some stressed how television writing demanded the vision and skill set of a smart, soft-hearted woman, while others deflected criticism by publicly grieving—or joking about—their inability to marry, have children, and be a "normal" woman. Whether the latter move was tactical or toothless, the fact remained that the woman professional needed to accommodate a male-dominated industry while avoiding the alienation of viewers at home.

The postwar white, middle-class woman television writer would circulate through industry and popular discourses as an illustration of the career woman writ large. The figures of Selma Diamond, Margaret Cousins, and Shirley Gordon all reveal that to cultivate a workable persona in publishing, radio, and, television, women writers needed to balance self-confidence with self-effacement, be special while remaining relatable, and contribute to on-screen representations that exposed the problems with the status quo without offering radical alternatives. And, in the construction of their scripted lives, Diamond, Cousins, and Gordon all authored rich, multilayered portraits of women at work, the stories they told about themselves ultimately supported or sustained by their scripts. These narratives of working women—creative, ambitious, imperiled—thematize the sacrifices women made to fit into a sexist industry and to gain acceptance.

WRITING JOKES AND EMPTYING ASHTRAYS:
THE SCRIPTED LIFE OF THE POSTWAR
CAREER WOMAN

In a 1953 sketch from *The Buick-Berle Show* (NBC, 1948–1956), *Dragnet*'s Jack Webb made an appearance as his character Sergeant Joe Friday investigating joke theft.[75] Webb explains that television writers are the "unknowns of the industry," a joke compounded by the fact that the writers onstage are being played by actors. As he interrogates everyone in the writers' room, one man pleads to be left out of it, explaining "I'm a family man. It's too near Christmas." Another says that he does not steal jokes because he's "got troubles enough . . . [being] engaged to three girls." A third confesses to a pill addiction. The character of "Selma Diamond," based on the real-life woman staff writer for *Berle*, is nervous and defensive, questioning Webb in return. "You think it's unusual, a girl writing jokes?" she asks. "Do you think I stole the jokes? It isn't true. I'm a writer. I write jokes. That's my job. I write jokes, make coffee and empty ashtrays."

This scene puts television writing on trial, and each writer's alibi gives further definition to the profession, not only as a job description but also as a type. While the men writers explain who they are—heterosexual men who work to support their lifestyles (which involve women, children, and hedonistic pleasures)—Diamond's answer is predicated on *what she does*, a combination of creative and domestic labor.[76] The particular job of the woman writer is to be as much *woman* as *writer*, making the working space comfortable and enabling her male colleagues' creativity. Diamond may be "one of the guys," but she is also the one who has to empty the ashtrays and make the coffee. Lynn Peril details the "office wife" archetype that emerged in the 1910s and '20s, imagined as either a "pitiable old maid" or a "seductress" who "did what C. Wright Mills called the 'housework of [the boss's] business.'"[77] What if the "office wife" was simply a woman who did not feel the need to marry, since she spent her days playing the wife at work?

Selma Diamond was one of the most public-facing women writers in postwar television, later leveraging her celebrity to regularly act in film and television. As a figure in early television authorship, Diamond provides a model of how the woman writer combined the safe with the subversive in her self-presentation. Her real-life raspy smoker's voice and her rough-and-tumble humor could have been professional liabilities, except for two ameliorating factors. The first was her self-effacing humor about being a failed woman, and the second was her class and ethnic identity. Being a middle-class, Jewish college graduate made her like many of her male compatriots. It was only her gender that marked her off from them and that gave her a distinctive place in the male-dominated writers' room.

Indeed, many of the writers for 1950s television were Jewish, even as Jewishness was a target of Cold War anxieties, marked by leftist, socialist, and even communist associations. Early in the decade, ethnic, working-class families were represented on television, including *I Remember Mama* (CBS, 1949–1957), *Life with Luigi* (CBS, 1952), *The Honeymooners* (CBS, 1955), and *The Goldbergs*.[78] Susan Murray analyzes Jewish talent as a mainstay of early television in her work on vaudeo [vaudeville-video] stars including Milton Berle, Jack Benny, George Burns, and Sid Caesar. Berle's "signs of his Jewishness were read through his historical connections to such things as vaudeville [and] New York," while the effeminized masculinities of Benny, Burns, and others exemplifies television's "cross-fertilization between performers' onstage characters and their authentic identities."[79] And just as ethnicity for men like Berle permitted, even demanded, a more fluid mode of white masculinity, so too did Diamond's Jewishness allow for a more masculinized iteration of heterosexual femininity.

Diamond built her career around being the inverse of the effeminate male vaudeo star: the tough-talking, tomboy Jewess "so busy in this profession . . . [that she] miss[ed] all the Saks' shoe sales."[80] Having been deemed a "Television Rarity" by the *New York Times*, Diamond's pedigree was similar to many other writers in this period, while her persona was distinctly her own.[81] She held a degree from New York University and had published in the *New Yorker*. She had also worked her way up the ranks, in radio, an industry in which, she claimed, "nobody was waiting for me with open arms anywhere"; she would go to write for Groucho Marx, Gertrude Berg, and Tallulah Bankhead.[82] Diamond's claim of being a strange or different kind of woman positioned her to fail upward, gaining access to opportunities typically reserved for men. By saying she was better at writing for men than women—"Don't ask me why," she added—and labeling herself the kind of woman who had to "pa[y] for [her] own mink coat," she avoided being sidelined and treated as the room's token woman.[83] Diamond contrasted her conventional aspects—her Jewishness, her bourgeois class identity, her love of shopping and pretty things—with her unorthodox professional path, occupying those contradictions with brash and self-effacing humor. Diamond made jokes predicated on her familiarity with, but estrangement from, the trappings of gentility and girlishness, while poking gentle humor at anything performatively manly or macho. In a 1955 profile, Diamond cracked wise in response to the assertion that women do not have senses of humor, responding, "If a woman didn't have a sense of humor, how could she marry a man?"[84]

Diamond's public persona invites conflicting, though not mutually exclusive, readings. Was she a woman doing a man's job, a man trapped in a woman's body, a confirmed bachelorette, a hopeless spinster, or a perfect synthesis of female wit and male confidence? Quinlan Miller analyzes Diamond as a gender-queer figure, explaining that "Diamond transformed the social pressure to marry into comedy. . . . Diamond was 'again and again . . . asked why [she] never married,' and developed, in response, comic tactics for 'warding off nosy interviewers.'"[85] *Dick Van Dyke Show* (CBS, 1961–1966) creator Carl Reiner recalls her as "the one who actually said one day in a writers' conference, 'Why don't we go out and find some girls and get laid?'"[86] But for Diamond, as for many women writers in this period, any question of sexual orientation was overwritten by her professional status: married to her work. In a 1952 guest column for *Cue Magazine*, Diamond jokes that if "it weren't for the fact that, like all women, I have absolutely no sense of humor, I'd be ideally suited to my job."[87] This statement, a blend of self-mockery, masculine confidence, and pointed proto-feminist critique, epitomizes Diamond's comic point-of-view and her sardonic engagement with the tropes of the "girl writer." She emptied the ashtrays, yes, but she wanted the audience to see the effort behind the performance.

In the public choice between "work" and "love," Diamond definitively fell in the former camp. This dilemma finds a different resolution in the 1955 drama, "A Leaf Out of the Book," produced for the anthology drama *Climax!* (CBS, 1954–1958), adapted by Morton Fine, David Friedkin, and Shirley Gordon, from a Margaret Cousins story.[88] "A Leaf Out of the Book" takes the figure of the ambivalent career woman and imaginatively separates her into two extremes, generating a pre-second-wave feminist fable: women are allowed to have careers, as long as they remember to apologize for it. Cousins, a prolific writer and editor for such magazines as *Good Housekeeping* and *Ladies' Home Journal*, carefully managed a traditionally feminine persona, even as she ascended in the publishing arena. In 1965, Cousins was interviewed for a radio feature, "The Changing Attitude Towards Women," and told the journalist:

> Well, I'm a happy woman, I really am a happy woman, and I know I have missed the most important thing in life for a woman, and that's marriage. And I would have liked that. But since I didn't have that, I'm very grateful to be alive now when I have a chance to live life on the terms that I can cope with.[89]

It is unclear whether she is happy in spite of or because she did not achieve that "most important" rite of passage, marriage and children. Cousins seems to suggest that her career was a consolation prize for what might have been. But there lingers some ambivalence in her language, in that living life "on [her] own terms" as a writer and editor has only been possible because she passed up on becoming a wife and mother.

Patricia Bradley argues that Cousins's "work promoted patriarchy—men as the proper decision-makers ... [in that she] promulgated patriarchal values consciously, as an editor of a magazine that made no secrets of its values."[90] A woman in power, Cousins did not argue for progressive representations of femininity but, rather, "despite her obvious talents and discipline ... was chosen for positions of power primarily because her value system coincided with the value system of those in command."[91] It was this conservative value system—central to Cousins's own professional brand—that took narrative shape in the television adaptation of "A Leaf Out of the Book."

The drama centers on ambitious junior executive, Amy Lovell, whose last name foreshadows what she will choose when pulled between career and romance. In an argument with her beau, who expects her to put aside her career for him, Amy proclaims: "[Marriage] has to be on your terms, doesn't it? I have to fulfill all the dimensions you establish for a woman, don't I? Well, my career is precious to me. . . . If you don't accept that, you don't accept me." But Amy's resolve weakens after a glimpse into the life of villainous career woman, Sybil Morley. Sybil may inflict pain in the boardroom but proves to be the most injured party of all, having chosen a long-term affair with her boss, Harry Winters, over marriage and family. His gift to Sybil, a token engraved with the words, "To Sybil Morley, in gratitude for her years of service," only underscores the cold, transactional nature of their relationship. Sybil's feelings toward Amy are initially jealous ones—which Harry deems a "womanish" reaction—but Sybil later warns the ingenue of a life without love:

> There won't be any family portraits on your wall. . . . And come to the window. . . . No? Then I'll tell you what's out there. . . . No backyard with children. Boats. And a river. It's very beautiful; esthetic you'll bring your friends over and they'll say 'How very beautiful, Amy. How fortunate with a view.' And think of it, no backyard and no sound of husbands with the lawnmower. But boats.

As her name suggests, Sybil Morley is a modern update of Dickens's Marley, the character from *A Christmas Carol* (1843) who advises the miserly Ebenezer Scrooge to change his ways before it is too late. By observing Sybil's lonely life and the sacrifices she has made, Amy envisions her own future as an unmarried career woman. The boats outside Sybil's window signify a coldly curated life, while conjuring associations of drifting, of being untethered from things that matter, like husbands and lawnmowers.

Sybil may be sympathetic, but she remains a pernicious stereotype of the frigid, yet sexually accessible, postwar career woman. She is living proof that Amy—and, perhaps, the woman watching at home—cannot feel entitled to professional *and* personal satisfaction: she, and they, can only have one. Cousins did not present herself as immune from this dilemma, professing to have chosen career over love, and, like Sybil, claimed to regret the decision. Amy does what her boss and her creator did not by settling down with the man whose sweet talk includes: "Then marry me so I can beat some sense into you." While Cousins the author lives on her own flawed terms, her creation, Amy, condemns the terms of her boyfriend's ultimatum but chooses him anyway. But what do we make, as contemporary viewers, of this seemingly ideologically incoherent narrative, and what does it have to tell us about the woman author in postwar television?

Cousins's otherwise conservative persona is complicated by a thorny text like "A Leaf Out of the Book." Throughout the case studies in this book, we can see women writers' scripts pit female types against one another, mounting debates around women's roles in the workplace and the home; in the process, their characters approach contemporary cultural scripts with ambivalence or disdain. These shows usually failed to declare a victor, allowing viewers to entertain new viewpoints and have compassion for both sides. Other times, an episode will seem to cap the story off with a moral—in the case of "A Leaf Out of the Book," the rightness of choosing a man over a job—but the happy ending is problematic, even unsettling. As Cousins's biography borrows elements from romantic Amy and ambitious Sybil, this teleplay sheds light on how women television writers in this period constructed personas that reconciled, if imperfectly, those contradictions that arose between feminine ideals and the realities of professional life.

Cousins, after all, is not the only author of "A Leaf Out of the Book," nor is she the only woman writer. Shirley "Shirl" Gordon, one of the screenwriters who adapted Cousins's story for *Climax!*, had a career in publicity and radio writing before moving into writing for television sitcoms such as *Bewitched* (ABC, 1964–1972) and *My Three Sons* (ABC, 1960–1972), as well as authoring children's books. Gordon lived a quiet, if unconventional, private life, adopting a child as a single woman in her thirties.[92] Her extant work in radio and television, however, is revealing, as it is highly attuned to matters of gender, work, and the dangers professional women face. To that end, "A Leaf Out of the Book" serves as a compelling companion piece to Gordon's "The Statement of Mary

Blake" (May 4, 1950), a radio thriller on *Suspense* (CBS, 1942–1962) about male violence in the wake of female intellect. As its title suggests, the action is narrated by Mary, a laboratory assistant whose boss, Dr. Gregory Martin, frames her for murder. Dr. Martin's motive for killing his wife is rooted in professional jealousy: while her intellect and scientific insights have made his illustrious career possible, he is overwhelmed with resentment for her abilities.

In Mary's telling of the events, professional abuse fuses with sexual misconduct, Dr. Martin being a man who seeks out ways to demean the intelligent, capable women in his life. When the Martins throw a party, the doctor proposes a toast to his wife, in which he obliquely suggests he wants to share her with other men; later, he tries to pressure Mary into calling him attractive. In her study of radio thrillers, Allison McCracken analyzes the prevalence of "professional and/or intellectual men" who are villains, explaining that in the radio anthology drama *Suspense*, "the most 'civilized' men . . . are inevitably the most sadistic and treacherous . . . the conflating of the professional man with the controlling husband . . . [harboring] potential for social critique."[93] Not only is this doctor here ruthlessly working to condemn two women with a single plot, but his patriarchal entitlement spans the professional and the personal. A man who acts out at work is likely a brute at home, and vice versa, so why doesn't anyone stop him when his sadism is conducted in plain sight? As the party scene in "The Statement of Mary Blake" indicates, such abuse of power is possible because Dr. Martin has the support of other men at the party. With their hungry expressions and glinting gold teeth, they thrive on the doctor's humiliation of his wife, not to mention his presentation of a nubile young research assistant whom they can ogle. With all this support from friends, colleagues, and even the authorities, the doctor would plausibly get away with his wicked deeds, though Gordon does give the listener a happy ending. Justice is served because Dr. Martin's guilt is so intense that it renders him legally blind (a cute nod to *Jane Eyre* and its brooding, bigamist hero, Rochester), and he confesses to his crimes.

"The Statement of Mary Blake" is a radio thriller, "A Leaf Out of the Book" a television drama, but their underlying message is shared: the choice between love and career is a false one, because all women live in peril under male control. Gordon's radio play presents the darker conclusion to this setup, both women finding there is no escape from Dr. Martin's ego and destructiveness. On its own, "A Leaf Out of the Book" advises women to choose love over career, but, in the context of

Gordon's radio play, Amy's boyfriend's joking threat of violence echoes the doctor's sinister behavior, and, in the milder case of Harry Winters, an inappropriate, philandering boss makes for a bad boyfriend. Rather than think they will find safety as "wife" or "colleague," women must shift between registers, balancing different modes of professional and private femininity, switching up the performance when it wears thin. In this respect, the woman on-screen—but the career woman in particular—becomes a proxy or surrogate for the woman television writer who invented her, a figure always adjusting to a set of changing, sometimes hazardous, circumstances. This link between production culture and cultural production runs across broadcasting genres and threads throughout the case studies in this book. Women's need to deceive, disguise, and transform are central in all genres of postwar television programming, but it lies at the affective heart of its slapstick comedies and suspense dramas.[94]

Just as Gordon's work on "The Statement of Mary Blake" draws out the complications and dissonances beneath the surface of the seemingly retrograde "A Leaf Out of the Book," so too does focusing on the work of women writers in postwar television, particularly their renderings of women at work, open up the varied and "polysemic" meanings of the medium. The narrative indeterminacy of "A Leaf Out of the Book" is compounded by the fact that only a script survives. Unlike recordings, television scripts do not typically reveal how the camera framed the subjects, the particular intonation of actors' voices, or if the performers delivered their lines with conviction and earnestness or some degree of irony. Without being able to see the show, it is impossible to know whether this production pushed this scripted cautionary tale in the direction of horror or camp or played it totally straight, curtailing a closer inquiry into the episode's postwar gender politics. But Jeanine Basinger at least offers a way to understand the narrative arc of the episode through her discussion of the classical Hollywood women's film. Basinger explores how "plac[ing] a woman at the center of the story . . . provid[es] a temporary visual liberation of some sort, however small—an escape into a purely romantic love, into sexual awareness, into luxury, or into the rejection of the female role that might only come in some form of questioning."[95] Amy's pushing back against her fiancé's expectations is not canceled out by the story's conservative conclusion or the revelation of Sybil's regrets. According to Basinger's model, Amy's moment of articulate rebellion provides a "temporary visual liberation" to the viewer at home, an alternative possibility, a road not taken, even if it is too radical to let stand.

The scripted life of the woman writer—her creative work and her public persona—presented women with their own "temporary liberation" imagining a life of fulfillment through creative work. But the woman television writer as a cultural text was not seamless or coherent: quite the opposite, which in many ways was the point. This was also a phenomenon in early cinema, Giuliana Muscio describes how women scenario writers "achieve[d] important positions on the professional level, but not without contradictions. Their biographies reveal their originality, their restless search for a balance ... between creativity and domesticity."[96] So too did Diamond, Gordon, and Cousins all struggle with that "balance." Selma Diamond made fun of her marital status while joking about the trap of domesticity, while Margaret Cousins publicly bemoaned her life without a husband or a lawnmower but never paused her career in response. The least is known of Gordon's private life, but her work responds to the same set of cultural scripts, and, in the process, she does not pull her punches. Her writing suggests that the pressure on women to choose between career and family is a distraction from indicting the patriarchal systems that controlled wives and secretaries alike. The rhetorical indeterminacies in these writers' scripted lives reveal how they—and, indeed, how all women television writers—simultaneously responded to and created their own postwar feminine ideal, one rife with oppositions but held together by compulsory whiteness and middle-class identity. They performatively strained against the binaries of home and work, romantic love and intellectual fulfillment, mothering children and nurturing scripts and shows. After all, it wasn't supposed to look *too* easy. (If it was, they might have joked, then maybe a man could do it.) And American audiences knew these women writers were there—except when they didn't.

ESTABLISHING AN ARCHIVE OF FEMALE AUTHORSHIP IN POSTWAR TELEVISION

Women writers were paradoxically both absent and present on postwar television, underpinning many of the medium's playful self-disclosures and its meta-humor. In one such instance, one episode of *The Bob Cummings Show* (NBC, CBS, 1955) features a character named Margaret telling her friend, Carol, that "she has been watching too much *Burns and Allen*. Carol asserts that she can't believe any woman is that dumb, and Margaret answers, 'Of course not. It is written by men.'"[97] By Richard Irvin's account, these lines were certainly penned by the show's woman writer, the aforementioned Shirley Gordon.[98] And it might well be a sly criticism of *Burns and Allen* for having an all-male writing staff. With this punchline, the team at *The Bob Cummings Show* suggests that television needs women writers if it wants to feature smart, plausibly written female characters. Yet Margaret and Carol's exchange could just as easily imply that women don't write for television, so, just as the figure of Gordon and the woman television writer is evoked, she is erased. This moment mirrors the *Berle* writers' room sketch, in which Diamond and the other television writers are both seen and unseen, real and imaginary.

The woman writer in postwar television moves in and out of the historical record, and, thus, studying her presents its own series of historiographic challenges. In certain ways, the television industry lives up to the "Wild West" mythology created by the industry and its employees, the archival documentation plastered with freelancers' names, many of which leave little to no paper trail. In contrast, however, select television *auteurs* have archives, biographies, and numerous resources dedicated to their work. In the case of the woman writer in postwar television, we know she is there, but she can be hard to find and, even when found, the information can be limited. Liz Clarke notes the particular "double bind" that comes with studying woman scenario writers in early cinema due to "screenwriting's marginalization in the film industry and the erasure of women from film history," compounded by the fact that the "collaborative aspect of scenario departments both erased many writers from film histories and obscured the contributions of those who received credit."[99] Many of the same issues arise in the study of the woman writer in early television, particularly the common institutional and popular disinterest in collaborative women's work. Furthermore, the ways in which women writers framed their labor in obliging, congenial ways—when they had a platform at all—contributes to their contemporary obscurity. Piecing together this history requires scholars to write around these unanswerable questions of intent and authenticity, while grappling with those gaps in the archive that can never be fully closed, the missing "leaves out of the book" of television history.

One of the difficulties of archival research is that there is both too much material and not enough: thousands of boxes of uncataloged material, uncredited typescripts and screenplays, and black-and-white photographs of anonymous staffers, writers, and chorus girls. The way in which materials are organized further determines and delimits meaning. Institutional collections like the National Broadcasting Company

Papers at the University of Wisconsin, foreground a top-down account of television history, in which the major players are network decision-makers. Personal collections, such as the papers of Gertrude Berg, Peg Lynch, and Lucille Kallen, highlight a single writer's work and vision but cannot produce a broader portrait of a network of women writing for television or navigating the media industries. Volumes and online exhibits that center on women's contributions to television as stars and producers do not yield a framework for understanding authorship, rereading canonical texts, or reckoning with how women writers respond to industrial or historical change.

For me, uncovering this history has meant establishing what Allan Sekula would call a "shadow archive" of female authorship in early television. Sekula defines the "shadow archive" as a collection of materials that "encompasses an entire social terrain while positioning individuals within that terrain."[100] This mode is not new to feminist historians and media archaeologists, who have long sought to go beyond the simplistic directive to "add women and stir." Reorienting early film historiographies has required going outside of official modes of archival evidence to materials ranging from diaries to dollhouses.[101] For this study, I have drawn from network and personal, as well as commercial, archival collections. Oral histories and interviews play a central role in establishing this history of early television and letting women writers from this period tell their own stories. However, even as memoirs and testimonials promise to reveal what official documents obscure, they present their own set of shortcomings and confusions. Miranda Banks relays the observation of one screenwriter, who describes the oral histories of television history as together producing "'a kind of Rashomon'" narrative.[102]

The contrasts between individuals' accounts can make it impossible for the historian to reach any empirical truth as to how networks treated their female employees. But this is only a testament to John Thornton Caldwell's reminder that any "monolith [of "the entertainment industry"] does not exist."[103] For example, in her memoir, *I Love Lucy*'s Madelyn Pugh tells a story of how her female friend, writer Kathleen Hite, received informal mentorship from a woman executive at CBS, who told her that "CBS didn't hire women writers ... [but] offered her a job as her secretary ... [since] the only way she could make it was to start from within."[104] Yet writer-star Gertrude Berg (chapter 3), an established radio personality, was a CBS writer and star, so was a single allowance made for Berg, or were other factors at play? Women writers like Berg, Pugh, and Hite assembled careers—sometimes prolific, often precarious—rooted in chance and circumstance. Each woman's story is inflected by how they were hired, whether they found allies in their place of work or with a devoted fan base, and if their contributions were institutionally rewarded. The history of women television writers, to quote the poet Emily Dickinson, must be "told slant," this being the only way to reflect women's varied experiences and speak to the uncodified, informal ways in which gender politics impact labor practices in a creative industry.

Tracing women writers' credits poses its own host of obstacles, the research "trap" sometimes as simple as a woman using initials instead of her first name. Jay Presson Allen is a woman, even though her name is traditionally male, while a name like Shelley could be a man or a woman. In one instance, I found that a digital search of the writer "Lois Balk" failed to bring up a revealing item, just because her name is misspelled as "Louis" in the article. Here, we see the double threat of loss: that the woman writer's contributions might be lost through sheer bureaucratic error, and, even if found, be misrecognized. The result is that the archive of women writers is sometimes more wide than it is deep, evidenced by the wealth of knowledge available about Selma Diamond and the comparatively sparse literature on Shirley Gordon.

Additionally, in terms of broadcast content, many television programs have simply vanished, are only available on-site at libraries and university archives, or were shown live and thus never recorded. Incomplete television listings from newspapers give historians some clue as to which extant scripts were filmed and broadcast and which, most likely, have sat in a filing cabinet for the past seventy years. Without grants or commercial digitization to restore what recordings do exist, obscure series disappear from historical memory, and there is no one to champion their renaissance. This phenomenon is exacerbated by the fact that kinescope recordings of the live shows that made up much of the decade's programming are so fragile that, as media historian Cary O'Dell notes, it is "the one and perhaps only method of television recording technology to be completely obsolete in the industry today."[105] By contrast, television shows recorded on 35 mm film, such as *I Love Lucy*, have maintained their visual quality over time and are more easily rebroadcast and syndicated.[106] Scholarship is driven as much by the availability and quality of extant recordings as it is by academic curiosity, Alexander Dhoest pointing out that "television historiography has tended to focus on supply rather than demand"; as a result, much of early television—and its writers—has been and will continue to be forgotten.[107] Noting this scarcity, Maggie Hennefeld argues that a "lack of archival evidence corroborat[es] the ideological limitations of how history comes to be understood."[108] The scattered nature of the archive has hindered scholarship on the woman television writer, perpetuating the misconception that the industry was populated by male writers, directors, and executives, with women occupying the role of on-screen talent. This understanding of industry past neatly maps onto a cultural nostalgia for a "simpler time," in which white, middle-class men went to work and women stayed home. The scripted lives of women writers offer a corrective both to television industry history and the gender politics of work in postwar America. Their work went beyond writing scripts and story reports to include persona fashioning for the benefit of the industry and the general public. Erin Hill reminds us that, in the media industries, a woman's work is "never done"; likewise, any feminist inquiry into television history is an ongoing project in the rereading and reclamation of that which has been misplaced or underestimated but not yet lost.

CHAPTER 2

"A Sea of Male Interests"

Your Show of Shows *and the Comedy of Female Mischief*

"Think of it . . . as the Harvard of Television": this is how Lucille Kallen described her time as a writer for the comedy-variety hit *Your Show of Shows* (NBC, 1950–1954).[1] *Your Show of Shows* has long stood as a paragon of the Golden Age of Television, with its commitment to quality and liveness. But it is best known for its zany comedy sketches; for its leads, Sid Caesar and Imogene Coca; and for its storied writers' room, peopled by playwright Neil Simon, writer-director Mel Brooks, writer Mel Tolkin (*All in the Family*), and hyphenate-talent Carl Reiner (*The Dick Van Dyke Show*).[2] Kallen, the only woman writer on staff, is afforded a minor mention in these histories, upstaged by these more distinguished film and television alumni. But it is not only the success of Simon, Brooks, and others that relegated Kallen to a minor role in the histories. The romance of the postwar writers' room as fraternity house and masculinity machine has proved too compelling a narrative.

The wild comedy in a sketch like "This Is Your Story" (1953) dramatizes this vision of the Caesar writers' room as fueled by male camaraderie and competition.[3] This parody of the proto-reality show *This Is Your Life* stars Sid Caesar as Al Duncy, a regular Joe pulled from a television studio audience to be reunited with estranged family and friends. As the six-foot-tall Al embraces his elderly uncle Goopy (a wiry, compact Howard Morris), their affection turns to desperate, hysterical sobbing, cuddling, and wrestling. Who can love the other harder and weirder? The strait-laced host (Carl Reiner) can do little to pry them apart. Al's aunt Mildred tries to join the group hug, it is not long before she stands helplessly by as the two men re-reunite, the uncle wailing as he latches onto Al's leg. Aunt Mildred does not or cannot roughhouse with the boys. Watching these actors play and build their zany homosocial world together is the great appeal of both the on-screen gags and the off-screen writers' room it allegorizes.[4]

Just as Aunt Mildred enters the frame but fails to find a place, so Lucille Kallen's role in the proceedings does not conform to a nostalgic myth of white, Jewish men high-spiritedly inventing television all by themselves. Where Kallen is remembered, she is too often demoted to accessory status in the collaboration. In his 2003 memoir, *Caesar's Hours*, Sid Caesar writes of the "very smart and very businesslike . . . [Kallen, who] provided the woman's point of view, which was crucial."[5] Caesar refers to her role as one of taking down the lines from the writing brainstorms and assembling them into scripts but insists that she was a "skilled writer," and not a secretary.[6] But the line between "secretary" and "scribe" was always being blurred or moved for Kallen, in contemporary accounts and even during her day-to-day work in the room.

In his book on production culture, John Thornton Caldwell describes how "writing by committee functions as a lab for creativity focused on freeform speculation, critical dialogue, personal contestation, and professional oneupsmanship."[7] Calling writers' room a laboratory conveys the trial-and-error nature of comedy writing work, while, in the case of *Your Show of Shows*, the writers, through debate and competition, worked to establish a future of the medium and who was best suited to write for it. Felicia D. Henderson, a woman-of-color working in contemporary television, issued an on-the-ground self-ethnographic treatment of the writers' room, explaining, "Inside this ground zero [of the writers' room] . . . ideas are negotiated, consensus is formed, and issues of gender, race, and class identities play out and complicate the on-screen narratives that eventually air on network and cable television."[8] Here, Henderson gestures to the larger representational stakes of the writers' room: identity politics inform the stories that are told, gendered dynamics seeping into the scripts themselves, which, in turn, can critique or even alter the cultural status quo.

Kallen's fraught relationship with being a woman in the writers' room speaks to broader conversations around the limits of postwar femininity, as well as the challenges of being a woman writer for television. Kallen attests to being "a source of both annoyance and entertainment [to her male colleagues]. . . . It engendered both resentment and self-conscious swaggering, it manifested itself in both condescension and protective affection," concluding that, "in short, those guys were confused."[9] Kallen's presence, then, was not separate from the testosterone-fueled antics of the writers' room but one of its causes. The woman writer is privy to the disorder of the room, even a provocation of this wildness, and yet, Kallen's scripted life was focused on maintaining control in the face of chaos, in cloaking wildness in a mid-priced fur stole.[10] Kallen strove to wear her gender lightly, putting it on and taking it off when appropriate, playing the little lady at one moment and bluntly grabbing for editorial control in the next. The aggression and gendered rivalries of *Show of Shows* fed into the energy of the program through Kallen's sharp satires of contemporary womanhood and all its petty, crushing demands, including that women must be ladylike so they will be listened to—only to have men promptly shout over them.

By her own account, Kallen found her greatest success and made her greatest impact on the show by working the outsides of the writers' room, cultivating intimate, one-on-one collaborations with the show's head writer, Mel Tolkin, and its lead actress, Imogene Coca. Disentangling an individual author's voice from a collaborative effort can be tricky, but existing oral histories and working scripts begin to reveal which sketches and musical numbers were written for Coca by Kallen, which sketches were cowritten by Kallen and Tolkin, and which sketches speak most directly to Kallen's comic sensibility: silly, musical, and, as Tolkin later described her, "feminine and feminist."[11] Her work with Tolkin on the recurring sketch, "The Hickenloopers," as well as with Imogene Coca on a wide range of character sketches and songs, created a space in a male-driven comedy show for subversive, girl-power portraits of egalitarian marriages and women driven mad by the pressures of domesticity and monogamy. If Kallen and Coca's work on *Your Show* narrativizes the constraints of being a woman professional through comic allegory, their partnership on the *Your Show of Shows*' star vehicle spin-off, *The Imogene Coca Show* (NBC, 1955) tells the story of a woman temporarily freed; the show lasted one riotous, if creatively incoherent, season.

THE EVOLUTION OF *YOUR SHOW OF SHOWS* AND THE CAESAR'S WRITERS' ROOM

Kallen met writer Mel Tolkin and producer Max Liebman at the Jewish resort Tamiment, where they all worked on the hotel's summer theatrical revue from 1947 to 1950.[12] Kallen's musical conservatory training prepared her to work on this weekly showcase, which combined song, dance, and comedy. Prior to Tamiment, Kallen organized a theater group in her hometown of Toronto. When she moved to New York City to attend Juilliard, she found that "[her] heart was not in [music]," so she decided to abandon her plans of becoming a professional musician to work in theater instead.[13] Kallen wrote a musical-comedy nightclub act for a small ensemble, and after having seen a performance of her show, Max Liebman interviewed and hired Kallen and one of the show's actresses.[14]

Historian Martha Schmoyer LoMonaco describes the Tamiment Playhouse as a "hybrid [theater that] grew out of such diverse influences as the burgeoning resort industry, the American socialist movement, the Yiddish Theatre, the American musical theatre, and popular entertainments such as revue and burlesque comedy."[15] Max Liebman subjected his employees to exceedingly high standards. In a later oral history, Kallen remembered Liebman as a "very demanding . . . perfectionist," adding that, "if he weren't, he wouldn't have achieved the quality that he did." She recalled, dryly, how he would roughhouse with her, "bang [her] head against the wall" as a form of affection, and make comically impossible demands, like that she somehow "write a completely original, fresh, new song that sounds exactly like" an existing popular song.[16] Though he worked behind the scenes, Tamiment reflected Liebman's humor, his vision, and his work ethic, as would the televisual adaptations that followed. Tolkin, Kallen, and Liebman were the only credited writers for the 1948 Tamiment revue, writing sketches and musical numbers for performers including Imogene Coca and the later Your Show of Shows choreographer James Starbuck.[17]

The original television adaptation of Tamiment, The Admiral Broadway Revue (Figure 4), debuted in 1949, running on Friday nights at 8 p.m. But when the show lost its sponsor in 1950, NBC rebranded the series, positioned Caesar and Coca as its leads and public faces, and changed its name to Your Show of Shows.[18] Your Show of Shows was broadcast on Saturday nights, from 9 to 10:30 p.m., following the comedy-variety program, The Jack Carter Show; NBC marketed the two and a half hours of programming as the Saturday Night Revue (Figure 5), a gesture toward the live theatrical playhouses that populated early television. Throughout its run, Your Show garnered Emmys for the show and its lead performers, and it remained in the Nielsen top 20 until its final season.[19] Both publicity images make the performers' faces

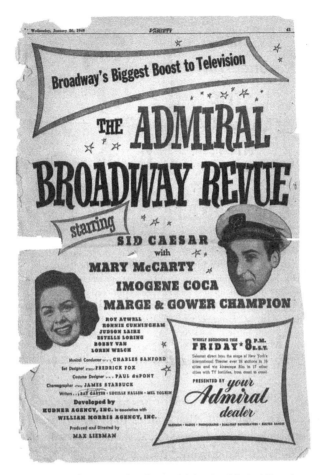

FIGURE 4. This promotional material for the *Admiral Broadway Revue* stresses the show's theatrical roots and its deep bench of talent, including, but not limited to, its stars. *Admiral Broadway Revue* folder, Tolkin Papers, WGF.

the focal point, with small and minimal text, a blank background, and no mention of sponsorship, indicating how much the network used star power to market the program and draw in audiences.

In the move from stage to screen, the explicitly socialist politics of the playhouse were dropped—or, at least, highly repressed. But much remained the same: the variety format, the pacing of the revue, and the triumvirate of Liebman, Tolkin, and Kallen. Tolkin claims that NBC executive (later network president) Sylvester "Pat" Weaver "lifted

2½ hours of
wonderful fun

**THE
SATURDAY
NIGHT
REVUE**

8 to 10:30 p.m.

SID CAESAR

IMOGENE COCA

JACK CARTER
and guests

FIGURE 5. This subsequent advertisement for "The Saturday Night Revue" doubles down on NBC's star power and its strong Saturday night lineup as a whole; it does not credit any other members of the cast and crew or even mention the shows by name (*Your Show of Shows, The Jack Carter Show*). Credit: "NBC's Saturday Night Revue," accessed May 15, 2016, http://1.bp.blogspot .com/-lvr1p_5WtZk/Ts4QfxZbK2I/AAAAAAAAIOo/Wyo _De9DcEA/s1600/Screen+shot+2011-11-24+at+1.37.48+AM.png.

[Tamiment], bodily, for *The Admiral Broadway Revue*," while Liebman told *Theatre Arts* magazine that, rather than simply translate theater to television, he believed "television . . . should also adjust itself to the values I intended to bring from the theatre."[20] Kallen felt the influence of sponsors and ratings when writing for television, two elements that did not factor in to her writing for Tamiment Playhouse:[21]

> I was not awed by the fact that we were on television because I didn't know what television was in those days. . . . I was not amazed, sitting there at "The Admiral Broadway Revue" and seeing this song and parody number that I had worked up in my little cabin at Tamiment being recorded for posterity![22]

Television functioned under a different set of commercial and ideological pressures from Jewish theater, but the newness of the medium allowed for more aesthetic and formal experimentation. One 1950 episode, for example, included an original opera number for the show's leading lady and an abbreviated adaptation of Oscar Wilde's *The Importance of Being Earnest* alongside contemporary comedy sketches.[23]

Elements of highbrow art, specifically opera and ballet scenes of *The Admiral Broadway Revue*, remained a part of *Your Show of Shows*, but theatrical adaptation did not. And as the show found its voice and increasingly relied on original material, more writers were hired, including Brooks, Stein, and, when Kallen went on maternity leave, Neil and Danny Simon.[24] When Kallen returned, she was thrust into a new role: the only woman in the bustling, all-male Caesar writers' room, her partner, Tolkin, at the head. This shift in power dynamics meant that Kallen had to work all the harder to contribute to the conversation and make herself heard.

FOXHOLES AND FRATERNITIES: THE GENDER POLITICS OF COLLABORATIVE AUTHORSHIP

The writers' room does not run according to a legislative body's set procedures: the collaboration can feel raucous, even dangerous, when any act of domination or aggression can be laughed off as "just a joke." Carl Reiner, who would eventually write for *Your Show of Shows* as well as perform, would linger in the hallway outside the writers' room, as the writers did not initially want to invite the actor to join them.[25] And one much-repeated anecdote from the Caesar's writers' room centers on a pregnant Kallen, sick from her coworkers' cigar smoke. When producer Max Liebman set up a rack of pipes and tobacco in the room to accommodate her, Kallen recounts overhearing one colleague remark, "She wanted equality but not cigars."[26] She translated Liebman's gesture, generous but ineffectual, as expressing the male consensus: "We love you . . . [but] this is our house."[27] Likewise, Henderson pinpoints "cigar smoke [as] . . . the means by which the early writers' room was gendered and a female writer was othered and marginalized."[28]

Cigar smoke serves as an appropriately macho literalization of the abstract category that separated Kallen from the rest: the notion of comedy writing as *men's work*. The men who wrote for *Your Show of Shows* publicly discussed their work as an ideal hybrid of artist and office job, providing regular pay and creative fulfillment minus any of the preciousness or angst of the Romantic artist figure. In a 1974 interview, writer and star Carl Reiner addressed how the writers for Sid Caesar managed to be funny on a nine-to-five work schedule. Reiner explained: "Professional comedy writers and performers will be funny wherever and whenever they are brought together. They are programmed to produce laughter, and when there is a job at stake, a professional reputation involved . . . the comedic motor quickly turns over.[29] Reiner did not idealize the work: there were time restrictions and plenty of executives to please. That said, these writers felt they were making something in accordance with their own interests, tastes, and humor. Better than "yes men," Caesar's writers were "yes *and*" men, game improvisators and comedians for pay. *Caesar's Hour* writer Larry Gelbart would say of Caesar that "he encouraged us to just be ourselves and to be ourselves through our writing."[30] While the demands of the network, the sponsor, and the audience must be met, the writer was his own boss when it came to creating his own world through language.

Television writing required that men work collaboratively, and the bonds that formed were close but volatile. Caesar described the collaboration of the writers' room as working "in the trenches together . . . [when] in a foxhole under fire . . . these guys become your buddy."[31] The gendered analogy reveals how the writers' room functioned as a fraternity or single-sex army platoon. This fraternity, though, had its darker, psychodramatic dimensions. Tolkin would admit to *Newsday* that the brainstorming sessions were fueled by, in his words, "creative anger" stemming from a desire to impress the patriarch-star: "[Caesar] was the dad and we were all competing for his approval and his love."[32] Tolkin also recounted the writers' relishing of wild antics, feeling free to "make mistakes. . . . [Because] if we tossed out a lousy idea, everyone would jump on it, build on it, embellish it."[33] In his memoir, Caesar describes the enlivening process of collaboration as turning a lackluster Monday into a joyous romp, as they respond to the prompt of embodying "the psychology of a fly": "I started rubbing my wrists, the way a fly keeps washing his claws. . . . Lucille got interested and came up with something the fly could do. Then Tony Webster chipped in with a fly shtick. In another couple of minutes they all agreed it had possibilities and we went to work on it."[34] The writers took energy from each other, and the group worked to top itself as much as each man sought to top the other. But some writers recalled the high-octane collaboration with ambivalence or displeasure. Joe Stein is quoted in one oral history as saying: "There was a lot of screaming going on. Very often I thought I was saying a line that was funny, but I'd never get heard."[35] Neil Simon credits Carl Reiner for saving his career; Simon, with his quiet voice and reserved personality, whispered his ideas into Reiner's ear, who would then convey the jokes to the group.[36] Simon and his brother were not invited into the writers' room environment straightaway, instead beginning their time at *Show* working in a private "office" on a stairway landing.[37]

Tolkin believed the group's shared ethnic "outsider"-ness united them, recalling, "[I] was from the Ukraine, Kallen was a woman, Brooks was from the Bronx, and Webster was Catholic. . . . Most writers are outsiders . . . [so] it was an outsider's look at Earthlings' foolish, absurd behavior."[38] He added that it was because the writing team was "a little offbeat . . . [that it had] a fresher look."[39] Their harmony was established through a shared difference, their common experiences of being foreigners and strangers to the mainstream. In one interview, Borscht Belt graduate Mel Brooks recalls how Tolkin expanded his horizons:

> Mel Tolkin was the head writer and, you know, a very deeply intellectual, artistic guy who put me onto people like Andreev and Nikolai Gogol. . . . I was just a kid from Williamsburg, Brooklyn and I . . . should have been heading for the garment center, I should've been a shipping clerk, and here I was writing "The Admiral Broadway Revue" for Sid Caesar and so Tolkin got me a psychoanalyst.[40]

Joe Stein would confirm: "There was a lot of cigar smoke and a lot of talk about psychiatry. Every one of them was seeing a shrink, and his not seeing a psychiatrist, in this context, made everyone "look . . . at [him] like [he] was crazy."[41] The more time these men spent together, the more similar they became, while their differences bred *Your Show of Shows'* zany comic sensibility.

The recurring character of the "Professor" demonstrates how the Caesar writers' membership coalesced around Jewishness, a category tied up with whiteness and maleness, while also standing somewhat apart from prevailing definitions of American identity. The Professor is a parody of postwar pundit culture and intellectualism; with his heavy accent, he is typically introduced as a "distinguished Viennese expert" on decidedly nonacademic topics like mountain climbing and magic.[42] Tolkin and Brooks's subscription to psychoanalysis becomes relevant here, the oblique referencing to Freud turning the Professor into an inside joke as well as an occasion for satire.

The Professor also serves as an exhibit of recognizably Jewish comedy and the "wise fool" trope.[43] When the Professor is a magician in a 1951 sketch, his tricks fail at first, only to succeed more spectacularly: rather than making a pretty girl disappear, he makes a bevy of beauties appear in her stead. According to the men onstage, this is truly a providential mistake, far better than the initial outcome would have been.[44] As a mountain climbing expert in a sketch from 1952, the Professor advises those falling off a mountain to, first, scream all the way down so that they can find your body and, second, to flap their arms and fly.[45] When his interviewer (Carl Reiner) objects, the Professor replies that you'll never know if you can fly until you try: you might be the first person to succeed! And if this fails, he concludes, you can always go back to screaming. *Tablet Magazine* discusses the Professor as evidence of *Your Show of Shows'* "deep Jewish roots," as he was an Austrian character born out of the minds of a roomful of Yiddish-speaking comedy writers.[46] But, if the Professor was a parody of Freudianism or 1950s expert culture, it was also a loving tribute. Many other sketches accomplished the similar feat of poking respectful fun at higher art forms such as art-house cinema, opera, and ballet. The Professor illustrates the multi-voiced comedy of a writers' room where the members have different but complementary relationships to intellectualism and cosmopolitanism.[47]

As Henderson establishes in her study of the writers' room, a room of outsiders must establish its own hegemonic order by finding someone to marginalize, consensus built at the cost of shutting out others, and the excluded party in Caesar's writers' room would be the woman in the room. The tenor of the writers' room was incompatible with Kallen's desire to remain lady-like at work. Kallen would later say:

> I never was a Selma Diamond. Selma was . . . very forceful, grating. . . . She had a voice, and I was torn between preserving my femininity and preserving my career at the same time. So it was difficult . . . to be forceful enough to get through. I mean, these were big guys. . . . They were loud, they were noisy, they were ruthless.[48]

She would write for the *New York Times* in 1992 that the dilemma was that "nobody likes a pushy girl who bellows. But nobody hires a writer because she's dainty."[49] For Kallen, the problem was one of deciding how to behave and how to belong. While the men in the room needed only to focus on sharpening their comic prowess to find acceptance, she "walk[ed] a very fine line" at the office, puzzling over how to be taken seriously at work while maintaining a genteel demeanor.[50]

Writers' descriptions of the room draw up the space as a sexual battleground. According to Caesar, the room, which doubled as the dancers' changing room, overlooked Broadway and Fifty-Sixth Street and had "elevators . . . like steel cages. When you pulled back the gated door, it sprang back like a trap. We were writing amid women's underwear, socks, and jock straps."[51] Kallen recalled more specifically how they worked "in the boys' dressing room with the jock straps hanging over-head."[52] Caesar and Kallen's descriptions reveal how each understood their work. The elevators speak to the poverty of the production but also give television writing the high stakes of coal mining—very much matching Caesar's trenches metaphor—while the undergarment-scape suggests openness, even explicitness, in their conversation and com-edy. Specifically, Kallen's assertion that, starting out in television, she survived the *locker room talk*, composing comedy among "the sweaty jockstraps and discarded tights . . . without worrying about problems of gender" can only be read as a wry joke, the trappings of masculine anatomy literally dangling in front of her face.[53]

Kallen would say of her time in the writers' room that "at the time I felt it was one big happy family, but later I said, What an idiot! . . . There was a male phalanx, and then there was me."[54] She was excluded from this band of brothers: when the men went out to eat, or when they talked about women, she could not join in. (Years later, at a televised reunion, Kallen would be unable to attend due to family obligations, and the men on the stage—including Reiner, Brooks, and Caesar—made a point of explaining to the audience that they had in fact remembered to invite her.[55]) But Kallen was also quoted as saying that "when [they] were working, there was no difference," even as her recollections of the writers' room tell a different story.[56] The riffing, bantering and inter-rupting tempo of conversation that Neil Simon likened to an "auction," Kallen called "an all-out war."[57] The idea of forging her own voice proved a practical and a figurative challenge, as Kallen felt that she "couldn't override those big voices, and yet . . . had very definite ideas about what should and shouldn't be done."[58]

Kallen went beyond seeking a seat at the proverbial table—she liter-ally needed a place to sit down. The writers' room was a sty. The soggy plates, the half-eaten pastrami sandwiches, the coleslaw "abstract art decoration" on the wall constituted a space that was part *Animal House* and part studio space, only littered with Jewish deli food rather than clay or paint. To navigate this trashed room, Kallen learned to wear dark skirts so that the stains wouldn't show. Here is Kallen's "fine-line walking" in action, the compromising of her job and her femininity. It would be unthinkable to start dressing like a man but foolish to wear a "white sharkskin suit," as did one uninformed guest actress.[59] Strap-ping on the proper armor, for Kallen, made a difference. She wore a red scarf to the office, so that she could "break through the tumult to say something . . . [by] climb[ing] up on the couch and wav[ing] it," as, in

It all begins with a Monday conference. Writer Lucille Kallen unfolds the rough of a sketch for Max Liebman, producer and director of the show. Staffers look and listen, their brain cells working furiously.

FIGURE 6. Curious what it looks like in a (clearly staged) writers' room? Look no further. The caption reads: "It all begins with a Monday conference. Writer Lucille Kallen unfolds the rough of a sketch for Max Liebman, producer and director of the show. Staffers look and listen, their brain cells working furiously." Image from "Backstage with Imogene and Me" by Sid Caesar, *Coronet* magazine, December 1951, Mel Tolkin Papers, WGF.

Kallen's words, "Sid boomed, Tolkin intoned, Reiner trumpeted, and Brooks, well, Mel imitated everything from a rabbinical student to the white whale of Moby Dick thrashing about on the floor with six harpoons sticking in his back."[60] Using a red scarf as a tool of intervention was not a permanent fix, she noted, as, after the novelty wore off, the other writers began to ignore her again.[61] Herein lies the emblematic question for the woman in the writers' room: how and when did she need to reassess her circumstances and change her behavior, her tactics, her self-presentation?

Serving as the room's scribe turned out to be a promotion of sorts, leveraging her role as "secretary" into one of editorial power and control. In one publicity still (Figure 6), Kallen is the only one with pen in hand. And as Kallen was the best—likely, only—typist in the room, her transcribing duties became her mode of intervening into the chaotic collaboration.[62] Kallen recounts Mel Brooks's entrance into the writers' room: "I didn't know who he was for a time, and he thought I was the secretary. At a certain point he was allowed into the Writers' Room, and we came to accept him."[63] Caesar insisted on Kallen serving as the room's scribe, the team's calm center, while the rest of the writing staff was "jumping around, yelling and screaming ideas and dialogue."[64] Kallen diplomatically marshalled the voices of the room, inventing her own essential intervention in the back-and-forth without the need to stand on furniture or wave around her clothing. Kallen's imperative became braiding together all the voices of the room—including her own—into something cohesive and funny. But it was her one-on-one collaborations with Tolkin and Coca that provided Kallen the most meaningful escape from the pressures of the room, as well as the opportunity to be an equal partner in the creative process.

MARRIAGE OF TRUE MINDS: KALLEN AND TOLKIN AS "THE HICKENLOOPERS"

Tolkin would write of Kallen that "Lucille [was] the sitter, I the pacer. In addition to being very creative, she is a strong, rough editor. I heard a lot of 'NO's before she'd start putting words on paper."[65] Tolkin and Kallen's partnership was an equitable and harmonious one, Kallen later joking that their chemistry sprang from Tolkin's brilliance twinned with his willingness to follow her orders.[66] Most frequently, they collaborated on "The Hickenloopers," a recurring domestic sketch starring Caesar and Coca as married couple Charles and Doris.[67] Kallen described writing the sketches with Tolkin over the weekend or on Mondays, so the pair could present the work to the group in Max Liebman's office. Kallen and Tolkin drew on their lives and marriages to their respective spouses for inspiration.[68] He later told an interviewer that "with the domestic sketches, we discovered that whatever bugs me bugs the world. And the more detailed you are about these little things that bug you, the more generally interesting you become."[69] Kallen would affirm this, explaining "you could outline any of those sketches and people will fill them in mentally, because they dealt with the kind of life experience that lent itself to exaggeration."[70] Writing "The Hickenloopers" with Tolkin provided Kallen with a calmer alternative to the writers' room, and their working relationship speaks to how the woman writer in television forged alternative avenues for creative autonomy.

The stakes of these sketches had representational implications for the scripted life of the woman writer and for marriage in the postwar moment. Tolkin told *WGA Journal* that he and Kallen were "particularly proud of [their] domestic sketches. She helped give Coca, who played the wife, an edge of strength and feistiness." Working with Tolkin, Kallen did not need to repress or repackage her own "feistiness" but, instead, channeled it into Coca's Doris. As a result, "The Hickenloopers" provides a vision of egalitarian male-female partnership that bridges the personal and the professional, husband and wife interchangeable with creative collaborators or costars (Kallen and Tolkin, Caesar and Coca). "The Hickenloopers" interrogated a postwar ideal of marriage in which "[a man] held the authority, with a wife who would remain subordinate," by extension challenging the idea that the woman behind the typewriter was necessarily "subordinate" to the men in the room, the leading lady second to her leading man.[71] What if the relationship between men and women could be equal, respectful, and even fun?

Kallen credited the success of "The Hickenloopers" to the rapport between its stars, claiming, "Sid alone is like having a match without anything to strike it on. [Coca] was the perfect foil for him. She was diminutive, and he was large. She was stiletto sharp, and he was a roar and kind of bumbling."[72] While Caesar's Charles was prone to fits of rage, Coca's Doris can ably move between weeping, screaming, and sweet talking, depending on what will be most effective. The marriage—and the comedy—is one of well-matched adversaries gamely facing off. Coca, after all, is not the silly little woman, like Gracie in *The Burns and Allen Show* (CBS, 1950–1958), nor is Caesar a buffoon married to a sensible wife, like Jackie Gleason in *The Honeymooners* (CBS, 1955–1956). There was progressive currency to this choice, in that the question of who "won" the battle of the sexes was never settled, neither party dismissed as oblivious or unreasonable. Kallen vowed this even-handedness in portraying Charles and Doris's faults reflected the writers' commitment to realism, and was a testament to the actors' abilities.[73] To that end, the Hickenloopers sketches gave both actors time to shine, neither consistently playing the straight man or the dummy. According to Kallen, Caesar in particular strove to give his costar ample comic opportunities: "he was very . . . conscious of her getting what she deserved, and he was afraid of hogging."[74]

The domestic sketches were predicated on Charles and Doris meeting one another's challenges or energies, outdoing one another, and concluding with a reconciliatory compromise. In the "Chinese Food Sketch" (n.d.), Charles brings home Chinese takeout only to discover that Doris has spent all day cooking a fancy dinner.[75] Both insist theirs is the *true* dinner and demand the other's dinner be thrown in the trash. After mirroring one another's antics—screaming, insisting, sitting in stony silence—Doris tosses her dinner out the window into the arms of a grateful neighbor, while Charles's dinner is devoured by a friend stopping by. Finally, the couple happily settles on a third way: Indian buffet.

Similarly, in the 1951 scene "Auto Smash Up," Charles discovers that Doris has totaled the car and wrought major property damage on Main Street.[76] First, Doris tries to diffuse Charles's barely suppressed fury— "I'm very upset, and I'm very excited!" he informs her—by acting affectionate and omitting some crucial details. But when Doris is backed into a corner, having to explain how she drove into one building and, while in reverse, hit another, she bellows "Well, I had to back out, didn't I?!" She promptly bursts into tears, and, both spouses having been granted their chance to explode, the domestic scene is promptly resolved. Kallen called this sketch her favorite because it provided a

perfect situation for the two [performers. . . . It] catered to their strengths in both cases . . . Sid's ability to register . . . shock of tornado-like impact . . . and Coca's fudging with the truth; both of these things were very much a part of their repertoire, and it worked beautifully.[77]

Their meet-ness as a couple creates a liberal portrait of contemporary marriage, while voicing an implicit argument for the "perfect situation" of male-female partnerships in all areas of public and private life. The institution of marriage needs smart, strong women to thrive, and so does television, in staffing both women writers and performers. Here, the scripted lives of Kallen and Coca converged: both struggled, in different ways, with fame and working in the male-dominated world of comedy, and their work together crystallizes the pressures and travails of performing agreeable femininity day in and day out.

While the chemistry between Caesar and his writers, and even that between Coca and Caesar, has attracted decades' worth of fan attention, the connection between Kallen and Coca has largely gone unanalyzed. Writing for *Your Show of Shows*, Kallen experienced her gender as something imposed upon her—or seized from her—at work. Much of the comedy she wrote for Coca thematizes this experience and, by extension, provides commentary on postwar womanhood as a series of impossible expectations and contradictions.

A GATHERING OF TALENTS: KALLEN AND COCA ON *YOUR SHOW OF SHOWS*

Can a white man truly tell anybody how it feels to be negro?
Can a heterosexual truly tell anybody how it feels to be queer?
Can a twenty-year-old truly tell anybody how it feels to be
    middle-aged?
Yet we never question the fact that almost everything we see
    on stage and in films about how it feels to be a woman . . .
    is told to us by a man.
. . .Where is our showcase? Where is our gathering of talents?
    Where is our stage?

—Lucille Kallen, "Memo to Whoever Is Concerned" (undated)

The 1953 *Your Show of Show* sketch "The Clock" introduces the viewer to the tiny town of Bauerhoff, where the villagers "disagree . . . about many things"—except for their shared love of the local cuckoo clock. The community still regularly congregates around the clock to watch the Dutchmen figurines perform their "perfect" machinations.[78] The balance and symmetry of the set—a structure with the two arched doorways framing a giant clock—projects peace and order. The four little Dutchmen, played by Sid Caesar, Carl Reiner, Imogene Coca, and Howard Morris each perform their task, with Caesar as the primary hammerer and Coca as the water-girl whose job it is to cool off the hammer and anvil. If, by Chekhov's logic, a gun introduced at the beginning of a story must be fired by the tale's end, so, in comedy, must cream-pies fly, banana peels be slipped on, and ladles of water be tossed in the direction of unsuspecting Dutchmen.

"Other things in the world might fail, but [the clock] is perfect," the narrator assures the audience, only to have his words promptly overturned. A change in the musical key and the twitchy movements of the actors denotes the cuckoo clock's growing malfunction, which culminates in a frantic group-spasm and burnout. This scene at first calls to mind Henri Bergson's 1900 canonical treatise, *Laughter*. According to Bergson, we laugh when people behave like machines, when "something mechanical [is] encrusted on the living," and this kind of "automatism" serves as "a sort of social gesture . . . [to] correct men's manners."[79] Failed automation stands in for the chaos of comedy work: as with the candy assembly line in *I Love Lucy*, the mess and the yelling appear as failure, but the unraveling has been carefully planned.[80] So too did the Caesar writers' room, like the clock tower in Bauerhoff, run on conflict, debate, and disagreement, Mel Brooks labeling their comedy as real life "bent an inch or two."[81] The comedy of "The Clock" is born from the tweaking of wires, the grinding of gears, and a deepening technical maladjustment that descends into total disorder. Reading the scene alongside Brooks's statement, the clock becomes legible as a literal *comedy machine*, its paradoxical regime of conflict and chaos resulting in impeccably choreographed slapstick.

The devious little Dutch Girl lies at the heart of the hijinks, the skit speaking to the role of the woman in comic collaboration. At the scene's start, the Dutch Girl's primary function is to provide aid to the Dutchman as he works, pouring cool water on his hot metalwork. But as the wiring of the clock goes on the fritz, her task morphs into an act of sabotage. The viewer watches Coca splash Caesar repeatedly in the face, their expressions powerfully blank. Coca is the instigator, rather than the naive surveyor, of wild physical humor, as the Dutch Girl is revealed as a scene-stealer, unwilling to play the nurturer or the helpmeet, submissively performing her women's work. The Dutch Girl's behavior disrupts the operation, in one sense, but in other, makes the comedy machine go.

Like the Dutch Girl, Kallen operated as the odd-part-out in the writers' room, where her value as a participant and her role in the process was indeterminate. And yet her "confusing" presence as a woman in the writers' room branded and shaped the comic sensibility of *Your Show of Shows*. Reiner not only called Kallen "quite a talented girl . . . cute as a button too," but also said she imbued *Your Show of Shows* with a "woman's touch."[82] This female perspective manifested as a sharp, funny reprimand of conventional gender roles and "how it feels to be a woman," as Kallen says in the epigraph to this section above.[83] So, while all the writers wrote for both Caesar and Coca, of the latter, Kallen recalled: "I did write with her in mind, and I had a feeling of great kinship with the way she played things. I knew how she would do it, and it was easy for me to write."[84] Meanwhile, Brooks and Tolkin specialized in the "Sid Specialties," solo pantomimes for Caesar that focused on the male anxieties of work, marriage, and fatherhood.

Lucille Kallen used her mordant wit to create a mythical Westchester village where sleuth C.B. Greenfield solves crimes. She was also killingly funny as a writer for 'Your Show of Shows.'

Lucille Kallen (upper right) at work on 'Your Show of Shows.'

FIGURE 7. Imogene Coca (far left) and Lucille Kallen (far right) function as visual bookends to a tableau of men at work. From Michael Sauter, "Murder Most Civilized," *Suburbia Today*, November 11, 1984, Tolkin Papers, WGF.

Kallen's writing for Imogene Coca carved out an important space for female subjectivity and expression on *Your Show of Shows*. Coca was an ideal muse and instrument for Kallen's expressive and creative powers, the two women coming together to critique the constraints of postwar white, middle-class womanhood and, in its most audacious moments, offer a vision of a freer form of lived femininity (Figure 7). Kallen and Coca's creative chemistry was inextricable from their personal friendship, one rooted in common experiences and complementary personalities. As Kallen explained to one interviewer: "Imogene and I were two females lost in a sea of male interests, male behavior. That consolidated our relationship."[85] Kallen would recall how the otherwise shy Coca would encourage Kallen to buy expensive hats, and, once, convinced her to buy a two-piece bathing suit so the two could pose for a mock-scandalous photo, concluding, "She had a great sense of play, obviously."[86] It was Coca's silliness and Kallen's carefulness that allowed their skits and songs to tap into sources of female anger and frustration without transgressing the safe realm of "light" comedy. Kallen was bound by a sense of manners and gendered protocols in the writers' room, but Coca, within the confines of the television frame and her little-girl schtick, was able to let loose on the behalf of both of them.

Just as Kallen was hyperaware of when and how to deploy her femininity at work, Coca had made a career of performing gender for a viewing public. By the time she appeared on television, she had been working as a live performer for nearly thirty years, beginning as a child star on the vaudeville circuit before becoming a chorus girl throughout the 1930s and '40s. She also performed in a number of straight plays and even developed her own nightclub act, though Coca's quiet personality did not fit with the clubs' raucous atmosphere.[87] Her work at Tamiment and on *Your Show of Shows* allowed her to take her experiences as object of the "male gaze" and turn it into a spoof as she vamped for laughs. Kallen's sketches for the actress engage with the real-life travails of women at work and women at home: the frustrations of romantic relationships, the grind of domestic labor, and the countless day-to-day struggles of being a wife and mother. As cultural critic Lauren Berlant writes, "Love is the gift that keeps on taking," speaking to the process of bargaining, compromise, and disappointment that characterizes melodrama's "female complaint."[88]

One dance pantomime, "Pocahontas" (1950), combines Kallen's sharp wit and Coca's trademark goofiness to dramatize the "female complaint" and poke fun at the domestic ideal.[89] In this skit, Pocahontas falls in love with Captain Smith while preparing to marry a tribal brave. The number begins with the scene's narrator describing what her life as a married woman would look like:

And the Brave told Pocahontas
How their future life would be
He would hunt and fish for her
And stand on top a far-off hill
And look out over all the lands
In the meanwhile Pocahontas
As a wife would gladly do
Would be cooking, would be weaving
Would be chopping forest trees
Also it would be her task

To listen for the enemy
While she built the warming fire
While she cooked the hearty meal
While she weaved the Indian blankets
Listen for the enemy
While she skinned the animals, and
While she swept the tepee floor
While she chopped the forest trees
Listen for the enemy

She would plant the seeds for corn
She would take the harvest in
She would sit and grind the corn
And grind the corn and grind the corn
And he would stand on top a hill
And look out over all the lands . . .

The verses are structured to convey the extensiveness and drudgery of Pocahontas's wifely duties, evidenced by how each line starts out, monotonously, with "While she" or "She would." By comparison, her husband's responsibilities are easy: he hunts, but he also spends a good deal of time "stand[ing] on top [of] a hill and look[ing] out over all the lands." His work grants him access to a big and beautiful world, while Pocahontas is saddled with endless menial labor. In accordance with their responsibilities, the Brave dances fluidly and gracefully, pausing to nobly survey the lands. By contrast, Pocahontas's movements are frantic: chopping the trees, planting the corn, and slamming her body into the ground whenever she has to "listen for the enemy." At the conclusion of the verse, Pocahontas looks at her betrothed with a mixture of exhaustion and irritation, her body still swaying from the effort of grinding the corn and grinding the corn and *grinding the corn.* Presenting the labor of food preparation as grueling and unrewarding provides a humorous contrast with the notion that postwar wives should approach cooking as a way to "express their love [for others]."[90] Together, Kallen's lyrics and the actors' pantomimes undermine this cultural ideal, addressing the draining realities of housework, as well as the ease and arrogance with which men can move through the world.[91]

Pocahontas discovers John Smith in the forest, and a dance sequence ensues, in which they mirror one another and frolic. Their connection is more child's play than foreplay, Pocahontas is enamored with Smith's beard, exotic to her because the Brave is clean-shaven. The hard work of the previous sequence temporarily suspended, Pocahontas envisions a new life that is all excitement and no toil. Ultimately, as in real life, the Pocahontas-Smith romance cannot last, so her Brave offers her a consolation prize: Smith's beard, presumably scalped from his face. Whether Smith is alive is unclear, but Pocahontas is thrilled with her new acquisition nonetheless. Was it Smith she wanted, or just his beard? Coca's naive child-woman here takes on racist undertones, as it invokes the childlike savage trope, ignorant of Smith's possible suffering or too callous to care.

Yet, at the same time, Coca's Pocahontas is also a white woman and not only because of the performer's race. In his article on the transgenerational appeal of Pocahontas as a cultural icon, Philip Young refers to how she has served as "the archetypal sacrifice to respectability in America," and so here, Pocahontas is recast as a white, middle-class housewife, with all her attendant disenchantments: hard work at home, an oblivious spouse, and no possibility of escape.[92] John Smith and his exotic beard offer a temporary reprieve, and his detached beard provides what Berlant calls a "fetish object" to assuage the ambivalence she feels about her own life. As Young writes of Pocahontas and of the female reader: "We sense that the adventure has to end the way it does partly because we know the difference between what we dream and what we get."[93] If Pocahontas is stricken with the female complaint, the question becomes, what is the real-life correlate for Smith's beard? What "fetish object" enables the housewife's retreat into imagination and play, making her hard work and lonely existence easier to bear? The answer, conveniently enough, is the medium that carries the message: television. Television has the capacity to provide imaginative escape and to temporarily lift women out of their lives.

Another oppressive element of women's daily lives—and one that features prominently in the Kallen/Coca sketches—is that of female embodiment, meaning both the toll it takes living in a woman's body and the discomfort of failing to fit existing female archetypes. Elizabeth Matelski writes: "In the years following World War II . . . [women] refashioned their bodies through whatever means necessary . . . to fit an accepted cultural and pseudo-biological ideal."[94] As Coca physically contorts herself into the roles of fashion plate, glamour puss, and sexpot, she reveals these norms as artificial and impossible. One critic marveled at how, for Coca, "[a] movement of the nose or forehead could transform her from a demure aristocrat into a vicious gun moll." Kallen echoed this sentiment, raving that: "[Coca] was a mixture of so many characteristics—she was essentially very ladylike and refined. . . . And then all of the sudden, this tough lady would emerge . . . someone hard and grasping. . . . She was an actress![95] Coca's bodily elasticity and flexibility signals the ways women regularly twist and contort themselves to please others, to fit in, to make their bodies (and their bodies of work) palatable to others.

To that end, the Kallen/Coca sketch "Best-Dressed Woman" (1951) lampoons the absurdity of beauty culture and the ridiculous demands women place on themselves. "If you want to be truly well-dressed, wear clothes!" advises Coca's unhinged fashionista.[96] This demented inverse of Coco Chanel offers terrible fashion tips in an off-key warble: wear all of your stylish attire at once; if fringes are the newest fad, then the more fringe, the better; if one dab of perfume is sufficiently intoxicating, any woman-about-town should carry a seltzer bottle's worth. Her confidence is as unfailing as it is misplaced, what Ted Sennett calls an "image at grotesque odds with her delusions of grandeur."[97] But even as Coca plays the fool, "Best Dressed Woman" is a joke for women as much as it is about them, as the comedy foregrounds the style industry's absurd control over women's minds. Caesar's Professor character effortlessly straddles categories of class and even ethnicity, an exemplar of assimilation in that it is a Jewish joke but not to the point of exclusivity. "Best Dressed Woman" grapples with the question of what makes a woman but cannot offer a neat or happy resolution. The "masquerade" that constitutes gender performance—the girlish laughter, the stylish wardrobe, the ability to flatter men without being flattened by them—unites the experiences of the women watching at home and the women writing and performing on television.[98] "Best-Dressed Woman," then, is about how women, in their efforts to fit in and please others, must always be looking at themselves from the outside, judging and reevaluating their performance of self. Gender identity is not just the occasion for a joke; as the clownishly large seltzer bottle of fragrance suggests, gender *is* the joke.

Imogene Coca ameliorated the sharp edges of Kallen's scripts through her gentle, madcap comic delivery. Coca's non-threatening presence had been established prior to her arrival on *Your Show of Shows*, one that Sennett calls a "parody of sexiness . . . [and] sexy ladies."[99] She even adapted her mock striptease from the club circuit for *Your Show*. In this dance, Coca hides behind a curtain, prances around in an oversized trench coat, and covers her face with her hands in embarrassment, only to then use the belt of her coat to awkwardly frame her bottom. When she takes the pins out of her hair, her locks do not cascade downward but stick out from the sides of her head. But even as the audience claps and cheers her on, she will not lift her hem higher than her knee. Coca finally steps offstage and drops the coat onto the stage from behind the curtains and emerges . . . wearing another identical coat. The audience laughs and claps in response.[100] In a real striptease, the performer offers to show some, but not necessarily all, of her body; by contrast, the mock-striptease jovially replies to hoots and hollers with *no, nothing*. Therein lies the covertly political significance of the mock striptease, a tease-of-a-tease that blocks the viewer from objectifying the performer. Barthes makes this argument in his essay, "Striptease," in which he explains how the stripper conceals as she reveals with the aid of her bejeweled costuming and her "cosmetic of movements."[101] It is the inexperienced amateur "debutante"-stripper who exposes herself artlessly, having lost control, and whose dance is truly obscene.[102] Coca plays the gawky, shy amateur, but her dance is not risqué, and her amateurishness is a ruse. This "distancing" or "covering," as Barthes describes it, is compounded by the literal "covering": the fur coat *under* the fur coat.[103]

Recordings like these help us to imagine the actress's performance where only the script remains; we can envision Coca's silliness and picture how it might sweeten Kallen's acerbic words. In the Kallen-authored musical number, "Yours, Only Yours" (1950), for which the script is extant, Coca again vamps and vogues, though here, her movements are presented as survival tactics, designed to deflect unwanted advances. Coca is described as "slink[ing]" on screen to the tune of "torch music" and, decked out in jewels and a sexy get-up, adjusts her body into an "attitude of despair" and, finally, sings:

I'm Yours
Only Yours
Exclusively Yours . . .
I am a Slave to You
I wish I were Dead[104]

Her many admirers, including a millionaire, a gangster, and a bartender, all demand her attention and love. Each man threatens to kill her if she will not commit to him alone, and she replies with the lyrics, "I'm Yours, Only Yours . . ." Since Coca cannot belong to all of these men exclusively, she decides "this number will never be over." Coca's singer mobilizes this sexed-up schtick as protection, though the part about "wish[ing she] were dead" might be true. The singer fears retribution, and, it is implied, her own domestication, monogamy being a compulsory rite she will avoid as long as possible. In this sketch, as in so many of Kallen's works, postwar femininity is presented as a set of behaviors that ask women to constantly defer to or circumvent male control, dislocating their own bodies and personalities in the process. Here, as was so often the case, Kallen wrote to Coca's strengths as a plucky actress with a springy, gamine frame, while Coca was the performer par excellence for Kallen's "very feminine, very feminist" authorial perspective.

In 1954, NBC canceled *Your Show of Shows* and gave both leads their own programs. With Caesar headlining *Caesar's Hour* (NBC, 1954–1957), and Imogene Coca *The Imogene Coca Show* (NBC, 1954–1955), the thought was that two stars could produce two more hit shows for the network.[105] Kallen served as Coca's head writer, freer than before to compose challenging, complex female characters and create a less chauvinist writers' room. While the scripts for *The Imogene Coca Show* successfully challenge mainstream representations of the day, the series was creatively disjointed and never found its audience. It was canceled after a single season. That said, *The Imogene Coca Show* remains an important exhibit in understanding not just Kallen and Coca's relationship but the generative possibilities of the woman writer and star working in close collaboration.

HER SHOW OF SHOWS: THE FAILED PROMISE OF *THE IMOGENE COCA SHOW*

Lucille is an attractive brunette, very feminine.
And feminist, but out of her guts, not as a joiner.
—Mel Tolkin writing to the *WGA Journal*, February 17, 1989

The proto-second-wave feminist themes that Kallen and Coca brought to *Your Show of Shows* became the central organizing principle of their work together on *The Imogene Coca Show*, which debuted in the fall of 1954 but was canceled by the following spring (Figure 8). Years later, Kallen would explain how she ended up as Coca's head writer:

> [We writers] were all given our choice, whether to go with Sid or Imogene. I went with Coca because I felt a little bit put upon by the predominance of male points of view. The men thought of Coca as inferior, too. They had three categories of females—mother, whore, and if she had any brains, lesbian. Mother and wife were the same. Those were good women. Anybody who was sexy had to be a tart. Anybody with brains had to be not female.[106]

While the show began as a situation comedy, it reverted to Coca's strengths in short-form comedy, presumably in the face of low ratings.

FIGURE 8. An advertisement for *The Imogene Coca Show*, which premiered on NBC on Friday, October 2, 1954 at 9 p.m. Again, the face of the star is the primary marketing tack, as is the case with the earlier "Saturday Night Revue" advertisement. *Imogene Coca Show* one-sheet, Box 380, Folder 62 (*Imogene Coca Show*), NBC Papers, UWM.

The show went further than *Your Show of Shows* in examining the sex lives and inner lives of American women. In one sketch, Coca plays ingenue Betty, a nice girl with a colorful romantic past. Her fiancé is scandalized by the sheer volume of men to whom she has been engaged or attached and threatens to dump her. The switch comes when one of his former lovers approaches the couple mid-fight, an exchange that reveals the depth of his hypocrisy—and hers too, as she stalks off angrily. This sketch troubles the binary of "good girl" and "tramp" by presenting Coca as a former good-time gal who remains pretty darn sweet. Backed into a corner, Betty admits to her fiancé that, while he's the only man she has ever loved, "I had to meet *somebody* before I met you."[107] That a woman could separate sex and love without being labeled a vixen goes further than anything from *Your Show of Shows*. While the Doris Hickenlooper character is married but chaste, Coca's Betty is single, a sexual dynamo, and marriageable too.

The episode "Lemon Pie," written by Kallen, Ernest Kinoy, and Max Wilk, focuses on a different Coca character, a frustrated housewife and beleaguered American consumer. Coca goes to great comic lengths to satiate her yen for lemon chiffon pie—it involves stealing a public bus—but we are introduced to her in the episode's opening, as she flips through a magazine and encounters, in this order:

1. a story about a sexpot temptress that "other women envied—feared—loathed—despised—hated: Men liked her";

2. an ad instructing mothers to buy "Cousin Sarah's Quik-baked, triple whipped, whole-wheat Lemon Chiffon Pie";

3. a feature about a married couple that starts their own university;

4. another ad for lemon pie;

5. a cosmetic exposé on removing freckles;

6. and, of course, another lemon pie endorsement.

Coca looks out the window and distractedly watches the gangsters and thugs in the building across the way; all she can think about is pie. This scene, similar to the "Best-Dressed Woman" sketch on *Your Show of Shows*, seems at first to mock its protagonist but proceeds to issue multiple arguments about femininity and consumer culture. Jessamyn Neuhaus writes of the relationship between women's grooming and cooking, quoting one 1947 marital sex manual that read, "'If you see food well prepared . . . your appetite will be tickled, and you will eat with great joy. . . . The same applies to the appearance of your body . . . ,'" specifically when it comes to "inspir[ing] desire in your husband."[108] The intended (female) reader of this manual is not merely asked to be attractive but to equate herself with food, to consent to being figuratively consumed. The problem is that Coca wants to eat rather than be eaten.

Further, all the women in Coca's magazine spread are either femmes fatales or pie-baking Cousin Sarahs, and nothing in-between, like Betty from the previous sketch. The Cousin Sarah's lemon pie ad targets mothers, selling not only the food itself but also a set of expectations that can never be fully satisfied. Coca's character explains to her friend: "Look, Sabrina—somewhere—somewhere out there in the night—out there—in this vast sprawling jungle called New York City—somewhere amidst the steel and concrete, amidst the hustle and bustle of this great metropolis there is a piece of Lemon Chiffon Pie with *my* name on it."[109] She doesn't want to make the pie for others, she wants to eat it herself, the heightened, melodramatic language speaking to a more down-to-earth, everyday unhappiness. After all, Coca's character doesn't want fame, fortune, or even epic romance: all she wants is pie. This "pie in the sky" plot is rooted, then, in the reality of how mass culture seduces women's senses while crushing their self-esteem. With all the crippling expectations placed on women by mass culture, isn't it enough to make a woman go wild? Isn't it enough to make her hungry for something different or, at least, something fattening? By this logic, Coca's desire to have a pie *all to herself* is a radical gesture, and that the ad for Cousin Sarah's lemon pie could provoke anarchy in the heart of the American housewife is a comic bonus.

Despite all the promise and talent on board, *The Imogene Coca Show* never found its voice or its audience, nor did the writing staff find its footing. The reasons were manifold, ranging from the personal— Coca's mother and husband were both ill during the show's run and died around the time of the show's cancellation—to the aesthetic.[110] One *Variety* review diagnosed the show as "something frantic and almost desperate," while Kallen explained it more simply: "Coca's show didn't work. The combination of Sid and Coca was a miracle,"[111] adding in another interview, "You couldn't duplicate it, and Coca wouldn't buy anything less than that."[112] Coca did not spark with costar and former game show host Hal March, whom she hand-picked for the role.[113] While NBC executives argued about how to best use her talents, Coca herself was not fully committed to the program, noting: "I wanted my own show like a hole in the head. I never did find out why the show went off."[114]

Interpersonal problems further plagued the show's writers' room. Working with staff writer Mel Brooks on *The Imogene Coca Show* presented a threat to Kallen's authority. She would later say of Brooks's work on *Your Show of Shows* that "Brooks was insecure.... He had this overpowering need to dominate, to impress. He would come up with forty lines every day, two would be brilliant; the rest would be forgettable."[115] In one interaction on *The Imogene Coca Show*, Kallen hired Brooks to punch up the gag lines, but when she rejected one of his jokes for not fitting the needs of the scene, he allegedly replied: "Don't you tell me what's funny, you just type."[116] With this single retort, Brooks reduced Kallen to the secretary he had first mistook her for on *Your Show of Shows*. It speaks to the pigeonholing that reduced women in the postwar workplace to a particular "type." As Lynn Peril writes: "By the turn of the twentieth century, the association between woman and machine was so complete that the term 'typewriter' could mean either the physical object or the woman who operated it," such that any woman with a typewriter could easily be misrecognized as a "typist"; here, Brooks uses Kallen's place at the typewriter as a pretext for undercutting her authority and bolstering his own.[117] The producer of the show, under Kallen's direction, banned Brooks from the room, who then had to submit his jokes in writing.[118]

The beauty of collaborative work in the writers' room is, ideally, the power is shared, not hoarded by the "boss," but the danger lies in how easily and nastily power can be seized from others. Kallen won that particular battle against Brooks, but then again, she never headed up another writers' room, refocusing her energies on writing fiction instead. Neither Kallen nor Coca would regain the heights of commercial success they had on *Your Show of Shows*. While many of the male writers of *Your Show of Shows* went on to illustrious solo careers in Hollywood, Kallen did not. Kallen's private correspondence with Tolkin reveals a shared resentment, manifested through various rivalries, jealousies, and vendettas with others. In private correspondence, Tolkin would write to Kallen: "Fuck 'em, both Carl [Reiner] *and* Mel [Brooks]. . . . Mel has lost the talent he never had but has made millions from."[119] Writer Greg Garrison would later tell oral historian Jeff Kisseloff: "The two people who get the least amount of credit did all the work. That was Lucille and Mel Tolkin."[120]

Lucille Kallen navigated her workplace by developing particular strategies for making herself heard in Caesar's writers' room and by cultivating relationships where her perspective as a wife and a woman were most valued, namely her partnerships with writer Mel Tolkin and actress Imogene Coca. Through these collaborations, Kallen established a place on television for women's comedy—both by women and for them—on *Your Show of Shows* and *The Imogene Coca Show*, even as she was deeply outnumbered on the former program. The scripted life that traversed Kallen's work life and her creative oeuvre was rooted in playfully dismantling the expectations and conventions of postwar femininity through Coca's doe-eyed performances voicing female cunning, frustration, and even rage. In this respect, Kallen and her work become a microcosm or analog for the figure of the woman writer in postwar television, navigating the boys' club of the writers' room and the industry writ large. Throughout this study, we will see how women found ways to survive, even thrive, in postwar television, building gendered expectations of creativity and care into their personas and their scripts. But the scripted lives of women like Kallen and others are complicated archives, full of irresolvable tensions and gleeful subversions that speak to the messy ideological commitments of early television and postwar culture.

EPILOGUE: PEOPLE AS HIDDEN HISTORIES

"It's as exciting as an Egyptian tomb that's been opened. . . . Did they find any dead writers in there?"[121] These words, spoken by Carl Reiner, are in reference to the discovery of lost *Your Show of Shows* scripts in 2000. The closet from Max Liebman's office contained forty-seven boxes of scripts—137 of *Your Show of Shows*, along with 160 episodes and scripts from other programs—alongside various memorabilia, including one of Liebman's signature toupees. *The New York Times* published an essay on the unearthing of this archive, reporter Glenn Collins touting the materials' value to media historians. Collins asserted *Your Show of Show*'s place in the television canon through quotes from curators at the Paley Center for Media (formerly, the Museum of Television and Radio) and mentioned that the collection will "shed new light on the contributions of some less-famous comedy writers like Lucille Kallen." Sid Caesar's and Liebman's heirs went on to donate many of these materials to the Library of Congress. Subsequent research on *Your Show of Shows* and the Golden Age of Television have only been possible through the uncovering of this closeted archive and others like it.

Collins frames his reportage with "what Mr. Reiner described as 'a very good mystery': Why were the documents in the closet, and how could this room in such a prime piece of Manhattan real estate have gone undisturbed for so long?" Here, we might pull on the theoretical threads implied by this "mystery" and ask how documents, people, and history get lost. This closet of television history was discovered by an operating engineer for City Center, who had never heard of the show but alerted a supervisor who was familiar. What if he had not? What if someone else had found these papers and, in a rush to clear the space for new tenants, threw the papers in the dumpster? That is how history becomes garbage or as good as trash: when an archive has been lost for so long that everyone stops looking for it. As the *Times* headline reminds us, this "mother lode" was not so much misplaced as it was forgotten.

What is most compelling about this feature, however, is the discovery that the reporter doesn't realize he is making: that of Natalie Chapman Goodman, Max Liebman's personal secretary from 1949 to 1955. If Coca and Kallen are undervalued participants in *Your Show of Shows*, then Natalie Chapman is effectively invisible in the history of 1950s television. I first came across her in a feature for a 1951 issue of *Coronet* magazine (Figure 9). This spread, told from Sid Caesar's point of view, details the behind-the-scenes process of *Your Show of Shows*.

The caption in the image reads: "After we cut, add to, then rewrite one of the five weekly comedy sketches, secretary Natalie Chapman types it out. All hands give her the hawk treatment—eagerly watching to see if and when she'll laugh." Chapman was not a writer, but she impacted

After we cut, add to, then rewrite one of the five weekly comedy sketches, secretary Natalie Chapman types it out. All hands give her the hawk treatment—eagerly watching to see if and when she'll laugh.

FIGURE 9. Natalie Chapman typing up a Sid Caesar script. Sid Caesar, "Backstage with Imogene and Me" by Sid Caesar, *Coronet* magazine, December 1951, Mel Tolkin Papers, WGF.

the show in important ways. She was a sounding board for the writers, an ideal viewer that didn't look like Charles or Doris Hickenlooper, but was, instead, an unmarried career woman. Chapman occasions an important reminder that, while television narratives and sponsors held tightly to the image and interests of the American family, many television viewers, not to mention the industry's workforce, did not live out the domestic ideal portrayed on-screen. Chapman played another vital role in the office by preserving the show's kinescopes, recounting to the *Times*: "it was my job to water the film every two weeks so it wouldn't disintegrate." With that end in mind, she regularly doused the films with a watering can. (Unfortunately, this was not pictured for the *Coronet* feature, though we can see its fictional incarnation with Coca as the Watergirl. See Figure 10.)

In 1955, Chapman, referred to in one newspaper as "Imogene Coca's Girl Friday," eloped with television writer Hal Goodman.[122] That same year, she quit Liebman's employ to work on *The Imogene Coca Show*. Paperwork from the show would describe her as a "Production Assistant, worked full week. . . . Salary $166.66," making more than fellow production assistant, George Harri, who made $125.[123] The idea of Chapman

FIGURE 10. A woman waters the comedy in "The Clock," *Your Show of Shows* (September 15, 1953). © 1953 NBC Television. *The Sid Caesar Collection: The Magic of Live TV* (Beverly Hills, CA: SidVid, LLC., 2000), DVD.

following the women of *Your Show of Shows* into the feminist experiment of *Coca* is intriguing, even as her duties at work are unclear. Presumably, she was at least temporarily unemployed by year's end. Chapman drops out of historical record until the *New York Times* discovers her anew almost fifty years later, casting her as second banana to the real star of the show: the boxes of scripts and memorabilia in Max Liebman's closet. What elapsed for Natalie Chapman Goodman in the intervening decades remains obscure, in large part because the reporter did not ask.

CHAPTER 3

Gertrude Berg, Peg Lynch, and the "Small Situation" of the Stay-at-Home Showrunner

"People get tired of the jazzy, slapstick humor. They like the kind of thing that reminds them of their own family jokes. Maybe they don't laugh as loud, but it leaves them feeling better."[1] This is how television host Robert Q. Lewis, in 1953, explained his preference for "human humor" in American television. He offers as examples *The Goldbergs* (CBS, NBC, DuMont 1949–1956) and *Ethel and Albert* (NBC, CBS, ABC, 1953–1956), two shows developed and written by their stars, Gertrude Berg and Peg Lynch, respectively.[2] *The Goldbergs* and *Ethel and Albert* were written and produced in New York, having been adapted from their original radio shows, the former having run from 1926 to 1946 on NBC, the latter beginning on local radio before broadcasting on the NBC Blue Network and ABC from 1944 to 1950.[3] By the time the television versions debuted, listeners of the radio series were invested in the joys and tribulations of Berg's Molly Goldberg and Lynch's Ethel Arbuckle, adventures that ranged from difficult dinner guests and pesky toothaches to aggravating domestic disputes and struggles with low self-esteem. But fans also knew that Berg and Lynch, two women who made careers playing and writing about being housewives, were in fact full-time professionals in the growing field of broadcasting.

The shows' shared attention to the minutiae of domestic life established these two women as pioneers of female-centered realism in the first decade of commercial television, as they innovated an aesthetic both for and by women. But *The Goldbergs* and *Ethel and Albert* were also implicit endorsements of woman writers and all the love, care, and ingenuity they had to give to television. By teasing out the resonances between the showrunners' public faces and the shows they wrote, we see how their scripts function as allegorical plays about women television professionals. Through the scripted lives Berg and Lynch engineered—both the stories they told about themselves and about their fictional alter egos—they simultaneously spoke as the woman at home *and* the woman at work, suggesting that smart, motivated women might not have to choose between career and family. In that respect, the cultural work that Lynch and Berg did in the postwar moment antedates the second-wave feminist question of how women might "have it all," and answered it by arguing that the full-time homemaker and the professional writer require overlapping sets of traditionally feminine skills and insights.

If women's responsibilities to nourish and support the American citizenry is a matter of public welfare, then television is all the more in need of women's voices and stories. Donna Halper speaks to the quietly female-empowering narratives of Berg and Lynch's radio programs: "Owing to radio, women as musicians, as actresses, as businesswomen, as politicians, and above all, as thinking human beings went from staying entirely within the domestic sphere to at least having a chance to make themselves heard in the public sphere."[4] Before they graced television screens across America, the characters of Molly and Ethel, not to mention the women who played them, had already been established as "thinking human beings." Berg and Lynch argued that what television needed was a set of dish-pan hands and a woman's sense of purpose. The ideal television writer, then, did not need to be a man in a suit, but could be instead a woman in an apron.

Both opted out of broader, more masculinized conversations about television as an art or the television writer as an artist, situating themselves within a medium committed to its robust female and family audiences. Lynch maintained that she was disinterested in matters of aesthetics, while Berg stated that her goal as a writer was to convey the words and emotions of her family, neighbors, and community. Berg told one reporter: "A woman's career doesn't necessarily have to cause her to neglect her other responsibilities. . . . In fact, in my case, I really believe that being a wife and mother made it possible for me to write in a manner which only a mother could."[5] Rather than convince readers that a woman can write as well as a man, Berg explains how a woman can provide television with a deep and detailed rendering of home, family, and community.

In the process of making such arguments, Berg and Lynch confronted a series of cultural expectations and constraints: that a working woman couldn't possibly juggle work with her other responsibilities at home, that television writing was a man's game, and that television was either fluff or art—not, as Berg and Lynch preferred to frame matters, a cozy reflection of everyday life. In response to these pressures, Berg and Lynch authored personas that reconciled the domestic and the professional, but they never apologized for their careers either and thus provided a model for future second-wave feminist discussions around women who want to work. The female protagonists of *The Goldbergs* and *Ethel and Albert* serve as crucial complements of their writers' public faces, Berg and Lynch's scripted lives joining together the categories of "domestic" and "professional."

I have coined the term "stay-at-home showrunner" here as a way to explain this purposeful conflation of work and home, the creative and the maternal, that Berg and Lynch cultivated in their personas and on their programs. Miranda Banks identifies Berg as "arguably the first and foremost example of what a television writer would become in the contemporary era. Berg embodied the hyphenate as a television pioneer: she was a writer, producer, and actor, and true show-woman."[6] (Lynch, by contrast, was not a producer of *Ethel and Albert*, but she did maintain the rights to her characters, even after the television show's cancellation.) In defining the term, Banks writes that the showrunner

> gives a series—and just as importantly, those who work for the series—a sense of structure and direction. . . . The job demands the skills of a visionary: someone who can hold the entire narrative of the series in their head; who is the gatekeeper of language, tone, and aesthetics on the set and behind the scenes; who knows where the series has been and a sense, if not a plan, for its future.[7]

These managerial, literary, and emotional tasks converge with the responsibilities of the caring wife and mother: to run a show is not so different than to run a home. The stay-at-home showrunner brings her domestic or feminine skills into the work world and, at the same time, creates a warm, family dynamic on set. And the job of the showrunner, not unlike that of the wife and mother, is to have a vision for the "future" and to gently maneuver others in the service of that goal.

The publicity stills below (Figures 11 and 12) show Lynch and Berg performing their writerly identities while at home, Lynch comfortably curled up on a floral sofa, while the caption with Berg's picture reads "Gertrude Berg—Molly Goldberg to you—writes her scripts over a 6 a.m. teacup." Berg's routine required both discipline and flexibility, Cary O'Dell explaining:

> To write so many scripts, Berg relied on working habits which were both rigid and legendary. She rose at 6:00 A.M. to write scripts (usually three weeks in advance) in a longhand cursive legible only to her and her daughter, who usually typed the finished product. Gradually her scripts grew more detailed, but in the beginning they were often little more than outlines which Berg and cast improvised live on air. Once, when a key actress failed to show up for the show, Berg devised a new script in eight minutes.[8]

Like any good housewife, Gertrude Berg is prepared for any contingency, and, by bringing her daughter into the work, demonstrates how her show is truly a family affair. In the cases of both Berg and Lynch, their writerly processes exude an air of domesticity and coziness, both women working from home and getting up early to write, presumably before any of their familial obligations commence.[9]

The move from radio to television forced Berg and Lynch to reckon with the implications of the visual track, even as they opted out of conventional discussions of writerly craft. How does the figure of the woman writer come into focus when she is placed in front of the lens, and how do the on-screen characters of Molly and Ethel serve as doubles for both the viewer at home and the writers who made them? Berg and Lynch leaned into the dual meaning of the word *voice*. Their series, having been adapted from radio, explore how the woman's voice is not only a mode of communication but also an instrument of her creative perspective, happily unburdened by male arrogance or ego and characterized instead by modesty and authenticity.

Lynch and Berg both worked with director Walter Hart to establish a visual language of the domestic that complemented their dialogue and narrative "smallness," as the heart of Berg and Lynch's works stem from character dynamics and domestic disputes. Their complementary strengths—Hart's stage direction pedigree, together with Berg and Lynch's ways with words—underscored the collaborative and gendered nature of making television in the postwar moment. And the tactics of the "stay-at-home showrunner" surface in the scripts themselves, as Berg and Lynch speak on their own professional behalf through the characters they played each week.

FIGURE 11. Peg Lynch curled up on the sofa with script in hand. *TV Guide* picture, Scrapbook, PLP.

WINDOWS, MIRRORS, AND WIRETAPS: THE MOVE FROM RADIO TO TELEVISION

Of these two series about the day-to-day minutiae of marriage and family, *Ethel and Albert* more closely resembled what would become television's default, described by Vincent Brook as a parade of "relentlessly white, middle-class, suburban sitcoms."[10] Lynch, like Berg, began in radio as a teenager, and in 1938, at the age of twenty-one, she devised *Ethel and Albert* as a recurring sketch for a Minnesota radio station.

Gertrude Berg — Molly Goldberg to you—writes her scripts over a 6 a.m. teacup

LAZARNICK PHOTO

bergs are their "favorite neighbors," the family next door, the folks back home. Because Mrs. Berg believes fervently in racial understanding, she is delighted that the Goldbergs win as warm a response from Christian as from Jewish listeners. Her favorite fan letter came from the Mother Superior of a Catholic convent.

"One of the pleasures that the Sisters have given up for Lent is listening to the Goldbergs," she wrote. "We would all be deeply grateful, however, if you could send us the programs we missed—after Lent is over."

Somehow, I feared that off the air Mrs. Berg might turn out to be a garrulous, nosy gossip, operating behind a barrage of gagmen, ghost writers, and high-pressure salesmen. But when I telephoned her for an appointment "at her office," a tinkle of laughter greeted me. "But, darling"—she calls everybody "darling"—"I'd be lost in an office. I work right here at home, on a card table. Come on over. . . ."

I went—and made the acquaintance of one of the swellest people I ever met. On the radio Molly Goldberg is kindly, generous, tolerant, and philosophical in a comfortable, homey way, but she keeps both feet firmly on the ground and she usually manages to edge her family along the lines she has thought out in advance. That's Mrs. Berg, in real life, to a T. She's as smart as a lightning calculator, and as industrious as an eight-day clock, but you get the impression that her bosom, like Molly's, is big enough for the cares of the whole neighborhood.

Her curiosity about people is matched only by her honest affection for them. First day I spent with her I think she asked me more questions than I asked her. It happened that my wife had just gone to the hospital, expecting her first child some time that night. Mrs. Berg called the hospital three times during the night to find out how things were going, and she was the first person to congratulate me in the morning—at 6:45 A. M. (It was a six-pound girl, and mighty handsome, too, thank you.) If some other person I was interviewing had done that, I might have suspected the gesture was as phony as a plug nickel. With Mrs. Berg, that never entered my mind.

Like Molly again, Mrs. Berg is wrapped up in her family—her husband, Lewis, a modest, mild-mannered fellow who used to be an engineer in a sugar refinery and now designs bridgework for a dental firm, and their two children, Cherney, 19, (Continued on page 118)

by William A. H. Birnie

FIGURE 12. Gertrude Berg—"Molly Goldberg to you"—balances home and work, as the caption reads, by "writ[ing] her scripts over a 6 a.m. teacup." From "Molly Goes Marching," *The American*, November 1941, Box 54, GBP.

Ethel and Albert went on to air on stations in Virginia and Maryland before landing in New York in 1944 as a fifteen-minute radio serial on ABC; it was upgraded to a half-hour program in 1949.[11] The next year, *Ethel and Albert* made the move to television as a ten-minute recurring sketch on *The Kate Smith Hour* (NBC, 1950–1954) and *The Kate Smith Evening Hour* (NBC, 1951–1952). Two years after that, *Ethel and Albert* premiered as a full-length, half-hour show on NBC, though, over the course of its run in the mid-1950s, *Ethel and Albert* played on all three networks.[12] Throughout her time on radio and television, Lynch remained attentive to her target market and wrote programs to move sponsors' products. Lynch's daughter would later describe *Ethel and Albert* as "initially a sort of commercial, . . . Peg having discovered that a husband-wife format could be adapted to sell a variety of products."[13]

Ethel and Albert made some notable changes in moving to television, including the erasure of a daughter that had been voiced by a child impersonator on radio. As a result, the plots of television's *Ethel and Albert* focus on the dynamic evolutions of an equal, happy partnership in which their sole responsibilities are to one another. The television version also removed the radio preamble, which explains the show's focus on the small details of married life; presumably, audiences from radio already knew the premise, and new viewers would be immediately placed in the familiar world of the Arbuckles through visual cues like set design, costume, and performance.

Berg's career did not begin in radio. She started writing as a teenager in the 1910s, piecing together entertainment for the guests at her father's hotel resort. She went on to study playwriting before moving into broadcasting, selling scripts to radio networks throughout the 1930s and '40s. Her first program, the very short-lived *Effie and Laura*, debuted on CBS radio in 1928, a program described by Berg in her memoir as "about two young women who worked in the Five and Ten. . . . [It was] a sophisticated slice of life full of stark realism, economic problems, and the endless search for the meaning behind life"; it lasted a single episode.[14] *The Goldbergs*—initially titled *The Rise of the Goldbergs*—was first broadcast by NBC Radio on November 20, 1929.

But the groundwork for the character of Molly Goldberg had been set many years prior. At the age of fourteen, Berg invented for the stage the character of Maltke, "a woman with an inferiority complex . . . [and with] a husband who was a no-good."[15] In her memoir, Berg describes "Maltke Talnitzky . . . [as] a figment, an illusion, and a combination of all the Maltkes I had ever met."[16] In one sketch Berg wrote in this time,

Maltke put her husband's mistress on trial and explained to the judge, "I'm a woman, a plain everyday woman, and you think my husband is such a Beau Brummel he needs something better? He doesn't. Believe me. For the kind of man he is, I'm good enough."[17] Maltke, like *Your Show of Show*'s Professor character (chapter 2), was a "wise fool" in the Yiddish or Jewish tradition, someone who employs faulty or flawed logic to arrive at her deep, if rough and ready, insights into life.

Radio-television's Molly Goldberg borrowed from the stage character of Maltke a "plain everyday[ness]," but Molly lacked Maltke's acid tongue and was blessed with a devoted husband. If Maltke was an inside joke, restricted to a Jewish hotel clientele, Molly was, according to Vincent Brook, a "cuddly, Yiddish-accented matriarch," half-assimilated for a mainstream American audience. (*The Goldbergs*' final season only accelerated the assimilation of the family, moving them out of the tenement apartment and into the suburbs, as the series' name changed to *Molly*.[18]) At the peak of *The Goldbergs*' success, Berg was the highest-paid woman in radio, earning $7,500 a week, fellow Jewish soap writer Irna Phillips following close behind.[19] In 1948, Berg wrote and starred in a Broadway version of her radio play, *Me and Molly*, and this stage play provided a "springboard" for Berg to premiere *The Goldbergs* as a television serial in 1949.[20]

A number of marriage and family–centered radio serials, comedies and dramas alike, were making the jump from radio to television at this time, *The Life of Riley* (ABC Blue, NBC Radio, 1944–1951, NBC 1949–1958), *Easy Aces* (NBC Blue, CBS, 1930–1945, DuMont 1949–1950), and *One Man's Family* (NBC Radio, 1933–1949, NBC-TV 1949–1955) being only three such examples.[21] Writers who had made their names and reputations in radio had to find new ways to tell their stories for television. Daytime writers in particular sought to write television that the housewife could follow without having to look up from her cooking and cleaning, as she might have done listening to the radio.[22] Television also required the writer to find new, cleverly unobtrusive ways to place sponsors' products.[23] Amid all this change, when a show moved directly from radio to television, fans still needed to discover in the new incarnation all they loved from the original radio version.[24] These concerns manifested for Berg and Lynch on the level of their "small" storytelling: how would they preserve the intimacy and company-keeping quality of their radio programs with the move to television?

In many ways, radio's Molly and Ethel came even closer to their fans through the power of television, opening up the opportunity for

FIGURE 13. Molly chats with her neighbor, the viewer. Still from "Mother-in-Law," *The Goldbergs* (May 14, 1951). © 1951 CBS Television.

audiences to become invested in the real-life women who played them. While other shows might incorporate the sponsored item into dialogue between characters, Berg advertised sponsors, including Sanka coffee, through a direct address to the audience (Figure 13). Week after week, the character of Molly Goldberg leaned out of her window—a box within the larger box screen of the television screen—and confided in the viewer-neighbor, detailing the minutiae of her life and how, incidentally, the extra cost of Sanka is "like a drop in the ocean" compared to the lift it gave her.[25] This product placement worked in part because the audience had a long-standing relationship with Molly Goldberg and her warm, familiar way of speaking to the listener over the radio.[26]

The television versions of *The Goldbergs* and *Ethel and Albert*, through the tool of visuality, both offered a window into and a mirror up to the American family. Lynn Spigel explains in *Make Room for TV: Television and the Family Ideal in Postwar America*, that as "[a] new 'window on the world,' television was expected to bind public and private spheres, making trips into the outside world an antiquated and even redundant exercise."[27] She goes on to describe how the marriage of the private and public spheres in *The Goldbergs* was analogous to the linking of reality and fiction:

> The commercial ends as Molly turns away from the window frame (as well as the frame of the television image) to enter the Goldberg living room, where she now takes her place in the story. The transition from commercial

to story is made absolutely explicit in the program because Molly literally *turns her back* on the advertisement's enunciative system and *takes her position* in the tale as she walks into the living room where her daughter, Rosalie, now addresses Molly as a character in the story.[28]

Making the shift "from commercial to story" was more jarring on television than in radio, requiring a bold and definitive breaking of the fourth wall. This aesthetic crash of the public and private realms occurred with Molly/Berg's move from neighbor to performer. Conceiving of television as "window on the world" suggests a naturalistic mode that reminded the viewer of "real life," yet this gesture of walking onto one's mark and launching into the scene taps into the reflexive, even avant-garde, possibilities of television. Spigel proceeds to write that "the world onto which Molly Goldberg's window opened was, as in all television, an alternate view, an endlessly self-referential world as opposed to a document."[29] This "self-referential world" looked a whole lot like a real apartment, but it also resembled a soundstage or a set—because it was.

Michele Hilmes writes of radio's "ability to escape visual overdetermination," allowing for the subversive undermining of categories like gender and race, but this does not mean that television circumscribed the potential for progressive representations. Early television's "visual determinations" had its own capacities to open new avenues of meaning and showcase female talent, as it did in *The Goldbergs*.[30] When Molly moves from the window to the living room, there is a brief, visible moment in which she becomes Gertrude Berg, a flicker of the writer-star as she steps on her mark, before she is Molly again. In this way, *The Goldbergs*' move from radio to television made Berg the writer *more* visible, not only as a figure on a screen but as a professional playing a part. This tiny instance encapsulates the multiple ways in which Molly Goldberg (the character) and Gertrude Berg (the writer/performer) speak for one another, in one voice, establishing the homemaker as a creative force and the woman television writer as a nurturing matriarch. This move is subtler than that of George Burns cracking wise at the edge of the proscenium on *The Burns and Allen Show*, embodying the good-humored husband-comedian more at home on a stage than in the woman's realm of the domestic space. Berg's stay-at-home showrunner was a more disruptive invention than that of the bemused husband, so it required a delicate touch.

Ethel and Albert broke the fourth wall as well, though her use of it was largely for humorous effect, a sly acknowledgment of the show's being a realistically styled work of fiction. Critics were fixated on the show's mimetic qualities, one article from *News of Radio and Television* entitled "Housewives See Selves Reflected on TV" containing the caption: "The TV screen becomes a mirror in which couples see themselves when 'Ethel and Albert' are on the air."[31] The episode of *Ethel and Albert* entitled "Free Tickets to a Movie Premiere" (NBC, October 24, 1953) builds the comedy around this aspect of the story, going so far as to explain how the show should be interpreted. In "Free Tickets," the Arbuckles feign illness so as to cancel plans with friends and attend a movie premiere instead.[32] But when their friends come over to check on them, a dressed-up Ethel and Albert (Alan Bunce) have to hide. "I wonder if anyone has ever done this to us," Ethel muses. It is as though, in this moment, Ethel sees her own life, to borrow Spigel's terms, as both window and mirror—as private but also public, in that shared experiences bond individuals as couples, families, and communities of listeners and viewers. In as much as Peg Lynch articulated a literary perspective, it was that of writing stories that women viewers would relate to and see themselves in.

Yet, straightforward, plain-spoken Ethel is more than she appears. The key difference between Ethel and the woman watching at home is that Ethel happens to be Peg Lynch, a woman who writes and stars in her own television show. This disjuncture comes up as early as the first television episode, "No Pencil by the Telephone" (NBC, April 25, 1953), when Ethel wiggles away from Albert's embrace, explaining "somebody can see right through the window." She points toward the invisible fourth wall, eliciting quiet laughter from the audience. This exchange speaks to what Lynn Spigel calls the "theatricalization of the domestic world," meaning the ways in which mass culture "represent[ed] . . . the family's interior world . . . [as] merged with a view of public exteriors."[33] This "theatricalization" was not only a way to "negotiate [the] conflict between women's domestic isolation and their integration into social life" but, for the purposes of the woman television writer, to reveal how domestic matters are of literal and literary interest to the general public.[34] And to spotlight this moment even closer, we might ask: who or what is Ethel really pointing at? The viewers? Her neighbors? Or the camera, the very thing that makes Ethel and Albert *Ethel and Albert*? And is the person observing through the window the viewer or the writer of this scene, Peg Lynch? In these brief moments of *Ethel and Albert*, verisimilitude uneasily coincides with meta-humor, a product of the stay-at-home showrunner's presence on-screen and the purposeful blurring of Ethel and Peg within the diegesis of the program. It is a reminder that Ethel is an illusion but an implicit suggestion that, if an Everywoman can create and produce her own television show, then any woman who runs a home could do the same.

In line with the lives and voices of their creators, *The Goldbergs* and *Ethel and Albert* convey story through vernacular and, at times, circular dialogue. Paired with stationary camerawork and character-driven storylines, Lynch and Berg engineered a television realism that focused on housewives' experiences and concerns. But underneath these realist stories were sophisticated, multilayered narratives that implicitly endorsed the woman writer and her ability to do worthwhile work outside the home. In that way, Berg and Lynch's scripts serve as a gendered counterpoint to a work like Paddy Chayefsky's "Marty" (NBC, 1953), a teleplay typically held up as exemplary television craft but has a secondary purpose of endorsing male television authorship.[35] Berg and Lynch's shows are unlikely to find a place in a Criterion boxset collection, as do those of Chayefsky, Rod Serling, and Reginald Rose. But their female-driven slice-of-life serials demand to be put in conversation with such work, with attention to both the ways in which they echo one another and how they meaningfully diverge.

In the dialogues below, we see an exchange from "Marty" and one from a 1954 episode of *Ethel and Albert*. In the Chayefsky scene, the two men's circuitous language reflects habitual indecision and their seeming paralysis, stuck, as they are, in the same booths in the same diners, eating dinner at the same friends' houses. In Lynch's script, Albert's conversational middle-man status provides humor at the expense of the domesticated married man, tethered to the telephone like a hausfrau. These scenes together illustrate Lynch and Chayefsky's common interest in how ordinary speech shapes one's life and dictates its rhythms, for better or for worse. In Chayefsky, these conversations indicate the characters' boredom and personal stagnation, but, for Lynch, this back-and-forth patter is the stuff of domestic life and emotional intimacy. While both dialogues are comedic, only in "Marty" is the humor tinged with sadness.[36]

From Paddy Chayefsky's "Marty," *anthology drama* (air date: May 24, 1953):

Marty: I don't know, Angie. What do you feel like doing?

Angie: Well, we oughtta do something. It's Saturday night. I don't wanna go bowling like last Saturday. How about calling up that big girl we picked up inna movies about a month ago in the RKO Chester?

Marty: [Not very interested] Which one was that?

Angie: That big girl that was sitting in front of us with the skinny friend.

Marty: Oh, yeah.

Angie: We took them home alla way out in Brooklyn. Her name was Mary Feeney. What do you say? You think I oughtta giver her a ring?

Marty: It's five o'clock already, Angie. She's probably got a date by now.

Angie: Well, let's call her up. What can we lose?

Marty: I didn't like her, Angie. I don't feel like calling her up.

Angie: Well, what do you feel like doing tonight?

Marty: I don't know. What do you feel like doing?

From Peg Lynch's *Ethel and Albert*, "Dutch Treat" (air date: May 8, 1954):

Albert: [Annoyed] Oh. [Gets up. Goes to phone which is on desk. He lifts receiver.] Hello. Yes. Well, call you back? Well, hold on. [Calling.] Ethel!

Ethel: [Off.] Yes?

Albert: [Raising voice.] It's Myra! She wants to know how much she owes you.

Ethel: How much she what?

Albert: [More precisely] How much she owes you.

Ethel: Does she mean for lunch this noon?

Albert: [Into phone.] Do you mean for lunch this noon? [To Ethel] Yes.

Ethel: Well, tell her I don't know exactly. Tell her I paid eight dollars and thirty-five cents for the whole thing.

Albert: [Into phone.] Myra? She says she paid eight dollars and thirty-five cents for the whole thing.

Ethel: Ask her if she had the lobster Newburgh.

Albert: [Into phone.] Yeah–Yeah–Yeah–hold on– [To Ethel] What?

The ways in which writers talked publicly and deliberately about craft were gendered; Paddy Chayefsky would say of his screenwriting practice that he "tried to write the dialogue [as if] it had been wire-tapped," espousing his aesthetic philosophy to realism on television.[37] Lynch, by contrast, jokingly treats the video camera as a surveillance device, lightly engaging with this trope of televisual realism through humor—and through putting the line in Ethel's mouth, not her own. Lynch could not trumpet her authorial prowess in the same terms as Chayefsky, but spoke through her creation instead, rendering Peg-the-writer invisible except as a comical neighborhood gossip, a Peeping Tom hiding in the shrubbery. In 1953, TV pundit Lewis argued that "the good plays, like Paddy Chayefsky's great 'Marty,' are really a new dramatic form. They're extended character studies. Couldn't be done except on TV."[38] But the same must also be said of *The Goldbergs* and *Ethel and Albert*. *Marty* is a play about a man learning to speak up and find his own voice, but *The Goldbergs* and *Ethel and Albert* are not so different: they are about giving the ordinary woman a voice and a platform, ideally a network one.

VOICING THE CONCERNS OF
THE STAY-AT-HOME SHOWRUNNER

Berg and Lynch did not labor in obscurity: their names graced their shows' credit crawls, and both women did interviews and wrote guest columns for publicity, Berg appearing on Edward Murrow's *Person to Person* and writing for *Everywoman's* magazine, while Lynch was profiled by the *Boston Globe* and the *New York Daily News*, among others.[39] Within the universe of the show, Berg explained away her presence with a wink and a nudge. In the first episode of *The Goldbergs*, when Molly's husband warns her to be quiet and let him speak when a business acquaintance arrives at the home, Molly asks, "Do I ever talk?"[40] The joke is twofold: the only person in the *Goldbergs* universe who talks more than the gregarious Molly is her real-life counterpart, author Gertrude Berg, who speaks through all her characters.

But, Berg preferred to say that her characters spoke through her, not the other way around. In this way, she disavowed the language of craft, opting instead for a humble, maternal rhetoric. In 1949, she wrote in *Variety*:

> "The Goldbergs" must have had the ingredients of showmanship to have survived 17 years in radio, but I don't know what they are. I have no conscious technique in writing the script, nor has it been necessary to write any differently for television than for radio. In writing the story of the Goldberg

family I simply try to develop situations and employ dialog that are true to the life of a people I know so well and love. If it comes out showmanship, that is my good fortune. . . . Through all the years in radio I would go down to the lower East Side, visiting cafes and homes, attending meetings at such places as the Educational Alliance and Cooper Union. This way I kept in close touch with the people I wrote about. Besides, I love them.[41]

In this statement, Berg denies having any "showmanship" or literariness, but goes on to detail a writerly process that spans personal and ethnographic registers. Her assertion that she does not write to be funny only makes her more like Molly—earnest, sincere, and only humorous by accident. Banks explains that the "autobiographical storytelling [of the showrunner-*auteur*] is self-evident, but it always depends on the audience's extra-textual knowledge about the television author for its legitimating effects."[42] Thus, when Molly talks, she speaks for her community and gives us a glimpse into the life and perspective of her creator, Gertrude Berg. Berg further demonstrated loyalty to her roots by hiring neighborhood "elevator operators, grocery clerks, and delivery boys" to play these roles on her show, letting them speak (or not) in their own voices in the service of filling out or supplementing her own.[43]

The principle of the "voice" in both *The Goldbergs* and *Ethel and Albert* contained multiple meanings, marking what made Berg and Lynch, as well as their characters, so ordinary (their speaking voice), but also what made them singularly valuable to television (their authorial voice). From their time in radio, Berg and Lynch were accustomed to telling stories through dialogue, be it through women socializing with neighbors and friends, wives conducting petty arguments with their husbands, or couples taking issue with the etiquette of a relative, neighbor, or guest. Molly's Yiddish-inflected rhythms and flawed grammar helped her to register as endearingly "real" to listeners and viewers, though the accent itself was put on. This was a voice to which radio listeners and even television viewers would be accustomed, one that straddles the categories of contemporary representation and nostalgia for the past. As George Lipsitz writes, "the subgenre of ethnic working-class situation comedies in early network television evoked concrete historical associations and memories in their audiences," *The Goldbergs* being a central example.[44] According to Berg, Molly's heavy accent and malapropisms were a loving tribute to her community's elders, in particular an homage to her mother and grandmother. To make ethnicity visible in this moment of mid-century assimilation required Berg to invoke a Jewish past. Berg parroted the speech patterns of previous generations in her performance, even as the task before her as a writer was updating the character of Molly, "born" on radio in 1929, for the postwar moment. This tension between past and present did not exist for Peg Lynch, who spoke in the same relatable—and contemporary—midwestern twang as her creation. Lynch played Ethel in the radio version but claimed she only decided to occupy the role on television when auditions for the part went so poorly, telling *TV and Radio Magazine* that "listening to [the actresses'] beautiful, lush voices, I knew I simply couldn't write for anybody like *that*."[45]

Berg and Lynch, with their accessible speaking voices as Molly and Ethel, distinguish themselves and their shows from slick, aspirational mass-market entertainment. Their public personas and the shows they wrote challenged the constraints of postwar beauty ideals and argued that a woman does not need to be glamorous to be successful, fulfilled, or beloved. This brand of self-acceptance was accompanied by a hefty dose of suspicion toward Hollywood's lofty standards for sex appeal, as their shows suggested that women showrunners could craft more wholesome and compassionate programming for women watching at home. One writer, profiling Gertrude Berg toward the end of *The Goldbergs* in 1956, notes the discrepancies between the writer and the character. Berg *appears* different from her role: "On [television,] Mrs. Berg looks the epitome of circularity ... but in person, while retaining a certain impressive solidity, she appears younger, smaller, less matronly. She had on a black dress, a black silk scarf, and a huge diamond ring."[46] This description of Berg as sophisticated and urbane only emphasizes Molly's soft, unpretentious appearance. Molly and Ethel are similarly approachable—modestly attired and coiffed, exceedingly feminine—which made them beloved to their fans and rendered their creators' professional accomplishments less threatening. Having made their names in radio, Peg Lynch and Gertrude Berg were largely exempt from the pressure to look glamorous and, instead, embraced their approachability to a white, female fan base.[47]

In her discussion of women stars in 1950s television, Mary D. Desjardins discusses the careful balancing act female television personalities had to strike between elegance and ordinariness, writing that "the television and radio fan and trade publications demonstrate a willingness to arbitrate among different forms of glamour that the female film star might bring to television."[48] Desjardins's argument elaborates on the work of Susan Murray, who explores how on-screen personality Martha Raye "combined the intimacy of television through the female audience's identification with her as 'ordinary' within the spectacle of Hollywood glamour."[49] Denise Mann historicizes television's initial rejection of Hollywood glamour, arguing that "advertising claims reinforced the view that mass media images of housewives were 'natural' and images of glamorous Hollywood stars were unnatural."[50] If movie stars are gods, then, television stars are neighbors whom viewers invite into their homes and talk to through the window.[51]

One *Ethel and Albert* episode in particular reads as a swipe at actresses' "beautiful, lush voices," the phoniness this voice betrays, and the insecurity it provokes in real-life women. In "Ethel is Jealous of Hildy" (NBC, April 10, 1954), Ethel finds herself at her wits' end with her houseguest, an actress who goes by Googie LaMer.[52] Ethel's husband, Albert, is at first charmed by Googie, as are the rest of the men in the neighborhood: she is the epitome of class and charm, taking every opportunity to sing at the piano and demonstrate her prowess in French. Her habit of flirting with married men annoys the neighborhood wives, and Ethel's patience runs out when Googie tries to steal Ethel's role in the Women's Club theatrical production. Googie's excessively feminine "masquerade" is geared to the tastes of Hollywood and of men, and she ruthlessly competes with Ethel and her friends, both for male attention and for roles.[53] In that respect, she not only represents a danger to decent women and the state of marriage but to the stay-at-home showrunner-star, to the Ethels of the world but also the Pegs. When Ethel's theatrical aspirations are challenged, she commits to turning Albert against the high-maintenance Googie. By the episode's conclusion, Ethel has been restored to her rightful place, in the home and in the Women's Club show, as a wife and a star performer. This episode implicitly supports Lynch's rhetorical point: for *Ethel and Albert* to capture her authorial voice, it needed her own plain voice to say the lines.

Berg responds to her own appearance in an episode of *The Goldbergs* (August 14, 1953) in which Molly frets about her looks:

Enter Rosie with movie magazine.

Rosie: Gloria Swanson, Ma, is four years older than you are. Just look at her, Ma.

Molly: So what are you saying?

Rosie: She looks like a young girl: look at her figure.

Molly: I'm not a moving picture star.

Rosie: There's nothing wrong with *your* figure, Ma.

Molly: And if *yes*, what can I do? So M.G.M. won't renew my contract.[54]

Here, Molly and Gertrude Berg speak in unison: Molly, who knows she is not a glamour queen, and Berg, who recognizes that the movies demand from their stars a level of sophistication that television does not. (There's a disingenuous, if jokey, element to this dialogue: a film of *The Goldbergs* had come out three years prior, in 1950, from Paramount.) Molly suffers a series of indignities around her looks, leading her to consider a makeover. Molly goes to a salon but ultimately decides against dying her hair. Expecting her husband, Jake (Robert H. Harris), to be disappointed, Molly discovers he is relieved. Jake explains to her: "As you are and what you are is all I ever asked, is all I ever wanted." But the message of this episode is best articulated by Uncle David (Eli Mintz), who understood the profound pressures women face:

> I don't know what you expect from women these days. I don't know, to be a good housekeeper, to be a good cook, a good mother, good mother-in-law, read books, have culture and also to look like motion picture stars. I don't know. From my wife I expected supper on the table, a kind word, a—a—I don't know. Who would want to be a woman in this time and age? I don't know who—not me!

Uncle David thus expresses solidarity with the put-upon homemaker who has been dismissed as frumpy or frazzled, cowed by the "millions of dollars spent on diet foods and books, reducing support groups, youth 'fat camps' and exercise salons . . . [of] the 1950s and 60s."[55] (A later episode of *The Goldbergs* would center on Molly's trip to one of these weight-loss "farms."[56]) The frankness of this critique is softened by its being delivered by a male voice, less likely to be dismissed as shrill or bitter. That said, what Berg communicates to her women viewers in this moment—even as the lines are spoken by Uncle David, not by Molly—is that she is just like them and understands their struggle.

For Lynch and Berg, this lack of glamour grounded their scripted lives, how they marketed themselves and how they wrote scripts that treated everyday women's lives as worthy of note. Many of these writers' strongest, most pointed statements on writing for television was not delivered by themselves but, rather, expressed through their homemaker alter-egos. *The Goldbergs* and *Ethel and Albert* articulate their showrunners' philosophies of writing, which prized a paradoxically artless craft and a feminine commitment to authenticity that has no room or time for creative posturing.

NOT AN IMITATION: ARTLESS AUTHENTICITY AND THE WOMAN TELEVISION WRITER

For both stay-at-home showrunners, but Berg in particular, the commitment to aesthetic and literary naturalness was partnered with a fiercely curated public face. In his biography of Gertrude Berg, Smith underscores the disconnect between her persona and the "'impressing and imposing' person [she was] . . . a woman . . . described as tough, sophisticated, demanding, bright, tyrannical, fair, and shrewd."[57] Whether Berg was truly "only out for Berg," as writer Gerald Nachman described her, is indeterminate and fraught with judgment, so we might instead consider how Berg's public persona diverged from her documented behaviors at work.[58] As a radio professional, she was said to have "insist[ed] her name appear on each script and be announced at the beginning of each episode, . . . demand[ed] for more time to prepare and deliver each script . . . [and] charged for repeated broadcasts."[59] But even as she played the pushy perfectionist at work, Berg cultivated the "image [she] *wanted* to portray to the public," one in which attention to detail is framed as a gesture of love, not ambition.[60]

Berg played Molly for the fans, but she made sure that Molly returned the favor. Molly Goldberg was put to work explaining Berg's artistic vision and authorial perspective, couched (as it had to be) in the language of homespun wisdom. As Molly asks herself at the end of the first episode of *The Goldbergs*, "What is a lie? A lie is the truth a little exaggerated. . . . Some people have a talent for exaggeration—I have a talent in the opposite direction."[61] That talent is the same as Berg's: to tell the truth, even when it's "small," even when it's drab and unglamorous. In this moment, Berg and Molly again speak in one voice, the realism of *The Goldbergs* falling in line with Molly's predilection for "exaggeration in the opposite direction." And, it must be noted, it is only through Molly that Berg can describe this work as a "talent" or a gift rather than an act of service.

In a later episode of *The Goldbergs* (September 25, 1953), Berg makes a more sustained and forceful case for why her show and her work matters. In this episode, Molly wants the family to help her write to Sammy, her son who is away in the Army.[62] Molly thinks long letters with elevated diction are best, while daughter Rosie (Arlene McQuade) wants to keep the correspondence casual and light. Rosie and her friend try to secretly record the Goldbergs' dinner conversations, so they can capture the family's authentic voice, but, every night, there is some sort of argument, be it about Jake's business or Rosie's dating life. After several nights of contentious dinners, Rosie angrily informs her family: "I've been trying to get a recording to send to Sammy. Maybe you'd like to hear yourself. . . . Maybe you'll learn something from them. . . . I thought Sammy might like to hear his family at home. A typical night in our life. Listen to it." Once the family knows they are being recorded, everyone refrains from gossip, negativity, or stress—in other words, the recordings become unrecognizably genteel. The family accidentally sends the quarrel-ridden recording to Sammy, a mistake that turns out to be providence. Sammy writes back that the recordings are "delicious," adding "I hope you don't mind, but I had all the fellows listen. We all felt we were back home and it felt good." He weighs in on all the Goldberg family debates and asks if they can plant a recorder in the local candy shop. Uncle David explains the moral of the story, that "Sammy wanted his family, not an imitation."

Once again, Uncle David's wisdom resonates, and through him, Berg expresses her show's higher purpose: to offer viewers a *real* family and "not an imitation." (That the realness comes through the power of recorded sound speaks to *The Goldbergs'* roots in radio.) The servicemen's appreciation emphasizes how such radio and television renderings of the home and family are necessary for maintaining the "American way of life" these boys are fighting to protect. Moreover, Berg welcomed, even encouraged, this blurring of her character and herself, as it allowed her to express her creative perspective through her beloved fictional counterpart and in episodes like this one. One 1951 article refers to the actress as "Molly Berg," combining the two names into a single moniker.[63] If the best television writing stems from an intimate knowledge of "small situations," then who could be better qualified than a wife and mother like "Molly Berg"?

Unlike Berg, Peg Lynch was known to resist this conflation of real and fictional, explaining: "Ethel is more like me than I am her."[64] By saying this, Lynch asserts her own authorial intent and ownership—*she* is the creative wellspring for the world of *Ethel and Albert*, drawing on her own experience but also on her imagination. This was quite different from Berg, who would say that the "answer [to *The Goldbergs'* appeal] always comes out that it's because we [Molly Goldberg and Gertrude Berg] are the same."[65] And while Berg was married years before her radio career took off, Lynch began writing *Ethel and Albert* when she was still single. When a journalist seemed surprised that a woman like her could invent fictional situations she had not herself experienced, Lynch answered back by inquiring how many detective writers are murderers and added that her husband was not similar to Albert anyway.[66] The difference in terms of tone and approach was likely a matter of practicality as much as personality. Berg needed to protect herself against scandal, stating that she avoided "anything that will bother people . . . unions, fund raising, Zionism, socialism, intergroup relations. . . . I keep things average. I don't want to lose friends."[67] As a Jewish woman who worked closely with an accused Communist, Philip Loeb, in the era of Julius and Ethel Rosenberg and the Red Scare, Berg needed to operate in a more protective, defensive mode.[68] By contrast, white, midwestern transplant Lynch, a woman who lived without a whisper of scandal, was freer to stray into sharp, direct rhetoric, in her own voice and especially through her characters.

Lynch's ironic edge is on full display in "Fixing Up the Den for Albert" (NBC, June 6, 1953), in which she sets her satiric sights on the difference between male authorship and female ingenuity.[69] This episode makes for a fitting companion to the previous episode of *The Goldbergs*, as both make strong cases in favor of the woman writer but from disparate comic viewpoints. The opening credits for this episode of *Ethel and Albert* begin with a His and Hers armchair graphic, followed by a title card for writer Lynch, decorated with the image of a paper and pen. This foregrounding of Lynch's authorship is crucial for understanding the armchair/pen-and-paper dialectic that follows, a comedy that explores the eternal conflict between work and home from a female point of view.

"Fixing Up the Den" begins with a restless Albert complaining that his office life does not fulfill him and that he needs a creative outlet. He believes he has a talent for writing but that their cramped home is not conducive to his artistic aspirations. "A man really needs a place of his own," he tells Ethel. "There are times when a man wants to get away from a family." Rather than a woman needing a "room of [her] own," as Virginia Woolf famously averred, it is the man who needs a refuge from woman's domestic territory, presumably so he can write virile, tough-guy prose. This male, white-collar anxiety—that work belongs to one's boss, that home belongs to one's wife, and that there is no place where Albert can, in his words, "commune with his soul"—is similarly rendered in a satiric column by Reginald Rose, published in *Variety* in 1955. Entitled

"How Not to Write a TV Play," Rose portrays himself as plagued by his own procrastination, aggravated by every family member and each ring of the doorbell while, at the same time, craving these distractions.[70] Rose's no-nonsense wife, as he depicts her, has very little interest or time for his overblown musings on the hard life of a television writer, busy as she is managing a home and family. In this essay, Rose pokes fun at his own ineptitudes and absent-mindedness, but the gender binary is clearly drawn up: the home is not a place for creative thought, and the homemaker is not intellectually or creatively productive.

Lynch's script for "Fixing Up the Den for Albert" takes Rose's premise in a different direction by showing how making the home *is*, in fact, a creative endeavor, even if men don't recognize it as such. In her effort to please Albert and support his dream, Ethel transforms the den into his new study. The room is plastered with university pennants, leather furniture, and wallpaper that Ethel's friends call "darling." Albert wants to be a maverick, a creative loner, but he needs his wife to step in and help, implying that the average American man cannot achieve his dreams of independence and autonomy without a woman's help. While Albert wishes he were a profound, misunderstood artist type, the fact remains he does not want to—and cannot—write. It is Ethel, with her flair for interior design, who is the creative one in the family, as is Lynch, the show's semi-stealth author.

The comedy of "Fixing the Den" derives from Albert's pretentious writerly ambitions, born out of male ego rather than a drive to create or communicate. While Lynch's treatment of Albert is gentle, even affectionate, the irony is still piercing. A masculine preoccupation with the process and romance of writing is antithetical to literary or aesthetic authenticity. The woman writer may not have the time or cultural permission to meditate on craft, but she does the work just as well, if not better, than a man caught up in his own self-image. One can imagine, using Lynch's episode as inspiration, Rose's essay rewritten from the point of view of a "housewife-writer," who fits in her writing between baking casseroles and putting the baby to bed, without delay and without complaint. Lynch's critique predates second-wave feminist conversations around women juggling home and career, but she lays the groundwork by suggesting that women writers (like herself) are too busy balancing these things to *talk* about writing. Just as Lynch's star persona was one of "natural"-ness, so her professed instincts for writing television were a product of clear-eyed competence, not tortured genius.

Reading this episode through Lynch's own words provokes the question: is a philosophy of craft necessary for producing art, then, or is it just vanity in a field where "no imitation" will suffice? But even as Berg and Lynch fought for their place in television, neither worked alone. Their common collaboration with director Walter Hart publicly mounted the familiar 1950s industry fixture of the male-female creative union, Hart sustaining the writers' visions with his homey staging and photographing of the domestic hearth.

MASCULINE DOMESTICITY AND
THE WORK OF WALTER HART

James L. Baughman explains of the postwar moment in broadcasting that "all four of the networks, in at least one critical regard, expected television to resemble radio. TV would rapidly become a mass medium and prove profitable by selling airtime to advertisers."[71] And as radio networks owned the television stations, it only made sense that talent from the former would find a place in the nascent industry of the latter.[72] While early television hoped to maintain viewers and fans from radio, questions remained about how to adapt radio's stories to the new medium. Writer Charles Lawsome recounts how, initially, writers not only took inspiration from radio but even directly lifted radio scripts for their teleplays. Lucille Ball, who had performed on radio and film before becoming a television star, worked with her writers to address the challenge of adapting radio scripts: "In the beginning Carroll and [Pugh] Davis borrowed storylines from their old *My Favorite Husband* scripts but learned that television was different. They had to move the characters around and not depend on the sound effects as much. Primarily, they had to learn to think visually."[73] For Ball's writers, this involved devising comedy that was visual rather than solely auditory, and, for Pugh, that involved testing out Ball's stunts herself, including being dangled out of a window rolled up in a carpet.

But for Berg and Lynch to "think visually" and find a scheme to match their language, they needed help—and it came in the form of director-producer Walter Hart. Hart established the closeness, warmth, and financial comfort of both the Goldberg and Arbuckle households. Hart directed for both shows, as well as the film version of *The Goldbergs* (1950), and produced *Ethel and Albert*. But his career began in the New York theater scene. In 1937, Hart stepped down from his place as head of New York production for the Federal Theatre Project, explaining to *Variety*:

I am tired—tired of the constant reorganization, tired of the constant change in rules and regulations, in orders and counter-orders. Most of all I am tired of passing miracles. I want to go back to the simple little matter of producing or directing one play at a time in what is amusingly called "private industry."[74]

One month later, he would write a similar editorial for the *New York Times*, claiming that the Federal Theatre Project was "too large and unwieldy to be efficient" and calling for reform.[75]

As Hart was based in New York City, he established himself in the city's television scene, not only working on *Ethel and Albert* and *The Goldbergs* but *Studio One* (CBS, 1948–1958) as well.[76] In many ways, *The Goldbergs* and *Ethel and Albert* resembled theatrical productions: each episode is short and self-contained, centered on a prescribed set of characters and locations, with action largely restricted to the home or the immediate neighborhood. His directorial oeuvre resonated with that of the *Philco-Goodyear* directors who staged the works of Chayefsky, Horton Foote, and Gore Vidal, among others, and whose "niche," as Erik Barnouw describes it, lay in telling "compact rather than panoramic stories, in psychological rather than physical confrontations."[77]

Hart articulated his vision of television production and direction in a 1951 issue of *Theatre Arts* journal. In it, he emphasizes the nature of collaboration in the new medium:

> Almost no one knows how to distinguish between writing, directing and acting. Indeed, often they cannot be distinguished. And perhaps that is all to the good, for the only real direction that is worth anything is work which is so completely collaborative, so wedded to the material, that you cannot tell where one begins and the other ends.[78]

Hart's collaborations with both women were amicable and constructive. He described Berg as a "wonderful person—warm, charming, and sympathetic," while Lynch would say of her scripts "I take everything I write from my family, Alan Bunce's or Walter Hart's."[79] In his direction of *The Goldbergs* film, one reporter noted Hart's signature moves as a director, his habit of "cutting the film as he went along" a product of his time in television; furthermore, Hart "made the camera crews do intricate movements during dialogue . . . [and] eliminated breaking of the acting continuity for the usual camera shifts."[80] While Hart's style is in many ways unobtrusive, even invisible, *The Goldbergs* and *Ethel and Albert* both bear the imprint of Hart's contributions, including camerawork that privileges performance and dialogue over action or effects, as well as his attention to detail in framing domestic space.

FIGURE 14. The Goldberg apartment on display in the September 5, 1949 episode, of *The Goldbergs*. © 1949 CBS Television. *Ultimate Goldbergs*, DVD.

FIGURE 15. Ethel and Albert Arbuckle enjoy quiet time in their upscale, suburban home in "Should a Wife Try to Change Her Husband?" *Ethel and Albert* kinescope, PLP.

The Goldberg and Arbuckle homes are more than simple backdrops: they are carefully configured and designed in relation to the characters on-screen and the viewer watching at home. When the scene is filmed straight-on, the set appears flat and static, making the characters and their conversation the focal point for the viewer. But when shot at an angle, the depth of the domestic space is emphasized, the oblique orientation showcasing the details of the interior design and conveying a sense of "lived-in"-ness (Figures 14 and 15). In the set of *The Goldbergs*, there are numerous figurines, paintings, even a back room that, while barely visible, appears decorated, while *Ethel and Albert*'s set features items on the mantel and lamps arbitrarily distributed throughout the room. These rooms are neither pristine nor squalid, possessing a plausible amount of clutter, and the attention to detail suggests a feminine, even feminist, politic that asserts the attention-worthiness of the domestic space, down to each and every *tchotchke* on Molly's coffee table.

Spigel writes of how postwar culture contended with "multiple anxieties . . . [around] the ability of the domestic environment to be made into a site of exhibition," but Walter Hart shoots the homes in *The Goldbergs* and *Ethel and Albert* as humble yet inviting spaces where the viewer can figuratively put her feet up.[81] Hart films the homes of the Goldbergs and the Arbuckles in similar ways, though their material circumstances differ. The Arbuckles have no children and cohabitate with an elderly aunt in a stand-alone house, indicative of their upper-middle-class status, while the Goldbergs are a working-class family cramped into a city apartment until the final season, when they move to the suburbs. The Goldbergs' apartment runs counter to Hollywood representations of the sophisticated bachelor urban oasis, which Pamela Robertson Wojcik explores in her study of the postwar apartment plot, but neither does it decry the squalor of city life.[82] How could it, when the viewer is positioned as Molly's neighbor in addition to her friend? The Arbuckle's home is more luxurious and spacious than the Goldbergs', but both spaces project comfort and friendliness.

Thus, the tenement's open window becomes a cousin to the Arbuckle's high-end picture window. Both are surrogates for the television screen, that transparent portal between the public and the private that remedies female loneliness and promotes community, while sponsors and networks treat it as the vehicle for "giv[ing] the home audience . . . a *perfect view*."[83] Hart, Berg, and Lynch's collaborations "control and construct a perfect view," but where the "scientific management of the gaze in the home" is tempered by warmth and familiarity.[84] Through the director-father figure and the writer-mother, *The Goldbergs* and *Ethel and Albert* offer views of homes that are cluttered but never oppressive, with a look that is personal without being pathological or voyeuristic. These shows, industry marriages of male vision and female speech, offer a soft reprisal to those postwar concerns that any "failure in the authority of human vision [speaks to] . . . the man's [diminished] position of power in domestic space."[85]

Berg and Lynch wrote with advertisers' needs in mind, but their domestic spaces function as more than just showrooms for consumer products, in large part due to Hart's efforts. In *The Goldbergs*, the home serves as a powerful suturing device. As shown in Figure 16, the kitchen table is not only the vehicle for familial intimacy but also that which affectively links the show and its audience. The camera is stationed so the viewer is positioned at the kitchen table with Molly and Jake as one of the family. Just as the listener of the radio version invites the Goldbergs into her kitchen by tuning in, so the television version seats the viewer at the Goldbergs' table. In *Ethel and Albert*, the home becomes a barometer for character dynamics and development. In "Should a Woman Try to Change Her Husband?" (NBC, October 2, 1954), Ethel tells Albert, just as he is leaving for his boys' night, that he is not sufficiently attentive or romantic. While playing poker in an impossibly dark room, Albert feels guilty for leaving his wife home alone, as he pictures her struggling with some packages from their basement storage (Figure 17). When he comes home and finds that Ethel is sick, he puts on an apron and vacuums the house for her, transforming himself into the picture of a devoted housewife to make it up to Ethel (Figure 18), a sight

FIGURE 16. Eating around the family dinner table in the September 12, 1949 episode of *The Goldbergs*. © 1949 CBS Television. *Ultimate Goldbergs*, DVD.

FIGURES 17 & 18. Through the power of superimposition, Albert deliberates, ultimately deciding to stay home and nurse his ailing wife in "Should a Woman Try to Change Her Husband?" *Ethel and Albert* kinescope, PLP.

gag with sweetness at its core. These shots together reveal that the home is more than a place to live: it is the means and material through which Ethel and Albert demonstrate their commitment to one another. Margaret Marsh has referred to what Spigel calls the "more 'compassionate' model of marriage where men supposedly shared domestic responsibilities with women" as a postwar renaissance of "masculine domesticity," an ideal that first took root in the Progressive era.[86] Hart, with his keen attention to women writers' visions and worlds, establishes himself as a craftsman and the professional equivalent of a "masculine domestic."

Finally, *Ethel and Albert*'s "The Corner of Your Eye" (CBS, October 8, 1954) thematizes the act of looking at and around the home, and, in the process, comes as close as Lynch ever would to expressing a philosophy of visual storytelling.[87] Unlike most episodes of *Ethel and Albert*, "The Corner of Your Eye" relies on slapstick, sight gags, and physical comedy. While their aunt Eva goes to the movies, Ethel and Albert decide, after many nights of watching television or playing bridge, that they will invite a couple over for the evening. The abrasive husband is introduced with an uncharacteristically tight close-up shot that highlights his loud voice and his noisy wardrobe, in stark contrast

FIGURE 19. At the end of a long, chaotic evening, what better ending than curling up in front of the television, as evidenced by the conclusion of "The Corner of Your Eye"? From "The Corner of Your Eye," *Ethel and Albert* kinescope, PLP.

with Albert's conservative suit. The couples are playing bridge when the husbands get into an argument over a local news story in which a man claims that a burglar broke into his home, bound and gagged his wife, and stole the family's jewelry. Albert insists this was a case of insurance fraud, because any man would see an intruder out of the corner of his eye, even if, as their guest argues, he was watching television at the time. "You have to consider the psychological factor!" his guest insists. The men draw a diagram of the living room, as pictured in the paper, and decide to reenact the incident to test its veracity. In the effort to stage this play, Ethel is bound and gagged. But when Aunt Eva comes home, she mistakes their guest for a real burglar and knocks him out cold.

Ethel's rhetorical question—"What earthly difference does it make what you can see out of the corner of your eye?"—is directed at her husband and guests but invokes the corollary question, "How must the story change once there is something to *see*?" This episode serves as an allegory for how the promise of the visual fundamentally alters the future of broadcast storytelling and comedy. "Let's be grateful we had a little excitement around here," Eva remarks before all three of them settle in to watch some old movies on late-night television (Figure 19). At first, Ethel and Albert both resist the pull of the television but ultimately succumb. It is just too alluring, too compelling, to be denied. So, as the viewer begins the episode by watching Ethel, Albert, and the rest of the characters *be* television, it ends with the couple watching television, the program once more operating as a window into and a mirror up to its audience.

Even as Berg and Lynch remained tied to their dialogue-driven modes of radio storytelling, the humor and heart of the television versions was also developed through visual means. Critics appreciated Hart's direction, generally thought to complement Berg and Lynch's scripts and to capture the minutiae of the family's daily routines, what a *New York Times* television critic called "the small situation in married life."[88] Other critics at the time seized on Hart's contributions as well, calling his work on *Ethel and Albert* "smooth and facile" and his direction of *The Goldbergs* film (1950) as "employ[ing] the television technique of using three constantly shifting cameras simultaneously—[and] achieving a warm feeling of intimacy and movement."[89]

Male-female partnerships in early television not only became a fixture of industry gender politics but also wove themselves into the public narratives around television. An industry narrative that touted the combination of female wisdom with male craft was one that left space in television for both men and women: if Berg and Lynch had the ear to write their stories, Hart had the eye. This trope of the egalitarian partnership—rehearsed behind the scenes as a work relationship and staged as a marriage—lay at the heart of both programs, as *The Goldbergs* and *Ethel and Albert* served as forceful antidotes to stereotypical representations of authoritative patriarchs and submissive wives.

"BABES IN THE WOODS": THE STAY-AT-HOME SHOWRUNNER PLAYS DUMB

If "Corner of Your Eye" suggests that Lynch was thinking about craft, privately if not publicly, *Ethel and Albert*'s "Women's Club Buys a New Club House" (CBS, July 4, 1955) provides further evidence that the stay-at-home showrunner knew when to keep her lips sealed. In this episode, Ethel and Albert are at odds when Ethel's women's club buys a house that rests on the same lot of land that Albert and his business buddies wish to develop.[90] The men at first think it will be easy to buy the land from the club by dazzling them with a fair price—these women, they say, are "babes in the woods" when it comes to the high-stakes world of real estate. But Ethel and her club-members are uninterested in the potential for financial gain, having fallen in love with the meeting space. What would they do with more money if all they want is the house they already own? "Men are such dreamers, it's a good thing that we women keep our feet on the ground," Ethel pronounces. In her work on Peg Lynch, Lauren Bratslavsky has noted that Ethel often wins in arguments against Albert, and, in the end of "Women's Club Buys a New Club House," the women's seeming naivety—their unwillingness to get lawyers involved, their indifference to financial gain—rewards them handsomely in the end.[91] The men decide to buy the land around the home for a hefty price, so the women's club makes money while still being able to keep the building for their meetings. Still, Albert and his associates, sore from having lost so much ground and cash, describe the women as the "sharpest, slickest . . . operators" even as "the women don't know they're being smart . . . they blunder through their victory!"

But was it such a blunder? Toward the middle of the episode, to win Ethel's favor, Albert gives his wife a bouquet of roses, warning her, "Careful, they have thorns." So, perhaps, Ethel has thorns—Peg certainly does. There is great value to "playing dumb" as a wife or a woman in the professional ranks: when you are drastically underestimated, no one sees you coming. If the scheming housewife is a familiar trope in midcentury mass culture, how might this approach speak to the tactics of the woman television professional who wrote for her? Lynch claimed that both she and Ethel Arbuckle lacked any mathematical aptitude—"To me . . . five times zero will always be five"—but she knew enough to keep ownership of her characters and her program, just as Ethel knew enough to keep ownership of this prized women's clubhouse.[92] Under these circumstances, Ethel's assessment that women know how to "keep their feet on the ground" seems more earnest: both the character and her creator knew to hold on to that which will generate revenue. (Lynch's daughter would say of her mother that refusing to sell the rights to her show was "possibly the only smart business move [her] mother . . . ever made."[93]) In this way, Ethel and Lynch have similar approaches to business, privileging space and creative autonomy over short-term financial gain.

Both Gertrude Berg and Peg Lynch operated *entrepreneurially*, to use Jon Kraszewski's term, generating multiple streams of revenue through and as their characters. And while these women did not project the "lone-wolf" personas of male television writers like Chayefsky or Serling, they too moved between genres and formats, raising their profiles with each appearance.[94] Berg performed as Molly Goldberg across multiple media platforms and even made an in-character cameo on a 1954 episode of Milton Berle's *Texaco Star Theater*.[95] Lynch's *Ethel and Albert* teleplays were published by Samuel French concurrently with the show's run, just as a collection of Rod Serling's scripts were published by Simon & Schuster in 1957.[96] And after the cancellation of *Ethel and Albert*, Lynch returned to her roots in radio, capitalizing on her persona and proven track record from television.[97] Much as these women distanced themselves from the business of television through playing housewives on-screen, their professional behaviors reflected a savvy concerning the longevity and financial rewards of their personal branding.

Thus, not only did *The Goldbergs* and *Ethel and Albert* leave a generic impact on the medium with their early articulation of the flexible, fungible form of the family sitcom, but Berg and Lynch anticipated the rhetorical and institutional power of the showrunner, a figure that would increasingly become the public's primary understanding of who a television writer is and what one does. Berg and Lynch scripted their careers and programs by expressing an alternative to the craftsmanship ideal as set out by men writers of the day and making artlessness into an expression of craft. Berg's success lay in pretending to be ordinary, a savvy move from a woman known for playing a guileless character. In 1950, one Kentucky newspaper explained Berg's appeal as that of an unglamorous "hausfrau triumphant in an era when career women have been winning most of the plaudits . . . but big, placid and comfortable as she appears, she is one of the most talented, astute and determined career women of her generation."[98] Berg smartly inhabited a peculiar contradiction, one that allowed her to play the homemaker without being deemed inauthentic and to be "astute" without experiencing backlash. And as Lynch, not one for aesthetic musings, would say about the move to television: "We didn't have to change a single line in the script; E. and A. was a natural for television, which made me think that all this hullabaloo about learning to write for television as if it were some weird new art is a lot of nonsense."[99] But many of her episodes suggest, even blatantly insist, that it took know-how to make the media leap.

Television writers Lynch and Berg "broaden[ed] sitcom history," as Bratslavsky writes, but, in the context of other women television writers in this period, these two figures also contributed to the television's public face of female authorship as a precursor to pop culture gender politics.[100] As cultural objects, their shows seem like traditional representations of female domesticity, but, as institutional artifacts, they reveal something far more challenging: a domestic sphere not only managed by women but authored by them as well. All of the characters lived and died by Berg and Lynch's pen, and each writer spoke through her creations, male and female, promoting gender equity in the home and criticizing Hollywood's stringent standards of beauty. By obscuring their attention to craft and channeling these discussions into the plots of their shows instead, Berg and Lynch revised the act of television writing as an occupation that rewards patience, attentiveness, and the quiet execution of hard work—in other words, a profession geared to the strengths and virtues of the American housewife.

CHAPTER 4

"What Girl Shouldn't?"

The Many Children of Irna Phillips

In 1947, radio and television soap opera writer Irna Phillips was embroiled in a heated exchange about the conditions of her employment at General Mills. In her impassioned letter to the company's vice president, Sam Gale, she wrote: "I am sure you will agree that even in the conduct of the affairs of big business, the human equation must play a great part. May I express an opinion which I have learned many years ago: That there isn't anyone that is irreplaceable."[1] These lines encapsulate the hopes and motives of Phillips, the radio powerhouse, and her strategic transition into television writing and creating. This move was not smooth for all of radio's writers and producers, but Phillips ultimately secured her place in the growing industry in the wake of *Guiding Light*'s (NBC Radio, CBS Radio, 1937–1956) well-received adaptation for television (CBS TV, 1952–2009). Her robust partnership with Procter & Gamble offered further security, Cary O'Dell writing of the latter that "between the two of them... they formed the biggest, toughest alliance daytime television had ever seen," producing not only *Guiding Light*, but also *As the World Turns* (CBS, 1956–2010), and *Another World* (NBC, 1964–1999).[2]

With each change—from radio to television, from Chicago to national broadcasting (New York and Los Angeles), from live to recorded—Phillips adapted her writing and her persona to her contemporary moment, proving adept at constructing a sentimental, emotionally accessible public face while remaining highly practical in private. In this way, she balanced the needs of sponsors and networks without losing the faith of her fan base.[3] But because, as Phillips notes, all writers are "replaceable," she was always advocating for herself both within the industry and through direct appeals to the public, even embedding these arguments in the shows she wrote and created. Phillips grew practiced in making the case that emotion, sentiment, and the "human equation" might coexist within the harsh climate of the entertainment industry, since the future of the soap depended on just this balance of passion and pragmatism.

Irna Phillips provides a focal point for synthesizing the many changes occurring throughout the first decade of postwar television beginning in 1949, and she further demonstrates how a professional woman might tactically position herself in relation to an ever-shifting media landscape. Through numerous public relations strategies and in writing, Phillips confronted questions such as: How can radio serials be adapted to the visual format of television? Where will the television industry be based? How much should television cost to produce? How will the medium be monetized? Is television best suited to social-educational or commercial purposes, to art or to entertainment? By setting stories of crime, divorce, and familial dysfunction within domestic settings recognizable to her white, middle-class, and overwhelmingly female audience, Phillips engineered many of the tropes of the early radio soap and its transmediation to television.

Like Berg and Lynch (chapter 3), Phillips in many ways antedated the contemporary figure of the showrunner, even though she only produced one of the shows she created, the television incarnation of *The Brighter Day* (CBS, 1954–1955). Industry and press coverage extended Phillips' "auteur" status, Michael Z. Newman and Elana Levine defining the showrunner as "an artist of unique vision whose experiences and personality are expressed through storytelling craft, and whose presence in cultural discourses functions to produce authority for the forms with which he is identified."[4] These discourses of artistic "legitimation" and "authority" were deployed by Phillips and her team to counter criticisms of daytime serials as lowbrow, its fans as ignorant or selfish, and Phillips (or her assistant writers, most likely) weaved her rebukes of soap opera's opponents into her scripts. This rhetorical strategy is one Phillips developed in radio, where, as Ellen Seiter explains, she "characterized her audience, and her defense of the soap as uplifting as well as entertaining."[5]

Phillips further attested to the respectability and social need for soap operas by linking her shows to her public persona, that of a dedicated nurturer, a keen observer of human interactions, and a woman of refined tastes. Soap opera has a reputation for being a multi-authored and, thus, "impersonal" genre in comparison with quality playhouse dramas of the 1950s and the premium or quality dramas of the present; still, Phillips insisted her shows were her own intimately "authored texts," even when she was operating in a primarily managerial or narrative oversight capacity.[6] In response to criticisms that soap operas were moral and aesthetic trash, Phillips and her allies foregrounded her training in education and psychology, from which sprung her "expert[ise on] the woman's audience."[7] Phillips's public persona underwrote her creative output, as she portrayed herself as a real-life, tough but tender, soap opera heroine. Indeed, these elements of her scripted life were mutually reinforcing: the respectability, authenticity, and emotional accessibility of the woman (Phillips) and the form (soaps) were tethered together, for better or for worse.

To soften the edges of a potentially sharp, entrepreneurial persona, Phillips allowed male collaborators and sponsor/network surrogates to speak for her on matters of sociological or business import. Elana Levine writes of how soaps permitted "a more gender-equitable blend of labor than was typical of most early TV dramatic production," but Phillips professed to know her own place, stating that "the happier marriages, friendships, associations of any kind result from an equality between man and woman, where a woman is a woman by her own right, and a man is a man by his own right."[8] This allowed Phillips to perform disinterest in the financial aspect of entertainment, demonstrating that her heart lay with her scripts and her fans. Yet, she still demanded to be a woman—and a writer—"by her own right," apologetically able to do her job without hindrance, like a loving, protective mother.

In this way, as well as through her private life as a single parent, in her conspicuous supervision of a team of secretaries (rather than being her own typist), and through the issue-based storytelling for which she would become known, Phillips anticipated numerous points and debates of second-wave feminism. But Phillips was vocally opposed to many of the movement's tenets as she understood them—or claimed to; one of her obituary notices read that "although she never married, Miss Phillips was not a feminist," believing that "'women are happier being dependent on men.'"[9] Phillips's persona straddled the descriptors of "retrograde" and "radical," and this was also true of her soaps, serials that subtly undermined postwar discourses of sexism and misogyny. With the postwar rise of "momism," a movement of cultural experts attributing the faults of American men to their mothers' failures, soap operas depicted mothers as sympathetic, multidimensional women who struggle to be neither overprotective nor frigid. Ien Ang writes in her book on the primetime melodrama *Dallas* (CBS, 1978–1991) that "although motherhood is presented in soap opera as a feminine ideal, at the same time it is a source of constant care and worry."[10] Irna Phillips foregrounded the strain of women's work and worry in her writing, centering mothers with rich emotional lives and personal travails. She also made space in her shows to consider how women balanced professional accomplishment with personal satisfaction, while illustrating how women of different class backgrounds, educations, and ambitions clash within their own families.

With her first foray into television, the short-lived *These Are My Children* (NBC, 1949), Phillips and director Norman Felton demonstrated their hopes and ambitions for the television soap. Their emphasis on psychological and aesthetic experimentation in soap operas, ideals typically used to describe quality, live dramas, resonated with the work of fellow television writers and producers based out of Chicago. Phillips is rarely discussed in conjunction with those who worked in the "Chicago School of Television," a micro-industrial community of television makers that favored low-budget, improvisational productions. These included the children's show *Kukla, Fran, and Ollie* (NBC, 1949–1957), the "seriocomic half-hour" *Studs' Place* (NBC, ABC, 1949–1951), and the variety program *Garroway at Large* (NBC, 1949–1954).[11] Phillips, while based in the same city, favored detailed, preplanned narrative universes and melodramatic storylines dictated by sponsors' needs and demands, so her programs are rarely discussed in conjunction with these "Chicago School" shows, which originated on local syndicates. But Phillips's work on television and her defense of the soap form bears the imprint of the Chicago School and, by extension, of postwar discussions around television's cultural and artistic legitimacy.

These Are My Children is an essential artifact in the history of Irna Phillips and women writers in postwar television. First, it marked the start of Phillips's television career, before assistant writers took over more of the day-to-day writing responsibilities, rendering it a central text for drawing out Phillips's authorial signatures. Second, *These Are My Children* innovated numerous fixtures of the soap genre, as adapted from radio, including conflicts between family members and generations, community among women, and voice-over sequences that placed the viewer directly in the mind of a character on-screen. The heart of the serial lies with Mother Henehan and her worries over her adult children, who sometimes need to leave the safety of hearth and home to make their way. The problems of her female characters are never diminished as "women's problems," nor are their responsibilities mere "women's work": this cozy corner of domestic space, as Phillips draws it up, captures the entire world in its scope.

Thirdly, and finally, *These Are My Children* functions as a creative master text for Phillips's scripted life, as well as her subsequent daytime successes, which thrived beyond the 1950s. *These Are My Children* illustrates Phillips's ability to speak on behalf of her career and of soap operas in general through the women on-screen. Phillips's strength as a writer and showrunner lay in how she devised worlds of women relatable to her female fans, those of mothers and daughters, neighbors, friends and rivals. Tania Modleski explains that the soap opera listener-viewer was addressed as an "ideal mother" with greater wisdom than her children, even as the on-screen narratives "invite identification with numerous personalities."[12] But it was not only the viewer positioned as the perfect matriarch in Phillips's soaps; it was the show creator too, Phillips caring and fretting over each of her shows like it was one of her brood. Phillips establishes numerous opposing proxies and stand-ins for herself in *These Are My Children*, illustrating the complexity and contradictions of her persona.

Just as she collapsed distinctions between conventional femininity and executive or managerial control in her public life, she framed the soap as a form that bridged art and commerce. Phillips resisted all binaries that pitted commercial success against literary quality, insisting that her body of work proved how prestige and popular appeal could coexist in the endlessly adaptable, flexible form of the soap. In this way, she both engaged with and upended contemporary critiques of soap operas as trashy, toxic, and ill-suited to the new television medium. In the construction of her scripted life, she used the contrasts within herself—unmarried but privy to intimacy, traditional in her gender politics but professionally ambitious—to articulate the ideologically messy, open-ended world of the soap opera. Elana Levine details how Phillips wrote stories that "contradictorily exposed the trauma of the very gendered ideals of traditional marriage and family life that she sought to uphold."[13] A high-powered career woman and single mother of two, Phillips herself did not fit into the "constructions of gendered identities" that the soap perpetuated, and the resultant tensions ripple through her authorial oeuvre.[14]

POSTWAR MISOGYNY AND THE SOAP OPERA
AS CULTURAL VILLAINESS

The soap opera has historically received its share of denigration in the public square, a 1940 edition of the *Saturday Review of Literature* referring to the radio soap as "serialized drool."[15] In his 1948 *New Yorker* essay series on "Soapland," James Thurber provides the following "recipe" for soap opera: "Between slices of advertising, spread twelve minutes of dialogue, add predicament, villain, and female suffering in equal measure . . . sprinkle with tears, season with organ music, cover with a rich announcer sauce, and serve five times a week."[16] Such snide assessments of radio soaps persisted when the form first moved to television with *These Are My Children* and others, with criticisms typically falling into at least one of three areas.

The first objection, largely propagated by journalists and writers, was that soap operas could not be art—the highest form to which mass culture could aspire—because they were written quickly and by committee. In 1959, *Variety* published a treatise on the cultural redemption of the soap opera, in which Robert J. Landry laid out the "snob's" case against soaps:

> Secretly or openly a number of the successful soap opera librettists employed ghost writers. One chap who owned the program and leased it to the advertiser was most business-like. He operated from a former Virginia plantation and used assistant writers in relays. While in residence these writers lived—not inappropriately perhaps—in the old slave quarters.
>
> Anne and Frank Hummers who were among the most successful wholesalers of serials "sketched" or "plotted" the daily episodes but turned the outlines over for completion to hired "dialoggers."[17]

This hierarchical, bureaucratic writing process is diametrically opposed to a romantic model of artistic production. Rather than the free, maverick writers of New York's anthology dramas, the "dialoggers" of the soap are compared to slaves, one show's operations conveniently centered, for the purpose of this analogy, on a plantation. (A regional bias, here, emerges alongside an aesthetic one, not to mention a staggering insensitivity to the racial implications of this metaphor.) Daytime soaps were scripted not only without writers' enthusiasm, by Landry's estimation, but also somehow without their consent.

Landry understood the mechanized, serialized nature of this kind of authorship to doom the soap to mediocrity: "Longevity generated creative fatigue. Everybody had to fight weariness and familiarity. The writer alone could not keep the daily performances fresh if the director professed open boredom or if the actors ridiculed everything but the money."[18] The workings of the soap opera mill and its lack of divine inspiration was said to bleed into all areas of the production, including direction and writing, and necessarily produced soulless storytelling. Dwight MacDonald reached this conclusion in his 1953 essay "A Theory of Mass Culture," writing that "unity is essential in art; it cannot be achieved by a production line of specialists, however competent."[19] While Landry focuses on how businesslike writing produces drama that is both boring and somehow *bored* by itself, MacDonald identifies what the soap opera lacks—a "unity" that can only be achieved through the work of a singular, artistic voice. This ideal of the inspired artist privileged male writers who were admired, even rewarded, for their aloof, independent personas. This left less space for women writers, who labored under different cultural restraints and expectations.

Secondly, critics described soaps as guilty of manipulating silly, suggestible audiences, luring women in with sentiment and melodrama to sell sponsors' products. Over 70 percent of daytime radio listeners were female, and, by 1936, 55.3 percent of radio programming during the day was "serial drama."[20] With the advent of commercial television, soap operas were initially outnumbered by other forms of daytime programming, but sponsors and networks knew there was a built-in audience ready to turn on the set. Marsha Cassidy explains:

> Daytime viewership . . . leaped from virtually zero in 1948 to 7.61 million homes tuned in *every minute*, on average, between 10:00 a.m. and 5:00 p.m. in 1958. That same year, 10.6 percent of the nation's total TV homes were already viewing television at 10:00 a.m. (per minute average) and the percentage of homes turning on their TV sets as the day progressed rose steadily, reaching 23.3 percent between 4 and 5:00 p.m.[21]

The audience was willing and growing apace, a boon to those sponsors looking to reach the women watching at home.

The aim of a soap, Thurber claimed, was to provide to these captive viewers an "engrossing narrative whose optimum length is forever . . . [and] to saturate all levels of [the viewer's] consciousness with the miracle of a given product, so that she will be aware of it all the days of her life and mutter its name in her sleep."[22] The soap operas hypnotizes its female viewers not so much to provoke reflection or elicit emotional identification but, as Thurber suggests, to plug the sponsor's "miraculous" product. In reference to the radio soap, Canadian writer

Bruce Hutchinson complains that the "net effect [of advertisements], and particularly the effect of the dreary serial stories accompanying them, is a massive lie . . . solely to make money for various manufacturers."[23] Robert Allen provides historical context for these critiques, but from the perspective of the networks and agencies: "Broadcasters had a vested interest in representing radio listeners—to advertisers, if not to the general public—as susceptible to persuasion. . . . It was particularly important that women listeners be depicted as malleable," as they are the ones buying goods for the home.[24] Though prime-time shows were also sponsored, including many of the highbrow theatrical playhouses, it was daytime's commercial objectives that critics framed as especially nefarious, as the messages were directed at impressionable women. The possibly lonely housewife might find solace in her favorite radio—later, television—companions and thus be persuaded to spend. Phillips was attuned to this dynamic, Marilyn Lavin explaining that "Phillips . . . wanted her listeners to develop an ongoing relationship with the central characters of her programs—they were to become surrogate 'friends' . . . [that] urged program listeners to purchase Pillsbury flour products as a means of showing friendship and loyalty."[25]

The third main indictment of soaps focused on the dangerously indeterminate line between this "surrogate friendship" with the characters on-screen and viewers' unhealthy removal from reality. Some experts and critics found this commercial imperative not just distasteful but dangerous. Mental health professionals described radio and television soaps as potential triggers for physical and psychological illness among women, producing, in turn, a diseased social body. Allen recounts one example from 1942 when one psychiatrist noted how soaps caused, in their female viewers an "acute anxiety state, tachycardia, arrhythmias, increase in blood pressure, profuse perspiration, tremors, vasomotor instability, nocturnal frights, vertigo, and gastrointestinal disturbances," adding that "radio programming ought to be contributing to the war effort . . . [rather than] proffer[ing] a surfeit of daytime fare that 'pandered to perversity.'"[26] It was soap's allegedly lurid plotlines, together with the self-indulgent escape into fantasy that constituted following one's "stories," that made the genre such a threat to the responsible, civic-minded American women of the 1930s and '40s.

These critiques of the soap opera speak to the tension between high- and lowbrow art, as well as the long-standing pattern of mistrusting mass culture as a corruptor of women's moral fiber. The marking of mass culture as a feminine and feminized sphere dates back at least as far as the Victorian period, in which, according to Ann Douglas, novel reading was viewed as a potentially threatening "form of leisure, a complicated mass dream life," sustained by women and clergy.[27] Andreas Huyssen further explores the relationship between femininity and mass culture in nineteenth-century Europe, explaining how women have been excluded from discourses of highbrow or literary art, and written off as the creators and consumers of vapid, effeminized mass art.[28] In particular, Huyssen pinpoints novelist Gustave Flaubert's invention of Emma Bovary, with her appetites for romance and her status "as [a] reader of inferior literature—subjective, emotional and passive," as a prime example of this cultural anxiety.[29] "The identification of women with the masses," Huyssen explains, was designated "as [a] political threat . . . [in that] the male fear of women and the bourgeois fear of the masses become indistinguishable."[30] The "movie-struck girls" of early cinema are only further historical proof of this fear, transposed into a more contemporary mediascape. At the turn of the twentieth century in the United States, independent working women could, for the first time, earn their own money and take up public space as moviegoers. Many women were more interested in attending a matinee alone or with friends than finding a fiancé.[31]

Novels, movies, and television have historically been marketed to the female consumer, offering the promise of a fantasy world where she might picture herself as the bold and independent heroine.[32] The banal soap opera, with its serialized format and materialistic emphases, was described by its detractors as particularly immersive and, thus, addictive, weakening the mind of the flighty, isolated American housewife. With the ascent of a postwar cult of domesticity, the widespread ideology of what Elaine Tyler May calls "domestic containment" encouraged white, middle-class women to revere their domestic and familial duties as a patriotic preservation of the free world.[33] Television, and the soap in particular, jeopardized women's focus and productivity and constituted a threat to their emotional health.

But how else would the dutiful housewife know which soap to buy if not from the mass media? Within this context of peacetime prosperity, Cold War anxiety, and heightened consumerism, the matriarch-homemaker could not win. The suspicion harbored against the soap opera was both a harbinger and an index of postwar misogyny. Philip Wylie's 1942 book *Generation of Vipers* marked the start of America's decades-long love affair with momism, which Roel van den Oever explains as "the idea that an overaffectionate or too-distant mother . . . hampers the social and psychodevelopment of her son," adding, "Momism has it both ways: Moms are blamed for working outside the house and for staying at home."[34] The postwar mother figure proved a particularly fraught "site of highly contradictory accusations: she is at once too hot or too cold," the over-sexed, ambitious mother in the 1962 film *The Manchurian Candidate*, adapted from the 1959 novel, being an exaggerated example.[35] A wife and mother who looked outside the home for meaning—even into the screen of a soapy serial—was liable to run too hot, importing such melodrama into her own life, or too cold, consumed by her imaginary life. Experts insisted that the stakes were just that high for the future of the American family, the margin for error that narrow.

To that end, the anthology drama *Matinee Theater* (NBC, 1955–1958) sought to capitalize on these anti–soap opera sentiments by creating a daytime program for the housewife seeking "intellectual and aesthetic loftiness."[36] The show's producer, Albert McCleery, promised "'naturalistic performances, frequent close-ups,' and dramas of 'character,'" but, as Marsha Cassidy discloses, McCleery's "commitment to sexual, familial, and adult themes; the advocacy of a new matinee viewing habit for women; and the vision of a populist theater within easy reach of everyone—all helped serial drama triumph on television."[37] The difference between "soaps" and "legitimate" daytime programming is primarily a matter of branding, and, accordingly, critics, creative professionals, and viewers did not always agree on what made a soap. Opponents of the soap dismissed it as aesthetic and narrative garbage, McCleery suggesting that *Matinee*'s "mission of uplift" ran counter to the spirit of the trashy, exploitative daytime serial.[38] But Phillips and her collaborators publicly emphasized the craft and care that went into the writing and production of each episode and did so in similar terms, communicating their own efforts to develop television form while providing solace and guidance to the women at home. Phillips's secret weapon in making the case for the television soap opera's respectability—its *own* "mission of uplift"—meant centering her own process, credentials, and persona in these conversations.

UNDERSTANDING SIMPLICITY: PHILLIPS AS COUNTER-EXPERT AND CRAFTSWOMAN

In a 1953 episode of the daytime soap *The Guiding Light*, a husband and wife sit at the breakfast table and discuss a murder trial that has touched their family (Figure 20).[39] The husband remarks on his wife's

FIGURE 20. The very picture of American domesticity, courtesy of *The Guiding Light* (March 25, 1953). © 1953 CBS Television.

nuanced take on the events, to which she replies that she is actually quite simple and that "the more simple people are, the more complex they seem to other people, 'cause most people are so complex, they don't understand simplicity." These lines, from the mouth of a self-proclaimed "simple" housewife, encapsulate the perspective of Irna Phillips, touted as the show's creator in the episode's opening. (No other writer is credited, inviting viewers to interpret this line as the creator's own commentary, regardless of whether Phillips herself wrote it.) Phillips, along with many of proponents of soap opera broadcasting, insisted that the simplest domestic affairs reveal hidden complexities, and the most profound wisdom can come from the unassuming housewife. This argument was in direct response to those cases made against soap operas and the women who loved them.

The same year this episode aired, Dwight MacDonald published the aforementioned "A Theory of Mass Culture." Robert Allen summarizes MacDonald's charges against the soap opera—that it constitutes a "diversion that brainwashes rather than uplifts, the misappropriation of creative skills, and even the misuse of the public airwaves."[40] This formulation sums up the gendered criticisms of mass culture and soaps at mid-century as entertainment so compelling and stupid as to constitute a public health crisis. In response to these expert criticisms, Phillips established herself as a *counter*-expert—on writing, on emotion, and on the women for whom she made the shows. In defending herself and her commitment to the work, Phillips safeguarded the soap opera as a legitimate form of entertainment and education. Along the way, she anticipated sarcasm and suspicion of her own shrewdness, so, where Phillips could not publicly offload discussions of finances or business to a male partner, she rewrote her economic savvy as analogous to household management or motherly care.

Phillips's efforts to erode the cultural stigma around soap operas through the shows themselves—as the line about "simplicity" slyly accomplishes in the aforementioned *Guiding Light* episode—were part of larger institutional efforts on the part of fellow soap writers, networks, and sponsors. Numerous professionals within the broadcasting and advertising industries sought out authorities in sociology and psychology to redeem the soap opera and relabel it a vehicle of social betterment. In 1946, in preparation for the television soaps that would follow, NBC hosted a convention of women's clubs called the FemConvention, held in Phillips's hometown of Chicago, though Phillips was not in attendance. Her soaps were shown to a live audience of fans, then a panel of executives and experts vociferously defended the soap opera. This was a key example of the industry finding an opportunity to preach to the proverbial choir and to have it covered by the press. One reporter for *Billboard* attested:

> Club women saw *The Guiding Light, Today's Children*, and *Woman in White*, then heard I.E. (Chick) Showerman, manager of the NBC central division; [Carl] Wester, and Dr. Freda S. Kehm, former professor in sociology at Carlton University, give pitches for the daytime tear-jerkers. . . . Showerman, who now commands thru his net, the heart of the soap opera field, made it plain he wasn't there to preside over the soapers' demise, even tho the tear-wringers have long been under sharp attack by both public and trade sources as appealing to immature minds.
> He told the women: "You are the final judges of what goes on the air and you have indicated to us what you want and you're going to get it."[41]

Showerman's comments clearly indicate defensiveness around the daytime serial and its perceived moral depravity. By expressing that female soap fans—and not critics like Thurber or disgruntled psychiatrists—were the "final judges," the network reinforced its commitment to the viewers and asked for their loyalty in return. It was not just the characters on *Guiding Light* or *Today's Children* that reflected, listened to, and understood them, after all, but NBC too. "The smart soap apologists," *Billboard* concludes, "are beginning to fight back with more than suds."

Dr. Freda S. Kehm's presence at the event speaks to the NBC's willingness to bankroll their own specialists on behalf of their daytime money-makers: "Dr. Kehm told delegates many social messages are being driven home via soapers, and cited several religious and civic groups who swore by the serials as morally uplifting. (Dr. Kehm is employed by the Howard Mayer flack firm here to promote Irna Phillips' soap opera dramas as a means of social education."[42]) *Billboard*'s full headline, "Chi Soapie

Flacking Lathers 400 GFWC FemConvention Reps," is a playful mouthful, and the off-rhyming phrase "flacking lathers" suggests some kind of daffy mischief afoot. The repeated use of the word "flack," a synonym for "publicity," also implies con artistry, with its flip sound and its echoes with the word *hack*. This reporter cannot help but underscore (and mock) how Kehm was paid to participate in "one of the smartest promotion gimmicks for soap opera yet seen in the Windy City."

Kehm's defense of the serial tracks with James Thurber's disapproval of those "proponents of soap opera . . . protesting, a little vehemently, that serials have always promoted in their dialogue and understanding of public welfare, child psychology, and modern psychiatric knowledge in general"; he tersely concludes that, in his own experience, he "found no instances of sustained instruction and uplift in soap opera."[43] In issuing this critique, Thurber singles out Phillips's dramas in particular and the cultural contradictions they inhabit, saying that her shows had been "described as vehicles of evil and also as documents sincerely devoted to public welfare."[44] Phillips often opted out of these cultural tussles, and with her absence from the 1946 panel, put the defense of soaps' honor in the mouths of other, purportedly disinterested, spokespeople like Dr. Kehm.

Phillips sometimes presented herself as part of a team, other times as the sole author or generator of meaning. In the former case, by signaling and stressing her professional partnerships with male peers in the field, Phillips enacted a retiring, ladylike stance toward the business side of television. She demonstrated to the public that she was not a man-hater, but, instead, an amenable creative collaborator who would never encode misandry or pleas for housewifely revolution into her programs. Her creative alliances also sent the message to the industry that her work was better as the result of her collaborations with smart and powerful men.[45] She entertained close and well-established partnerships with director-producers Ted Corday and producer Carl Wester. Corday directed and produced *As the World Turns*, among other Phillips programs; as Cary O'Dell writes of their collaboration, they together "create[d] an intimate style that emphasized the interior lives of her characters. Slow, lingering close-ups during intimate revelations became the visual paradigm of the serial and presented many possibilities for character revelation."[46] Phillips's attention to the visual language of the soap relied on Corday's technical know-how and artistic vision, while his aesthetic contributed to the reimagination of the soap for televisual storytelling.

If Phillips's collaboration with Ted Corday centered on artistry and aesthetics, her business partnership with Carl Wester allowed her to pass him the purse strings in full view of American audiences—even though, in truth, she was careful and protective of her own intellectual properties as financial investments in her future.[47] In his assessment of Phillips's business acumen, Thurber describes her as shrill and savvy: "Facing the hard commercial world, Miss Phillips developed a shrewd business personality. Her forthrightness used to frighten into numbed silence William Ramsey, of Procter & Gamble, perhaps the biggest sponsor's man in radio. They later became friends."[48] With no husband to soften Phillips's image, she needed an equivalent in her professional life. And Thurber's choice of the word *shrewd* to describe both Phillips and Gertrude Berg (chapter 3)—notably, both women of Jewish heritage—reveals a strain of calculated ambition that clashes with postwar female ideals of heterosexual love and maternity.

Ray Wilson's 1940 piece, "Irna Phillips as Big Business," seems to anticipate these criticisms with a subheading on how "Carl Wester Runs the Shop." Wilson writes of how when agency men come calling, it is "Carl Wester [who] answers the phone.... Irna Phillips is too good a business woman not to appreciate her need to remain detached, sheltered, feminine in the care of a trustee"; he goes on to compare their relationship to the "Kate Smith–Ted Collins set-up."[49] This "set-up" was one in which singer and radio/television star Kate Smith, "as a single woman outside the shelter of a patriarchal marriage ... [needed] a business partner who filled the role of protective father figure and husband"—enter her producer, Ted Collins.[50] But if Wilson is agnostic on the Smith-Collins pairing, his treatment of Phillips and Wester is more cynical, suggesting Phillips is masking her shrewdness with conspicuous (and false) "femininity." Wilson's tone alternated between admiring and arch, offering exaggerated praise for how she spins her folksy wisdom into big bucks for the sponsor. "Gad, how the soap sells!" he declares, mirroring Thurber's remarks that "no other woman writer of soap[s] ... has written as many words ... or made as much money" as Phillips.[51]

Other times, however, Phillips pointedly worked alone. Through documenting and publicizing her solo writing process, Phillips branded herself a woman of great discipline and emotional intelligence—ultimately, the source, brain, and heart for every serial that had her name on it. According to a 1960 piece in the *Saturday Evening Post*, Phillips routinely clocked into the office at 9 a.m., her very presence converting the humdrum room into a charged site of drama and emotion:

Every day at nine in the morning Phillips sat down at a rickety, brown card table—the same one she had used for years—and began to devise that day's scripts from projected story lines often set down months in advance. From there she would dictate dialogue to her secretary and close friend, Rose Cooperman. "I really don't think I write," she said. "I act." Occasionally sitting still and occasionally moving around the room, moving as the character would, Phillips assumed all the characters in the scene—male, female, adult, child—changing her voice to indicate a change in speaker.

The drab setting, evidenced by a worn, "rickety" desk, is magically transformed by Phillips's words and performance. Each of Phillips's characters speaks in her voice, as she literally conjures these figures to life.

As Phillips would talk, "Rosie," her secretary, would take down every word, following the various characters by following changes in I's voice and gestures. Rose filled in the punctuation along the way. Both women occasionally became so involved with the story line they were creating that they found themselves in tears.[52]

Within the framework of this profile, Rosie is not a scene partner but a stand-in for the viewer at home. The fact that both Phillips *and* Rosie are moved by Phillips's storytelling illustrates the affective appeal of the soap opera, not to mention the emotional effectiveness of the writing itself. This profile implicitly strikes back at accusations of "brainwashing": if the writer herself was moved, surely there must be genuine feeling behind it. And while Rosie plays a vital role in the transcription of the soap, there is only one artist or author in the room, and that is Irna Phillips.

This portrait of Irna Phillips executing her unique, all-encompassing vision lived uncomfortably alongside the reality of soap opera production, which often involved farming out the writing to others. Coverage of Phillips's "ghost writers" in radio, who in 1942 included Gertrude Prys (*Road to Life*), Howard Keegan (*Guiding Light*), and Janet Huckins (*Lonely Women*), was underplayed by trade coverage; a *Variety* profile initially presents this team of writers as a "closely guarded secret," but goes on to specify that "although Miss Phillips is not currently doing the actual writing on any of her five serials, she takes an active hand in the plotting of the shows and, of course, approves the completed scripts. All five of the programs are characteristically Irna Phillips's work."[53] The "of course" communicates that Phillips's primacy never was, and never could be, in doubt, while the idea that these programs remained "characteristically [her] work" begs the question of what makes a script any individual's "work." Parlaying her infamous micromanaging into a legibly artistic gesture, Phillips effectively erases the work of her "dialoggers." This profile speaks to how tightly Phillips managed her public persona, as well as the extent to which a trade magazine might provide flattering coverage of their subject in exchange for access. This piece promises an exposé—to reveal a "closely guarded secret" from inside the television industry—but all it does is ensconce Phillips's primacy as her shows' artistic center and ultimate *auteur*. The ghost writers of Irna Phillips, while named, remain specters.

Phillips presented as a professional, balancing her responsibilities to her viewers with a network-approved budget, not unlike the ideal housewife-viewer who managed the home and watched her soaps without giving her housework short shrift. In a 1944 item for *Billboard*, "Irna Phillips Tests Her Video Ideas on Radio Studio Audience," the reporter describes Phillips's pursuit of "the secret to the successful daytime serial of tomorrow."[54] In this period, Phillips staged her radio plays in front of a studio audience with the goal of "keep[ing the] audience which would only hear a show for a while and see and hear it for another while, and thus everyone—sponsor, net, audience, and husband—would be happy." Her desire to experiment with the formal possibilities and pitfalls of writing for television marked an attention to craft, as did her commitment to "giv[ing] the home audience a three-act play daily, using a small, inexpensive cast [without] losing dramatic content."[55] For Phillips, a story was only as good as her fans received it. In 1944, "letters from listeners . . . attested to the . . . fact" that staging the radio plays contributed to dynamic and enjoyable storytelling, suggesting that reception was an important barometer for what Phillips and her team produced.[56] One *Variety* reporter claimed that "[Phillips] doesn't believe there's a single dope in her audience," and, indeed, Phillips positioned herself as the intermediary between women listener-viewers and the network or sponsor, by her own account producing compelling character-driven stories on an economical scale.[57] It did not hurt, of course, that she figured in her own imagination—and those of her fans—as a compelling character herself.

"HER OWN BEST CREATION": IRNA PHILLIPS AS FICTIONAL CHARACTER

In 1930, at the age of twenty-nine, Phillips was ready to make a change—and to return to her roots. Having worked as a schoolteacher in Missouri and Ohio and taken graduate level coursework in theater, speech, and psychology at the University of Wisconsin, she moved back to her hometown of Chicago.[58] There, she got her start in broadcasting, "reading poetry and ad-libbing inspirational commentary" on radio's WGN.[59] During her time at WGN, she wrote what is sometimes referred to as radio's "first" soap opera, *Painted Dreams* (1930). After a disagreement over intellectual property at WGN, she moved on to NBC's Chicago affiliate, WMAQ, and wrote *Today's Children* (1932). Phillips became known for her steely, perfectionist ways, watching her shows and calling the network when she was unhappy with any aspect of the production.[60] Her personal life was no less unconventional, adopting two children in her forties but never marrying. She may have lacked the conventional trappings of feminine respectability or success, but, as female, middle-class audiences came to know Phillips as a writer and a television professional, they also came to see her as "one of them." To understand Irna Phillips became the same as understanding soap operas, and to love soaps, one had to love Irna.

Phillips's mythology—what fellow soap producer Agnes Nixon called the writer's "own best creation"—was spread across others' accounts of her and her own, sometimes melodramatic, self-disclosures.[61] As Ray Wilson wrote of her, "Both CBS and NBC give thanks . . . that the girl, by one means or another, saw fit to combine the [strong, homey] philosophy her mother taught her with the knowledge of people [her] psychology [degree] gave her."[62] Rather than present herself as a traditional domestic or a progressive career woman, Phillips constructed, in and through the press, an image of a woman who reconciled these two sides of herself in the service of creating female-centered entertainment. Her gift was one of being able to speak the languages of both mother and daughter, of femininity past and present.

The persona Phillips fashioned for herself in her unpublished memoir, *All My Worlds,* served as the basis for the public face she would present to journalists and other members of the press.[63] The manuscript, however, goes deeper, to a personal and psychoanalytic degree, into Phillips's formative years. She describes herself as an "ugly duckling" who owes her success to her homemaker mother, and writes: "We [me and my mother] would talk. And it was through these conversations late in the evening that I came to know Mama and began to see Papa through her eyes. . . . Mama had only one goal in life—to keep her family together." This gift of "seeing through . . . [her mother's] eyes" spoke to her writerly gifts and suggested that, through her intimacy with her mother, she was ideally positioned to observe and convey the intricacies of familial life. Phillips goes on to explain how her relationship with her mother shaped all of her writing moving forward:

> Those of you who are familiar with my work in radio and television know the value I place on marriage, home, and family. These have been consistent themes throughout all my work. I know for a certainty that these values are directly traceable to my mother's influence. . . . When there was no longer a man as head of our house, the children became the center of Mama's world. She ran her household with love and understanding, rather than with discipline and rules. . . . She always tended to accept things as they were and make the best of them.

Significantly, Phillips's shows not only reflect these values of love, understanding, and family unity through their "themes" but through the detailing of domestic space, specific to the visual realm of television, and the privileging of verbal self-expression and discussion, as inherited from radio.

In her memoir, Phillips presents herself as the extension of her mother's generative spirit, but also incapable of inhabiting her mother's traditional way of life. Phillips's mother becomes a central figure in her daughter's biography, a figure of both what might have been and what could never be. Phillips lightly suggested her mother might have made different choices, had they been available to her:

> I remember asking Mama about my name. Mama lived much of her life in German literature and poetry. Poems by Goethe and Heine were among her favorites. Gently my mother explained that she had named me after a German novel she had read. I was unhappy with this explanation. . . . I remember feeling that all I had ever been was a fictional character, but I never expressed this thought to my mother.

This inherited literary imagination and the desire to live inside poetry was passed down from mother to daughter. But it came at a price, Phillips's innate grasp of story and art inextricable from the pain of living "as a fictional character." This sadness extended beyond her public admissions that, as a child, she was "lonely . . . making up long and involved stories for her dolls to live out," only to grow up and play dolls with the actors on her soap.[64] Phillips suffered heartbreak as a young adult, getting jilted by a lover after getting pregnant, only to miscarry and be sterile afterward; this trauma, which surfaces in the unpublished memoir, echoes through her scripts and serialized storylines.[65]

But in her autobiography, she also states that, even before these darker turns in her life, she knew she was different from other girls. Phillips explains that she experienced a nagging feeling of apartness in her youth, and the comparative vividness of fiction made her "want . . . to be someone, something different than what [she] was." "I wanted to be an actress," she writes. "Not too strange a wish for a seventeen-year-old girl, but an obsession with me. Acting, I believe, is a form of escapism for many. As I look back on my high school years I'm certain I was constantly trying to escape from something." This passage calls to mind the role-playing that Phillips performed in the tearful scripting of her shows: she seems to have escaped a humdrum domestic existence only to "escape" into her own fictionalized version of that same life.

This book was never published, and the pathos of Phillips's coming-of-age, as presented in her own voice, was lost in the move from memoir to press coverage, as were some of her life's more intimate details. But media profiles pick up on these elements of Phillips's self-mythologizing, in particular her dedication to fans and her keen emotional intuition. A piece in one local paper, preserved by Phillips in a scrapbook, described her as follows:

> Irna Phillips is an amazing person. Her deep insight into the thoughts and emotions of others, her understand [sic] of all human nature, her strict code of fairness, and her sympathy for all mankind have endeared her to the hearts of all her listeners. . . . I would like to tell of my own observations on this bit of femininity. Irna Phillips is an idealist, but a practical one. . . . We grant that she is a very brainy person, but don't get the idea she isn't human—she is, immensely so![66]

Again, the divide between Phillips's intellect and her emotion—her "brain[iness]" and her "human[ity]"—is presented as a unique strength, the contradiction of the "practical idealist" remedied through the category of femininity. Women, after all, can and must be both pragmatic in the execution of their duties, while cooking, cleaning, and caring for their families with infinite patience and love. Phillips watched her mother care for a family while occupying an elevated, lyrical world in her mind, and, in the spirit of her beloved mother, combined intellectual discernment and emotional vulnerability in her public face. This rhetorical move positioned her not just as an innovator of the soap but also as its incarnate spirit: analytical yet emotional, colorful yet familiar.

Phillips used her own persona to deflect criticisms of the form that she engineered. How could soaps be too commercial when she remained so committed to dramatic conventions of theatrical storytelling? How could they be brainwashing women, when her relationship with fans was so intimate and strong as to nearly be *one of them*? But, at the same time, she rejected any notion that her work was lesser or more lowbrow than other programs of the day. The language and logic with which she framed her crafting of the soap opera, then, cannot be disentangled from the rhetoric of quality television and, more specifically, the work of the writers and producers of the Chicago School of Television.

ODD WOMAN OUT: IRNA PHILLIPS AND THE CHICAGO SCHOOL OF TELEVISION

In those accounts that trace television's move from New York to Los Angeles, the micro-industry of Chicago television often gets lost in the shuffle. An offshoot of Chicago broadcast radio, the postwar "Chicago School of Television" was widely acclaimed for its emphasis on live programming, educational content, and loose, improvisational structures, all produced on a shoestring budget.[67] Many of the shows associated with the Chicago School came out of the local NBC-affiliates:

> [WNBQ] pa[id] close attention to the problems of adjusting personal styles of writing, direction, and performance to television, and to the more theoretical questions of how television actually worked. . . . [With] an almost totally scriptless-improvisational approach reliant on interpretive camera work and creative use of scenery props and lighting, Chicago School practitioners produced successful programs in limited spaces with local talent and small budgets. [Station manager Jules] Herbuveaux provided the freedom for his staff to create, and [program manager Ted] Mills theorized and experimented with a variety of ideas including Chinese opera, commedia dell'arte, and Pirandellian forms of reality in his search for new and effective television forms.[68]

Chicago television makers' interest in producing quality, live television overlapped with the aesthetics and commitments of New York City writers and directors working on theatrical playhouse anthologies. Daniel Berger and Steve Jajkowski wrote of the show *Studs' Place*: "Staged in a diner somewhere in Chicago, and for the most part unscripted, *Studs' Place* is a prime example of the Chicago School curriculum. The natural acting and everyday story lines resulted in a program that felt like real life."[69] A number of the most acclaimed series coming out of Chicago were geared toward children—shows like *Ding Dong School* (1952–1956) and *Zoo Parade* (1950–1957)—or were news-informational programs like *Garroway at Large*, a joint venture with the national NBC network.

The decline of Chicago-based television, seemingly inevitable after *Garroway at Large* moved to New York in 1953, stemmed from a series of institutional and technological shifts.[70] Many of the Chicago-based television makers saw these changes as destructive to the future of the medium. At the same time that the Chicago micro-industry was losing talent to the bigger markets of New York and Hollywood, the coast-to-coast network cable disincentivized networks from airing Chicago productions, Berger and Jajkowski explaining that "it was cheaper [besides] to rerun off-network situation comedies than to produce a local television show."[71] Audiences came to expect and demand the high production values of New York– and Los Angeles–based programming, but Chicago professionals like Burr Tillstrom refused to overhaul their shows' style and point of view.

Professionals in Chicago television expressed their commitment to craft in the trades, further cementing their reputations as principled craftsmen-visionaries. WNBQ station manager Jules Herbuveaux combined ideals of practicality and artistry in describing the men of Chicago television, speaking both to the general public and the industry in the process. Technique, he explained to *Variety*, was a "myth . . . [born] out of the whole cloth of expediency."[72] Humility and artistic pride were braided together in the creation of this myth, including this line from Studs Terkel, who wrote of the Chicago "actor, director and writer [being] unencumbered by advice and off-the-top suggestion[s] from The Man in the Brooks Bros. Suit. . . . [Chicago Television relied on] the ridiculously simple formula of allowing artists to call upon their own, their inner resources. To be themselves." The commitment to marrying "technique" and "necessity," all while drawing on personal and emotional reserves, was not only the way Chicago School makers were talked about—it was the same way Phillips talked about herself.

Chicago was also the birthplace of the American soap. James Thurber conveys that, despite the fact that the soap opera capital for some time was New York City, "no other city has ever disputed Chicago's ambivalent claim to the invention of the story-coated advertising medium that either fascinates or distresses so many millions of people."[73] The city's "half-proud, half-sheepish" relationship to the soap emphasizes how the Chicago School of Television has been historically positioned as soap's polar opposite: erudite where soaps are frivolous, fresh where soaps are stale, and original where soaps are formulaic.[74] But, across the genre, Thurber describes how Chicago television makers faced the "wariness of advertisers, mainly, and the thin resources of talent in the

Middle West"—concluding that, in spite of these obstacles, "there was a smell of gold in Chicago, and the pioneers were indefatigable."[75] Making television in Chicago was always a struggle, even at the peak of the Chicago School's respectability and influence. With the gradual disappearance of Chicago as a hub of television production, some moved to the coasts for employment opportunities, hastening the micro-industry's end. But Phillips remained, primarily working from her home base of the windy city.

Few have considered Phillips's body of work within the micro-industry of Chicago's television scene, as her shows were rigorously planned as opposed to improvised and were unapologetically commercialist. Truly, only one of Phillips's television shows—*These Are My Children*—can be thought to belong to this "school," if only in terms of its local production and the personnel who worked on it. But throughout her career, Phillips shared with those Chicago-based "pioneers" a commitment to producing television realism on a budget, and the rhetoric of men like Ted Mills and Jules Herbuveaux made a lasting impression on how Phillips talked about the soap opera. While the Chicago School exemplified artistic integrity and obsolescence, however, Phillips's attention to mass appeal and professional adaptability demonstrated what it would ultimately take to remain a part of television's future.

Despite the quality discourses surrounding shows like *Studs' Place*, Chicago television industry players did care about ratings and profits. Chicago's AFTRA executive secretary, Raymond A. Jones, wrote that the city's most successful soap opera, *Hawkins Falls* (NBC, 1950–1955), made a financially savvy case for Chicago television: "Take a show like "Hawkins Falls," he wrote. "It has a top rating and a remarkably low cost-per-thousand. The boys who developed that program knew that there are plenty of fine professionals available, but when the 'right' one didn't show up for a specific spot, they sought him out by holding auditions."[76] Here, Jones stresses the vitality of Chicago's television production scene in 1953—one more embattled than he cares to admit—and *Hawkins*'s high ratings, in conjunction with its low cost. As Chicago-based advertising vice president J. Hugh E. Davis told the Chicago Television Council and Radio Management Club, *Hawkins Falls*, "'the top-rated soap opera,' gets better ratings . . . than *The First Hundred Years* out of New York and *Miss Susan* from Philadelphia which cost, respectively, $6,000 and $3,000 more per week than *Hawkins Falls*."[77]

Hawkins Falls was a soap in the Chicago School vein, characterized by improvised dialogue and aesthetic minimalism and entrenched in postwar discourses of quality television. Created by Doug Johnson, *Hawkins Falls* opens with a close-up on a book cover that reads "Hawkins Falls: A Television Novel." By calling itself a novel, the show draws on literary imagery and associations with quality, but it borrows a narrator from the middle-brow tradition of the radio serial. The grave male voice speaks directly to viewers, while, each week, a different, friendly everywoman opens the episode by proclaiming homespun wisdom such as: "The person who takes advice is often wiser than the one who gives it."[78] This particular folksy epigram suggests that the soap viewer could be even smarter than the soap she watches, while also signaling to her that she might stay attentive to what the show had to teach her. This episode proceeds to present a straightforward ethical lesson: a group of town busybodies vowing to tame their gossiping habit after they realize they share the same unreliable source. *Hawkins Falls* focused on character-driven situations and actions, even placing a bank robbery offstage so that the action focused on characters' reactions and recollections. This was presumably both to keep costs down—fewer actors, props, and effects are required—and to reinforce that television those meant to capture "real life," not sensational drama.

These Are My Children premiered in 1949, a year prior to *Hawkins Falls*, premiering on the local NBC affiliate, WMAQ-TV. The show was very much a joint effort between Phillips and director Norman Felton, the latter of whom is more often associated with the almost entirely male coterie of the Chicago School. Felton's statement on daytime television lays out their shared consensus on soap's "best practices." He writes, "Physical action must be motivated, never superimposed only as an attempt to bring 'action.' . . . Dialogue should be conversational . . . [and] our most successful scripts have been those in which the rising climax began *at the beginning*, and naturally culminated at the close."[79] Station manager Ted Mills responds to Felton's memo with some dubiousness, asking, "Would an audience be satisfied with sections of a room?" but follows up with the suggestion that "innovations," together with "lines—radio-like," could help "orient the audience" and presumably hold viewers' interest.[80] Mills became an important ally in Phillips's evolution. His interest lay in developing a specifically televisual aesthetic, in which the soap opera "must strive for a picture that looks a little different, and yet, while different, right for given characters and moods."[81]

Felton and Phillips, with Mills's input, articulated a series of principles for the television soap, much of which surfaced in the public coverage of

These Are My Children and Phillips's later programs. One critic wrote of how Phillips's shows "usually consist of a couple characters sitting in a living room, a preacher's study or a doctor's office discussing a simple problem."[82] Felton and Phillips co-formed their philosophy of television and used the same language, presenting a united front to the network, the sponsors, and the press. This, in turn, established continuity between Phillips's radio work and television experimentation. Together, Phillips and Felton expressed a series of aesthetic commitments that shaped how the programs would look and feel moving forward. Phillips's professional relationship with Felton established a strong, male coauthorial presence in her first television show and softened her public image, similar to her lengthier working relationships with Ted Corday and Carl Wester. But these collaborations with Felton and Mills also underscored the forethought that went into Phillips's serials and the soap's subsequent proximity to more respected, "quality" programming being broadcast live out of Chicago at the same time. Phillips's peripheral connection to the "Chicago School of Television" lent an air of respectability to her scripted life—both her persona and her shows—as her star ascended and those of many fellow Chicago television makers faltered.

These Are My Children, however, was not a success story for Phillips. In 1949, NBC notably lessened their commitment to transmitting local productions nationwide by enacting a "no-eastbound edict." This meant that Chicago-produced daytime series would no longer have a platform on NBC affiliates, as the AT&T cross-country cable was no longer available for daytime use.[83] So, while the local television scene was courting profitable daytime programming like *These Are My Children*, the networks would not broadcast any of it coast to coast. *Variety* reported that *These Are My Children* "had just completed a four-week run. However, it would have finished at the 4 p.m. hour . . . [and] NBC officials were satisfied with the program, but since it is soap opera, they felt it didn't warrant a night-time slot, and cancelled it to put efforts on other shows."[84] An item in *Variety* suggested that "'Children' [would] . . . go back on the screen when eastbound daytime is again available," but this revival never came to pass.[85] From then on, Phillips's shows would be produced in New York and Los Angeles.

These Are My Children remains a historically significant serial beyond its being the so-called "first television soap opera."[86] *These Are My Children* also set up many of the tropes and structures for which the American television soap would become known. Extant scripts from the series, together with the literature about its production and reception, reveal Irna Phillips's ability to bridge the divides between the local and the national, the artistic and the commercial, and numerous groups or factions within the mass audience. She kept her options open for further work on the coasts, and by the end of the decade, it would be Phillips and soaps that triumphed in the struggle for airtime.

THE "COMPACT LITTLE WORLD" OF *THESE ARE MY CHILDREN*

With television striving to find a visual counterpoint to the sounds of soaps, Lynn Spigel describes how early television soaps were written to be listened to as the housewife worked, adding that "their segmented storylines . . . as well as their repetition and constant explanation of previous plots, allowed women to divide their attention between viewing and household work."[87] Phillips was conspicuously attentive to the diligent homemaker-viewer ideal. In a *Variety* feature from that January, one reporter explained that *These Are My Children* would be a

> tele innovation in that Miss Phillips is writing it for both audio and video audiences—she feels it's unfair to ask housewives to stop work to watch daytime TV. It'll be a low-budgeter . . . [and] Miss Phillips's success may start trend to bring Chi back into major importance as net production center. Minimum sets . . . new lighting and camera techniques are planned.[88]

But unlike other programs coming out of Chicago's micro-industry, Phillips put commercial aspects at the forefront, with "characters . . . typed to permit integration of commercial into story."[89] (For example, *These Are My Children*'s cosmetologist character was given lines like "The most important thing for any woman, whether she's 20 or 60, is to always appear at her best."[90]) An item in *Broadcasting, Telecasting* described the program's momentum on a national stage: while "the program originally was scheduled as a local show . . . early rehearsals prompted NBC to add the series to the television network's schedule, Monday through Friday, 5–5:15pm."[91]

Extant critical reception is limited and skews negative. A reporter with the byline "Jose" asks, "how [the character of Mother Henehan] can take out the time to gab interminably—well, it ain't true to life."[92] Jose is indifferent to what Ien Ang calls soap's "emotional realism," and his pointed jab about the "gabbing" female not only indicates scorn toward feminized mass culture but also implies that the show lacks quality *because* female characters talk too much.[93] Despite this lack-luster review, the show did find an audience. In an interview years later, Felton commented that the show received a great deal of fan mail and letters of support from viewers.[94] A note from Felton to Phillips from nearly forty years prior supports his claim, reading: "Guest relations called to say that around thirty calls from telephone have already come in from irate women viewers who complained about 'These are My Children" being taken off! Maybe you'd like to know that it has been missed in Chicago."[95]

The endlessly chatty women of the Henehan family, along with their friends and neighbors, were a holdover from Phillips's work in radio, women's conversations and confessions serving as the primary vehicle for storytelling and the show's subject matter. Phillips's programs focused on the intimate relationships between women, and her storylines privi-leged female subjectivity and experience. For example, in Phillips's radio serial *Today's Children* (1933–1937), she focused on a cohort of profes-sional women and the choices that faced them, both at work and in their personal lives. Marilyn Lavin writes of the series: "Before mar-riage, Kay, Eileen, and Frances all worked outside the home. . . . Frances was a 'young modern,' who questioned whether it was "necessary for a woman to be in the home twenty-four hours of the day . . . to give up every other outside interest she may have—just because a wedding cer-emony has been performed?"[96] *These Are My Children* pursued similar questions and staged analogous debates around family, marriage, and contemporary womanhood. Building on the work of Neil Verma, Jason Loviglio writes that radio serials of the 1930s and '40s "negotiat[ed] the tension between emerging conventions of serial narratives, with their relentlessly domestic mise-en-scène and the exigencies of their industrial production schedules on the one hand, and the urgent chaos of contem-porary politics on the other."[97]

In writing and producing *These Are My Children*, Phillips and direc-tor Norman Felton, then, faced these very challenges: first, how to find a visual language for radio's "relentlessly domestic mise-en-scène," and, second, how to express the "urgent chaos" of the postwar moment through story and style. To address the former issue, Phillips and Felton begin their story of intergenerational cooperation and strife through attention to setting the scene. Felton described their set as just a simple living room, while Phillips describes in her script the television win-dow should open "out on a quiet street which might be a city suburb or a small town," a picture-perfect "average American" scene.[98] This setting established its primary characters, the Henehan family, as the archetypical middle-class family, creating a rapport between the diegetic world and the viewer at home. As with *The Goldbergs* and *Ethel and Albert* (chapter 3), the television screen functions as both a window into and a mirror up to real-life American families, and, like the opening of *Hawkins Falls*, the opening credits of *These Are My Children* prominently feature a book. Notably, in this case, it is not the cover of a literary tome or a "television novel," but, instead, a family Bible. Martha Nochimson writes, "Patriarchal historical discourse interprets the feminine as disruption and the linear as continuity," but the family Bible is a chronological document that is distinctly feminine, an object of maternal meaning-making, archiving, and familial care.[99] And, after all, what is the Bible if not a family serial about birthrights, tribal loyalties, and mothers who suffer for their children?

Second, *These Are My Children* explored the "urgent moment" and the woman at the center of it by mapping the political and the historical onto the personal and the intergenerational. The soap is often conceived of as both ahistorical and apolitical, Ien Ang writing that "the soap opera generally ignores too concrete social or cultural references because it concerns itself with a completely different aspect of life . . . that of 'personal life'" and concluding that stories in soaps are "always from the standpoint of the private sphere."[100] But as Elana Levine explains in her historical account of the television soap, "[The new soap] was . . . a resonant microcosm of the questions surrounding gender, marriage, and family life in postwar America."[101] Phillips and Felton captured all of the uncertainty of postwar America by channeling these feelings into stories of the domestic and familial.[102] Reporter Dan Goldberg articulates this sentiment as early as 1940, writing that the day-to-day of homey life was by definition self-contained and serialized, and "[the] real desire and aim of the average woman is to build a compact little world; certainly, it proves she is intensely interested in any factor which might tend to break into it."[103] Just as Phillips constructed a contained, "compact little world" for her viewers, so too did her fans, through the act of viewing, treat the soap as an occasion to examine their own lives and families. The on-screen home becomes a site of argument, reconciliation, and interpersonal exchange, while Mother Henehan, her professional daughter, and even her educated daughter-in-law are all pieces of and proxies for actual women—not only for the viewers at home, but also for Phillips: the woman, the writer, the real-life "fictional character."

In the first episode of *These Are My Children*, Phillips foregrounds that her story is one born of the "Atomic Age," and, in the process, she conflates planetary destruction with volatile familial dynamics. Mother Henehan's neighbor, the gossipy Mrs. Berkowitz, worries about her son's obsession with the nuclear bomb. Mother comforts her by saying, "'Tis this business of growin' up in an age like today that makes our young people a little less—well, how can I say it?" The women struggle to express the anxieties their children face, their "want[ing] everything better than what we got," Mother concluding. "Times are hard for all the young people," she explains "all the children. All we can do is—is guide them—show them the way."[104] The children of the show's title, then, are Henehan's own, as well as a reference to all the confused, struggling postwar youth. Finally, this line is a testament to Irna Phillips's performatively maternal dedication, demonstrated by how she "guides" all the characters within the "compact little worlds" she creates.

Mother Henehan and Mrs. Berkowitz do not worry about the world outside their homes, but this is not apathy or provinciality. Rather, the home *is* the world, on the part of the woman viewer and the woman writer too. Likewise, when Mother Henehan's daughter, Pat, complains that the family treats the birth of a new grandchild like "a world-shaking event," Mother replies, "Havin' a baby is just what you said and don't ever forget it." What really *shakes* the world, then: the threat of nuclear annihilation or the birth of a child? *These Are My Children* comes down firmly on the side of the latter—birth, child-rearing, and family life. The Cold War is just in people's (mainly men's) heads, after all.[105] As Seiter explains, radio serials taught listeners that "women are responsible for the physical and psychological well-being of those around them," but in the context of Cold War television, Phillips goes so far as to suggest women are doing the *most* important work, combatting the fear and precarity that threaten to overtake the American order, American men in particular.[106] Rather than compulsively reading about the Communist enemy, Mrs. B., Mother Henehan, and their neighbor, Little Mary, exchange local gossip, a ritual about which Mrs. B jokes, "If [Mary] ain't getting news, she's bringing it."[107]

Compared to radio programs where "the source of wisdom is a patriarchal figure," the mother protagonists in Irna Phillips's serials were framed in "grateful reverential terms," their priorities and concerns held up as paramount.[108] As Phillips adapted these maternal archetypes to television, she began the cultural work of revising or answering back these misogynistic cultural scripts. Momist literature focused on the impact that a flawed mother might have on her son, while the daughter of such a woman "await[ed] only two terrifying fates . . . feminism and lesbianism"; but, in *These Are My Children*, the relationships between mothers and daughters are just as important as those between women and their sons, if not more significant.[109] This attention to relationships between women allowed Phillips to create equally complex and sympathetic female characters with which different kinds of viewers could identify with or root for. When these relationships transpired within the unit of the family (between women and their daughters or daughters-in-law, or between sisters), the conflicts spoke to the high-stakes, intimate world of family conflict.

The "relentlessly domestic mise-en-scène" visualizes such intrafamilial tensions for the small screen, gesturing to the problems and differences that caused strain in so many American families. Phillips's stage directions described "Mother Henehan's home [as] . . . a peculiar potpourri of memories, relics, and new, modern furniture."[110] Phillips and Felton demonstrated a shared commitment to economy in storytelling. Felton brought to the partnership "ideas about visuals [that] were rooted in more than production efficiencies [but] . . . were also connected to the narrative and affective dimensions of the program; like Phillips, he understood the need to get viewers invested in the characters on screen."[111]

Middle-aged wives and mothers could see themselves in and learn from the loving but helpless Mother Henehan, as "intergenerational tensions demanded their own therapeutic interventions. Often, soaps modeled how the older generations could counsel their adult children, providing the healing insights the middle-aged characters needed to be fulfilled."[112] *These Are My Children* cleaves to the trope of Mother Henehan having to help and advise her children without fully understanding them. In that way, soaps intended to train their fans to be better wives and mothers, not only through representing healthy family dynamics but also by presenting the distant intimacy that exists between a viewer and her soap opera as a design for the mother-child relationship. Just as the viewer at home can watch the action unfold but never intervene, so too Mother Henehan hopes her children will make good choices without her interfering, never "too hot" or "too cold" in her maternal concern. The space of the home serves as a metaphor for the comfort and discord of family relations, particularly those between members of different generations.

Any change to the Henehan homestead was treated as a threat to all the values it represented, as when Pat considers moving outside the cramped family home to live with her friend, Alice. Carol Lopate writes that "daytime television . . . promises the family can be everything, if only one is willing to stay inside it," and this comes through in Mother Henehan's reaction to the news.[113] She tells Pat: "There's nothin' so important as a family gettin' along one with the other. Then you can fight anything on the outside. Once something's happened to that harmony on the inside anything can happen on the outside and don't you ever forget it."[114] The home and the family are a single organism, and to leave the home is to abandon the family in favor of an alluring "outside" (friends, career, cheap thrills). But, at the same time, Pat is not the show's villain, nor is her desire to share a bathroom with one roommate, as opposed to seven other family members, presented as unreasonable. Her competence as a cosmetologist is treated within the show as a point of pride, rather than an unattractive signal of female ambition. According to Tania Modleski, "Soap operas invite identification with numerous personalities," and in the case of These Are My Children, women at home could identify or agree with different characters over the course of the series or even a single episode.[115] Importantly, the show allowed, even elicited, that openness of interpretation. Just as Phillips played all the parts when dictating scenes to her secretary, the viewer is invited to imaginatively inhabit all the characters at different points, while the scene voices both sides of every argument without comment.

In that way, the women within the "compact little world" of These Are My Children find empowerment through different avenues of labor—wifehood, motherhood, success in school or the work world, or even a combination of these. Phillips pushed back against such cultural restrictions or binaries—wife or spinster, domestic or professional—in her own life and persona. One 1941 profile of Phillips begins with the lines: "A single woman is never entitled . . . to live the way she wants to. So says Irna Phillips, radio's highest-paid soap opera librettist."[116] In this item, Phillips insists that, although she is an unmarried career woman, she wants to have a comfortable home where she can cook and enjoy the finer things. The reporter remarks that "Miss Phillips gets mad . . . [because] she knows, and so knows every other single woman who likes to keep house, that married women think unmarried ones have no right to possess silver spoons, good bed and table linen, comfortable sofas and chairs, an address, a phone number." A professional woman like Phillips should be entitled to establish her own home, and a woman's right to possess and curate her own space is something These Are My Children's Kay and Pat discuss while gossiping about

Jean, Pat's educated sister-in-law.[117] Pat believes that, because "Jean's a college graduate, she's come from a home very different from ours," and she resents Jean's unhappiness having to live with the entire Henehan family. Despite Kay's pleas to be open-minded, Pat gripes that all her brother's personal and professional failings fall at the feet of his high-maintenance wife. But only moments later, these two single career girls are discussing their own futures without judgment: "You should have a home of your own," Pat tells Kay, and Kay replies, "What girl shouldn't?"

This rhetorical question—"What girl shouldn't?"—speaks to the multivalence of postwar femininity in its efforts to resolve the tension between the figure of the demanding harridan and that of the retiring ingenue. In line with Phillips's public persona, *These Are My Children* undermines the retrograde binary between good girl and bad woman. Even the otherwise traditional Mother Henehan is glad that her daughter Penny will be "thru with her school soon and . . . standin' on her own two feet."[118] Phillips takes the recurring cultural inquiry of "what do women (even) *want?*" and reframes it from the female perspective: *What am I, as a woman, allowed to want? What should and shouldn't I have?* Levine explains that "in much of the psychological research of the day, in the soaps, characters' emotional problems were closely linked to assumptions about appropriate gender roles," and Phillips's phrasing of the question focuses on what women are entitled to want, the answer being *everything.*[119] Is it not a woman's prerogative to have her own home, like Phillips with her "good bed and table linen"? Why *shouldn't* she build a career that fulfills her? Write and control her own soap opera empire? What girl shouldn't want all of it? Phillips sought to reconcile all these contradictions through a scripted life that combined her public face and her creative work. She claimed to regret never marrying (again, what girl shouldn't?) while also suggesting, in her memoir, that she was not equipped to play a traditional domestic role in real life. Phillips's performed guilt around her single status—authentic, exaggerated, or some muddled mixture—lay in the "shoulds" and "shouldn'ts" of white, middle-class femininity.

The problems of being a man, by contrast, are not looked at so closely in the postwar soap opera, and *These Are My Children* is a key case in point. Frustrated young men and lost boys become the subject of women's talk, but they are rarely themselves autonomous, dynamic characters. As early as 1950, cultural critic Gilbert Seldes was commenting on this cliché of soaps:

So the technique of production, parceling out small bits of action from day to day, has given to the daytime serial one of its most remarkable qualities: it abounds in weak characters, usually men, who cannot make up their minds and stand undecided at every fork in the road. The will has atrophied, they are at the mercy of events, torn by indecision, pushed into action without the sinew and fiber to carry action through. . . . The weak man required by the structure of the daytime serial is peculiarly useful because he is, obviously, impotent, and although a woman may wear at suspected infidelities, she is never deceived.[120]

Seldes's reference to the "technique of production" seems to speak to both the serialized nature of the soap and the kind of thrifty, *feminine* authorship it requires, with its careful "parceling out small bits of action." Seldes suggests that men in soap operas are weak because of how the shows are plotted and structured, but, in his description, he suggests that soap writers emasculate fathers, husbands, and sons, all for the pleasure of the entertainment at home.

That women on soaps are "never deceived," insofar as this was true, could have served other purposes as well: it would maintain a wholesome, un-sordid narrative universe; it could provide a sense of escapism and relief to those female viewers who feared and, in fact, *were* deceived in their marriages and lives; and it sustained a world of women in which men were not threats, leaving women to do battle with—or to embrace—one another. John, Jean's husband and Mother Henehan's son, passes through the first episode of the show briefly, saying little except that it "looks like always the females are doing things around here."[121] This line is all the more significant with a woman writer at the helm, one who, despite her partnerships with men like Felton and Corday, was known for her tight grip over every aspect of her shows. Just as Gertrude Berg, in the voice of her character Molly, asked, "Do I ever talk?" on *The Goldbergs* (chapter 3), so Phillips speaks through one of her characters, making her presence keenly felt.

Still, the specter of masculinity—neither vividly present nor completely absent—hangs over this world of women, in their every conversation and thought. Mother Henehan, a devoted widow still married in her heart, prays to her husband, Michael, through a voice-over, which Phillips called "a key technique for providing viewers access to a character's inner life."[122] Mother utters:

I've tried so hard, Michael, to keep the family together under the same roof in harmony. but I'm proud of them, all of them, fighting their way in such a mixed-up world. . . . Even if I don't know what's in Pat's mind, whether

she's goin to be leavin home or not, or what's goin to happen to John and
his family, I have faith I have, that problems work themselves out if you let
them alone.[123]

In this moment, Michael is reinstated as family patriarch, but Mother
Henehan remains the head of the household, as she likely always was.
Levine echoes Seldes's earlier point, writing that Phillips, like other soap
writers of the day, "made the experiences of the female characters the
significant ones; the man at the crux of the tribals was dispensable."[124]
Here, the idea of the husband and father subsumes the man (Michael):
by this logic, men's primary function is to make women wives and
mothers. Again: what girl shouldn't? To that end, the primary male
characters of These Are My Children are a clueless husband and father
living at home with his mother, a neurotic son paralyzed by the fear of
nuclear war, and a ghost.

The most radical potential takeaway of These Are My Children is
that women are better equipped to run the world than are the men who
actually do. The show never actually says as much, but with its claims
that the home is the world and that every baby is a "world-shaker," all
the women watching could understand themselves as the executives and
head writers in the "compact little worlds" of their own homes. Phillips, Henehan, and the female viewer all share the same racial and class
identities (white and middle-class), but the women of These Are My
Children conspicuously span age, profession, and marital status. Not
only do the differences between characters generate many of the soap's
conflicts, but these characters also experience complex, even competing,
emotions within themselves, as they strive to live up to a postwar gender
ideal. Phillips invented herself as someone equipped to express the needs
of American women, as she personally broke and bent social norms
along the way. She wrote about white, middle-class women struggling
to find their place in postwar culture, telling stories without easy resolu-
tions, conclusions, or closure.

BUILDING A CAREER WITHOUT CLOSURE

In February of 1949, Norman Felton sent a letter to Phillips encour-
aging her to continue in television and warning her of challenges she
would inevitably encounter along the way. He wrote:

The future holds great promise . . . and I am filled with unfounded confidence in my future in television. It is inevitable that you must continue to

build your place in the new medium. . . . Be careful not to make enemies. . . .
They will . . . be in a position to criticize you . . . but they will respect you
for asking for their opinions. The wretches *should* be roughly treated and
hamstrung . . . but I'm afraid they would creep away, lick their wounds, and
leap to their typewriters to harm you.[125]

Felton's words might speak to Phillips's outsider status in the industry,
her reputation for being demanding, or, alternatively, to the challenges
she faced as a woman writer in television. Felton eventually left the
Chicago television scene to make a career for himself in Hollywood,
producing such shows as *Dr. Kildare* (NBC, 1961–1966) and *The Man
From U.N.C.L.E* (NBC, 1964–1968). After their paths diverged, Phillips and Felton never worked together again.

The next soap opera Phillips wrote for television, *The Guiding Light*
(CBS, 1952–2009), was adapted from radio and had a historically
lengthy run. The show's seventieth anniversary, "inspired by a true
story," moved between the contemporary universe of the show and a
flashback that showed Phillips inventing the television soap. In this telling, *Guiding Light* was Phillips's first television show, projected to be
a flop by everyone but the woman herself.[126] It makes sense that *These
Are My Children* would be eliminated from this narrative, especially
with the threat of *Guiding Light*'s imminent cancellation, which came
two years later. Networks were canceling low-rated soap operas in the
new millennium and replacing them with talk shows and cooking programs. So, in an effort to paint the future of the soap opera as bright,
Guiding Light looked back to its past and capitalized on the persona of
one of soap's original leading ladies: Irna Phillips. In this vision, she was
a plucky, irrepressible visionary who ruled with "heart, warmth, and
an iron fist."[127] When an executive tells her that no one has successfully
translated a radio soap to television, she says, "Good, I'll be the first."[128]
A romanticization, to be sure, but one that accesses an important truth:
Phillips engineered the soap opera so as to give herself the best possible
chance of survival.

Along with numerous other men and women, Phillips invented the
soap opera as a genre predicated on delay, distraction, and deferral
until tomorrow, next week, next year—what Martha Nochimson calls a
"narrative without closure."[129] Ien Ang reiterates this point:

It is inherent in the form of soap opera that in principle it goes on endlessly . . .
this constant deferment of the ultimate "solution" . . . all those elements in a
narrative which pose a problem or effect a delay in the solution of a problem:
obstacles, errors, devious behavior, deceptions, half-truths, and so on.[130]

Traditionally, this has been understood as a product of soap opera's profit motive. The soap auteur creates a world of heroines and villain-esses, mothers and children—familiar but still "another world"—to sell romance and detergent and hook the starry-eyed viewer-consumer.[131] The lack of an ending further results in a slipperiness of meaning and morality, rendering soap opera narratives difficult to analyze. Good characters can break bad but become good again in a week or a year's time. Modleski explains in the case of a canceled radio serial that it is "impossible to tie up all the loose ends . . . what [Roland] Barthes calls the 'discourse's instinct for preservation' ha[ving] virtually triumphed over authorial control."[132]

But did the discourse really escape Irna Phillips, or were fans wit-nessing the author's own entrepreneurial hustle? Madeleine Edmondson and David Rounds argue that "deep in the very nature of soaps is the implied promise they will last forever," and Irna Phillips worked toward building a career that could last forever, a perfectionist who wove her own persona into the DNA of her shows and maintained an unyielding hold on her authorial image.[133] A *career without closure* amounts to the endless, if lucrative, grind of job security. It calls to mind the image of Imogene Coca playing the dance hall performer (chapter 2), forced to never stop singing because, as soon as she does, she will have to choose which of her lovers is her one-and-only and endure the wrath of the spurned others.

How did the women writers of daytime and prime time keep singing? The industry was changing, moving away from radio for good and out of New York City, into Hollywood modes of storytelling and production. Phillips's commitment to commercially viable storytelling for women, together with her willingness to work with productions on both coasts, allowed her to build a career that weathered the industry changes of the 1950s and '60s. Phillips went on to create *As the World Turns* (CBS, 1956–2010) and *Another World* (NBC, 1964–1999), as well as to write and advise on a host of other soaps until her death in 1974. Seiter asserts that Irna Phillips's "aggressiveness, her instinct for self-protection, and her dedication to the sponsor made possible her success and longevity within the broadcasting business," while fellow radio soap writer Jane Crusinberry (*The Story of Mary Marlin*) "lacked the business savvy, the ability to make alliances, and the foresight of Irna Phillips."[134] But it was not only Phillips's temperament or her assertiveness that secured her future, one rife with successes and network squabbles alike; it was also a testament to her ability to harness the cultural conversations around television and turn them to soaps'—and her own—advantage. She smartly described the television soap as a form that straddled the binary between the intimate and the universal and constructed, in the public eye, a colorful scripted life that braided together her own biography and reputation with that of the American soap. All the while, she combatted anti-soap rhetoric by deploying discourses of quality television informed, in part, by her fellow television writers and producers in Chicago. Unlike fellow radio-to-television personalities like Gertrude Berg and Peg Lynch (chapter 3), she publicly shared the details of her craft, but, akin to this pair, she performed a disinterest in the business side of entertainment. (Of course, in private or internal correspondence, it is clear that matters of money and intellectual property were always at the forefront of Phillips's mind.) So, while Levine concedes that "everyone favored the TV soap once it was indisputably profitable," Phillips's longevity speaks to her own strengths in legitimizing the soap opera and, through doing so, making a place for herself in the field of television.[135]

CHAPTER 5

"Knowing All the Plots"

Presenting the Woman Story Editor

Florence Britton, story editor for the anthology drama *Studio One* (CBS, 1948–1958), was as known for her "green thumb with writers" as she was for her boozy martini lunches.[1] Producer Bette Chichon recounted Britton's gift for "br[inging] something out of writers":

> [Florence] would work with the writer and that was pretty much the rela-
> tionship. . . . She radiated an enthusiasm. I can see her eyes twinkling if you
> were to give her an idea or she were to give you a suggestion and you would
> come up with something even better. I believe Rod Serling, I believe that she
> helped him come along.[2]

Britton started her career in show business as a film actress, and, after stints in theater and advertising, moved into television. As a story editor at *Studio One*, Britton served as the gatekeeper for the show's tone and quality.[3] Britton believed in the talent of writer Rod Serling and encouraged him to give up his insurance job in Cincinnati to pursue a full-time career writing for television. Serling would go on to write "Patterns," which was broadcast on *Kraft Television Theater* (NBC, 1947–1958) on January 12, 1955.[4]

On the surface, "Patterns" is an exposé of a ruthless corporate culture that pits young upstarts against aging patriarchs. The main character, Fred Staples, is a transfer from his company's Cincinnati office with the opportunity to advance professionally, but only at the expense of a senior colleague. While "Patterns" focuses on the epic conflicts between

FIGURE 21. Marge Fleming (Elizabeth Wilson) and Fred Staples (Richard Kiley) converse as equals, each wielding their own pen. From "Patterns," *Kraft Television Theater* (January 12, 1955). © 1955 NBC Television.

two men at work and within each man's conscience, the play affords screen time to the secretarial infrastructure of the company—in other words, the women behind the men. Secretaries and assistants gossip, seek out "genius," and give support to the men in the office they champion. The story may not center on secretary character Marge "Miss" Fleming, but her understanding of the corporate world is on a par with that of the men in the office, as portrayed in the scene shown in Figure 21, and her character exhibits a degree of morality and compassion that marks her point of view as feminine.

As a result, "Patterns" documents the power of male-female partnerships in the postwar work world generally and in the television industry specifically. Fleming proves a revealing stand-in for Britton, as Staples is for Serling, their relationship an analog for the increasingly predominant model of institutional authorship: the male writer and female story editor, the latter, all too often, uncredited.[5] It is the job of the female administrator—or, as the case may be, the woman story editor—to deploy her knowledge of the industry to help men advance in the field. It is also worth noting that, as old men and young battle for dominance, the women in "Patterns" survive these shifts and even steer outcomes; so, although these characters do not work in the entertainment business, they might as well. Recognizing the resonances between a figure like Miss Fleming and the real-life Florence Britton transforms "Patterns" from a story about male competition to one about the female support that makes corporate-creative work possible.

To pay keen attention to the work of women story editors like Britton, Dorothy Hechtlinger (*U.S. Steel Hour*), Alice Young (*Climax!*), and Janet Wood (*Studio One, Playhouse 90*) is to rewrite the histories of television authorship in the first ten years of commercial television and to interrogate how gendered forms of work are rewarded or ignored.

Sexist conceptions of story or script work have long rendered the labor of these women invisible, both in the present and in their own time, and created a significant blind spot within the study of television. Too often, women story editors have been largely ignored in accounts of early television, upstaged by the maverick (mostly male) writers they mentored. But the woman story editor was a crucial fixture of television from the industry's beginnings, and she strove to navigate various institutional and generic changes with caution and care. New York live anthology dramas needed script professionals to manage the flow of story and script, and the job only became more demanding as television production ramped up in Hollywood.

With television's move to the West Coast, the women of the network script departments—story editors, analysts, supervisors, and secretaries—became scapegoats for television's transformation into a middle-brow commercial art form, what FCC chairman Newton Minow dismissively referred to in 1961 as a "vast wasteland." The wisdom seemed to be that, now, anyone could write for television, even the hack writer, even the *woman secretary*, as long as the bureaucratic machinery remained in perpetual motion. With the rights for creative properties increasingly concentrated in studios, television writing relied more than ever on what Miranda Banks calls "non-writers—perhaps secretaries or associate producers—[who] took scripts from one series and switched around characters and locales, thereby turning what might have been a detective series into a Western."[6] The question remains: how much writing and rewriting were these "non-writer" secretaries doing? Were they the ones choosing which scripts had universal—or, at least, adaptable—elements? As J. E. Smyth documents, television "offered qualified opportunities for women who had achieved a certain power in Hollywood, but who, as secretaries in a shrinking studio job market, had found it difficult to rise to heads of story or producing departments."[7] Is it possible, then, as with Lucille Kallen working behind the typewriter at *Your Show of Shows* (chapter 2), that the scribe was again being mistaken for the secretary?

These women were not what *Your Show of Shows'* producer Max Wilk called "pencil[s] for hire."[8] Story editing, as opposed to credited screenwriting, was an integral entry point for women with literary inclinations and abilities. At their most powerful, women story editors operated autonomously as creative executives in television, wielding great editorial and managerial control in their day-to-day work. Some advised and championed the most successful screenwriters of the day, and those working on anthology dramas cultivated the program's overall voice by nurturing a curated stable of writers, source materials, and scripts. At their most disenfranchised, women story editors struggled to make their job responsibilities understood to colleagues who viewed them as competent, if uncreative, administrators. The "private secretary" figure of the early twentieth century, "entrusted with a very broad range of jobs ... [and] distinguished by [her] initiative, responsibleness, interest in work, and executive ability," was followed by the postwar "office wife" that dominated representations of work culture.[9] The female story professional fails to adhere to these cultural scripts: on top of being a competent clerical worker and supporting player, she exhibited in-depth expertise of genre, audience, and network or program identity. It was the story editor's knowledge and inventiveness that could determine what made it onto television.

To properly accord these women "writer" status and to explain how some were able to parlay their clerical-editorial roles into official writing positions requires reading trade periodicals and items alongside internal documents including memos and coverage reports. How did women story editors institute creative continuity and coherence in the shows they worked for, and how did they explain or conceive of the work they were doing? The blurring of administrative and creative work was nothing new for women in the creative fields, as they had long peopled and even headed up film studios' scenario and script departments.

But as the work of film and television story editors is difficult to define, and the work is largely done in obscurity, their names drift in and out of the historical record. The figure of Janet Wood at CBS TV is a prime paradigm for those women who fell through the cracks of the film business, then television, and, finally, feminist media history, due to historical and institutional movements much bigger than themselves. Still, some story analysts, including Sonia Chernus and Maria Little, weathered the changes that came with the move to Los Angeles, even becoming television writers themselves. As Jane Gaines writes, there has been a "rationing of the women credited in the industry story of triumphant corporatization ... [resulting in an] unequal distribution of narrative wealth."[10] This concept of "narrative wealth" only underscores how the historical record must expand to include fictional figures as well, including the aforementioned Miss Fleming and the character of Betty Schaefer in the 1950 film *Sunset Boulevard*. Such a reconfiguration showcases the work of women story editors and draws attention to the limits of official studio and network archives. Media texts reflect and revise industry gender politics, and, to that end, "Patterns" and *Sunset Boulevard* thematize male-female collaboration and the professional and personal precarities under which women in particular suffer.

NOTES ON TERMINOLOGY

Job titles in film and television have not retained the same meanings over time. Today, television's story editors are both staff writers and "production executives," with one pamphlet for the Writers' Guild explaining that story editors are "better paid, better recognized writer[s]" who may or may not "spend a significant amount of time doing any real story editing."[11] By contrast, the same pamphlet emphasizes that "in the 1960s, [when] freelancers dominated the market . . . 'in-house' writing staffs were small, generally consisting of a producer and a story editor or two," and it seems that this model took root as early as the 1950s.[12] This means that story editors in early television were working primarily in a development capacity: selecting story properties, working with writers on individual scripts, and establishing a show or network's voice alongside other members of the production team. The story editor in postwar television, then, has more in common with a story editor at a contemporary film studio—managing scripts and, often, assisting upper-level executives—than a current television story editor.[13] So, while contemporary television showrunners may be said to serve as their shows' story editors, the focus here is on women story editors in postwar television who were not themselves staff writers but, rather, worked in a script and story development capacity.

For the purposes of clarity and historical accuracy, then, I have adhered to the following principles when using these terms:

- Numerous trade publications from the 1950s and '6os use the titles "story editor" and "script editor" interchangeably, as in the cases of Arthur Heinemann (*US Steel Hour* as editor, *Kraft Theatre* and *Suspense* as writer) and Janet Wood. In a 1951 editorial, ABC script editor Peter Martin argued for "invest[ing] in writers instead of . . . story properties," describing his role the same way that a story editor might.[14] A 1964 piece from the British trade magazine *Contrast* defines the script editor as one who "handle[s] the perpetual problem of providing a constant flow of produceable material . . . [and] has to commission plays and work on them with the authors."[15] Looking at these items together, it seems that these titles were often conflated or mixed up. To make matters more confusing, "script" employees in film, including "script girls," were employed by continuity departments and were not technically story or scenario workers.

· When given the choice between using the term "story editor" or "script editor," I use "story editor," as it is the more widely understood and explicitly defined term in the industry literature. I have referred to individual story and script editors according to how they are credited, and, whenever possible, have given additional detail about their responsibilities at work.

· Story analyst and reader are the same job. Hill explains in *Never Done* that "since its inception, the job of reader—variously referred to as 'screen analyst' or 'story analyst'—has been seen as drudge work, even thugh it was also a stepping stone to screenwriter or story editor roles."[16] Unlike the in-house story editor, the analyst often works on a freelance basis and does not manage a team of fellow readers.

The descriptors *editing, reading*, and *analyzing* gesture to—and, at the same time, obscure—how story editors were functioning as authors, working closely with writers to develop individual episodes while maintaining the voice of the show or the network. This interchangeable, often muddied terminology speaks to the industry's newness, the instability of industry guilds and unions in this moment, and the nature of the labor as feminized and, thus, imprecise and invisible, this latter point being a problem that goes back as far as the beginnings of cinema.[17]

GENDERING MEDIA LABOR PRACTICES: FROM SILENT FILM TO POSTWAR TELEVISION

The collaborative nature of film and television making often results in some authors receiving more attention than others, and the distribution of that credit can be gendered, raced, or subjected to other cultural categories. Christine Gledhill and Julia Knight write that "one of the key methods of organizing film texts—namely, individual authorship—is, as we have seen, irrelevant to the ways many women work," adding that "crucial to [this] project is the possibility of viewing the products of women's labor or films that were significant to women as audience."[18] These comments extend to the work of women story editors in early television, first, in how television authorship, despite the cult of the contemporary showrunner, must be continually reaffirmed as collaborative and, second, in how television demands to be reread as not only *for* women in the post–World War II period but also *by* them, even if the credited author is male.

The scripted lives of women story editors in television resembled those of female scenario department employees during the rise of the film industry and, later, the secretaries of the studio system.[19] In early Hollywood of the 1910s, the openness of the new field—comparable, if not identical, to the nascent television industry—had space for women to write scripts of their own and even head up studio story departments. The industry logic ran that women had the unique gift of speaking to other women, of telling stories with great heart and emotional depth, and of contributing within a detail-oriented workplace.[20] Screenwriter June Mathis wrote for a 1925 issue of *Film Daily* that women were particularly equipped to perform "careful, fine detail work of scenario writing. . . . [And] after some little time there appeared the woman script clerk, for just the same reason; because women watch the smaller details better than men."[21] Such an assessment is an obviously backhanded compliment: women take to scenario work in part due to its menial nature, the process of fixing scripts is akin to darning socks.

As story and scenario departments at film studios contended with the advent of "talkies" in the late 1920s and the capitalization of the system, a larger labor force of story specialists were needed on the lot and in the offices, and many of these positions went to women.[22] Erin Hill delves into the figures of the studio secretary and the reader, exploring how secretaries were expected to balance narrative know-how with affective or "emotional labor." One 1936 *New York Times* article described the studio secretary's duties as follows:

> Almost anyone can write, but few can be studio secretaries. The one you have has worked for three or four hundred dramatists, knows all about screen technique, camera angles, exits, suspense, climax, the clinch and fade out to full orchestra music. But since she isn't known as a writer she remains forever a secretary—to your good luck.[23]

The reporter's arch language here—"she *isn't known* as a writer"—indicates that the studio secretary is an author in disguise or one laboring in obscurity. This phrase, "to your good luck," is directed to the studio executive who is fortunate enough to exploit his secretary's talents with impunity, without promoting her or giving her due credit. Indeed, readers for studio story departments occupied various roles amounting to creative work, Hill describing the work this overwhelmingly female labor force performed as "filtering incoming material for producers, directors, and executives."[24]

Women story editors and secretaries did much the same work in television as they did in film, precipitated by the decline of the studio system and the rise of independent telefilm production in Hollywood. As Christopher Anderson explains, "the motion picture industry during the 1950s was less an empire on the verge of ruin than one struggling, under unsettling conditions, to redefine its frontiers," television being a major part of this redefinition.[25] The antitrust Paramount Decision of 1948 forced movie studios to divest themselves of their profitable theater chains. As the Hollywood studio monopolies were forced by law to dismantle themselves, the industry pivoted to package-unit production, in which movies became collaborative, one-off efforts between studios, agencies, and talent. Once the FCC freeze on studio acquisitions thawed, companies like Paramount and Disney were free to enter into the television game, which resulted in television's ultimate relocation to California.

Thus, the defunct production-unit system—in which the studios cranked out movie after movie, all "in-house"—found new purpose and life in the production of telefilms in Los Angeles. Film-television conglomerates were thoroughly entrenched by the end of the 1950s, an alignment that was arguably mutually beneficial for both film and television's financial bottom lines and which runs counter to any "media history that isolates cinema and broadcasting from one another or from the other cultural institutions in a particular era."[26] Story departments were closing or shrinking at movie studios in the late 1940s and early 1950s, just as they were opening and growing in Los Angeles–based television operations. The production-unit mode of production at movie studios, in which A- and B-movies were cranked out quickly and with an eye toward cost-cutting, had provided film story analysts ample preparation to work in television.[27] Television networks' story departments needed readers to choose writers and scripts and to nurture these properties through development, and women story editors' experiences in film, as well as those gendered, administrative-emotional dimensions of the work itself, made them eminently employable. And in the beginnings of television, some women, such as Dorothy Hechtlinger, moved to New York in the hopes of rising through the ranks quicker than they had in the film industry. Tracking women's movements through film and television, however, is difficult, which speaks to how the culture industries self-mythologize by touting the achievements of some and marginalizing those of others. The figure of Janet Wood exemplifies how media industry changes can sideline careers, screening off the realities of collaborative authorship in postwar television.

WHATEVER HAPPENED TO JANET WOOD? THE STORY EDITOR IN FEMINIST MEDIA HISTORIOGRAPHY

In 1953, *Billboard* published a small, seemingly insignificant item with the headline "Three Quit CBS Story Department":

> Arthur Heinemann, script editor; Janet Wood, story editor; and Bernice Galland, her assistant, this week resigned from the CBS-TV program department. They will be replaced by Don Moore, formerly Eastern story editor for Warner Brothers, who now becomes head of the TV story, script and rights clearance department. Mr. Heinemann, Miss Wood and Miss Galland have not announced their future plans.[28]

The historical reader of *Billboard*, likely an industry professional in music, film, or television, might have brought more insider knowledge to this piece, but from a contemporary reading position, several questions remain: who were these people, why did they leave, and what other pieces of the puzzle are missing? Related news items begin to fill in the gaps: Wood and Galland had been with the network for three years, and the entire office reported to television programming executive William Dozier.[29] Wood's and Galland's job titles are not consistent across sources; Wood is described in *Billboard* as the script editor and in *Variety* as the story editor, while Galland is typically referred to as an assistant or aide but, in *Variety*, is called the department's "chief reader." More research into these figures, then, does not resolve the mystery: while Wood's and Galland's professional moves are worth tracking within the industry at large, their titles are ever-changing and ambiguous, and none of the coverage of this walkout reveals their motivations for leaving.[30] The team's sudden departure and quick replacement raises the question of whether their exit was entirely voluntary or unforeseen. Heinemann would go on to have a successful career in television writing, particularly with *Star Trek* (NBC, 1966–1969), but the most senior woman in the department was not so lucky.

What happened to Janet Wood, and why does it matter in constructing a history of women writers in television? Parsing the history of early

Hollywood, Jane Gaines writes that "'what happened' to [women] is a question of how they persisted but also how they finally relinquished the hope that they once had of participation in a creative venture that became the world-dominating industry that left them behind."[31] In the case of Janet Wood, skipping ahead in the historical record reveals a short-lived career in publishing, during which time she authored a cookbook and was allegedly ousted from her job at Avon Publishing.[32] Moving back in time reveals an equally unfortunate narrative, that of a long-running career in the film industry that suffered gravely during the decline of the Hollywood studio system throughout the 1950s. To follow Wood's professional trials and disappointments through the archival record, then, is to rehearse Foucault's experience of reading seventeenth-century criminal notices; he notes how these "obscure men" were "able to leave traces—brief, incisive, often enigmatic—[only] . . . out of the discourses that, in sorrow or in rage, they exchanged with power."[33] In the case of Foucault, power is embodied by governmental agencies, judicial system, and the prison complex, while the power mobilized against Janet Wood comes from the culture industries: film, television, publishing. We only know of her because of her disciplining and dismissal—her "exchanges with power"—not for her successes or professional victories.

Because the story of women's movements in and out of media industries is subsumed by larger industrial and cultural shifts, Wood's career has been rendered doubly invisible, by virtue of both her gender and her feminized occupation. Her brushes with power occurred in moments of industrial overhaul and often resulted in her facing a professional setback. Unfortunately, Wood lives on in the literature as a peripheral casualty of film and television's developments. Her tale begins cheerfully enough with a 1940 blurb from *Variety*. The headline reads "Antidote to Agents": "Janet Wood, assistant eastern story editor of Metro, claims to have found the real solution for scaring agents. She appeared in the office last week wearing a badge ('Bradford, Pa., Special Police'—it's genuine), a fancy cartridge belt and a cap pistol hanging from her side."[34]

This joke speaks to a growing hostility among studio folk toward agents. But by the end of the 1940s, the mood in Hollywood had shifted, as the power of agencies was growing in conjunction with the move to independent production, putting the livelihood of story professionals like Janet Wood in jeopardy.[35]

When studios made budget cuts in the late 1940s and 1950s, story and script departments were among the hardest hit.[36] Edward Jay

Epstein explains that, "with the collapse of the studio system . . . , independent producers largely replaced the studio story departments and assumed much of the job of initiating projects by optioning and developing scripts."[37] J. E. Smyth further explains the many ways and reasons studios had to scale back, ranging from television to star price tags:

> Scenario, costume, and research departments downsized as studios attempted to cut costs in a shrinking market following a series of economic crises forced by expensive new star contracts . . . the rise of percentage deals, government-spearheaded trust-busting initiatives (in *United States v. Paramount Pictures*, 1948), competition from television, independent production companies, and shifting competition in overseas markets. Even in departments where women predominated, their positions were no longer mentioned in *Film Daily*. Some women, sensing the diminishing opportunities in a dying industry, moved to theater or television work.[38]

Studio story departments were rapidly becoming obsolete and, with them, the many women who worked in this sector became dispensable, even invisible. Even their presence in trade periodicals was fading, evidenced by the short and cryptic language of the "Three Quit CBS Story Department" item.

Janet Wood's career, then, attests to the decline of studio story departments, how significantly studios were altering their structures in the wake of the Paramount decision, and how script employees were fleetingly represented in the trades, their struggles described without detail or comment. The second half of 1947 illustrates a condensed account of Wood's rise and fall. In August, Columbia Pictures, the studio for which she was working, cut its theater office and combined it with Wood's division, the eastern story department. By September, Wood, her assistant Beatrice (then Aronson), and reader Albert Johnson were fired on a Friday, but then, mysteriously, rehired the following Monday. According to one reporter, "the economy axe swinging through the film industry has struck particularly hard at eastern story departments," cataloging the cuts to such departments at Paramount, 20th Century Fox, Universal and Columbia.[39] By December, the entire Columbia story department was gone, as was the one at Universal; the only film studio that committed to preserving their story department happened to be Wood's former home, "Metro" or Metro-Goldwyn-Mayer.[40] The days of teasing and scoffing at Hollywood agents were past.

Film elitism against television still rippled through the press coverage. In a *Variety* item from 1957, "Today's Story Editor Buys to Please

World," reporter Henry Klinger explained that "the Big Ones," meaning the big ideas for films, were still being hunted for in "publishing houses, Shubert Alley, and the forests of dram and prose."[41] The "Little Ones," or more minor properties, were only good enough for television. Klinger goes on to issue the following menacing proclamation: "the voracious appetite of television consumes [stories] at a pace fearful to contemplate. Typewriters pound incessantly for this avid market with an accompanying blackout of creativeness for other media," adding that "the young writer . . . and the experienced craftsman" have been seduced by the easy work that television provides. The antagonism previously reserved for agents in Hollywood is thus displaced onto television, a lesser medium luring talent away from cinema. Members of a film industry, that, in its heyday, relied on an assembly-line mode of story management and production, now condemned the same practices in its rival television. It was under these circumstances that Wood landed at CBS, where her job consisted in choosing material for such programs as *Suspense* (CBS, 1949–1954), *Playhouse 90* (CBS, 1956–1960), and *Studio One*.[42]

Writer Margaret Buell Wilder was like Wood in that she also began her career in Hollywood, providing the source novel for the 1944 film, *Since You Went Away*. She was handpicked in 1950 to serve as the script supervisor for a show from Young & Rubicam, where the supervising producer was the former assistant to MGM'S Dore Schary.[43] The show does not appear to have taken place with Wilder at the helm, since she would go on to serve as story editor for Columbia's TV branch, Screen Gems, in 1952 and was still keeping her hand in "script work" for Universal-International in 1954.[44] (She was also hired to write a script entitled "A Day Called Tomorrow," a film that was supposed to star Rock Hudson but does not appear to have been made.)[45] If Wood's traces in the historical record are ones of professional disappointments and endings, then Wilder's are a series of close calls: shows unaired, films not made, and a career with an unceremonious tapering off of credits.

Wood and Wilder together gesture to the opportunities television offered women from the film industry and also how, in such cases, the burgeoning industry offered but a temporary reprieve from precarity. Many other women's stories are more ambiguous. The relegation of their careers to the margins of television history, their sudden appearance and disappearance from historical record—all these speak to the variability of the positions they were encouraged to occupy. Too many of these women story editors' careers are only revealed in their brushes with network power or, when historians are lucky, in obituaries. In the effort to understand these editorial support positions as inherently creative, rather than sheerly administrative, historians can only refer to the documents these women left behind, such as readers' reports, correspondence, and public statements. Rather than emphasizing feminine intuition or a woman's touch, women story professionals in television demonstrated fluency with formula, genre, and network voice to remain relevant and employed. Women story editors followed numerous paths, some meeting with great success in the field, others moving on to staff writing jobs, returning to film, or leaving entertainment entirely. However, what they shared was the responsibility of managing scripts and, through their curatorial and writerly authority, determining the form and content of postwar television.

A "SHAMEFUL OMISSION": THE STORY EDITOR SPEAKS

One of the most difficult aspects of historicizing the work of story editors in film and television is how often their labor was necessarily hidden from view. One *Variety* item from 1962 insisted that the story editor "is critical to the success of a show . . . [the] function of the story editor [being] to stimulate writers to submit scripts, to work on the scripts and to oversee the overall balance of the series so that viewers with differing interests might be captured."[46] That said, the piece mentions writer-producer hyphenates like Rod Serling (*The Twilight Zone*) and Stirling Siliphant (*Naked City, Route 66*) and incorporates a CBS vice president of programming into the reportage, but no story editors are interviewed or even mentioned by name. This item underscores Hill's point about story editor Kate Corbaley and the MGM story department in the studio era, particularly in the 1930s and '40s, that "despite readers' pivotal role in discovering the material that would ultimately become MGM films, those films would be credited to their writers, producers, directors—and to Thalberg."[47] Giving Corbaley too much attention would only dilute the mythos of Thalberg's genius and suggest that story editors deserved a more secure and prestigious place in the industry. This would be an unthinkable move from the business side and a risky argument for trade magazines to publish.

There was no single career trajectory for professionals moving from story departments to screenwriting. Lois Jacoby, for example, began as a departmental assistant at the Theatre Guild in the 1940s before working as a script editor on *The Ford Theater Hour* (CBS, 1948–1951) and a writer for *NBC Matinee Theater* (NBC, 1955–1958) and *Studio One*.[48] Audrey Gellen Maas and Jacqueline Babbin worked together as script editors for David Susskind at Talent Associates from the 1950s into the early '60s, in particular "adapt[ing] literary classics ranging from *A Tale of Two Cities* to *Ethan Frome*, to fit into the ninety-minute television specials Susskind produced."[49] Maas went from typist to writer for *The DuPont Show of the Month* (CBS, 1957–1961) and *The Play of the Week* (NTA/syndicated, 1959–1961) and produced, among other television shows and movies, Martin Scorsese's 1974 film *Alice Doesn't Live Here Anymore*, before her death in 1975.[50] Babbin would ultimately create her own production company and produce the miniseries *Sybil* (NBC, 1976).[51] Fella Phillips, another script editor on *Dupont Show of the Month*, wrote for *Joseph Schildkraut Presents* (DuMont, 1953–1954.[52] But, just as often, the story of a woman story or script editor ends with her abrupt disappearance from historical record, leaving no paper trail behind.

Some women story editors were empowered at and through their work, however, as we see with *Climax!* (CBS, 1954–1958) story editor Alice Young, who worked under the supervision of producer Martin Manulis. Young came up through the CBS story department and, in her work for *Climax!*, did research and story work for the show, composing reports on potential storylines and literary options.[53] In one memo, she wrote to Manulis about a magazine feature that possessed "sincere and strong human interest values, and . . . [a] great . . . simple" story, making it an appealing source material for *Climax!*[54] As the story editor, Young sometimes took on the role of program spokeswoman, explaining to *Variety* in a 1956 article that *Climax!* and its sponsor, Chrysler, "shouldn't present a viewpoint, just entertainment" and that the show "does not want any stories which deal with racial tensions or any other such conflicts."[55]

Young might have been sincere, but she was not entirely accurate. The *Climax!* episode "Sorry, Wrong Number," which aired on November 4, 1954, presents a veiled critique of conservative gender roles and "domestic containment," although these politics were admittedly domesticated through the genre conventions of suspense drama.[56] Rod Serling took a page out of Young's playbook three years later, making the claim in an interview with Mike Wallace that *The Twilight Zone* (CBS, 1959–1964), set to premiere in a few weeks' time, lacked a political viewpoint or agenda. Numerous scholars and critics have ably drawn out *The Twilight Zone*'s trenchant critiques of postwar conformity and anti-intellectualism, among other recurring themes.[57] So, was Young in earnest or disingenuous when she cast *Climax!* broadcasts as mere "entertainment"? Regardless of motive, her job reconciled two conflicting responsibilities, privately selecting rich and dramatic scripts, while publicly defending the show and, by extension, the network.

To program challenging but plausibly "safe" television was just one of Young's roles as story editor. She also worked on the short-lived anthology series *Front Row Center* (CBS, 1955–1956) and oversaw a team of readers at CBS.[58] This team included network story analysts Maria Little, Miriam Geiger, and Sonia Chernus, whose reports served as creative gestures and editorial interventions into the tone and tenor of network programming as a whole. Their coverage demonstrates these readers' collective knowledge of the CBS brand, the individual tone of different network series, and television narrative and style as a whole. Little, Geiger, and Chernus gave CBS's anthology dramas their coherence and voice and, in that way, executed more creative control than any individual freelance writer for CBS. Little reported on an adaptation of Marcel Pagnol's *Topaze*, for instance, that "this is still a delightful play, and since it is more of a character than a plot drama, the parts which seem a bit dated now could be easily revised. It should be a good bet for PLAYHOUSE 90 or CLIMAX."[59] In this brief passage, Little reveals her grasp of the *Playhouse* and *Climax!* brands, as well as her understanding of how dramas work.

The format of the readers' reports elicited a great deal of imaginative and editorial input from its authors. In one report, the Comments section asked the reader—in this case, Miriam Geiger—to complete the following tasks: "Describe main characters briefly. Suggest star. Point out possibilities of three acts and finale high-points. Give overall feeling of story." In response to these demands, Geiger named her dream cast and laid out what were, to her mind, the two ways the story could be told. She also remarked how her "attached synopsis is overlong but in no other way can the overabundance of dramatic incident be told."[60] Each report testifies to the reader's individual writing style: if Geiger's comments are concise and forceful, Chernus's summary of *Climax!*'s "Pale Horse, Pale Rider" (CBS, March 22, 1956) reveals a more playful, indirect authorial voice. Chernus opens her report with the lines: "Yesterday MIRANDA saw two pairs of trouser legs waiting beside her desk. She knew they had an air of borrowed importance and that their business was somehow important."[61] Chernus's use of metonymic and ironic description—trouser legs to stand in for men and the ironic assessment of the character's "borrowed importance"—demonstrates how these reports indicate each reader's point of view or voice and thus serve as more than mere support documents in service of the production. Not only are these reports giving an "overall feeling of story" but are reflecting, even shaping, it through their coverage.

All three of the aforementioned readers remained in television after *Climax!* and became story editors and script writers in their own rights.[62] Young later served as story editor for *Perry Mason* (CBS, 1957–1966) before leaving television for a career in public relations, while Chernus served as story assistant and consultant for the 1960s shows *Rawhide* and *Mister Ed* and wrote scripts for both series. Both Little and Geiger wrote and served in various story capacities for the television series *Lassie* (CBS/syndicated, 1954–1974). From there, Little became a prolific writer for the show *Flipper* (NBC, 1964–1967) and served as the longtime story editor for the program, while Geiger became the story editor for the television series *National Velvet* (NBC, 1960–1962).[63] In their time as story editors, women like Little and Geiger sustained and supported the growth of numerous television writers, many of whom were, unsurprisingly, men.

Coverage exposes the artistic interventions of the network reader, while memos further reveal the scripted life of the television story editor, disclosing the performative elements of production culture. Women story employees strained against or sought to transform these environments, as becomes apparent in an extant memo authored by one Dorothy Hechtlinger. Prior to her career in television, Hechtlinger ran Paramount's stenographic department in 1929, based out of Long Island, but she is best known as Darryl Zanuck's story coordinator at 20th Century Fox from 1934 to 1945.[64] She was profiled in a 1942 feature for *Variety* with the headline "The Women Who Run the Men," which also describes MGM'S Ida Koverman, "confidential advisor and buffeteer-in-chief for the Metro production head," as one whose "unseen hand . . . pulls the strings that makes the puppet dance."[65] Just as Koverman "knows what Louis B. Mayer is going to do with his day before L.B. does," so do Hechtlinger and Bess Bearman constitute the "Col. Zanuck's inner-shrine . . . [with] Miss Hechtlinger . . . [serving as] his coordinator of scenarios in addition to further executive duties . . . having to do with production."[66] A 1943 news item announced Hechtlinger's departure from Fox and her plans to go to New York for an "extended vacation."[67] From there, she went on to work under William Goetz at Universal-International before settling in New York to run the story department for the television anthology drama, *The U.S. Steel Hour* (ABC, CBS, 1953–1963) from 1954 to 1955.

The U.S. Steel Hour was produced by the New York–based theatrical society, the Theatre Guild, and was sponsored by the United States Steel Company, these organizations having previously partnered to produce the radio program *The Theatre Guild on the Air* (ABC Radio, NBC Radio, 1945–1953).[68] A 1956 listing for writers in the *Ross Reports—Television Index* lays out some of the procedures and preferences of *U.S. Steel Hour*'s titled "script editor," Dorothy Hechtlinger: "[Series] uses adaptations of stories, novels, most interested in originals, preferably on American themes and locales."[69] Hechtlinger is also credited for one of the anthology drama's first episodes, the 1955 "No Time for Sergeants." This military barracks comedy stars Andy Griffith and was adapted from the novel by Mac Hyman. Also featured in the end credits is the supervising producer, Armina Marshall, who ran the Theatre Guild alongside her husband Lawrence Langner and who was one of the few (if not the only) indigenous women of color working in postwar television.[70] The episode speaks to Hechtlinger's own thematic preoccupations and objectives in curating the series. First, "No Time for Sergeants" encapsulates the "American themes and locales" mentioned in the above listing, with its focus on a small-town country boy, sometimes referred to as a "hillbilly," thrust into the complicated politics of the military-industrial complex. Rube comedies were popular both in silent film and as a genre of radio entertainment in the 1920s and '30s, and the conventions of the genre are repurposed here for television. Secondly, although "No Time for Sergeants" is part of a longer tradition of what Tim Hollis calls "rural entertainment," the teleplay is also an undisguised demonstration of the medium with its use of the laugh track and the protagonist's direct address to the camera.[71] Finally, as Will's friend Ben (Eddie LeRoy) lectures him on how to be selected for the infantry, the branch of the military they both believe is the most prestigious, he asks Will with some frustration, "Ain't you ever seen no war movies?" "No Time for Sergeants" obliquely proposes that its goofy televisual description of military life might be more truthful than the dignified, overly romanticized depictions in film. Make no mistake: the scope of the story may be slight and comic, but its satire is razor sharp. "No Time for Sergeants" takes an ironic look at the military-industrial complex, as its simpleton protagonist unknowingly reveals the armed forces' hypocrisies, its exploited hierarchies, and its tendency to prey on those yokels who have been tricked and brain-washed by Hollywood.

Hechtlinger was not one to shy away from denouncing unequal environments, evidenced by the strongly worded memo she wrote to one "Bill," likely H. William Fitelson, the Guild's managing director.[72] The letter opens with Hechtlinger forcefully lodging the complaint that she was excluded from an important meeting:

> Dear Bill: I think that what happened this morning when, for the first time since the operation started, I was prevented from attending the weekly meeting, was an indignity that I did not deserve. Had it been a high escallop private meeting—without John, Mark or me—it would have been another matter, but to be singled out not to attend is, frankly, something that I did not expect from any of you.

Her pointed note that "John" and "Mark" were included, while she was not, suggests (without explicitly condemning) sexism. She continues by explaining her duties at *The U.S. Steel Hour*:

> For one thing, the Story Department is an integral part of the production unit and there is no one who is fully equipped to discuss it. . . . I would have reported that I have been working with outstanding writers in an effort to get material tailored for us. Specifically I have worked on the following which are due in the immediate future. . . . I spent an average of two hours with each of these writers and I think we may expect important properties from them. Also, since it is my province to keep track of projects pending, I would have reported that [list of programs] had been received.[73]

By expounding on the intellectual and interpersonal demands of her work, Hechtlinger explains the nature of her job to someone who may or may not have known what she did for the show. In the process, she asserts her authorial significance to the larger functioning of the series.

Was Hechtlinger excluded from the meeting because she was a woman, because the story department was not deemed important, or because of the compounded stigma of story work being unimportant as the territory of women and administrative laborers? She proceeds to demand access to these meetings:

> Do you think it is right that I should be the only member of the staff not present when Ira Avery is introduced as successor to Ted Rogers? Or that I should be absent when it is important for me to get to know Charles Under-hill better? Do you think they can have a proper respect for the department when it is not represented? It certainly would appear that I was not considered a key member of the staff, under these circumstances, and it does not help to increase my interest or enthusiasm.

If future meetings are held, and other staff members are present, I wish to be present, too, and I think it was a shameful omission that I was not permitted to attend today's meeting.[74]

Here, Hechtlinger definitively expresses her reading of these institutional politics and her sensitivity to being excluded. Her experience resonates with that of script editor Peggy Chantler, who, according to *I Love Lucy*'s Madelyn Pugh Davis, faced a similar strain of sexism at work. She writes: "On one show when [Chantler] was the script editor, the executive producer held a meeting to discuss where the show was headed and not only didn't invite her but barred her from the all-male room. She said she quietly cleaned out her desk and went home."[75] Chantler, later Chantler Dick, would go on to write for *Dennis the Menace* (CBS, 1959–1963) and serve as the head writer for *The Courtship of Eddie's Father* (ABC, 1969–1972).[76]

Hechtlinger remained a prolific and in-demand story editor and associate producer at CBS Television throughout the 1950s and '60s at CBS, including on the *Desilu Playhouse*.[77] She was responsible for bringing director Ralph Nelson on board at *Desilu*, where he wrote and directed the 1960 teleplay, "The Man in the Funny Suit," based on the behind-the-scenes drama on the set of *Playhouse 90*'s "Requiem for a Heavyweight."[78] Hechtlinger never achieved the professional autonomy in television that she had hoped for and ultimately returned to Hollywood to serve as the chief story editor for Universal Studios, retiring from the industry in 1967.[79]

Historians rely on limited documentation to recover women story editors' work, both their experiences on the job and the imprints they left on the scripts they supervised. Readers' reports, memos, and other artifacts begin to show what motivated story editors' selections and the degree to which they shaped the content that aired. But much remains inaccessible, as their work was done out of public view and without institutional acclaim. So, to fully grasp the pathos and the affect behind these editors' chosen scripts, the extant history must be joined with the interpretative impulse.

WHEN THE STORY EDITOR MAKES A CAMEO

On-screen representations of female creative labor fills out a history of postwar television authorship in two ways: first, by providing a look into how postwar feminine norms within the industry and the culture at large informed one another and, second, by examining how these images and characters fill in significant historiographic gaps. These gaps include the practical, as Dorothy Hechtlinger lays out her job duties in an internal memo, as well as the affective. What did it look and feel like to be a woman story editor in this moment? To that end, Betty Schaefer of Billy Wilder's 1950 film *Sunset Boulevard* is the best-known, if fictional, Hollywood reader, and one who lends insight into the history of women in television. With her neatly pinned-back hairdo, her crisp, Peter Pan collared blouse (topped with a sensible tweed blazer), and her linen-laundry signature scent, Betty offers a fresh, young alternative to all the grotesque feminine excesses of forgotten film star Norma Desmond. Having flunked a screen test in her much-younger years, twenty-two-year-old Betty is happier behind the camera and believes her near-miss with stardom has at least left her with some "sense"—again, something Desmond never has and will completely lose by the end of the film.

Though a failed actress, Betty knows how to *play*, a crucial skill for any script employee or, for that matter, any leading lady. As she and protagonist/narrator Joe Gillis flirt, she moves deftly between melodramatic role-playing and responding to her present reality. At a party, she gently rejects his advances by intoning, melodramatically: "No, Philip, no. We must be strong. You're still wearing the uniform of the Coldstream Guards. Furthermore, you can have the phone now," the former being "in character" the latter spoken as her normal, practical self. Betty's ear for dialogue and facility with genre convention show her to be clever without necessarily being worldly. Joe teases Betty for "know[ing] all the plots," but her intellect does not make her any less naive, as she is blind to his toxic romantic arrangement with Norma. Joe and Betty's compatibility is reflected in their playful banter, in how the camera cuts out her fiancé Artie when the two are deep in conversation, and in how they productively cowrite a romantic script about a man and woman who keep missing one another (Figure 22). The plot for Joe and Betty's screenplay draws obvious parallels to the couple's own love affair, but the two are unable to write themselves out of the film noir in which they are mired. The last the viewer sees of Betty, Joe has chased her off, overpowered by his feelings of unworthiness.

But theirs is not the only doomed love affair that poor Betty must endure: the other is with Hollywood itself. In a declaration of purpose and ambition on the level of Dorothy Hechtlinger's scathing memo, Betty explains to Joe why she wants him to return to screenwriting,

FIGURE 22. Joe (William Holden) and Betty (Nancy Olson) meet cute but work even cuter in *Sunset Boulevard* (1950). © 1950 Paramount Pictures.

telling him, "It's not your career, it's mine. I kinda hoped to get in on this deal. I don't wanna be a reader all my life. I want to write." Betty, typically light and flip, delivers these lines with great gravity and an upturned chin—she takes her work seriously. We know that from our very first encounter with Betty, when she tells Joe in her boss's office, "I think a picture should say a little something."

With institutional sexism and the looming decline of the studio system, not to mention her own insecurity and inexperience, Betty stands a slim chance of becoming a screenwriter without Joe at her side. The nighttime stroll that Joe and Betty take through the abandoned soundstages foreshadows studio closure—the inevitable shuttering of doors, tightening of budgets, and dissolution of story departments. Betty may love her "cubbyhole" of an office, but how long will she and the other Hollywood readers have rooms to call their own? Betty is Janet Wood, fictionalized for the silver screen—both women whose days in the industry are numbered. Then again, what if Betty forgets all about following her fiancé to Arizona and makes the jump to television instead? With her tidy, modest self-presentation and her flair for economical storytelling, Betty would do great in television: she *is* Television, making Norma Desmond, in all her decaying grandeur, Studio Cinema in the flesh.

Through Betty Schaefer, we see how the Hollywood reader was seen in this cultural and institutional moment. But not all portraits are so literal, and recovering the woman story editor from the historical and fictional records means synthesizing oral history insights within an industrial allegory framework. The scripted lives of women story editors circulated within the industry, in line with institutional expectations around women's clerical and administrative work, and characters like Betty Schaefer provide insight into how these archetypes migrated into the popular imagination. Still on the fringes of public view, women story editors exerted a great deal of influence over postwar television and left indelible marks on both the industry and its storytelling practices. Fictional characters supplement archival finds such as Alice Young's public statements, Dorothy Hechtlinger's memo, and the reports of the CBS reader pool—all in the service of revealing an underestimated history of women's labor in film and television. And carefully moving between archival and historical sources and that of the fictional or representational renderings helps to reconstruct a postwar history of television authorship in a pivotal period of transition and upheaval.

CHAPTER 6

"A Girl's Gotta Live"

The Literate Heroines of the
Suspense Anthology Drama

In 1954, the anthology drama *Climax!* (CBS, 1954–1958) aired the teleplay, "Sorry, Wrong Number," adapted by Lucille Fletcher from her own
1943 radio play.[1] In this episode, actress Shelley Winters plays Leona Stevenson, an unfaithful, materialistic wife who, while laid up at home with
a broken leg, discovers on her telephone party line that her husband has
hired someone to kill her. The cozy home is rapidly transformed into a
site of claustrophobia and danger, in line with Helen Wheatley's description of Gothic television's "prison-like qualities of domestic space . . .
an overarching analogy between body, home and entrapment . . . [and]
the notion of marriage as imprisonment."[2] Leona's frilly bedding, the
jewels on her vanity, and, especially, her telephone, are framed in menacing close-up. As unlikeable as Leona is, the stakes of the drama hinge
entirely on her survival, and the episode seems unwilling to let her go
until its very final moments, as the camera pans across an unfeeling
cityscape, a roaring train smothering Leona's calls for help.[3] Violence
could be going on next door without the neighbors even knowing, the
episode argues, and many women—even those watching at home—
might be suffering untold horrors in their marriage. With narratives
that center in and around the home, the postwar suspense text presents
bourgeois respectability as a set of cruel rituals, chivalry as a form of
oppression, love and family as institutions of violence.

In this way, "Sorry, Wrong Number" functions as a *meta*-tale, forging a connection between the victim on-screen and the viewer watching

at home through the act of listening and recognition. When Leona first stumbles across the murder plot by picking up her phone, she tries to warn the police of the impending danger; at this point, she has not yet realized she is the hitman's target. "This is nothing to do with me personally," she insists to the police. "I'm just upset for someone else." The telephone on which she overhears this conversation serves as a surrogate technology for radio, on which "Sorry, Wrong Number" was earlier broadcast.[4] The demise of Leona Stevenson, Matthew Solomon writes, is "ideally suited to the perceptual peculiarities of radio drama" in all its aesthetic limitations.[5] But even as the narrative was adapted across media, including television and film, the premise remained the same: it is about a woman who does not realize that the story she is hearing is her own. By extension, "Sorry, Wrong Number" is about the woman listener-viewer for whom popular media has hard and pressing truths to tell.

Postwar suspense anthology dramas persisted throughout the first dozen years of commercial television and were, in many ways, envisioned with women audiences in mind. One study from the *U.S. Steel Hour* found that mystery was the preferred genre for female viewers, westerns for men.[6] The "half-hour mystery anthology" was a particular strength of CBS, "*Suspense, Danger,* and *The Web* . . . referred to around the Grand Central studios as the 'Three Weird Sisters.'"[7] The category of "Three Weird Sisters," a reference to the three witches of *Macbeth*, speaks to television's lingering high art aspirations as well as to the idea that a show for women was in itself a feminized object.

But the television industry was in the midst of major changes, and any writer stuck in bed with a metaphorical broken leg would be eliminated: such immobility was lethal. With television's move to Hollywood, women writers in particular had to adhere to a new professional "type." Negotiating the intricacies of a male-dominated writers' room became secondary to navigating the business as a whole and purporting an understanding of "real" families and the rhythms of domestic life was replaced by the need to be facile with genre and industry standards. As the demands of the television writing profession changed, women writers had to accommodate their voices to the shows' needs, not the other way around. Women writers facing professional precarity and contingency within the Hollywood television scene wrote across medium and genre to generate multiple revenue streams or became writer-producers working in conjunction to industry powerhouses. Enter the women of *Alfred Hitchcock Presents.*

Alfred Hitchcock Presents debuted in 1956 on CBS in the 9:30–10:00 p.m. EST timeslot, switching to NBC's 8:30–9:00 p.m. slot in 1960, and ran until 1962, after which time it was replaced by *The Alfred Hitchcock Hour* (CBS, NBC, 1962–1965). The numerous women who wrote for *Alfred Hitchcock Presents*, often working underneath or alongside the show's producer, Joan Harrison, were part of a new crop of television professionals navigating a television industry being gradually subsumed into the Hollywood dream factory. *Alfred Hitchcock Presents* was of a different breed of anthology drama than *Climax!*—prerecorded in Los Angeles and subscribing to a Hollywood model of teleplay production, as opposed to being broadcast live out of New York City. The writers of *Alfred Hitchcock Presents* are easily misread as delegates for the show's namesake, Jan Olsson calling the show Hitchcock's "authorship by commission."[8] While Hitchcock was a "palpable presence" on the show, it is more accurate to describe Hitchcock as the prompt or inspiration for the show's many writers and creative agents.[9]

The story of *Alfred Hitchcock Presents* is one of how women adapted, institutionally, professionally, and literarily. With the move to Los Angeles, nearly all television writers found themselves enmeshed in a new job market that offered less in the way of intellectual property ownership or autonomy, but more in terms of money and potential job security. The women who wrote for *Alfred Hitchcock Presents* worked on a freelance basis but made money writing across media platforms in literature, film, theater, and radio. Their careers serve as evidence of the increasing synthesis and cooperation of the culture industries at mid-century and how writers benefited by adapting their skills and stories across platforms. Meanwhile, Joan Harrison, the associate producer of *Alfred Hitchcock Presents* until 1960, worked under the aegis of executive producer Hitchcock, but the show's voice was largely an index of her own taste and ability, relying on literary adaptations to establish the show's cultured tenor.

In its engagement with an Anglophone literary tradition, *Alfred Hitchcock Presents* weaved together a Gothic past and a noir present and established a pulpy form of women's entertainment that straddled genres and media platforms. Mary Ann Doane writes that the genre of the woman's film is "not . . . 'pure' . . . [as it is] crossed and informed by a number of other genres or types . . . and finds its point of unification ultimately in the fact of its address."[10] With its preoccupations with femininity and the family, *Alfred Hitchcock Presents* spoke to female viewers by adapting the tradition of the woman's film for the small screen. Much of the humor and pathos was spoken for the wife and mother watching at home—and, in those cases, it was often a woman writer doing the talking. Television narratives can easily speak directly to and about the viewer watching in their homes, while the contained field of the television screen visually embodies the snug (or oppressive) smallness of domestic space.[11] It is television's reception context and its aesthetic, then, that made small-screen suspense an ideal vehicle for expressing postwar female angst in the years following the war and anticipating the politics of second-wave feminism of the 1960s and '70s.

Women's scripts for *Alfred Hitchcock Presents* functioned on two levels, telling stories of wives in danger while also revealing the drama of writers in peril. In his discussion of the feminization of paranoia—from the male-centered formulation of the conspiracy theory to the dangers and frustrations of domestic terror—Sianne Ngai writes that "paranoia [is] . . . defined here not as mental illness but as a species of fear based on the dysphoric apprehension of a holistic and all-encompassing system."[12] In such a reading, the "holistic and all-encompassing systems" of *Alfred Hitchcock Presents* are the twin patriarchal-industrial complexes of marriage and entertainment.

A concentrated look at the women writers on *Alfred Hitchcock Presents* offers a way forward for what Tania Modleski calls "the feminist critic's search for definitive answers about the nature and extent of the female collaborator's contributions," a task she deems "inevitably thwarted."[13] But when their contributions are taken in aggregate, the impact women like Charlotte Armstrong, Marian Cockrell, Helen Nielsen, and others made on postwar suspense television, on *Alfred Hitchcock Presents* and shows like it, is undeniable. Their anti-heroines, villains, and survivors fit comfortably in Hitchcock's filmography while drawing on a longer tradition of women-centered—and women-authored—literary and dramatic expression. The show further bore the impression of Joan Harrison's noir sensibilities, which she articulated as an assistant to Hitchcock in her early career and as a solo producer in Hollywood's studio era.

Just as the woman story editor needed to "know all the plots" (chapter 5), so too did the women of *Alfred Hitchcock Presents* devise "literate heroines" as their on-screen ambassadors. The figure of the scrappy, bookish literate heroine surfaces regularly in the show, across different authors' episodes, functioning as a stand-in for both the viewer at home and the writer in television with her implicit understanding of genre and her ability to read and write her way out of danger. Women writers' scripts adapted male-authored stories to the small screen, and, in doing so, transformed misogynistic subtext into text and switched narrative perspectives from male to female, all while crediting a man as the story's ostensible originator. Their quietly subversive rewriting of stories from John Collier and John Cheever offered cutting, at times grotesque, portrayals of toxic masculinity and liberating visions of respectable womanhood run amok. Collectively and collaboratively, then, the women writers of *Alfred Hitchcock Presents* adapted on the page and in the workplace, conflating personal and professional forms of containment in their scripted lives. Through thematizing literacy and genre-savviness in their creative works, they provided arch, ruthless survival guides to literate heroines both real and imaginary.

TEARING DOWN THE WALLS: MAKING AND REMAKING THE SUSPENSE GENRE

What lies beneath the slick and placid surface of the television image? The second episode of *Alfred Hitchcock Presents*, "Into Thin Air" (October 30, 1955), not only hazards an answer to this question but references how television built on the literary traditions that preceded it. The teleplay follows Diana Winthrop (Patricia Hitchcock) and her mother as they travel to Paris to attend the 1900 Grand Exposition. When Diana's mother falls ill from her travels and takes to bed, Diana visits the local pharmacist, and by the time she has returned with medicine, her mother has vanished. Even more strangely, the hotel insists that neither she nor her mother have ever been in the establishment. Diana fears she has lost her mother—or her mind—but she is, in fact, the victim of a wide-ranging conspiracy. She is only able to expose the deception by proving she has been in a room that the hotel quickly remade to look unrecognizable. To demonstrate she is sane, Diana pulls the wallpaper from the wall, revealing the familiar design and the cool, still-fresh glue underneath. This quick redecoration is an instance of *gaslighting*, a term popularized by the 1944 thriller film, *Gaslight*, in which a woman is likewise made to question her reality. The twist in "Into Thin Air"? Diana's mother died of the bubonic plague and, to keep public panic to a minimum, the hotel staff promptly disposed of her body and pretended she did not exist.

Scripted for *Alfred Hitchcock Presents* by Marian Cockrell, the adaptation of "Into Thin Air" fits into a larger network of women's fiction and suspense texts. Hitchcock introduces the episode with an acknowledgment that the story is "a classic of its kind," and that the episode had "borrowed this legend" from two sources. Only one of the texts is mentioned by name: Alexander Woolcott's *While Rome Burns* (1934). The other source can only be author Ethel Lina White's *The Wheel Spins* (1936), which had served as the basis for Hitchcock's 1938 film *The Lady Vanishes*. While the plot specifics for White's novel are different, the film version "retained the basic threat to the young heroine," according to one White biographer, who noted that "Hitchcock's own analysis of White's plot brought it back to its modern origins, the story of the Vanishing Lady, which dated from the Paris Exposition of the 1880s. . . . That plot, as carried forth by White, [was] later utilized" in movies and television long afterward.[14]

Stories, like viruses, are contagious, traveling across bodies and bodies of work, transmitting ideological messages through time. To that end, the image of the wallpaper being torn down in the television episode alludes to an even older, canonical tale of female hysteria, Charlotte Perkins Gilman's 1892 "The Yellow Wallpaper." In Gilman's story, a nervous woman's condition deteriorates as she is forbidden from leaving the home and comes to believe there is a figure who lives behind the pattern of the wallpaper in her room. In the story's climactic moments— in which the narrator surrenders to madness—she peels the wallpaper from the wall to reach the person she imagines trapped behind the pattern. "Into Thin Air" channels the image of the mad woman tearing the wallpaper down, a symbolic strike against her domestic containment, and rewrites it. Rather than an act of insanity, Diana's tearing down of the wallpaper (Figure 23) is one of clear-eyed sanity that results in her vindication. This single gesture turns a hysteric narrative into a story where the heroine can emerge triumphant, even though the ending is not a happy one. Diana pulls the paper down and, in the process, peels away the walls that confine her, while the television screen appears to be stripped along with it. Television may be a mass art, but that does not mean it is flat: television contains secret depths. The image also recalls the form of the palimpsest—the medieval manuscript form in which one text was laid or written on top of another—remnants of the past still visible underneath the present.

What came to be called "suspense" broadcasting in postwar radio and television conspicuously drew on a lineage of artistic and cinematic expressions, and *Alfred Hitchcock Presents* relied on literary adaptations in particular. The hour-long *Alfred Hitchcock Hour* typically looked to novels and novellas for episode inspiration, but the thirty-minute *Alfred*

FIGURE 23. The old wallpaper is revealed underneath the new, exposing the hotel's plot—as well as the borrowed "plot" of many prior source materials and generic stories. From "Into Thin Air," *Alfred Hitchcock Presents* (October 30, 1955). © 1955 Universal Pictures.

Hitchcock Presents based episodes on short stories more often than it solicited original teleplays. As producer Norman Lloyd explained, Hitchcock "liked to know that a story had been published, [so] you had something to begin with. He was not one for developing stories, as is mostly done today."[15] Show writer Henry Slesar echoed this sentiment, adding that it was the "English style of doing things."[16] Optioning these stories was primarily the work of Lloyd and Harrison, as supported by a team including consultant Gordon Hessler and Hitchcock's literary scout from the United Kingdom, Mary Elsom.[17] According to Harrison, this process was also more "economical" than seeking out new works, telling one reporter: "We only use material which has already been published . . . [and] by using published materials we obtain a quality we couldn't hit by ordering originals."[18] This quality, presumably, describes not just the sophistication of the material but the *literariness* they wished to capture and capitalize on.

In both its adaptations and its original teleplays, *Alfred Hitchcock Presents* articulated a postwar amalgam of gothic literature, melodrama, and pulp fiction for the small screen, a continuation of Hitchcock's film oeuvre. In her work on Gothic literature, Tania Modleski explains how the mode dramatized the "exceedingly private, even claustrophobic nature of [women's] existence. . . . The Harlequin [romance] heroine's feelings undergo a transformation from fear into love, whereas for the Gothic heroine, the transformation is from love into fear."[19] She locates a "second 'Gothic' revival," born of cultural fears around personal, sexual, even societal corruption, in the 1930s and '40s, "at the same time that 'hard-boiled' detective novels were attracting an unprecedented number of male readers."[20] But the noir mode continued to circulate and develop in the postwar years, internalizing fears around race, gender, and urban spaces.

Film noir and what Modleski calls the "gaslight genre" were indebted to the gothic tradition but were also part of a pulp literary tradition that featured female protagonists and included women writers in its ranks.[21] As Livia Tenzer and Jean Casella write in their introduction to the Evelyn Piper's 1957 novel *Bunny Lake Is Missing*:

> Women write pulp? It seems like a contradiction in terms, given the tough-guy image of pulp fiction today. . . . But women did write pulp, in large numbers and in all the classic pulp fiction genres. . . . And while employing the conventions of each genre, women brought a different, gendered perspective to these forms. Women writers of pulp often outpaced their male counterparts in challenging received ideas about gender, race, and class, and in exploring those forbidden territories that were hidden from view off the typed page. They were an important part of a literary phenomenon, grounded in its particular time and place, that had a powerful impact on American popular culture in the middle of the twentieth century, and continues to exert its influence today.[22]

Mystery writers such as Miriam Allen deFord (*Alfred Hitchcock Presents*) and Dorothy Salisbury Davis (*Alfred Hitchcock Presents, Suspense*) made the transition to television writing, while *Alfred Hitchcock Presents* adapted the work of numerous women crime and suspense writers, including Dorothy L. Sayers, Helen Fislar Brooks, and Lillian de la Torre. These women and their works brought the lurid, pulp sensibility to the broader, sponsor-centric medium of television and to a wider audience of women and families. *Alfred Hitchcock Presents* conspicuously braided together these creative traditions, and Hitchcock the silhouetted *auteur* was its organizing principle, as the show combined noir and thriller elements from his Hollywood filmography with "heritage" Gothic narratives as a nod to his British pedigree. In its coordination of these different generic influences, *Alfred Hitchcock Presents* maintained a highbrow television brand while attracting the traditional consumers of these modes: women.

The *Alfred Hitchcock Presents* episode "You Can't Trust a Man," an original teleplay written by Helen Nielsen and broadcast in 1961, exemplifies the series' female-centric pulp-noir register, as well as its direct appeal to women viewers. "A girl can't wait around forever. A girl's gotta live." So says singer and trophy wife Crystal Coe (Peggy Bergen), as she justifies deserting her ex-con husband.[23] Nielsen worked as an aircraft draftsman during World War II and moved to Los Angeles afterward to begin a career as a novelist and television writer. Sarah Weinman writes of Nielsen: "Many of [Nielsen's stories] featured a hard-boiled detective, Mike Shelley, solving murderous crimes, but on occasion Nielsen would switch to tough-minded, cigarette-smoking female protagonists who try their best to get out from under the passions that ensnare them to unavailable men, but never manage to escape."[24] The story of "You Can't Trust a Man" is about one woman's desperate passion to survive in an indifferent world. While Crystal's husband, Tony (Joe Maross), is incarcerated, she marries an older, richer man who can support her and her musical ambitions. When Tony reappears on the scene and threatens to expose her bigamist secret, Crystal does what she must to protect her new life: she murders Tony in cold blood and claims self-defense. The police believe Crystal's story, but when they tell her that Tony came into a fortune before his death, and they must investigate his next-of-kin, Crystal's face reveals a mixture of fear at being discovered and disappointment at the money that could have been hers.

Crystal's glamorous look and her cutthroat worldview render her a small-screen femme fatale in the film noir tradition. Yet, it is Tony who arrives from *out of the past* to disrupt Crystal's life and livelihood. Doane asserts that "unlike the film noir, the 'woman's film' does not situate its female protagonist as mysterious, unknowable, enigmatic," and in that respect, the episode is a comment on what women's drama does: expose the inner workings of the most "enigmatic" female.[25] Crystal behaves like a cornered animal, lacking any moral or ethical commitments, and she is similar to the protagonist of "Sorry, Wrong Number," in that viewers are necessarily emotionally aligned with her, even though her behavior and values are established early on as abhorrent.

The episode's title, "You Can't Trust a Man," performs a number of functions, one being the irony that it is the woman, not the man, who commits the murder. While the "You" of the title suggests a line from a conversation between two women, the speaker is likely voicing the perspective of our anti-heroine or, possibly, the woman author (Nielsen) as well. In this way, "You Can't Trust a Man" embodies the vindictive, cautionary tone of many *Alfred Hitchcock Presents* episodes, tales that center on women who transgress dominant modes of domesticity, femininity, and even morality, where female subjectivity is privileged over objectification, and where, in many cases, the heroine survives the closing credits after having inflicted violence—or justice—of her own.

In discussing the women story editors and screenwriters who worked with Hitchcock in his film career, including Jay Presson Allen (*Marnie*), as well as Hitchcock's wife, Alma Reville, Modleski writes:

> How much of the ambivalence toward women seen in Hitchcock's films is owing to the input of ambivalent women living in a male-dominated society and working with a dominating male director? In what ways might women have complicated his vision—or even helped to establish it? How much of what we call a Hitchcock movie drew on the contributions of women who were so often either uncredited or subordinated in the credits? A number of other Hitchcock films thematize women's collaboration with men's stories, whether or not these stories prove to be true.[26]

By calling these relationships "suspicious collaborations," Modleski marries the genre (gothic, suspense) with the authorial tactics and emphasizes how Hitchcock's films "thematize" male-female partnerships behind the scenes, in all their uneasiness and danger.[27] The model offered by the unapologetic Crystal, the "girl [who's] gotta live," encapsulates the movements of many women television writers piecing together careers through writing, translating work across media, and adapting to a new breed of Hollywood hustle.

A COTTAGE INDUSTRY OF ONE'S OWN: WOMEN WRITING ACROSS INDUSTRIES

The postwar culture industries are often portrayed as being at odds, but a closer look at television authorship offers the opportunity to reconsider this history as one of conglomeration, not competition. Matthew Solomon writes of how, by the 1930s and '40s, "the business of radio broadcasting had an important impact on the history of the film industry, while radio itself constituted a crucial intertext for the production of films," adding that "the narrative of radio and film often shared similar generic and thematic commonalities."[28] Not only did these radio genres and subjects carry over into the medium of television, but also the institutions of film, radio, television, and publishing were all financially intertwined. Their audiences were also shared, but this did not necessarily amount to a zero-sum game. Maria LaPlace defines the 1940s cycle of women's films as constituting "a circuit of female discourse which, although mediated by patriarchal institutions (such as publishing companies), is largely originated *by and for women*."[29] By expanding the idea of a "circuit of female discourse" to include radio, television, and print, LaPlace's term bridges melodrama studies and industry studies, providing a framework for understanding how women writers built sustainable careers in the postwar culture industries. Their texts, in print and on-screen, gave voice to a "subordinate 'women's culture'. . . [that] promoted discourse . . . subversive to patriarchy."[30]

Austrian-born writer Gina Kaus is one example of a woman writer whose contributions to the postwar "circuit of female discourse" included writing for *Alfred Hitchcock Presents*. Kaus was indifferent to the distinctions between "high" and "low" art, launching into her screenwriting career upon arrival in Los Angeles; at this point, she and her husband were separated, and she had the sole custody of (and financial responsibility for) their two children. As Regina Christiane Range writes:

> The former novelist not only determined to make a living . . . she tirelessly attempt[ed] to figure out the market demands of the Hollywood film business. . . . Kaus . . . managed to adapt and transfer her talent and expertise as a successful author and playwright to the medium of film and script writing. . . . [*The Wife Takes a Flyer* and *Three Secrets* being two scripts that] called into question normative and dominant discourses, especially in regard to the understanding of 'inherent' gender roles.[31]

Kaus's episode of *Alfred Hitchcock Presents*, "The Legacy" (May 27, 1956), does not make such a bold intervention into contemporary gender roles as these aforementioned scripts, but it does make a trenchant case for how fictional representations can empower women viewer-consumers.[32] In this episode, a frumpy society wife gains confidence and sartorial elegance after being wooed by a con artist. The man's accidental death makes her believe he killed himself after she jilted him, allowing her to live under the misapprehension that she was the object of deep, life-destroying passion. She becomes a happier, more confident woman as a result, the episode demonstrating how a lie (or a fiction) can have a lasting impact or "legacy" on individuals, institutions, even genres. The "woman's film," and its television translation, invites the female viewer to project herself into the story and imagine herself as stronger, more secure, ultimately safer in a dangerous world. The scam in "The Legacy" becomes a stand-in for entertainment: fake, perhaps, but capable of provoking real and lasting change.

What challenges faced the woman writer in television as she assembled her own fictional escapes and sought to secure her own professional "legacy"? Multiple changes were occurring in television by mid-decade: production was increasingly relocated from New York to Los Angeles, with programs going from predominantly live to prerecorded, and the industry drawing on Hollywood, as opposed to radio or theater, talent. Contemporary renderings of the culture industries at mid-century sometimes pit film and television against each other, as rivals. A 1955 item from *Variety*, "Mags Must Pitch Entertainment," describes the publishing world's "wonder about and . . . dread of television" and calls television "the malaria which is giving the magazine people the shakes," concluding that the publishing and journalism fields had commenced with an "over-all appraisal of themselves as an entertainment medium."[33]

What this reporter neglects to mention is the growing power of agencies in the wake of the film studios' decline, placing more power into the hands of writers, actors, and non-executive talent. *Alfred Hitchcock Presents* was in fact the brainchild of MCA "super-agent" Lew Wasserman, as Harrison biographer Christina Lane explains:

> Wasserman's plan was to edge out the competition by creating original content that employed his clients—actors, writers, and directors. He was in the process of convincing one client in particular to host a suspense series on CBS: Alfred Hitchcock. The thirty-minute filmed anthology series would create a perfect tie-in to the new *Alfred Hitchcock Mystery Magazine* (which Hitchcock himself had almost nothing to do with) and would launch Hitchcock as the first director of his stature to make a long-term commitment to the small screen. The "Master of Suspense" was not particularly enthusiastic about being associated with what he regarded to be an extremely low art form.[34]

Film studio story editors had a great deal to lose with the ascent of agency power (chapter 5), but this was not necessarily the case for writers. Writers—both women and men—could benefit from the increasing connections between film, television, and print entertainment, as could the agents taking a percentage from their clients' paychecks. So, even as writers' work was subsumed by the Hitchcock brand, women like Helen Nielsen, whose story graced the cover of *Alfred Hitchcock's Suspense Magazine* in 1958 (Figure 24), generated their own literary cottage industries, writing across media and ramping up their professional visibility in the process. At the same time, producers for *Alfred*

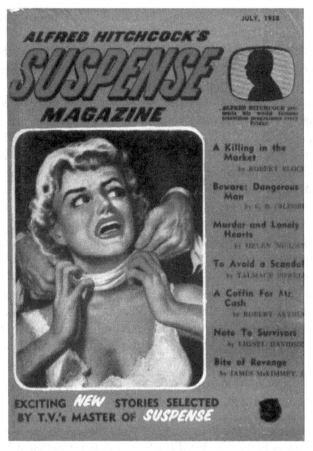

FIGURE 24. This cover of *Alfred Hitchcock's Suspense Magazine*
spotlights a story by Helen Nielsen, "Murder and Lonely Hearts."
Note how Hitchcock is referred to as "T.V.'s Master of Suspense"
and the icon of Hitchcock's profile in the television screen in the
upper right, suggesting that the magazine was more geared to his
television fans than to cinephiles. *Alfred Hitchcock's Suspense
Magazine,* © 2022 Penny Publications/Dell Magazines.

Hitchcock Presents could turn to their own magazine for source material or potential collaborators.[35]

Like New York–based writers including Paddy Chayefsky, Gertrude
Berg, and Peg Lynch (chapter 3), writers for *Alfred Hitchcock Presents* developed portfolios that included television as just one "hustle"
alongside publishing, film, and even theater, and this was an even more
essential move for freelancers without steady day jobs. Writer Charlotte

Armstrong, primarily a mystery novelist, wrote for *Alfred Hitchcock Presents*, while her fiction had been adapted by others into four films: *The Unsuspected* (1947), *The Three Weird Sisters* (1948), *Talk about a Stranger* (1952), and *Don't Bother to Knock* (1952). Lucille Fletcher, who began as a publicity writer at CBS, was able to adapt *Sorry, Wrong Number*, into a novel, a film, a one-act play, and multiple television broadcasts.[36] (Rod Serling also gave her story credit for his *Twilight Zone* adaptation of her 1941 radio play, "The Hitchhiker.") And author Margaret Manners, who worked as an editor for *Good Housekeeping*, was hired to write the novelization of the soap opera *Love of Life* (CBS, 1951–1980), and contributed to *Alfred Hitchcock Presents* in both script and story form.[37] Gone were the days of the woman stay-at-home showrunner, nesting in her sound stage. The woman writer of television's future needed to demonstrate the same drive as her male competition, even if she dressed that ambition up in a chic outfit, as was the case with *Alfred Hitchcock Presents* producer Joan Harrison.

JOAN HARRISON: HOLLYWOOD'S "FEMME NOIR" PRODUCER

Joan Harrison began in the film industry as Hitchcock's personal assistant and had a solo career as a producer in the Hollywood studio system before her work on *Alfred Hitchcock Presents*. John McCarty and Brian Kelleher write that "[Hitchcock] decided to bring in an ally, someone who knew him, his work, and his methods implicitly and who had as firm a grasp as he did of the British irony and understatement he wanted the show to have," while Lane writes that it was Lew Wasserman who pushed for Harrison's hire.[38] Until *Alfred Hitchcock Presents*, Harrison's primary work in television had been on *Janet Dean, Registered Nurse* (NBC, 1954–1955), a show that focused on the value of women professionals to public health and social ills. It was on *Janet Dean* that Harrison learned how to work on the quick production schedule that television demanded.[39] Regardless, Hitchcock and Harrison shared a taste for what McCarty and Kelleher call stories of "ordinary people caught up in extraordinary circumstance, with touches of British gallows humor, a macabre tone, a certain degree of suspense, and, most crucial of all, a twist almost 'to the point of shock' that arrives in the last scene or even the last lines."[40]

With Hitchcock as the executive producer, associate producer Harrison headed up a core team for day-to-day operations that included producer Norman Lloyd (whom Harrison fought to hire, in spite of his being blacklisted), story editor Gordon Hessler, and secretary Yvonne Hessler (who was also Gordon's wife). Writes Lane, "Joan's purview extended well beyond finding stories, cultivating writers, and developing scripts. There was little, in fact, for which she wasn't ultimately responsible."[41] These duties ranged from selecting stories to adapt to casting to working closely with the art direction or costume departments.[42]

In the area of script and story, Harrison and Lloyd favored experienced writers but offered new writers opportunities as well.[43] According to Lloyd, he and Harrison both wrote up reports on short stories and scripts, which Hitchcock would then read and evaluate. After his approval, the two would collaborate on the story with a hired writer who would compose the script. Harrison, then, served as the middleman between Hitchcock and the writers, injecting her own authorial contributions on the way. Lloyd also recalls the great amount of sway that Harrison held over Hitchcock, calling him "Hitchy" and gently suggesting he look at a particular property. According to Lloyd, "[Hitchcock] never refused her suggestions," their partnership akin, writes Lane, to that of "'work wife' and 'work husband.'"[44]

As much as the show relied on Hitchcock's executive decision-making and his respected brand name, it was Harrison's "gothic 'femme noire'" mode that encapsulated the show's voice and maintained the "continuity of the Hitchcock brand."[45] Harrison formulated her tastes and developed her skills under Hitchcock's tutelage, but, as Lane writes, "the [solo] films Joan had made in the 1940s were a perfect precursor to the 'television noir' of *Alfred Hitchcock Presents*. Her preferred style had always been intimate and had valued character-based studies over action. And for her, story ruled."[46] A preoccupation with "women's knowingness" was a hallmark of Harrison's work at Universal Pictures and RKO, which included writing and producing *Phantom Lady* (1944), producing *They Won't Believe Me* (1947), and producing *Dark Waters* (1944) from a screenplay she cowrote with later *Alfred Hitchcock Presents* writer Marian Cockrell.[47]

It was also during her time at Universal that Harrison cultivated a public persona in line with that of studio starlets and leading ladies: smart in her presentation and her style, capable of making competence look glamorous. Universal fabricated Harrison's scripted life as a real-life icy blonde, "mak[ing] mysteries 'from the woman's angle.' She would be the 'Mistress of Suspense'—a female Hitchcock."[48] Her image graced a multitude of fan magazines, with publicity stills of her

FIGURE 25. Harrison always looked her best, be she at work (in 1945, bottom) or at rest (in 1944, top), the latter presaging Grace Kelly's sexy negligee a decade later in Hitchcock's 1954 film, *Rear Window.* © 1945, 1944 Universal Pictures.

well-dressed and at work (Figure 25). The press bought in, a 1946 profile in the *Miami Post* quoting Harrison as saying: "'I have to convince the men that I'm not a woman, just a producer.'" The reporter editorializes: "(Frankly, I think that would be a tough job. Statistics: height 5 feet, 4; weight 104; blonde hair, blue eyes. Comment: neat dish.)"[49] Gossip columnist Hedda Hopper called Harrison a "a 33-year-old, golden-haired ball of fire with a temper of a tarantula, the purring persuasiveness of a female archangel, the capacity for work of a family of beavers, and the sex appeal of a No. 1 glamor girl"; Hopper's snide headline, "An Exception to the Rule," referred to Harrison being the rare woman producer who could do her job properly—and, presumably, could look good doing it.

Harrison took great pains to manage her look and style, her clothes being an important mode of her self-fashioning within an industry and cultural moment ambivalent toward professional women. Lane explains how Harrison "walked [the sartorial line] between feminine looker and tough businesswoman. . . . For an entirely new generation, Joan modeled a recalibrated version of the working woman."[50] For Harrison, this meant resisting any whisper of man-hater or killjoy status: she wanted others to know she enjoyed being a girl and didn't mind being treated as one, provided she also got her way. Harrison emphasized how her gender was a boon in her work rather than a hindrance. She described her professional life as one in which she was happy as the sole female in a male workplace, telling one reporter that she wore a more feminine wardrobe on the set to win over her male crew. Harrison also claimed that the chivalry of her colleagues had served her well in her career, such that the journalist marveled at how she "manages to perform her duties without any loss of her femininity."[51] On the set of *Alfred Hitchcock Presents*, one member of the production team remembered:

> If there was ever a question, [Harrison] would be involved. She was very efficient, attractive, pleasant, and businesslike, and we never had any great problem resolving the issue. There was never a knockdown, drag-out fight of any kind. It was all very congenial. Very British. Sometimes, Hitchcock would join us for these meetings, and on these occasions, we would even have tea. Miss Harrison would act as hostess, and it was she who served the tea.[52]

Her Britishness informs her particular strain of femininity, mutually supporting the characterization of Harrison as sophisticated and lady-like, demure but steely.

Harrison's public statements about stereotypical postwar femininity ran the gamut from supportive to harsh. Her early experiences working in a dress shop ended with her "loathing women," according to historians Martin Grams and Patrik Wikstrom, with her ultimately deciding to transfer to secretarial school, through which she met Hitchcock.[53]

A recurring element of Harrison's self-fashioned biography is that she was an inadequate secretary to Hitchcock, her strengths tending toward story development and production, not administrative women's work. Such stories underscore Harrison's aptitude as a creative executive alongside her disinclination toward traditional forms of feminine labor. Her career, in this telling, naturally led her into the work of a producer, since she claimed to think like a man and prefer the company of men. Harrison was also quoted as saying that "women [viewers] must have something to pull for, you know, whether it's a dog, a horse, an old beggar—even another woman," a backbiting remark that, ironically, takes aim at woman-on-woman cattiness.[54] Yet Harrison revealed support for something resembling gender equity within the entertainment industry, saying: "I think very few women make good directors but producing is different. Directors must at times be able to shout in a way women can't or shouldn't. But no production which does not satisfy the feminine point of view is a success."[55] Women were needed for a film or television show's success, but there remained the matter of finding the proper, gendered division of duties.

Harrison's statements on traditional marriage and family were even more guarded, at times contradictory. She was quoted in a 1957 *New York Times* article as saying: "I'm not a great believer in marriage, as I see it today. . . . I'm a great believer in marriage as it might be."[56] She married writer Eric Ambler a year later. Harrison tempered her ambitious persona with a softer side, as in the Hopper column, in which she was quoted as saying "I would rather produce a baby than the greatest picture ever made!"[57] Harrison never had children of her own, having married at the age of fifty-one. One writer described Harrison as holding far more "unconventional views" than her mentor, Hitchcock, while wielding her femininity carefully and always turning it to her advantage.[58]

Knowing her interests as a storyteller and filmmaker, Harrison's influence on "Lamb to the Slaughter" (April 13, 1958) comes into sharp focus. This teleplay rehearses many of Harrison's thematic inclinations—dark humor and merciless criticism at the expense of traditional marriage and domesticity—while narrativizing the particularly female superpower of self-reinvention. Written and adapted by Roald Dahl, "Lamb to the Slaughter" stars Barbara Bel Geddes as a pregnant housewife who bludgeons her husband to death with a frozen lamb shoulder after he decides to leave her for another woman. When the police come to investigate, she feeds them a roasted lamb dinner, her guests never

FIGURE 26. Barbara Bel Geddes as the happy housewife satisfied with a job—and a lamb shoulder—well done. From "Lamb to the Slaughter," *Alfred Hitchcock Presents* (April 13, 1958). © 1958 Universal Pictures.

realizing they are consuming the murder weapon. According to Jan Olsson, this episode, a parade of adultery, murder, and symbolic cannibalism, "effectively rips asunder the notion of happy life in suburbia."[59]

The musical soundtrack cues us into a sitcom world far less sinister than the plot would suggest. Our protagonist is a homicidal Donna Reed type, capable and quick-witted when it comes to covering even her messiest tracks. Mathieu Macheret writes in *Cahiers du Cinéma*, "If Mary realizes the perfect crime, it is because she is 'mistress of the house': . . . she controls her space."[60] At the end of the episode, Mary is symmetrically framed against the dizzying, aggressively cute backdrop of her kitchen (Figure 26). She delivers a chilling smile—but at whom? Mary not only "controls her space," it would seem, but, in this moment, controls the viewers' space as well, peering into their homes with an eerie smile on her face. Her life up to this point has been a rehearsal for this performance, and her skillful deployment of these cultural scripts allows her to take revenge *and* escape retribution. Like Harrison, Mary knows that playing into expectations can, paradoxically, become the means of escaping the very same set of constraints.

Hitchcock publicly stated that "Lamb to the Slaughter" was an ideal archetype for an *Alfred Hitchcock Presents* episode, but it was in many ways Harrison's mean-spirited baby. Producer Norman Lloyd explained in one interview that it was Harrison who "chose . . . episodes [with] English humor like 'Lamb to the Slaughter.'"[61] In Harrison's story notes to Dahl, she advises him to make the woman pregnant so as to "keep a basic sympathy for [her]" and writes: "Hitch and I both feel [the police investigation] could be prolonged and made more suspenseful."[62] Dahl's misanthropic worldview, epitomized in his fiction and his short-lived television series *Far Out* (NBC, 1961), dovetails with Harrison's suspicion of domesticity and marriage; together, they created a compelling narrative in which the viewer has to root for a murderess. Harrison herself had said women needed someone to root for, and, in this episode, the underdog is a wife who has been pushed too far.

Bel Geddes became known for her portrayals of unassuming, treadupon females, cursed to love unworthy men, notably in her portrayal of Midge in Alfred Hitchcock's *Vertigo* (1957), which debuted the same year as "Lamb to the Slaughter" first aired.[63] These two leading ladies, Midge and Mary, and their respective journeys reveal what set *Alfred Hitchcock Presents* apart from Hitchcock's body of films and how Harrison's point-of-view further altered Hitchcock's formula. In his description of "Lamb," Mathieu Macheret calls Bel Geddes's character a "poor" woman who, like her character Midge in *Vertigo* "is always the one that men ignore."[64] But being the object of desire holds graver dangers than being undesired or ignored, a formulation that "Lamb to the Slaughter" takes to its bloodiest conclusion. Heartsick Midge mocks her own invisibility to Scottie (James Stewart) by painting herself into the portrait of his love object, Madeleine (or Carlota). "Midge's all-too-human face inscribed upon the idealized portrait of femininity punctures the illusion . . . reminding [Midge] of her own inadequacy."[65] Wounded by her seemingly cavalier joke, Scottie—who previously dismissed Midge as "motherly"—cancels their plans and stalks off. Rather than follow Scottie, the camera stays with Midge, who, in despair, pulls her hair, calls herself names, and violently slashes at her painting with a brush.

Midge is the victim of these cultural narratives in which some women are disposable, others cherished, but the latter is more likely to end up dead or irreparably broken. Mary, on the other hand, recognizes that playing the "motherly" housewife gives her power, because women who are not *seen* cannot get caught. Mary has watched her share of housewives on television and inhabits the role flawlessly. Why not embrace the opportunities that come with moving through the world undetected, which, for her, will likely include collecting her police husband's pension? This sly commentary on gender performance was a testament to Harrison's priorities for the show, just as Bel Geddes's particular gift, best displayed in creepy close-up, was giving the viewer quick, private glimpses into a demented inner life. Because television is about and for women and the domestic space, the character of Mary is enfranchised, even powerful, in a way that *Vertigo*'s Midge never could be.

Joan Harrison knew about story and style, her scripted life merging adroitness in her profession with feminine allure and appeal, values that seeped into the stories she championed and advised. She was versatile in telling stories and in turning herself into a story. In that way, Harrison was the avatar of what I am calling the "literate heroine," a type that not only characterizes the savvy murderess Mary but also many of the female-authored protagonists on *Alfred Hitchcock Presents*.

THE SCRIPTED LIFE OF THE LITERATE HEROINE

What—or who—is the literate heroine? She is controlled and calculating, never resorting to histrionics or violence. What sets her apart from other crafty leading ladies, though, is her specific knowledge of suspense genre conventions, which allows her to recognize the danger she is in and fight back. In that way, she is an ideal stand-in for the woman writer whose adaptability and literacy are key to her professional survival. If suspense or mystery fiction can be easily dismissed as lowbrow and mindless, these narratives argue for their own life-altering relevance to the women in the stories, not to mention the women watching at home. While often understood as the reader/viewer projected or transported into the action, the literate heroine also brings the viewer into intimate contact with the woman television writer and what it means to read and write like your life depends on it.

Two innovators for this archetype on *Alfred Hitchcock Presents* are Marian Cockrell and Charlotte Armstrong. Both women, like fellow scribe Helen Nielsen, began by writing novels and short stories, with Armstrong also writing for the theater. Armstrong would tell one interviewer in 1971:

> You build to your climax. You may not let down. . . . You have to be very careful with your organization. Otherwise you lose your grip. And that won't do. And, of course you do so much with action and dialogue in the suspense story and that's what the playwright must do.[66]

Armstrong extolled the virtues of the "well-made play," an orderly, cohesive writerly ideal that fits with the precise rigors of the mystery-suspense genre. She would say of the suspense novel: "It's so flexible that anything I want to say . . . I can say in this form. . . . I was trained to be lucid."[67] By contrast, Cockrell did not come from a suspense background and wrote novels in the romance, fantasy, and Western genres. Cockrell, whose husband, Francis, also wrote and directed for *Alfred Hitchcock Presents*, got the writing job for Hitchcock through her agent.[68]

The women's professional profiles, then, reflect different areas of expertise and interest. Armstrong wrote for multiple suspense television series, including *George Sanders Mystery Theater* (NBC, 1957) and *Thriller* (NBC, 1960–1962), and Cockrell wrote for *Suspicion* (NBC, 1957–1958), from Hitchcock's Shamley Productions, as well as *G.E. Theater* (CBS, 1953–1962), *Perry Mason* (CBS, 1957–1966), and TV's *Batman* (ABC, 1966–1968). The Cockrells wrote separately and together for many of the same shows; Francis is credited as the solo teleplay author on eighteen episodes of *Alfred Hitchcock Presents* and the director for two episodes, while Marian wrote nine episodes for the show by herself (mostly adaptations) and eleven total with coauthors. The Cockrells also collaborated on the film *Dark Waters*, which was produced by Harrison. Amanda Cockrell, daughter of Francis and Marian, described their partnership on the project:

> While Mama was working on the film, Daddy was in the Marine Corps overseas. They collaborated by correspondence, but I think Mama made most of the decisions just because he wasn't there. They actually used the collaboration to evade the military censors—he could let her know where he was or where he was heading (a no-no that otherwise would have been censored out) by disguising the info as part of plot suggestions, either for the film, or for short stories she was working on: "What if Fred gets sent somewhere in the Pacific, like for instance Iwo Jima?" It didn't usually actually have anything to do with the actual plot of the story in question, it was just a dodge to get info by the censors.[69]

Francis and Marian Cockrell both grew up in the South, where *Dark Waters* was set as well. Their daughter noted how "Most of [Marian's] books written in the forties were set in the South just for that reason—it was territory she knew."[70]

The Cockrells' iteration of the literate heroine comes in the character of Julia in "The Rose Garden" (December 16, 1956), adapted from a Vincent Fotre story by Marian and directed by Francis.[71] Julia (Patricia Collinge) is the meek spinster sister of Mrs. Cordelia Welles (Evelyn Varden), a widow whose rose garden can only be a sly reference to the British matriarch par excellence, Mrs. Miniver. Cordelia controls Julia in every respect but one: Julia's writing. When a publisher visits the house and reads Julia's "fiction" about a domineering, homicidal housewife whose husband goes mysteriously missing, he rightly suspects that Cordelia is the real-life inspiration for Julia's tale. In order to disclose Cordelia's criminal nature, Julia masks the truth in the form of a suspense story. Julia ultimately earns her freedom from her sister's clutches, as the episode makes a bigger claim about how the suspense genre can reveal social hypocrisy and the dark underside of middle-class, bourgeois life. The drama's resolution comes through a harmonious male-female pairing between Julia and a (male) publisher who recognizes the truth in her writing and with whom she can share an equitable and trusting partnership. The scripted marriage of the Cockrells shines through in this adaptation, the episode itself an exhibit of how a man and woman can read and write together.

Like the Cockrells, novelist Charlotte Armstrong and husband Jack Lewi moved to the Los Angeles area to write for Hollywood, but, unlike them, her marriage was not a professional boost.[72] On top of the inconsistent nature of television work, Armstrong suffered professional setbacks as a result of her husband's advocating on her behalf. In the correspondence between two agents working on her behalf, Ben Benjamin and Carol Brandt, Benjamin complains of how a given "Television Department has put a hex on her" and mourns not having protected Armstrong from the network. He goes on to describe Lewi as "a very aggressive husband who is a frustrated television writer, packager and idea man . . . [who] can't understand why we have never been able to sell some of his various projects and on one day I think he called me four times about this whole thing." Lewi was more a liability than an asset, according to Benjamin, as he "always trie[d] to run Charlotte's business."[73] Brandt follows up in a 1956 note: "I feel gloomy that we haven't been able to pull something off for her. . . . We might set up something of a campaign between us on this lady. Surely she is gold."[74] Armstrong worried that these perpetually failing deals would create bad buzz around her, telling Brandt: "Trouble is . . . when every deal they make for me gets into some kind of mess . . . how many TV or Movie people around and about are going to be left who will ever hire me? Surely by this time the word is around that Charlotte Amrstrong [sic] is a bitch to deal with. This seems unjust."[75] Even so, Armstrong put together an impressive resume in the entertainment world. Her relationship to Hitchcock began with a 1950 meeting, which she detailed in a piece of personal correspondence: "Mr. H. is just as fabulous as he is rumored to be. It seemed to me that we saw eye to eye on this whole suspense racket and had we talked much longer the corpses would have been thick upon the floor."[76] Armstrong would go on to write three episodes for the series.

While the Cockrells collaborated on a more collegial portrait of male-female partnership and the literate heroine, Armstrong offered a more embattled, "suspicious" portrait of marriage in "Sybilla" (December 6, 1960), adapted from a story by Margaret Manners and directed

FIGURE 27. Sybilla (Barbara Bel Geddes) is a fan—and a fixture—of the *suspense anthology* genre in "Sybilla," *Alfred Hitchcock Presents* (December 6, 1960). © 1960 Universal Pictures.

by Ida Lupino. Set at the turn of the twentieth century in a wealthy Victorian home, the story centers on a newly married couple and their rocky journey to marital bliss. The title character, played by Barbara Bel Geddes, is the devoted new bride to an indifferent husband, Horace (played by Alexander Scourby), who despises her patience and attentiveness and would murder her for it. He decides, at first, to poison her, a plot that fails when Sybilla replaces the tonic he has left for her, without necessarily knowing it had been tampered with.

Horace's anxiety and paranoia only increase after a conversation with Sybilla about horror and suspense literature. He approaches her in the salon as she reads a suspense anthology entitled *Night of Horror* (Figure 27). Horace dismisses the book as "rubbish," and she replies, "I know. Still, it's psychologically interesting, Horace." She summarizes the story she has been reading: a man believes his friend is trying to murder him, so as a form of insurance, the man puts in a letter to his attorney detailing these suspicions, to be opened upon his presumably mysterious demise. The man then tells his "friend" what he has done, ensuring his safety through this blackmail. Moments later, Sybilla lightly mentions to Horace that she has a duplicate key to his desk drawer, where Horace stores his diary. Horace, convinced she knows his plot and is politely threatening him, must now keep her healthy, happy, and alive. In time, their marriage finds a contented rhythm, and when Sybilla dies years later of natural causes, Horace discovers, first, that the letter of insurance had been a bluff (or a misunderstanding), and, second, that in the intervening years, he had fallen in love with Sybilla after all.

It is Sybilla's reading habit that secures her husband's loyalty, buying her the time to eventually win his heart. Horace finds genre literature silly, but Sybilla understands the deep and accurate "psychology" these stories provide. In many ways, this episode belongs to what Doane describes as the "cycle of films . . . labelled [as] the 'paranoid woman's films' . . . in which the wife invariably fears her husband is planning to kill her—[so] the institution of marriage is haunted by murder."[77] But, unlike those rightfully anxious women or the doomed wife in "Sorry, Wrong Number," Sybilla never reveals whether she is wise to her husband's plans. All her actions and dialogue suggest calculated self-preservation, but neither the character (Sybilla) nor the performer (Bel Geddes) shows her hand. Modleski describes how "over-subtle emotions . . . constitute a classic paranoid trait" in Gothic literature; this excess of care and caution only underscores how the literate heroine is a consummate reader who refuses to be legible, a woman who resists becoming a readable exhibit of evidence, which is to say, a corpse.[78] In fact, their marriage flips the gender roles from its Gothic inheritance, masculinizing Sybilla by making her the opaque husband and feminizing Horace as he becomes the paranoid wife. While, initially, this leads to some distress and resentment on Horace's end, his domestication— via oblique intimidation—results in marital harmony.

In the end, "Sybilla" is about how the reading habits of the literate heroine have not made her sentimental or soft, but, on the contrary, deeply sensitive to the wickedness all around her. To return to Modleski's term, Sybilla and Horace's marriage is one of the most "suspicious [marital] collaborations" in the series, one which can never be fully resolved or redeemed. As Richard C. Allen describes the "female-focalized narratives" in Hitchcock's works, "When recognition is achieved it exposes a profound, even unbridgeable, gap between the world as it is and the world as we would wish it to be, in a manner that punctures the romantic ideal."[79] The only way to maintain the union, then, is to defer that recognition indefinitely, for the two to live in unspoken fear and anger toward one another until those feelings melt into love. If Sybilla knows

Horace's murderous intentions, she forgives him and gains the upper hand in the process. If she does not suspect, then perhaps her ignorance was bliss. "Sybilla" demonstrates how the literate heroine survives by reading shifting alliances and circumstances, not through placing blind faith in others, and by knowing that the genre she occupies never gets an easy happy ending.

Circumventing roadblocks through ingenuity, generic fluency, and tact, the literate heroine becomes an on-screen surrogate for her creator, the woman writer navigating a changing television mediascape. The literate heroine has roots in gothic and film noir traditions, but *Alfred Hitchcock Presents* reinvented her as a commentary on the contemporary industry culture and television's move to a Hollywood mode of production. In the episodes above, literacy is a mode of survival, but Marian Cockrell and Charlotte Armstrong mobilized their own literacy to adapt male-authored source materials for *Alfred Hitchcock Presents*. In doing so, they turned the stories' focus to the interiority of the female characters and to the horrors of life under patriarchy.

UNFAITHFUL WIVES: ADAPTATION IN *ALFRED HITCHCOCK PRESENTS*

As women writers adapted to a changing job market, so too did they adapt in their work, translating their skills into writing suspense for television and turning short stories into screenplays. In her essay on adaptation and "gendered discourses," Shelley Cobb writes that "feminist translation theory . . . has led the way by critiquing the gendered nature of the language of fidelity," in which the source text, usually a work of prose, is held up as the authentic or "original" work.[80] Under this model, the task of a screen adaptation becomes to "*translate . . . feeling*, [which] is a feminine approach to adaptation studies and, consequently, has all the attendant characteristics."[81] Thus is the source deemed a sacred male original, the adaptation its submissive feminized attendant, "the film [functioning] as faithful wife to the novel as paternal husband."[82] Cobb offers an alternative model: adaptation as a kind of "conversation," in which the novel and the film are engaged in a respectful exchange.[83] A gendered language of adaptation theory is particularly apropos in the case of *Alfred Hitchcock Presents*, where men and women are so often pitted against one another in life-or-death struggles. In their adaptations of male-written works, Marian Cockrell and Charlotte Armstrong hijack the gender politics of their source materials, privileging female subjectivity and experience over the violence of the male gaze. These scripts are *unfaithful wives*, sometimes "conversing" with their source materials, other times functioning as complaints or counterarguments.[84]

Sometimes these adaptations rely on a small recalibration, other times an extensive overhaul that highlights out the shortcomings of the original story. Cockrell overwrites the gender politics of John Collier's story in "Wet Saturday" (September 30, 1956) through subtle means, emphasizing the sexist underpinnings of the American aristocracy. Collier's story, first published in the *New Yorker* in 1938, centers on rich patriarch Mr. Princey, as he works to cover up his daughter's crime of passion, the murder of her indifferent tutor. The third-person narration is allied with Princey, whose habit, as Collier writes, was "to walk through the village, touching his hat, not smiling. . . . But now all this was threatened . . . because Millicent, his cloddish daughter Millicent, had done this shocking and incredibly stupid thing."[85] Cockrell's television adaptation is not filtered through Princey's point of view, allowing for a more flexible affiliation with the characters on-screen. Meanwhile, Cockrell adds a single line of dialogue that does not exist in the story where Princey scolds his daughter: "Our family has held a position of respect in this community for generations, a position I do not intend to have destroyed by the stupidity of one foolish female."[86] This explicit disapproval of Millicent (actor), not simply for being foolish but for being female, pulls on a thread of Princey's misogyny that lingers beneath the surface in the Collier story. In a single line of Cockrell's adaptation, the masculinist resonances of power and money come to the foreground rather than receding politely into the scenery.

Charlotte Armstrong's adaptation of John Cheever's 1954 *New Yorker* story "The Five-Forty-Eight" (October 25, 1960) involves a more extensive rewriting of its inspiration, revamping the perspective of the source material and, in the process, establishing a visual language of male brutality and female retribution.[87] In both versions, executive Blake is held at gunpoint by his former secretary, Miss Dent, on the 5:48 p.m. commuter train. Dent, a troubled young secretary with a psychiatric history, is pushed to her limit after Blake makes love to her, only to spurn and fire her afterward. She rouses herself from her bed-ridden depression to assault Blake, who has been dodging her ever since the sexual encounter. As Dent struggles to maintain composure and mental clarity in this confrontation, readers come to recognize Blake's truly monstrous nature. In the end, Dent does not shoot Blake but forces him out of the train and demands he lie with his face in the mud. She decides to spare Blake, because, unlike him, she finds she is capable of mercy and kindness: "Oh, I'm better than you, I'm better than you, and I shouldn't waste my time or spoil my life like this," Dent says, as Blake lies, Cheever writes, "in the filth . . . on the ground, weeping."

Cheever's prose does not reveal if Blake has been changed by this encounter: does he understand the depth of his cruelty, to the women in his life, whom he treats with open disdain? Is he desirous or capable of change? The ending is left open, though the final line—"He got to his feet and picked up his hat from the ground where it had fallen and walked home"—suggests that Blake will return to his regular routine and that ordinary American life is so rife with danger, violence, and madness that even this incident is business as usual. Blake is a World War II veteran, and the atrocities of war hang over the story like a ghost, coexisting alongside the more commonplace inhumanities women and men inflict on one another in civilian life.

Armstrong's version differs from Cheever's in two important respects, the first being in its development of Miss Dent as a character. Cheever's Dent is deranged, forcing Blake to read her rambling letter that opens with the words "Dear Husband." Her musings only grow stranger from there: she asks if "human love leads us to divine love," details a dream she had "of a volcano erupting with blood," and claims to be psychic. This letter is comparatively de-emphasized in the television version— the viewer can only spy snippets of the page—and Miss Dent, while agitated, is not delusional. In both the story and the show, her name, "Dent," connotes abuse, like an object that has been carelessly tossed about and damaged in the process. In Cheever's version, Blake was unlucky enough to wrong a woman already detached from reality, while Armstrong's telling suggests that Blake preyed on a vulnerable woman and, as a result, drove her to madness.

The second major difference between the source and the teleplay is where the drama's loyalties lie. Cheever's version is closely aligned with the perspective and emotional life of Blake, even as the author shows him in a deeply unflattering light. Armstrong's adaptation is initially more even-handed but ultimately sides with the character of Miss Dent. Cheever's story uses a third-person narrator inflected by Blake's point of view, a more extreme version of Collier's narrator in "Wet Saturday." Cheever writes of how Blake avoided Dent on the street, because "she had no legitimate business with him. They had nothing to say." He thinks to himself, as he dodges into a men's bar to escape her, "Oh, it was so simple!" The narration does not just reveal

Blake's thoughts and feelings but is allied with him, wanting what he wants and thinking what he thinks.

Armstrong's television retelling is not narrated by either character, but it accounts for Miss Dent's experience and emotional life in a way that Cheever's narrator does not. The cinematography supports the action in the script, Dent's feelings of betrayal and fury conveyed through multiple close-ups on the face of actress Phyllis Thaxter. Viewers are given direct access to her pain, rather than only seeing her through Blake's eyes. In Cheever's telling of Dent's seduction, we see her shabby apartment and her mousy self-presentation through Blake's eyes. He surveys her apartment and seizes on what the narrator calls her "lack of self-esteem." After the two have slept together, the reader can barely access Dent's pain through Blake's callous and dismissive perspective: "When he put on his clothes again, an hour or so later, she was weeping. He felt too contented and warm and sleepy to worry much about her tears." The story's narrator cares little for her tears, because Blake does not, and the reader is, by extension, distanced from her suffering. This is not the case in the television episode. A sex scene would not be passable by sponsors in an era where on-screen married couples slept in separate beds, so Blake and Dent's interplay (or conversational foreplay) is stressed, as is Dent's misguided tenderness and excitement, as she entertains her guest, almost crying with happiness.

Blake's decision to have Dent fired warrants a brief mention in Cheever. Firing the secretary he has slept with is the "only sensible thing," so he puts in the order to terminate her contract and takes the rest of the day off. In the television version, a flashback is rendered through Dent's point of view, the camera lingering on her devastation as Human Resources delivers the news; the figure of Blake occupies the distant background, protected by a wall of glass, before disappearing entirely. If, in the story, Dent's suffering is merely referenced, it becomes the focal point in the television adaptation, and the viewer experiences Dent's abandonment along with her. This betrayal sheds light altogether on the episode's ambiguous opening, in which Blake ducks into a bar to escape Dent, who is following him. The neon sign above the door reads "Ladies Not Admitted" (Figure 28), foreshadowing the story of professional misconduct that follows.

When the episode begins, it is unclear whether Dent is the villain or the victim. But reading her firing scene against the episode's opening constitutes an aesthetic and thematic motif of Dent's being blocked from moving freely. This theme is illustrated through her repeated

FIGURE 28. The tavern that Blake (Zachary Scott) ducks into to escape his angry former lover (Phyllis Thaxter) is itself an imaginative proxy for the kinds of male-dominated writers' rooms and industry spaces that women professionals in television faced. From "The Five-Forty-Eight," *Alfred Hitchcock Presents* (October 25, 1960). © 1960 Universal Pictures.

longing gazes through a transparent pane—a "glass ceiling" that is, in fact, a window. Blake's rejection and the subsequent loss of her liveli-hood breaks down her sanity and spirit, illustrated by the distortion of Dent's face by the window's flower carving, a notably feminine decorative touch for a men's bar (Figure 29). Before Dent's backstory is revealed, this moment reads as one of narrative tension, temporar-ily establishing her as a monstrous villain. But, when the full story is revealed, the image more accurately speaks to the fractured and fractur-ing experience of being a woman—a woman at work, a woman in love, a woman destroyed by her desire to achieve both personal and profes-sional success. (Incidentally, Billy Wilder's film *The Apartment* [1960], released in the same year, also uses broken or fragmented mirror imag-ery to convey the psychic breakdown of the working woman. Shirley MacLaine's broken-hearted elevator girl claims she likes her makeup mirror to be broken: "it makes me look the way I feel.")[88]

The recurring imagery of windows and glass is part of Cheever's original telling but is also a visual trope throughout different episodes of *Alfred Hitchcock Presents*. Jan Olsson observes of the series that "reflected surface[s] stand ... in for the easy access to a character's inner world that the narrator in a novel can offer [and] ... mirrors rep-resent an indispensable prop."[89] Olsson further emphasizes the show's "ludic repetition, the recycling of names and story elements ... [and] a recognizable stable of characters ... [that] shaped the construction

FIGURE 29. Dent stares at Blake from through the bar door in "The Five-Forty-Eight," *Alfred Hitchcock Presents* (October 25, 1960). © 1960 Universal Pictures.

of a show universe," which "operated in tandem with an obsessive use of meaningful props, especially mirrors."[90] Mirrors not only highlight what Olsson calls the "doubling" or "surrogation" that the serialized format of television demands, but mirrors are also "doubles" of the television screen.[91] Just as the character looks in a mirror to see herself, so too may the viewer look into the screen and witness her own reflection—and, unlike Leona of "Sorry, Wrong Number," she will recognize the story is about her.

Finally, these reflection shots serve as battlegrounds or contested screen-spaces over which Blake and Dent fight for dominance. As Blake attempts to insert distance, Dent squeezes herself into the reflective field with him. In a storefront window, Blake can escape her, but when she has him at gunpoint on the train, Dent finally has the leverage to invade his space and make him listen. In this way, the television screen surrogate—in the form of these reflective surfaces—becomes a site of female expressiveness and agency. The mirror, the window, the television screen: these are territories that can be wrested from masculine control, presenting the viewer with a metaphor for female authorship in a male-dominated industrial context. If the female leads in "Wet Saturday" and "The Five-Forty-Eight" are particularly unhinged, this only speaks to the show's overarching argument that insanity is an understandable reaction and a reasonable recourse to life under patriarchy.

These individual episodes or texts fit into the larger framework established by the show's Hitchcockian brand and its associate producer, Joan Harrison. The show was recognizably Hitchcock, Hitchcock telling one reporter that his work focuses on "murderous action and passionate interests, albeit sometimes illicit, in [his] films" because he is such a pacifist.[92] But Harrison's cynicism toward marriage and domesticity, paired with her arch sense of humor, constituted an important dimension of the show's voice and appeal.[93] Harrison fashioned a public persona—that of the stylish, sardonic career woman—that followed her through her decades of work in film and television. Harrison's distinctive persona and her creative preoccupations determined the kinds of stories she nurtured to fruition for *Alfred Hitchcock Presents*. And the female authorship on *Alfred Hitchcock Presents*—work by Marian Cockrell, Charlotte Armstrong, Helen Nielsen, Gina Kaus, and others—collectively created a space on television to narrativize personal and professional frustrations, to create a surrogate figure in the literate heroine, and to rewrite both source materials and cultural scripts from a woman's point of view. The scripted lives they invented—about themselves and for the small screen—not only begin to fill in the gaps of the history of women writers but also provide an affective dimension to this industry narrative, articulating what could not be said in more direct terms. What did it feel like to navigate the culture industries in this moment? What did it take to survive?

CODA: CAKE BAKERS AND CRIMINALS

I end, then, as I began: with Shelley Winters. In *Alcoa Premiere*'s "The Cake Baker" (ABC, January 2, 1962), written by Peggy and Lou Shaw, Winters stars as an unhappy housewife who lapses into eerie trances when faced with domestic drudgery.[94] When she volunteers to write a script for the school pageant, this creative pursuit gives her life renewed meaning. Unfortunately, her husband is threatened by her new hobby and forces her to quit. If the wayward wife Winters played in "Sorry, Wrong Number" was punished for wanting more, her character in "The Cake Baker" is granted a reprieve, her husband later deciding to support her in her quest for self-actualization. In addition to sharing a star, "Sorry, Wrong Number" and "The Cake Baker" are complementary texts; the former is a classic case of domestic horror, the latter, conversely, lays out the horrors of the domestic. The interplay between these programs elicits the question: is the anti-heroine of "Sorry, Wrong Number" petty and shallow because she lacks the artistic or intellectual outlet of writing and reading? Maybe the literate heroine needs literature not just to live but also to live well.

Shows like *Climax!* and *Alfred Hitchcock Presents* laid the groundwork for a second-wave feminist televisual manifesto like "The Cake Baker." The suspense genre allowed for postwar television to broach real issues of marital dysfunction and domestic frustration through the safe distancing of genre and convention. Meanwhile, the women authors of *Alfred Hitchcock Presents*—who faced their own containments, restrictions, and pressures, at work and at home—played a central role in giving shape to these sentiments through an amalgamation of gothic, noir, pulp, and melodrama. They were masters of adaptation, shaping their careers to the needs, expectations, and workflows of the Hollywood television machine, while adapting literary sources to an evolving television aesthetic. Their scripts facilitated viewers' escapes into settings both exotic and familiar, while tapping into emotional registers familiar to female writers and audience members alike: justified paranoia, perpetual frustration, and the stubborn will to navigate hostile systems of patriarchal power.

Conclusion

Better Than It Never Was

In the "Rosemary's Baby" episode of *30 Rock* (NBC, 2006–2013), contemporary comedy writer Liz Lemon (Tina Fey) meets Rosemary Howard (Carrie Fisher), a television writer from the 1970s and Liz's childhood idol.[1] Liz is initially starstruck by the gutsy, smart-talking broad, a woman who encourages her to take risks as the head writer of NBC's comedy-variety show, *TGS*. "We pushed the envelope!" Rosemary crows, recalling an edgier comedy past, before network comedies took their orders from corporate parent companies like NBC's General Electric. "You're not a cog in their machine!" But Liz soon discovers that Rosemary is a rotten role model: a lonely, unstable alcoholic who lives in an imagined glory age of television. When Liz cuts ties, Rosemary lashes out, accusing her of being like her—"married to your job"—before settling into the role of embittered mother, yelling, "I broke down barriers for you! You're my kid who never calls!" Liz returns to the television studio, back to her job and to what her boss, Jack Donaghy (Alec Baldwin), calls "work[ing] inside the system."

In assembling a history of television's past, there is the impulse to fast-forward to the present. What use do we have now for an account of women television writers way back when? The 1950s was a moment of media transition from radio; so too is contemporary television in need of writers to create programming for cable networks, streaming platforms, and multiple other avenues of internet content, branded or otherwise. If the past was committed to finding water-cooler shows to

attract mass audiences, our current moment allows for more niche programming for and by women of color, queer women, and trans women,
a wider coalition of women writers than existed in the postwar moment.
The similarities are there, but so are the differences.

The "Rosemary's Baby" episode of *30 Rock* suggests how to frame
these historical and institutional distinctions, dramatizing how women
television writers can be both indebted to and hindered by an indeterminate television past. Just as the Rosemary in Roman Polanski's 1968 film
both loves and is repulsed by her demon baby, so Liz Lemon and Rosemary Howard are stuck in their own toxic mother-daughter dynamic.
How can Liz honor Rosemary's contributions without destroying her
own (it is noted, well-compensated) career? Much of the episode follows
a paralyzed Liz, caught between Rosemary and Jack, choosing between
being a rebel and being a follower. The episode explores how Liz's experiences working in network television diverge from Rosemary's, even as
sexism and misogyny persist through the years.

This has always been and will likely always be a tricky history to
document. In 2005, the Paley Center launched "She Made It: Women
Creating Television & Radio," a "three-year initiative celebrating the
achievements of creative and business women in the television and radio
industries."[2] This extensive archive is an invaluable resource to historians of media seeking primary sources such as interviews and extant
recordings, but the curation of these materials illustrates the troubles
with compiling a comprehensive history of women in broadcasting. "She
Made It"—the very name conjuring up the image of Mary Richards
(*The Mary Tyler Moore Show* [CBS, 1970–1977] tossing her hat into the
air—but what "it" (success) looked like in the postwar moment is different from the 1970s television of Mary Richards and from television in
the twenty-first century. Critic A. O. Scott writes that the "Rosemary's
Baby" episode is about "the anxieties of female comic influence"[3] if
Aaron Sorkin's shows are testaments to slick male competence in television (*The Newsroom, Sports Night, Studio 60 on the Sunset Strip*), Tina
Fey and *30 Rock* examine the guilt-ridden, cross-generational sisterhood of female survival. The irony of this episode is that, in wanting to
follow in Rosemary's footsteps, Liz is forced to abandon her and leave
that history of television behind. If television was once a nervy form of
entertainment where the executives deferred to the writers and artists—
itself a dubious premise set up by Rosemary—in Liz's day, it has since
become a corporate property, and "G.E. Followship" award-winner Liz
has to play along to stay in the game. The industrial knowingness of

30 Rock is in full effect here: Fisher's character is named after Rose Marie, the actress who played television writer Sally Rogers on *The Dick Van Dyke Show* (NBC, 1961–1966), and Sally, in turn, is based on the real-life figure of Selma Diamond, the woman writer in the room of the comedy-variety program, *Caesar's Hour* (NBC, 1954–1957), among other shows.[4] But while Selma scripted her own jokes and persona, Sally was a product of an all-male writers' room.

If Rose Marie lent the figure of the woman television writer a compelling screen presence, the character of Sally Rogers resonated with pre-existing sad single girl tropes: being professionally driven and able to hold her own in the writers' room but unlucky in love. (It is no coincidence that this description sounds a lot like that of Liz Lemon.) Unlike *Dick Van Dyke*'s happily domestic and model-beautiful wife, Laura Petrie (Mary Tyler Moore), Sally was desperate for a date on her birthday, pleaded for a husband on live television, and underwent numerous other romantic humiliations.[5] To some extent, these narratives were inspired by Selma Diamond's comedy schtick, but Sally diverges from Selma primarily in our access to her as viewers in private moments. Sally—not to be confused with Selma—suffered private bouts of regret and loneliness when no one was watching, the stereotypical cat snuggled on her lap.[6] Sally Rogers, then, was simultaneously progressive and retrograde, Sally's professional successes necessarily coming at a steep personal cost.

"Rosemary's Baby" suggests a matrilineal line, then, that goes from Selma to Sally, through Rose Marie, to Rosemary, then Liz Lemon—who is actually Tina Fey. Also in the mix is Carrie Fisher, a comedienne, writer, and script doctor in her own rite, and even the whisper of Mary Richards, Fey having herself referred to *The Mary Tyler Moore Show* as the "template . . . of a great show, obviously, but also of a show that is all about the relationships in the workplace."[7] All of these women—both scripted and real—broke down barriers for one another, but only half of these women are real people. Rather than meticulously pull apart representation from reality, the Selmas from the Sallys, we must recognize that the history of women television writers requires movement between private dealings and public personalities, industrial realities and imaginative renderings. Fictional representations have long served as a useful, if incomplete, archive of television history and of the scripted life of the woman writer.

What happened to the woman writers of *Their Own Best Creations*? Who remained in television, and what precipitated their continuation in or departure from the industry? The decreased visibility

FIGURE 30. Who is the "faceless" woman writer in *A Face in the Crowd*? © 1957 Warner Brothers.

of the television writer, together with the industry's move to Hollywood and the masculinization of the television writing profession, impacted women's prospects in the field. Feminist media historians have begun to recuperate the authorial work of story editors and secretaries, uncovering the day-to-day writerly work these women accomplished. The television writers' room scene from the *A Face in the Crowd* (Elia Kazan, US, 1957) features such an unnamed woman, positioned just left of center (Figure 30).[8] Head writer Mel Miller (Walter Matthau) jokes that the lowly writing staff is composed of "men without faces," but here is an anonymous woman in profile. We return to the story of Lucille Kallen (chapter 2): is she a secretary, or is she a scribe? With models of television authorship ranging from credited writer to uncredited secretary-contributor, particularly in the latter half of the 1950s, is such a distinction even worth making?

Misunderstandings about television's past can make it more difficult to set benchmarks for an industry future. So, recognizing the contributions women writers made to a nascent medium and to a pre-second-wave feminist conception of the working woman is crucial for seeing how these legacies continue into our present. Contemporary women writers and showrunners continue to script public lives and personas that bridge the needs of industry and audience, while their shows narrativize and critique the pressures of being a woman who works. Recent lawsuits, journalistic exposés, and other artifacts of scandals remind us of the violent machinations of industry sexism that only exist at the periphery of postwar television historiographies—the stories too secret and sordid to be included in a light-hearted memoir or journalistic puff-piece.

The trouble with measuring "progress" in entertainment is twofold. First, what constitutes growth? We must consider if there are more women than before but also if these hiring efforts are intersectional and if the women hired have as much autonomy and agency as their male counterparts, all of these being challenging elements to count or quantify. Second, the industry's push for "progress" with hiring programs and the publication of data collected by the Writers' Guild, comes in conflict with the open secret economy of film and television and the intangible circumstances that result in women's careers being minimized, thwarted, or ended altogether. Just as postwar programs tell the story of the woman television writer in otherwise unsayable ways, so contemporary shows can obliquely and even directly speak to being a woman writer in television.

POSTSCRIPT: ON THE WOMEN OF *THEIR OWN BEST CREATIONS*

My aim in bringing together the works and public faces of women writers in postwar television has been to collate their experiences without collapsing the meaningful differences between them. In her study of women screenwriters in silent film, Giuliana Muscio writes that her "objective is to provide a historical account that encourages the creation of accurate portraits of each woman at work, but within a collective fresco."[9] The "collective fresco" of *Their Own Best Creations* is the cultural work that women television writers did in postwar America, writing and producing television while at the same time circulating as cultural texts themselves. Across the course of the 1950s, women television writers had to make the case for their roles in the television industry, and they did so in their public personalities, in their private dealings at work, and through the shows they wrote, supervised, and edited.

Women television writers—overwhelmingly white and middle-class—looked a lot like the archetypal mid-century homemaker in terms of race, ethnicity, and class, and they emphasized many of the same idealized traits. They argued that television needed their compassion, care, and frugality in the writers' room and behind the typewriter, conveying the stories that women at home most wanted to see. Through genres comedic and dramatic, in serials and anthologies, women television writers told stories of domestic frustration and male chauvinism that anticipated pre-second-wave feminist inklings and allegorized the struggles of being a woman at work. What sets the scripted life of women television writers apart during this era is how their scripts thematized the strain of being creative, professional, and female, as they themselves worked to reconcile those tensions and contradictions in the workplace, as well as in their public personas.

The chronological organization of this book tracks how women writers' tactics and rhetoric had to evolve over the course of the decade. Lucille Kallen (chapter 2), Irna Phillips (chapter 4), Gertrude Berg, and Peg Lynch (chapter 3), all benefited from the idea that a feminine perspective—at work and in their writing—produced better television. Kallen collaborated with *Your Show of Shows'* head writer, Mel Tolkin, to tell stories about marriage as creative male-female partnership and developed vehicles for *Your Show of Shows* star Imogene Coca. Berg and Lynch wrote minor, intimate stories about domestic and family life, and their relatable star personas conflated with the characters they played on-screen. All three women made the case for television writing being a form of women's work, requiring a blend of maternal-feminine energies and the comedic outlook of one who watches and listens, rather than one who is always asked to talk. Their scripts reflect those sensibilities, turning female anxieties into fodder for comedy and treating the domestic space as a canvas for self-expression.

As the television industry moved to Los Angeles and was absorbed into the production culture and scheduling of Hollywood's dream factory, the requirements for television writers changed. Irna Phillips (chapter 4) serves as an important transitional figure in this history, her scripted life combining a soft, womanly public persona with unapologetic business savvy and a team of writers working under her auspices. This is where the industry and the history of daytime television notably diverges from that of prime-time television. In no area of network broadcasting would courting the female audience remain as central as with the daytime soap. Women writers continued to play an important role in the development of daytime past the postwar era and even established their own literary lineages, as with Phillips's mentorship of Agnes Nixon (*One Life to Live*, *All My Children*). *Days of Our Lives'* head writer Dena Higley described Nixon as a "tiny lady, but a force of nature," a sentiment that makes Nixon sound like one of her show's fiery, passionate heroines.[10]

Comparing the soap opera to the prime-time genres of comedy-variety, domestic serial, and suspense anthology raises a larger question about genre: Did audience tastes really change over the course of the 1950s, or did Hollywood change them? Shows like *The Goldbergs* (which was only in the top 10 for the 1949–1950 season) and *Ethel and Albert* ceased to be of interest to networks and audiences with the move westward, while comedy-variety shows and anthology dramas, areas in which women writers had flourished, lost out to game shows and Westerns. To what extent audiences were demanding the new, Hollywood-adjacent programming that they got is impossible to know, though FCC chairman Newton Minow would famously dismiss the medium's devolution in his 1961 address about television as a "vast wasteland." Debates over what television would become and how it would be written drew to a close. As Miranda Banks explains, New York-based television writers were "primarily freelancers . . . concerned about minimums for piecemeal work" and protective of their editorial and creative autonomy; but "by the late 1950s, almost all of filmed television employees . . . had closed shop and moved to Los Angeles," where the pay was better and "writers with hyphenate positions on series had significantly more creative control."[11]

Women television writers now had to compete with the (often male) writers already entrenched at the film studios, and, as writers became increasingly invisible cogs in the Hollywood machine, so did women writers. Television was Hollywood's new B-movie, its writers asked to play the part of the unsentimental screenwriter-hack à la Joe Gillis in Billy Wilder's 1950 film, *Sunset Boulevard*. But every Joe needs his Betty Schaefer. To that end, women started in the story departments, working as secretaries and editors before possibly transitioning to full-time scriptwriting (chapter 5); some wrote alone or with a male partner, turning over scripts as freelancers, or were staffed in television writers' rooms; some scripted and adapted stories across different media to put together their keep; and still others held tight to their producer credits as a form of job security.

The women who wrote for *Alfred Hitchcock Presents* simultaneously worked as playwrights, novelists, and screenwriters, adapting their own and others' stories for television, while Joan Harrison demonstrated how a powerful producer, particularly one working under a big name like Hitchcock, could exert authorial and creative influence (chapter 6). But the anthology drama as a form peaked in the "Golden Age" of postwar television and was gradually supplanted by sitcoms and westerns, shows that demanded extensive knowledge of genre on the part of the author but still enabled casual, one-off viewing from audiences.

The rise of what Lynn Spigel calls the "fantastic family sitcom" in the 1960s exemplifies how a genre that previously foregrounded the woman's perspective came to embody bemused estrangement from domestic life and a more impersonal, streamlined process of television writing.[12] Nina Liebman writes of how shows like *Bewitched* (ABC, 1964–1972), *I Dream of Jeannie* (NBC, 1965–1970), *The Addams Family* (ABC, 1964–1966), *The Munsters* (CBS, 1964–1966), and *My Favorite Martian* (CBS, 1963–1966) represent the supernatural "hodgepodge" of the 1960s family sitcom.[13] Even as male television writers took inspiration and ideas for scripts from their family lives, they did not profess to be intense observers of the family, as did women writers in the 1950s.[14] In single-authored shows like *The Goldbergs* and *Ethel and Albert*, the home is transformed into a zone of intimacy and artistry, the family an ensemble cast, the marriage a creative partnership; Berg, in particular, claimed to write from her experience and was inspired by the people she knew and loved. By contrast, the new Hollywood sitcom was predicated on "consistency [and] duplication" and was assembled by committee.[15]

The "fantastic family sitcom" centers on a magic being or group of creatures failing, week after week, to perform normal, wholesome Americanness. The humor stems from the ways in which mothers, sons, and sexy genies neglect to understand or perform the social conventions correctly. Practically speaking, this premise allowed any proficient comedian or dramatist to step in and pen an episode. The very qualities that made a woman television writer appealing—her attention to the rhythms of life at home with a husband and children—were seemingly no longer necessary. So, while the "fantastic family sitcom" is often treated as television's campy adoption of second-wave feminist politics, this generic cycle devalued the postwar ideal of the woman writer and her voice; rather than having an intuitive knowledge of family and marriage, the Hollywood television writer needed to channel a denaturalized estrangement from those areas of life.[16] This is not to say that women could not or did not write for these shows but, rather, that they were not the driving creative forces behind this programming, nor were they asked to bring a particular feminine perspective to the process.

The absorption of television production into the film studios marked the television writer as male, more or less settling the gendered debate that had raged throughout the decade. But, if popular representation is to be believed, it was not a job for any kind of man: superficial man-boys were the institution's rank-and-file soldiers. In his 1960 satiric essay for *Variety* entitled "Why I Want to be a Television Writer," Sherwood Schwartz (*Gilligan's Island, The Brady Bunch*) claimed to have transcribed an interview with a ninth grader who aspired to be a television writer.[17] When Schwartz asked why, the boy replied that he was lazy, did not intend to go to college, and sought a profession where his "wise guy" talents would be rewarded with fancy cars, trips to Las Vegas, and dates with beautiful actresses. Schwartz claimed to be offended by this assessment, but the punch line of the piece reads: "I was so upset I couldn't work. I left my office, hopped into my Cadillac, picked up a glamorous actress, and headed for Las Vegas." Even as Schwartz feigns offense, he confirms that the stereotype is accurate. What does this kind of self-effacing humor achieve? Schwartz wants to project humility and self-awareness, but this gag fits into a larger cultural narrative in which television writers are no longer artists, nor do they deserve to be treated as such.

If fast cars and beautiful women are television writers' rewards, where does the woman television writer fit into this boys' club? At the Las Vegas blackjack table with Schwartz? Madelyn Pugh Davis, in *Laughing with Lucy*, tells the story of Selma Diamond being so immersed in her life with her male writer compatriots that, after a day of hard work, she followed up a suggestion to celebrate with, "Good idea. Where can we find some girls?" Pugh admits: "I never got to [that] point."[18] Ella Taylor explains that, "in television the group came to define both the meaning of family and the meaning of professionalism," the latter in particular referring to those "classical or 'free' professions [that require the] autonomous exercise of specialized skills."[19] This move follows what she calls the "rise of the professional work-family" genre.[20] In the 1950s, women writers created worlds in which domestic labor was rescripted as creative work. Nina Liebman argues that "in television, the familial world operates as an allegory for the social," meaning society more broadly but also, potentially, the social formations that exist within the industry (the writers' room, the studio set, the executive boardroom).[21] Moving into what Taylor calls the "corporate world of the 1960s," male writers engineered the inverse for television, literary attention is taken from the nuclear family—at least, allegorically speaking—and granted to the work family, the organization, and the system.[22]

A vast divide also emerged between the empowered writer-producer hyphenate and the rank-and-file television writer, the former overshadowing the latter in terms of power and visibility. In contextualizing the showrunner in television history, Newman and Levine state that "television producers and writers like Jack Webb, Rod Serling, Norman Lear, Larry Gelbart, and Steven Bochco have been public figures for decades. But it does indicate a change toward a greater role for the television creator within a culture that celebrates creative individuals in numerous areas of endeavor."[23] In 1950, Gertrude "Molly" Berg stood at the window-screen and raved about Sanka coffee, but Hollywood television was not compelled by such "small situations." So, by 1959, the vision of the television showrunner breaking the fourth wall was no longer a family matter. Instead of a middle-aged matriarch in an apron, the showrunner par excellence was Rod Serling donning a work-appropriate dark suit, inviting Americans to depart their homes and enter the flexible, imaginative "social" space of *The Twilight Zone*.

Some postwar women writers still continued in television into the 1960s and beyond, noteworthy names including story editor and writer D. C. Fontana (*Star Trek*, but beginning as a secretary at Columbia Pictures' Television), Irma Kalish (*The Facts of Life*), and Barbara Avedon (who cocreated *Cagney and Lacey* with Barbara Corday).[24] But the power and visibility of the Hollywood hyphenate—writer-producers and stars with producer power—overshadowed the figure of the hired television writer. Even *The Mary Tyler Moore Show*, an explicitly second-wave feminist television program, had women writers like Treva Silverman and Susan Silver reporting to creators-producers James L. Brooks and Allan Burns. (The show's casting director, Ethel Winant, would be promoted to CBS's vice president in 1973.) The actress-producer played an increasingly empowered role in authoring her own star vehicles: Moore had a great deal of say through her role at the show's production company, MTM Enterprises, while *Bewitched*'s Elizabeth Montgomery weighed in on storylines toward the end of the show's run and Marlo Thomas developed her own star vehicle, *That Girl*, through her production company, Daisy Productions.[25]

The women of *Their Own Best Creations* had different reactions to these changes. Both Lucille Kallen and Lucille Fletcher decided to concentrate on solo writing. Kallen occasionally wrote for television in the 1960s and even cowrote the play *Maybe Tuesday* with Mel Tolkin in 1958, but she chose to focus on her novels. Kallen contributed to *The Bell Telephone Hour* (NBC, 1959–1968) but otherwise only wrote sporadically for television after *The Imogene Coca Show*, for programs such as *Stanley* (NBC, 1956–1957), *The U.S. Steel Hour* (ABC, CBS, 1953–1963), and *We Interrupt This Season: NBC Experiment in Television* (1967); her focus was her fiction writing, in particular penning the C. B. Greenfield mystery series.[26] The closest she came to fictional-izing her time in television was with the 1964 novel *Out There, Some-where—!*[27] The story focuses on a dissatisfied housewife-turned-writer who is hired to adapt her story for television. In her collaborations with another writer (male, and in psychoanalysis, like Tolkin), the character of Ruth Bernard finds herself, just as Kallen did, "[sitting] in a tottering swivel chair . . . behind a typewriter."[28]

In interviews, Kallen would later explain that she left television for many reasons. She said that television had become "crummy" any-way and that she did not want to move to California.[29] Fiction writ-ing allowed Kallen to write what she wanted on her own terms. She explained to one *Newsday* reporter in 1993: "I used to sit there [at *Your Show of Shows*] when everybody used to tear into whatever it was I had done or had done with Mel, and I'd say 'Someday I'm going to write something that Sid can't get his hands on.'" She would similarly recall "wanting to get away from the domination of all those guys."[30] Suspense specialist Lucille Fletcher continued to adapt her work for the small screen but, like comedienne Lucille, preferred fiction writing. Her novels "all [had] . . . dark themes, but [were] more complex than her radio plays."[31] Fletcher was able to move into grittier territory with her fiction, areas where television did not dare to tread.

Peg Lynch and Gertrude Berg left television and returned to the familiar formats of radio and theater. Lynch returned to radio with *The Couple Next Door* (CBS Radio, 1957–1960), which allowed her to remain in New York and keep working with Alan Bunce on related advertising campaigns. When television made the move to Hollywood, Peg Lynch told interviewer-scholar Lauren Bratslavsky that she was ready to quit the breakneck timeline of television production.[32] Accord-ing to her daughter, Lynch was not interested in raising her child in Hollywood, and Lynch went so far as to tell one reporter, "I never liked television that much. Radio is more fun and more intimate. People can use their imagination."[33] Lynch was only able to take her characters back to radio because she had retained ownership of her show and the characters: "Before agreeing to appear on the Blue Network, [Lynch] turned down an offer from NBC, which wanted to co-own the show, 'possibly the only smart business move my mother has ever made,' her daughter wrote. Ms. Lynch retained ownership of 'Ethel and Albert' throughout her life."[34] But even though Berg and Lynch both owned the rights to their characters, this did not ensure longevity for either in television.

Berg's first effort to rebrand *The Goldbergs* as *Molly* in its final season and move it from the city to the suburbs was followed up by a second series called *Mrs. G. Goes to College* (CBS, 1961–1962), later renamed *The Gertrude Berg Show. Mrs. G. Goes to College* centered on a middle-aged woman with college-aged children who decides to finally earn her bachelor's degree.[35] If it sounds very much like "Molly Goes to University," that is because it was just that. Berg was an aging double, what Glenn Smith calls a "facsimile," of the beloved character that made her famous.[36] The concept of the show—a Jewish mama surrounded by a gang of educated teens—tried to combine Berg's approachable, ethnic star persona with the white-washed, youth-centric Hollywood product that television was becoming. It did not work, and Berg failed to fit into a vehicle tailored to her persona. With male-dominated, action-centric westerns like *Wagon Train* (NBC, ABC, 1957–1965), *Bonanza* (NBC, 1959–1973), and *Gunsmoke* (CBS, 1955–1975) topping the ratings in the 1961–62 television season, the sensibility of *The Goldbergs* was a relic, and Molly did not translate to the television's new production model or its audiences.[37] After the cancellation of *Mrs. G. Goes to College*, Gertrude Berg found her greatest critical acclaim as a stage actress, dying in her sixties in 1966.

The rest of the women in this study constructed careers predicated on versatility and flexibility. In spite of her strong voice and commitment to fighting for her intellectual properties, Phillips confronted professional hardships through the 1960s and '70s, her relationship to executives and networks growing increasingly fraught after her successful move to television in the 1950s. Phillips would create *Another World* (NBC, 1964–1999) with William J. Bell and *Love Is a Many Splendored Thing* (CBS, 1967–1973) on her own, only to leave the latter when the network refused to allow depictions of abortion and interracial romance.[38] She passed away in 1973 at the age of seventy-two.

Women story editors and women writers for shows like *Alfred Hitchcock Presents* had their own mixed record in television, some securely instituting themselves as contract players or power brokers within the Hollywood scene, others giving up on television altogether. Some women who began as secretaries and readers went on to longer careers in television writing and story development, such as Maria Little and Sonia Chernus, and Dorothy Hechtlinger returned to film; meanwhile, Alice Young pursued a career outside television, and the elusive Janet Wood bounced between media industries (chapter 5). The career paths of these clerical-creative professionals can be more challenging to reconstitute, as so much of the work they did was uncredited or done in an informal capacity. Freelance novelist and scriptwriter Marian Cockrell, together with her husband, Francis, collaborated throughout the 1960s, most famously on *Batman* (ABC, 1966–1968), and Helen Nielsen was a prolific writer in and outside of television in the postwar moment, but her last industry credit is a 1963 episode of *Kraft Mystery Theater*.[39] Charlotte Armstrong continued to write but not for television, her output including an opera libretto, and a posthumous novel *The Protégé* (1970).[40]

Joan Harrison left the industry on her own terms, but not without regret and disappointment. She retired to Europe in the 1970s with her husband, the writer Eric Ambler. While she did impressive work on *Journey into the Unknown* (ITV/ABC, 1968–69), a program her biographer calls "a daring experiment with gender and genre expectations that promised to be more radical than anything in the *Alfred Hitchcock* series," it was canceled after a single season.[41] Harrison's final film was an ABC Movie of the Week, *Love, Hate, Love* (1971), written by her husband, Eric Ambler. It received the network's highest ratings that week. Personal and professional obstacles converged: it was challenging to live with her husband, but even more difficult without him, and she would complain to friends: "I envy a talent that can work on its own—people like actors, directors, and producers can't!"[42] A 1960 profile published in the *New York Times* offers a glimpse of Harrison at her peak, while also gesturing toward a career that, like so many others, would slowly peter out. The reporter writes: "Occasionally, Miss Harrison reflects on the difficulties women face in television. Even in acting, the odds are against them these days. . . . But Miss Harrison has a suggestion: 'There is a great opening in television for a series about a woman private-eye.'"[43] It is only fitting that the figure of a female private eye would appeal to Harrison, the figure of a freethinking, problem-solving loner being an apt proxy for the persona she authored for herself in Hollywood decades prior.

The woman television writer did not disappear from television after the 1950s, but her presence in the cultural conversation waned. Feminist cultural and media studies of the 1980s and '90s, together with more contemporary conversations about gender discrimination in entertainment, has brought renewed popular and scholarly interest to the subject of industry politics and representation.[44] Putting the figure of the woman writer in her historical context, however, shows how little has changed, even in the wake of second- and third-wave feminist politics. The woman television writer still needs to explain herself and uses all the tools at her disposal—across press outlet and media platform—to do so.

SCRIPTED LIVES INTO THE TWENTY-FIRST CENTURY

In her 2015 memoir *Year of Yes: How to Dance It Out, Stand in the Sun and Be Your Own Person*, Shonda Rhimes co-opts the self-help memoir genre to burnish her brand as a nurturer-showrunner. *Year of Yes* echoes numerous moments in Irna Phillips's unpublished book that commingle her role as single mother with that of creative entrepreneur. Writes Rhimes: "In [my daughters'] world, mothers run companies. In their world, mothers run Thursday nights. In their world, mothers work. And I am a better mother for it."[45] She even explains that, as a shy person, she partially lives in the worlds that she creates:

> I create whole worlds in my head. . . . I birth babies, I end lives. I dance it out. I wear the white hat. I operate. I gladiate. I exonerate. I spin yarns and tell tall tales and sit around the campfire. I wrap myself in fiction. Fiction is my job. Fiction is it. Fiction is everything. Fiction is my *jam*.[46]

These tactics of self-invention—balancing softness and strength, living as joyously in her shows as her fans do, and articulating the relationship between writing and motherhood—are much the same as Phillips's and suggest that updated versions of the postwar cultural scripts persist into the present.

Rhimes, as a Black woman television showrunner and empire-builder, is under pressure to communicate a persona that elicits identification and affection, that, according to Eva Hageman, combines being relatable and being remarkable.[47] Rhimes does not demand privacy or elevate her writing to the level of highbrow art: rather, in a commencement address, she encourages graduates to "do" rather than to dream and jokes about her past aspirations to be the next Toni Morrison. She is a maestro of feeling, devoid of ego, a working mother who describes writing for television as "laying track for an oncoming speeding train."[48] (Or maybe, to hearken back to *I Love Lucy*, a candy assembly line?) Rhimes describes herself as retiring and camera-shy, preferring to speak only through her characters on-screen, but *Year of Yes* turned Shonda Rhimes into more of a public figure than she already was, inducting her into the order of her predecessor's scripted lives. By making herself and the work that she does legible to the public, Rhimes does what Phillips and Pugh and so many others in this volume sought to do more than fifty years prior: advance her career and combat any possible industrial obsolescence through writing herself into the story of television.

Postwar women writers sought to secure their spots in the television industry through forging public personas that sustained their careers and their scripts, and Rhimes demonstrates that not much has changed in this regard. Leading a scripted life is still a matter of institutional survival in the wake of industrial and cultural change. In their discussion of women in contemporary independent entertainment, Claire Perkins and Michele Schreiber assert that

> in making figures such as Lena Dunham, Jane Campion, Jill Soloway, Ava DuVernay, and Phoebe Waller-Bridge visible to a large, popular audience, conversations around women's television work also render the creators and their work accessible in an example of what Sarah Banet-Weiser calls popular feminism's "feedback loop." . . . The struggle to become at once visible and resistant is especially relevant to popular television feminisms of the current moment, as women practitioners negotiate how to pursue female-centric and feminist content within mainstream channels.[49]

The notion of a feminist "feedback loop" connects women television professionals past and present, their personas and also their shows. Being "accessible" means the shows and the women show-runners legitimize one another, together performing the cultural work of making women's media fun, entertaining, and open to all. But these figures must be both "visible and resistant," never fully succumbing to the institutional culture, always communicating their own indispensability to television while remaining relatable "outsiders" for their fans.

The history of women story editors like Janet Wood (chapter 5) demonstrates how quietly careers end, and in this era of nondisclosure agreements, scandal can be the vehicle through which historians recognize the specific obstacles facing women in entertainment. In 2004, Amaani Lyle, a Black writer's assistant at *Friends* (NBC, 1994–2004), sued the show's writers for creating a hostile environment in the writers' room with "graphic sexual and racist comments that left her too 'mortified to speak.'"[50] When the lawsuit was dismissed, Lyle quit the industry altogether, and her story resurfaced years later as the subject of #metoo-inspired public disapproval. Lyle's lawsuit resonates with the Golden Age of television anecdote of Lucille Kallen asking the men of *Your Show of Shows* to stop smoking cigars in the room—to no avail.[51] The "equality" Kallen and Lyle asked for, in both of these cases, required women to adapt to male behavior or, in Lyle's case, misbehavior. Their experiences together indicate why women writers might not stay in television—and why those reasons might be kept private. Lyle's failure in court in particular became "a tale that has been . . . whispered about across the industry in the decades since, as a reason to not speak up, not speak out, not seek help."[52]

Lawsuits provide one model of "resistant visibility," while exposés, like the one from *Designing Women* (CBS, 1986–1993) creator Linda Bloodworth Thomason, offer another. Thomason's career was derailed by CBS Chairman and CEO Les Moonves, while her column, titled "Not All Harassment Is Sexual," was published in the wake of the 2018 sexual harassment accusations against him and his subsequent resignation.[53] Thomason's essay looks at Moonves's aversion to her "aggressively feminist" scripts and the impunity with which he was able to tank her projects, despite her proven track record as a writer and showrunner.[54] According to Thomason, under Moonves's leadership, CBS, once known for its strong female vehicles such as *The Mary Tyler Moore Show*, *Rhoda* (CBS, 1974–1978), and *Murphy Brown* (CBS, 1988–1998), "loaded up the network with highly profitable, male-dominated series . . . mostly . . . presid[ing] over a plethora of macho crime shows featuring a virtual genocide of dead naked hotties in morgue drawers, with sadistic female autopsy reports." Thomason's confusion and misplaced efforts to make peace with Moonves, together with her lack of a public presence and fan base, resulted in her disappearance from the television scene for years. It is hard to read her exposé and not hear *Designing Women*'s Julia Sugarbaker (Dixie Carter) delivering one of her fiery, feminist rants; as Julia says about her pageant-winner sister, Suzanne, congeniality is "not something the women in my family aspire to anyway."[55] Thomason's career illustrates the veil under which industry decisions are made and enforced, as well as the relationship between industry gender politics and on-screen representation.

If behind-the-scenes struggles between male executives and female creatives are the subtext behind Julia Sugarbaker and her regular dressing-down of jerks and snobs, a corrupt entertainment industry trips over its own hypocrisy in the case of the *Good Girls Revolt* (Amazon, 2015–2016). This show, ironically enough, is based on a book by journalist Lynn Povich about sexual harassment and workplace discrimination in the 1960s. Sexism in journalism proved a fitting analogue to that in film and television; in a published conversation writer-editors Jessica Bennett and Jesse Ellison tell Povich: "There should also be absolutely no excuse for a lack of women writers on magazine pages—the old 'I don't get pitched,' 'I don't know any women writers,' is bullshit."[56]

Good Girls Revolt was canceled after a single season, allegedly by Amazon executive and workplace predator Roy Price. Amazon insisted that the show was canceled due to low ratings, but the network does not share these numbers with the public, and, according to the *Washington Post*, "[a]n outside firm that compiled audience estimates for Sony said the show was a hit, especially with women."[57] *The Hollywood Reporter* quotes *Good Girls Revolt* creator Dana Calvo's confusion and disappointment over the cancellation:

> "We were all so surprised because we were a hit," creator Dana Calvo tells *THR*, citing two metrics that Amazon execs told her they cared about: a high Rotten Tomatoes score (*Good Girls* has a 96 percent audience rating) and the ability to spur purchases on Amazon's retail arm: "Of the people driven from the entertainment sections to the commerce section, we were driving 55 percent, which was phenomenal."[58]

With the goal posts unclear and in flux, how can any writer succeed? Even before the Price accusations surfaced, *Good Girls Revolt* creator Dana Calvo had publicly stated that the executive "just doesn't care for the show. . . . He's representative of the Amazon culture in that he's just impenetrable."[59] This impenetrability is just good business, particularly if said business needs to protect bullies and sexists (or worse) at the helm. Decisions around network programming can be as much determined by personal taste as algorithmic intelligence, so writers' careers can be launched and ended in the course of a sour exchange or violent encounter, leaving no paper trail. As actress-writer Brit Marling wrote for the *Atlantic* about "gatekeeper" producer Harvey Weinstein, "Weinstein could also ensure that these women would never work again if they humiliated him. That's not just artistic or emotional exile—that's also economic exile."[60]

Women writers have begun to combat this secretive form of "exiling" not just through open letters and exposés like Thomason's but by making shows about the industry—by working, as *30 Rock*'s Jack Donaghy suggests, "in the system." The mockumentary *The Comeback* (HBO, 2005, 2014) follows washed-up television star Valerie Cherish (Lisa Kudrow) as she stages a comeback by taking a supporting role on a sitcom called *Room and Bored*. An antagonistic relationship emerges between Cherish and the show's head writer, Paulie G (Lance Barber), the show's woman writer, Gigi (Bayne Gibby) functioning as the tormented intermediary. Kudrow, a woman, and Michael Patrick King, a gay white man, cocreated the show and contributed to the scripts. King recounted to *Deadline* that the sadistic character of Paulie G encapsulates "exactly the kind of thing that's happening out there," that "thing" being a culture of misogyny and abuse.[61] Kudrow adds: "It was more reporting than anything else. We had five or six writers on that first season, and they all thought for sure they knew who Paulie G was, and it was a different person for each of them. It's a real type."[62]

The scripts of *The Comeback* are effective archives of reportage, accounts of industry toxicity verified by numerous writers' accounts and opinions. One of the major obstacles to studying film and television authorship is its collaborative nature: it is impossible to know which writer added what element, plus all the input from the producer, director, actors, or even the standards department. One remedy has been to scrutinize the "genius of the system" and read these texts as written by the industry rather than an indeterminate group of professionals.[63] But it makes sense to embrace the multi-vocal nature of a show like *The Comeback*, as it documents and collates a series of writers' firsthand experiences and secondhand horror stories. Labeling Paulie G as a "type" rather than a veiled depiction of a single, terrible person might at first seem like a defanged approach to predatory behavior in Hollywood: no one is outed, no individual held responsible. But by acknowledging that the industry is full of Paulie Gs, *The Comeback* implicates the entire industry through its dark, unflinching comedy.

Hollywood has a long history of strategic self-disclosure, of what Roland Barthes would call "inoculation": revealing some of the system's flaws or inequalities so as to mask its larger systemic failings.[64] *The Comeback* exposes the blatant ugliness of the "hate machine" that is the writers' room, while *Bojack Horseman* (Netflix, 2014–2019) strikes out at Hollywood's disingenuous commitment to gender equity. In an episode entitled "Bojack the Feminist," Flip McVicker, head writer of a fictional prestige drama, *Philbert*, tells the only woman writer on staff:

> Yeah, you're the lady who's gonna make my show less sexist, right? Here's what I need. Sit in my office, don't chew too loud, and collect your paycheck. Then, when the show comes out, people will see your name in the credits and say, "Huh, a lady worked on the show. Guess it's not sexist."

Having put her in her place, McVicker thanks her for "really making a difference." He has no interest in making his show or his writers' room less sexist, and neither do the producers or the network executives. Gigi on *The Comeback* is similarly sidelined, her contributions mocked or ignored completely. Both shows point to the entertainment industry's bad faith, as women writers are used as tokens and pawns in television's effort to present an enlightened face to the American public. Women writers provide cover while the industry remains as sexist and misogynist as ever.

So, how do we measure the progress of the entertainment industry in the wake of such deception and double-speak? The unknowability of careers gained and lost, of private conversations in executive boardrooms or hotel rooms—again, to borrow Allan Sekula's term of the "shadow archive"—makes it impossible to construct any totalizing or straightforward portrait of women in television. African American women filmmakers including Julie Dash (*Illusions*) and Cheryl Dunye (*The Watermelon Woman*) explored these issues in the 1980s and '90s, their films examining on how the irretrievable histories of Black women performers can only be reconstituted imaginatively through fictional means. To that end, television scripts and recordings must be instituted alongside official documents and personal accounts in assembling an incomplete history of women writers then and now. Through this synthesis of production culture and cultural production, a more revealing account of labor, culture, and gender comes into focus.

"DO WE CELEBRATE OR DO WE COMPLAIN?"
THE PROBLEM OF PROGRESS

So, as one colleague asked me, "Do we celebrate or do we complain?"[65] What does the data say? Aisha Harris has touted the "Shonda Effect" in reference to how Shonda Rhimes has inspired networks to hire more writers of color, reporting that a

> Writers' Guild of America report released earlier this year [2015] noted that staff employment for people of color actually *decreased* between the 2011–12 season and 2013–14 season, from a peak of 15.6 percent to 13.7 percent. The number of executive producers of color also decreased in those seasons, from 7.8 percent to 5.5 percent.[66]

Women writers of color are a percentage of that percentage, but the increase in writers from diverse backgrounds over time is not a consistently upward climb. The Writers' Guild of America has attempted to track these changes and turn them into metrics as early as the 1970s, in the wake of the second-wave feminist movement. According to a study conducted by the Writers' Guild in 1974, only 6.5 percent of all prime-time shows had had at least one female writer on staff. The next year, the Women's Committee at the Writers' Guild of America–West released a statistics report. Its preface reads: "We did not put statistics together to release numbers. We're concerned with what the statistics mean," the significance being that "television speaks to us and what it says shapes how we think."[67] With a sample set of 106 companies, only 45 had a documented record of hiring women writers. The report goes on to state that sometimes "where women are used they prove themselves as writers and are thus used again and again ... [while] some research indicates that where women are not given assignments, the companies involved take the position that they don't know women writers." The textbook catch-22 emerges: women writers need to have a job to get a job.

Of the three networks, ABC's female pool of writers led the pack at 10.8 percent, NBC and CBS trailing at 8.2 percent and 8.4 percent, respectively. This study looks at a range of programs, but the sample set is uneven, sometimes only referencing a single episode of a series. Story and teleplay credits are given equal weight in calculating percentage, though it is unclear whether those credits are compensated equally. *Marcus Welby, M.D.* (ABC, 1969–1976) has one of the highest percentages, with seventeen women writer credits with a sample set of twenty-nine episodes, but the series ran for much longer than twenty-nine episodes. Meanwhile, coauthorships and collaborations on these shows are neither explored nor annotated. As much as this report informs us as to the industry landscape at that moment, it also underscores the difficulties in gaining a full picture of women writers in the television industry at that or, indeed, at any other point in history.

Kate Fortmueller, in her study of labor unions in 1970s Hollywood, offers another possibility for why these metrics are so difficult to track: a lack of support from industry powerbrokers and even from within organized labor. Fortmueller describes the efforts of the women's committee working within the American Federation of Television and Radio Artists (AFTRA) as a "combative process in which dismissive institutions doomed women's committee efforts from the start ... [because] data collection of industry labor was often at odds with other union objectives."[68] By discouraging legitimate "accountability" with what data was accrued, the industry and the union thwarted any movement toward structural change.[69] Studio, agency, and union all benefitted from an indeterminate, hazy history, so it is easy to say that things were bad before and better now.

So perhaps the most meaningful element of the Statistics Report is that it documents the television industry's desire to broadcast progress—to audiences, and to aggrieved parties in the field seeking change. In 2015, the American Civil Liberties Union filed a petition objecting to the underrepresentation of women in Hollywood. This act brought attention to the issue of sexism in the film and television industries, legal experts arguing that "failure to hire" cases are difficult to prosecute for the very reason laid out in the Women's Committee Statistics Report—that Hollywood producers and executives hire who they know, in the process creating a self-perpetuating male-dominated environment. As one 1984 report from the American Women in Radio and Television and the United States Department of Labor reads: "The question arises whether sufficient numbers of women know about these jobs and are preparing to apply for them."[70] In the over seventy years since the advent of commercial television, the question of what qualifies and professionalizes the television writer—and how that might bear on the hiring and retention of women—is still being asked but not answered. Approaching this problem of progress historically eludes any straightforward schema. Is it more important for network executives to recruit more women writers or hire fewer but place them in greater positions of power? And how do intersectional feminist concerns factor into these metrics?

Scholars can contribute to the nurturing of meaningful, diverse representations on television. Media industry studies—as a methodology and as a body of literature—provides a persuasive logic for synthesizing the politics of production and television's logics and ethos. Thomas Schatz asks: "How do these industries systemically create both capital and culture? . . . What work is required to produce that content, and which work roles—and which works—are privileged in that process?"[71] These very questions demonstrate media industry studies' value to reading the woman television writer as a product of capital and culture, a producer of culture and a cultural text herself. Media industry studies further invites scholars and historians to recover lost histories through fictional artifacts that, in turn, archive their own cultural and institutional moment.

But historians' additional responsibility lies in setting up appropriate, ambitious benchmarks for progress and recognizing those continuities with the past without treating the industry as a static entity or a "monolith."[72] As television changes—its institutional formations, its technologies, its relationship to shifting audience blocs—writers must accommodate those shifts in their creative and scripted lives. Maya

Montanez Smukler explains in her study of women film directors in the 1970s that "progress [in the 1980s] was so miniscule it could be perceived as regressive."[73] That the widespread presence or cultural significance of the woman television writer would wane in the advent of second-wave feminism exemplifies "regressive progress" and points us toward those institutional forces that run alongside cultural ideologies. A more inclusive industry, then, asks that television networks be more accountable to the public and that historians and cultural critics hold them up to standards rooted in a documented past.

The proper course, then, can only be somewhere in between "celebration" and "complaint," since there is a longer history of women in television that must frame any conversations about a Golden Age of Television in the twenty-first century. And a purportedly conservative decade like the 1950s does not translate to a conservative industry culture, regardless of the on-screen representations circulating in that moment. Reading television through that lens not only limits our understanding of the medium but also that of the historical period from which these artifacts emerge. Classifying the 1950s as a "simpler time" imposes nostalgia on what was in fact America's conflicted postwar character and blocks off the avenues for more complex and revealing interpretations of its television. It is not enough to be better than before, especially if no one can agree what "before" looked like. Narratives of progress invite laziness and apathy from people in power, disproportionate gratitude for everyone else. By contextualizing and theorizing the needs that women have filled as authors from television's beginnings, broadcasting and media historians can better advocate for women writers in film and television today.

Notes

INTRODUCTION

1. Matthew Jacobson, Lecture for "Formation of Modern American Culture," Yale University, April 16, 2013. Credit to Najwa Mayer for this point.

2. Patricia Mellencamp, "Situation Comedy, Feminism, and Freud: Discourses of Gracie and Lucy," in *Studies in Entertainment: Critical Approaches to Mass Culture*, ed. Tania Modleski (Bloomington: Indiana University Press, 1986), 88.

3. Sianne Ngai, *Our Aesthetic Categories: Zany, Cute, Interesting* (Cambridge, MA: Harvard University Press, 2012), 181.

4. Miranda J. Banks, *The Writers: A History of American Screenwriters and Their Guild* (New Brunswick, NJ: Rutgers University Press, 2015), 127–128. See also Nina C. Liebman, *Living Room Lectures: The Fifties Family in Film and Television* (Austin: University of Texas, 1995), 48.

5. Tom Stempel, *Storytellers to the Nation: A History of American Television Writing* (Syracuse: Syracuse University Press, 1996), 47.

6. Madelyn Pugh Davis, with Bob Carroll Jr., *Laughing with Lucy: My Life with America's Leading Lady of Comedy* (Cincinnati, OH: Clerisy Press, 2007), 68–69.

7. Davis and Carroll, 147.

8. See Elaine Tyler May's term "domestic containment" in *Homeward Bound: American Families in the Cold War Era, 20th Anniversary Edition* (New York: Basic Books, 2008), here referring to the aesthetic and narrative containment of the situation comedy form.

9. Michael Z. Newman and Elana Levine, *Legitimating Television: Media Convergence and Cultural Status* (New York: Routledge, 2012), 38. Newman and Levine give historical context for the term "showrunner," explaining that the "'Showrunner' is not an official moniker. . . . It rarely if ever appears in trade papers or the popular press before the mid-1990s, and is seldom used even then. . . . By the middle of the 2000s the term was in wide use" (39).

10. Joy Press, *Stealing the Show: How Women Are Revolutionizing Television* (New York: Atria Books, 2018), 7.

11. Giuliana Muscio, "Clara, Ouida, Beulah, et al.: Women Screenwriters in American Silent Cinema," in *Reclaiming the Archive: Feminism and Film History*, ed. Vicki Callahan (Detroit: Wayne State University, 2010), 289–308. She writes: "Strangely enough, the lives of these women writers resembled the apparently contrived dramas they were writing. Powerful and professional as they might have been, their family life was often either quite traditional in roles, or full of secret dramas" (299). This resonates with the women writers of postwar television, for whom these "resemblances" were far from coincidental; their tactical constructions of public personas sustained their creative work, spoke to their proclaimed genre expertise, and communicated their ongoing value to the television industry.

12. Allison J. Waldman, "70 Years of '*Guiding Light*': Keeping a Bright 'Light' Shining," *TV Week*, January 22, 2007, accessed October 22, 2020, https://www.tvweek.com/in-depth/2007/01/70-years-of-guiding-light-keep/.

13. John Thornton Caldwell, *Production Culture: Industrial Reflexivity and Critical Practice in Film and Television* (Durham, NC: Duke University Press, 2008), 5.

14. This became possible only after the antitrust freeze on the film studios, achieved through the Paramount Decision of 1948, began to "thaw" as Hollywood moved toward independent production. For a thorough account of this, see Christopher Anderson, *Hollywood TV: The Studio System in the Fifties* (Austin: University of Texas Press, 1994).

15. Timothy Havens, Amanda D. Lotz, and Serra Tinic, "Critical Media Industry Studies: A Research Approach," *Communication, Culture & Critique* 2 (2009), 247.

16. See Anna McCarthy, *The Citizen Machine: Governing by Television in 1950s America* (New York: The New Press, 2010).

17. Lynn Spigel, *Make Room for TV: Television and the Family Ideal in Postwar America* (Chicago: University of Chicago Press, 1992), 32. See also David Farber and Beth Bailey, et al., *The Columbia Guide to America in the 1960s* (New York: Columbia University Press, 2001), 396.

18. Spigel, *Make Room*, 32.

19. Lawrence R. Samuel, *Brought to You By: Postwar Television Advertising and the American Dream* (Austin: University of Texas Press, 2001), 117–118.

20. Samuel, 238–239.

21. Spigel, *Make Room*, 122.

22. For more on television personalities and the role they played in forming the medium, see Mary Desjardins, *Recycled Stars: Female Film Stardom in the Age of Television and Video* (Durham, NC: Duke University Press, 2015).

See also Susan Murray, *Hitch Your Antenna to the Stars: Early Television and Broadcast Stardom* (New York: Routledge, 2006).

23. Horace Newcomb and Paul M. Hirsch, "Television as a Cultural Forum," in *Television: The Critical View*, 6th ed., ed. Horace Newcomb (New York: Oxford University Press, 2000), 564.

24. See Stuart Hall, "Encoding/decoding," in *Culture, Media, Language*, ed. Stuart Hall, Dorothy Hobson, Andrew Love, and Paul Willis (London: Hutchinson, 1980), 128–138.

25. Lynn Spigel, "The Suburban Home Companion: Television and the Neighborhood Ideal in Postwar America," in *Welcome to the Dreamhouse: Popular Media and Postwar Suburbs* (Durham, NC: Duke University Press, 2001), 52. For further context, see also Lynn Spigel and Denise Mann, eds., *Private Screenings: Television and the Female Consumer* (Minneapolis: University of Minnesota Press, 1992).

26. See May, *Homeward Bound*.

27. Allison McCracken, "Scary Women and Scarred Men: *Suspense*, Gender Trouble, and Postwar Change, 1942–1950," in *Radio Reader: Essays in the Cultural History of Radio*, ed. Michele Hilmes and Jason Loviglio (New York: Routledge, 2002), 193.

28. James T. Patterson, *Grand Expectations: The United States, 1945–1974* (New York: Oxford University Press, 1996), 644. See also Lynn Spigel, "From Domestic Space to Outer Space: The 1960s Fantastic Family Sitcom," in Spigel, *Welcome to the Dreamhouse*, 111.

29. Davis and Carroll, *Laughing with Lucy*, 39.

30. Joanne Meyerowitz, "Introduction," in *Not June Cleaver: Women and Gender in Postwar America, 1945–1960*, ed. Joanne Meyerowitz (Philadelphia: Temple University Press, 1994), 1–2.

31. Meyerowitz, 2.

32. Lizabeth Cohen, *A Consumer's Republic: The Politics of Mass Consumption in Postwar America* (New York: Vintage, 2008), 147, 148.

33. Elizabeth M. Matelski, *Reducing Bodies: Mass Culture and the Female Figure in Postwar America* (New York: Routledge, 2017), 17.

34. For more on this, see Barbara Ehrenreich, *The Hearts of Men: American Dreams and the Flight from Commitment* (New York: Anchor Books, 1983).

35. Erika Endrijonas, "Processed Foods from Scratch: Cooking for a Family in the 1950s," in *Kitchen Culture in America*, ed. Sherrie A. Inness (Philadelphia: University of Pennsylvania Press, 2000), 159, 167.

36. Jessica Weiss, "She Also Cooks: Gender, Domesticity, and Public Life in Oakland, California, 1957–1959," in Inness, *Kitchen Culture*, 215.

37. Spigel, "Suburban Home Companion," 48.

38. Spigel, 43.

39. Kathleen Anne McHugh, *American Domesticity: From How-To Manual to Hollywood Melodrama* (New York: Oxford University Press, 1999), 62.

40. Stephanie Coontz, *A Strange Stirring: "The Feminine Mystique" and American Women at the Dawn of the 1960s* (New York: Basic Books, 2011), xxiii.

41. See Daniel Horowitz, *Betty Friedan and the Making of "The Feminine Mystique"* (Amherst: University of Massachusetts Press, 1998), whose book

documents how Friedan's "intellectual and political circles" (21) were the breeding ground for the suburban second-wave feminism of *The Feminine Mystique*.

42. Betty Friedan, *The Feminine Mystique* (New York: W.W. Norton & Company, 1997), 108–109.

43. For more on the women of *Donna Reed*, see Joanne Morreale, *The Donna Reed Show* (Detroit: Wayne State University Press, 2012).

44. McHugh, *American Domesticity*, 6.

45. For more on the term *lifestyle feminism*, see Bonnie J. Dow, *Prime-Time Feminism: Television, Media Culture, and the Women's Movement Since 1970* (Philadelphia: University of Pennsylvania Press, 1996).

46. Maggie Hennefeld, *Specters of Slapstick and Silent Film Comediennes* (New York: Columbia University Press, 2018), 69.

47. This point will be explored at length in the book's conclusion.

48. Selma Diamond is discussed further in chapter 1.

49. Erik Barnouw, *Tube of Plenty: The Evolution of American Television*, 2nd ed. (New York: Oxford University Press, 1990), 213.

50. See Anderson, *Hollywood TV*, 257.

51. Anderson, 266.

52. See Erin Hill, *Never Done: A History of Women's Work in Media Production* (New Brunswick, NJ: Rutgers University Press, 2016). See also J. E. Smythe, *Nobody's Girl Friday: The Women Who Ran Hollywood* (New York: Oxford University Press, 2018). Further discussion of this history can be found in chapters 1 and 5.

53. Hennefeld, *Specters of Slapstick*, 55.

CHAPTER 1. CRAFTSMEN AND WORK WIVES

1. Katherine Laure, "TV Scripting 'For Men Only'?" *Variety*, September 12, 1956, 24.

2. Blanche Gaines, "No Tabu vs. Femme Scribes," *Variety*, September 19, 1956, 68.

3. Jon Kraszewski, *The New Entrepreneurs: An Institutional History of Television Anthology Writers* (Middletown, CT: Wesleyan University Press, 2010), 2.

4. Liz Clarke, "'No Accident of Good Fortune': Autobiographies and Personal Memoirs as Historical Documents in Screenwriting History," *Feminist Media Histories* 2, no. 1 (2016), 47.

5. Michele Hilmes writes similarly of radio historiography: "However, a tendency exists to accept as a given . . . [that] women are the audience, men the producers." See Michele Hilmes, *Radio Voices: American Broadcasting, 1922–1952* (Minneapolis: University of Minnesota Press, 1997), 131.

6. Jane Gaines writes that "no one knew that motion pictures would become big business. This was not yet a significant industry and with so little at stake (so little power, so little capital), much more could be entrusted to women." See Jane Gaines, "Of Cabbages and Authors," in *Feminist Reader in Early Cinema*, ed. Jennifer M. Bean and Diane Negra (Durham, NC: Duke University Press, 2002), 105.

7. Erin Hill, *Never Done: A History of Women's Work in Media Production* (New Brunswick, NJ: Rutgers University Press, 2016), 17.

8. Hill, 10.

9. Donna L. Halper, *Invisible Stars: A Social History of Women in Broadcasting* (Armonk, NY: M.E. Sharpe, 2001), 19.

10. Hilmes, *Radio Voices*, 132–133.

11. See Hilmes, xx. See also Allison McCracken, "Scary Women and Scarred Men: *Suspense*, Gender Trouble, and Postwar Change, 1942–1950," in *Radio Reader: Essays in the Cultural History of Radio*, ed. Michele Hilmes and Jason Loviglio (New York: Routledge, 2002), 184.

12. Hilmes, *Radio* Voices, 270.

13. Giuliana Muscio, "Clara, Ouida, Beulah, et al.: Women Screenwriters in American Silent Cinema," in *Reclaiming the Archive: Feminism and Film History*, ed. Vicki Callahan (Detroit: Wayne State University, 2010), 304.

14. Hill, *Never Done*, 10.

15. Hill, 10

16. Anne Morey, "Would You Be Ashamed to Let Them See What You Have Written? The Gendering of Photoplaywrights, 1913–1923," *Tulsa Studies in Women's Literature* 17, no. 1 (Spring 1998), 84.

17. Anne Morey, "Elinor Glyn as Hollywood Labourer," *Film History: An International Journal* 18, no. 2 (2006), 113.

18. Shelley Stamp, *Lois Weber in Early Hollywood* (Berkeley: University of California Press, 2015), 7.

19. Mark Garrett Cooper, *Universal Women: Filmmaking and Institutional Change in Early Hollywood* (Urbana: University of Illinois Press, 2010), 124.

20. Cooper, 181.

21. Cooper, 181.

22. A later historiographic response came when women writers from the silent film era published memoirs, Liz Clarke offering the example of Lenore Coffee, who framed her success in terms of it being "part innate talent and part training." See Clarke, "'No Accident,'" 49.

23. Hill, *Never Done*, 5–6: "Women were never absent from film history; they often simply weren't documented as part of it because they did 'women's work.' . . . [But] the stakes—pay, credit, workplace identity, and so forth— are too high to leave the past in the past." And in *Nobody's Girl Friday: The Women Who Ran Hollywood*, J. E. Smyth reorients Hollywood history through a counting and recounting of women's labor: managerial, creative, and emotional. See J. E. Smyth, *Nobody's Girl Friday: The Women Who Ran Hollywood* (New York: Oxford University Press, 2018).

24. Hill, *Never Done*, 128.

25. Catherine Martin, "In Their Own Little Corner: The Gendered Sidelining of NBC's Information Department," *Journal of Radio & Audio Media* 26, no. 1 (2019), 92.

26. Martin, 96.

27. This is discussed at length in Martin, and is analyzed further in chapter 5, which focuses on the writerly work of women story editors in early television.

28. See more on this in the conclusion.

29. See the Writers' Guild of America Records, 1921–1954, hereafter WGF.

30. *Studio One* [video]: Bette Stein Chichon, June 8, 1987. Paley Center for Media, NYC.

31. Box 383, Folder 22, NBC Papers, State Historical Society of Wisconsin, Madison, hereafter UWM. For more on the rise of talent agencies in 1950s Hollywood, see Denise Mann, *Hollywood Independents: The Postwar Talent Takeover* (Minneapolis: University of Minnesota Press, 2008). See also Tom Kemper, *Hidden Talent: The Emergence of Hollywood Agents* (Berkeley: University of California Press, 2010).

32. See Lois Jacoby, "The New York Market," in *TV and Screenwriting*, ed. Lola Goelet Yoakem (Berkeley: University of California Press, 1958), 114. Unlike radio, with its roots in amateur production and communication, television was divided between public and commercial interests from its beginnings. See Anna McCarthy, *The Citizen Machine: Governing by Television in 1950s America* (New York: New York University Press, 2010).

33. Jacoby, "The New York Market," 114.

34. Tom Stempel, *Storytellers to the Nation: A History of American Television Writing* (Syracuse, NY: Syracuse University Press, 1996), 45, 44.

35. See more in chapter 3.

36. For a comprehensive history of Black radio, see William Barlow, *Voice Over: The Making of Black Radio* (Philadelphia: Temple University Press, 1999). Black radio experienced a renaissance with the advent of television. Hilmes writes that "the networks' abandonment of radio for television . . . would provide opportunities for black voices on the air previously untenable, as the dominant cultural focus shifted to television" (Hilmes, *Radio Voices*, 264).

37. Cy Wagner, "Radio: LOCAL PROGRAM: Reviews & Analyses—Here Comes Tomorrow," *Billboard*, October 25, 1947, 13.

38. "Negro Writer Sues NBC," *Philadelphia Tribune*, October 16, 1956, 5. See also Sonja D. Williams, *Word Warrior: Richard Durham, Radio, and Freedom* (Urbana: University of Illinois Press, 2015), 111.

39. For more on this, see Bob Pondillo, "Racial Discourse and Censorship on NBC-TV, 1948–1960," *Journal of Popular Film and Television* 33, no. 2 (2005), 102–114.

40. "Negro Talent Coming Into Own on TV, without Use of Stereotypes," *Variety*, May 3, 1950, 40.

41. The Television Writers of America was supplanted by the Screen Writers Guild, with branches on the East and West. See Miranda J. Banks, *The Writers: A History of American Screenwriters and Their Guild* (New Brunswick: Rutgers University Press, 2015), for a more complete account. The leadership of the TWA came under fire by labor reporter Victor Riesel, who wrote in 1953 about how the TWA "has some intriguing leaders who've been real close to outfits cited in congressional records as Communist" and in particular targeted the group's executive secretary, Joan Lacoeur, and her associate Harry Bridges, who "gave the orders for the original left wing invasion of Hollywood back in 1936." See Victor Riesel, "Inside Labor," *Salisbury Times* June 8, 1953, 8. See also Michelle Hilmes, "Never Ending Story: Authorship, Seriality, and the

Radio Writers Guild," in *A Companion to Media Authorship*, ed. Jonathan Gray, and Derek Johnson (Oxford: Wiley-Blackwell, 2013), 195.

42. Carol Stabile, *The Broadcast 41: Women and the Anti-Communist Blacklist* (Cambridge, MA: MIT Press, 2018), xxii, 2–3.

43. Stabile, 160.

44. Banks, *The Writers*, 151.

45. Banks, xix.

46. Cary O'Dell, "Gertrude Berg," in *Women Pioneers in Television: Biographies of Fifteen Industry Leaders* (Jefferson, NC: McFarland, Inc. 2009), 47.

47. Morey, "Would You Be Ashamed," 86.

48. Andrew Hoberek, *The Twilight of the Middle Class: Post-World War II American Fiction and White-Collar Work* (Princeton, NJ: Princeton University Press, 2005), 8.

49. Hoberek, 5, 21.

50. See Barbara Ehrenreich, *The Hearts of Men: American Dreams and the Flight from Commitment* (New York: Anchor, 1983).

51. Hoberek, *The Twilight of the Middle Class*, 17, 17–18. Emphasis my own.

52. Hoberek, 19.

53. Kraszewski, *The New Entrepreneurs*, 2.

54. Kraszewski, 1.

55. Kraszewski, 21. According to Kraszewski: "Accustomed to making $1,000 from a television script, Chayefsky earned over $200,000 from the film version of *Marty*" (19).

56. See Morey, "Would You Be Ashamed"; see also Clarke, "'No Accident'"; and Jordan Brower and Josh Glick, "The Art and Craft of the Screen: Louis Reeves Harrison and the Moving Picture World," *Historical Journal of Film, Radio and Television* 33, no. 4 (2013), 533–551. Brower and Glick write: "[Critic Louis Reeves Harrison's] theorization of the medium through the concept of 'craft' . . . crystallized the . . . promotion of skilled labor and technical innovation as a way of bolstering the industry's drive for respectability and expansion" (534).

57. See Margaret Weiss, *The TV Writer's Guide* (New York: Pellegrini & Cudahy, 1952), 6.

58. Thomas W. Phipps, "Consider the Case of the TV Writer," *Variety*, July 28, 1953, 40.

59. William Kendall Clarke, "Consider the Case of the TV Writer," 35.

60. Paddy Chayefsky, "Consider the Case of the TV Writer," 35.

61. Chayefsky, 40.

62. "Marty" (*Philco Television Playhouse*), directed by Delbert Mann (1953; New York: NBC, Criterion, 2009), DVD.

63. Lucille Kallen, "A Comedy Writer Remembers Her Favorite Years," *New York Times*, November 29, 1992, H5.

64. Amos Coggins, "What It Takes to Be a TV Gag Man," *Milwaukee Sentinel*, July 10, 1955, 14.

65. Bennett Cerf, "Try and Stop Me," *The Dispatch*, February 14, 1956, 9.

66. Coggins, "What It Takes."

67. Cerf, "Try and Stop Me."

68. Giuliana Muscio writes of women screenwriters that "the public discourse by the fan magazines . . . [was] in favor of a normalized representation of them as good professionals *and* solid wives, as if one implied the other" (Muscio, "Clara, Ouida, Beulah, et al.," 301).

69. Lynn Peril, *College Girls: Bluestockings, Sex Kittens, and Coeds, Then and Now* (New York: W.W. Norton & Company, 2006), 336.

70. Hilmes, *Radio Voices*, 144–45.

71. "Advertising & Agencies: Radio, TV, Other Advertising Media Reported Facing Greatest Challenge," *Broadcasting, Telecasting*, July 2, 1956, 29.

72. "Advertising & Agencies," 30. For more on market research in postwar America, see Lizabeth Cohen, *A Consumer's Republic* (New York: Vintage, 2004).

73. "Grey Adv. Lady Execs Explain 'Woman's Touch.'" *Broadcasting, Telecasting*, August 8, 1955, 29.

74. Anne Morey, "'Have You the Power?' The Palmer Photoplay Corporation and the Film Viewer/Author in the 1920s," *Film History* 9, no. 3 (1997), 301.

75. "Berle's Writers 12/01/53," accessed January 27, 2020, https://www.youtube.com/watch?v=pC4EbJDXHlc.

76. See Clarke, "'No Accident,'" on "creative labor."

77. Lynn Peril, *Swimming in the Steno Pool: A Retro Guide to Making It in the Office* (New York: W.W. Norton & Company, 2011), 128.

78. For more on this, see George Lipsitz, "The Meaning of Memory: Family, Class, and Ethnicity in Early Network Television," in *Time Passages: Collective Memory and American Popular Culture* (Minneapolis: University of Minnesota Press, 1990), 40.

79. Susan Murray, "Ethnic Masculinity and Early Television's Video Star," *Cinema Journal* 42, no. 1 (Fall 2002), 102.

80. Leonard Buder, "Television Rarity: Selma Diamond Is Writer of Comedy for Video," *New York Times*, September 20, 1953.

81. Buder, X15.

82. Selma Diamond, "Notes on TV," *Cue*, September 5, 1952. Box 54, Folder "Cue," Gertrude Berg Papers, Special Collections Research Center, Syracuse University Libraries, hereafter GBP. See also "Selma Diamond, 64, Is Dead: Comedy Writer and Actress," *New York Times*, May 14, 1985, B8.

83. Diamond, "Notes on TV."

84. Sid Shalit, "Girl Can't Warm Her Feet on Back of Comedy Script," *Daily News* (New York), December 28, 1955, 61.

85. Quinlan Miller, *Camp TV: Trans Gender Queer Sitcom History* (Durham, NC: Duke University Press, 2019), 98.

86. Miller, 98.

87. Diamond, "Notes on TV."

88. "A Leaf Out of the Book," February 3, 1955, Box 65, Folder 2, Steven H. Scheuer Collection of Television Program Scripts. Yale Collection of American Literature, Reinecke Rare Book and Manuscript Library. This script was broadcast on February 3, 1955 on CBS. See William Hawes, *Filmed Television Drama, 1952–1958* (Jefferson, NC: McFarland & Company, Inc., 2002), 24. For more on television's "polysemy," see John Fiske, "Television: Polysemy and Popularity," *Critical Studies in Mass Communication* 3, no. 4 (December 1986), 391–408. Fine and Friedkin are men, Gordon is a woman.

89. Patricia Bradley, *Maintaining Separate Spheres: The Career of Margaret Cousins* (paper presented at the Annual Meeting of the Association for Education in Journalism and Mass Communication, Memphis, 1985), 1.

90. Bradley, 4.

91. Bradley, 4.

92. A 1959 article from the *Orlando Sentinel* refers to Gordon as a "bachelor girl" writing for the sitcom *Peck's Bad Girl* (CBS, 1959), a sitcom about a naughty girl in the vein of *Dennis the Menace* (1959–1963) but sharing its title with a 1918 film starring Mabel Normand. According to the reporter, writing for the show made Gordon so "interested in children . . . [that] she's adopted a Korean orphan boy." This framing of Gordon's choice to adopt as inspired by her writing for a one-season sitcom is, admittedly, dubious. Still, it speaks to how Gordon's private life is being mobilized by the entertainment press to publicize *Peck's Bad Girl*. See The TV Scout, "'Truth' Still Attracts Liars," *Orlando Sentinel*, June 23, 1959, 7.

93. McCracken, "Scary Women and Scarred Men," 203.

94. For more on this, see chapters 2 and 6.

95. Jeanine Basinger, *A Woman's View: How Hollywood Spoke to Women 1930–1960* (New York: Alfred A. Knopf, 1993), 13.

96. Muscio, "Clara, Ouida, Beulah, et al.," 298.

97. Richard Irvin, *George Burns Television Productions, The Series and Pilots, 1950–1981* (Jefferson, NC: McFarland & Company, 2014), 75.

98. Irvin, 75.

99. Clarke, "'No Accident,'" 48, 49.

100. Allan Sekula, "The Body and the Archive," *October* 39 (Winter 1986), 10.

101. Hennefeld writes: "In order to write this new history, feminist historians have drawn on alternative forms of evidence and documentation. Personal memoirs, fan magazines, and scrapbooks, urban street maps, women's club minutes, and subtler affective and aesthetic traces have helped establish the prolific but excluded records of female participation in every aspect of silent film making." Maggie Hennefeld, *Specters of Slapstick and Silent Film Comediennes* (New York: New York: Columbia University Press, 2018), 55. See also Amelie Hastie, *Cupboards of Curiosity: Women, Recollection, and Film History* (Durham, NC: Duke University Press, 2007).

102. Banks, *The Writers*, 2.

103. John Thornton Caldwell, *Production Culture: Industrial Reflexivity and Critical Practice in Film and Television* (Durham, NC: Duke University Press, 2008), 7.

104. Madelyn Pugh Davis, with Bob Carroll Jr., *Laughing with Lucy: My Life with America's Leading Lady of Comedy* (Cincinnati, OH: Clerisy Press, 2007), 109.

105. Cary O'Dell, "Kinescope," in *The Encyclopedia of Television*, 2nd ed., ed. Horace Newcomb (New York: Routledge, 2013), 1263.

106. See Stefan Kanfer, *Ball of Fire: The Tumultuous Life and Comic Art of Lucille Ball* (London: Faber, 2003), 126. For more on researching archival television, see William Lafferty, "A Note on Alternative Sources of Television Programming," in *Private Screenings: Television and the Female Consumer*,

edited by Lynn Spigel and Denise Mann, 273–276. Minneapolis: University of Minnesota Press, 1992.

107. For more on this subject, see Alexander Dhoest, "Breaking Boundaries in Television Historiography: Historical Research and the Television Archive, University of Reading, 9 January 2004," *Screen* 45, no. 3 (Autumn, 2004), 248. Dhoest writes of how a host of factors have shaped television studies and history, including availability, accessibility, and even state-suppression.

108. Hennefeld, *Specters of Slapstick*, 55.

CHAPTER 2. "A SEA OF MALE INTERESTS"

1. Interview of Lucille Kallen by Sunny Parich, Archive of American Television, April 25, 1998, Ardsley, NY, https://interviews.televisionacademy.com/interviews/lucille-kallen#interview-clips. See Box 1, Folder 1, Lucille Kallen Papers, *T-Mss 2000-026, Billy Rose Theatre Collection, The New York Public Library for the Performing Arts, hereafter referred to as LKP.

2. Woody Allen and Larry Gelbart are often credited as writers for *Your Show of Shows* in popular histories, but in fact, both men wrote for Caesar only in his later show, *Caesar's Hour.*

3. "Sid Caesar—'This Is Your Story' with Carl Reiner and Howard Morris (Full Sketch)," YouTube, accessed January 22, 2020, https://www.youtube.com/watch?v=gNbT9Lf9xZo.

4. For an extended discussion of this particular sketch, see David Margolick, "Sid Caesar's Finest Sketch," *New Yorker*, February 14, 2014.

5. Sid Caesar, *Caesar's Hours: My Life in Comedy, with Love and Laughter* (New York: Public Affairs, 2003), 131.

6. Caesar, 97–99.

7. John Thornton Caldwell, *Production Culture: Industrial Reflexivity and Critical Practice in Film and Television* (Durham, NC: Duke University Press, 2008), 216.

8. Felicia D. Henderson, "The Culture Behind Closed Doors: Issues of Gender and Race in the Writers' Room," *Cinema Journal* 50, no. 2 (Winter 2011), 146.

9. Lucille Kallen, "A Comedy Writer Remembers Her Favorite Years," *New York Times*, November 29, 1992, H5. Box 40, Folder 5, LKP.

10. For more on "unruly" comediennes, see Kathleen Rowe, *The Unruly Woman: Gender and the Genres of Laughter* (Austin: University of Texas Press, 1995).

11. "Letter from Mel Tolkin to Rowland (February 17, 1989)," Box 2, Folder 3, LKP.

12. "Finding Aid," LKP.

13. Parich, Interview of Lucille Kallen.

14. Parich.

15. Martha Schmoyer LoMonaco, *Every Day a Broadway Revue* (New York: Greenwood Press, 1992), ix.

16. Tamiment Playhouse Archives interview [Lucille Kallen]," conducted by Andrew Horn, April 27, 1982. Box 40, Folder 26, LKP.

17. See Playbills, Tamiment Playhouse Records, TAM 107, Box 1, Folder 11.

18. The program was reconceived as *Your Show of Shows* when the Admiral Corporation decided to put more money into television set production and less into program sponsorship. Mary McCarty, not Coca, was the co-lead of *Admiral Broadway Review*, as evidenced by the image in Figure 1. For more, see LoMonaco, *Every Day a Broadway Revue*. In *The Admiral Broadway Revue*, Mary McCarty was the second lead, but she did not make the jump to *Your Show of Shows*. Kallen attributes this change to the electric chemistry that quickly developed between Sid Caesar and Imogene Coca. See also Parich, Interview of Lucille Kallen.

19. Michael Tueth, *Laughter in the Living Room: Television Comedy and the American Home Audience* (New York: Peter Lang, 2005), 29.

20. Tom Stempel, *Storytellers to the Nation: A History of American Television Writing* (Syracuse, NY: Syracuse University Press, 1996), 36. See also "'A Broadway Revue Every Week'—Liebman, Max" *Theatre Arts* May 1953, Tamiment Playhouse Records; TAM 107; Box 7, Folder 16.

21. Tamiment Playhouse Archives interview with Lucille Kallen, LKP.

22. LoMonaco, *Every Day a Broadway Revue*, 112.

23. Karin Adir writes: "Opera was another target for Coca's uncanny sense of satire. She was able to send up the imperious nature of the opera diva with the raising of an eyebrow." See Karen Adir, "Imogene Coca," in *The Great Clowns of American* Television (Jefferson, NC: McFarland & Company, Inc. 1988), 101. See also: *Your Show of Shows* script (March 11, 1950), Box 1, Folder 3, Sid Caesar Papers, Manuscript Division, Library of Congress, Washington, D.C., hereafter referred to as SCP.

24. LoMonaco, *Every Day a Broadway Revue*, 12.

25. Susan King, "Comedy Writer-Actor Carl Reiner's Life of Laughter," *Los Angeles Times*, March 29, 2014, http://articles.latimes.com/2014/mar/29/entertainment/la-et-st-ca-carl-reiner-classic-hollywood-20140330. See also Allan Neuwirth, *They'll Never Put That on the Air* (New York: Allworth Press, 2006).

26. In some versions of this story, she is pregnant (see Henderson, "The Culture Behind Closed Doors"), which is why she is feeling sick. In Kallen's telling (American Archive of Television oral history), she suffers from allergies. Details aside, the anecdote has taken on great weight in the history, as it spatializes the contested—and gendered—territory of the writers' room. See also Kallen, "A Comedy Writer."

27. Parich, Interview of Lucille Kallen.

28. Henderson, "The Culture Behind Closed Doors," 150.

29. Carl Reiner, "Let's Put Another Laugh in Here . . . ," *Travel and Leisure Magazine*, March 1974. See also: James Robert Parrish, *It's Good to Be the King* (Hoboken, NJ: John Wiley & Sons, Inc., 2008), 101.

30. "Interview with Larry Gelbart." *The Sid Caesar Collection: The Buried Treasures/The Lost Episodes: Volume 1 The Impact of Sid*, DVD, 2004.

31. Caesar, *Caesar's Hours*, 124.

32. Allan Wallach, "The Show Behind 'Your Show of Shows,'" *New York Newsday*, November 22, 1993. Box 2, Folder 9, LKP.

33. Max Wilk, *The Golden Age of Television: Notes from the Survivors* (Chicago: Silver Spring Press, 1999), 170.

34. Caesar, *Caesar's Hours*, 99–100.

35. Jeff Kisseloff, *The Box: An Oral History of Television, 1920–1961* (New York: Viking, 1995), 312.

36. *Caesar's Writers*, dir. Michael Hirsh, VHS, Plus 8 Video & Michael Hirsh Productions, 1996.

37. *Caesar's Writers*.

38. Stempel, *Storytellers to the Nation*, 37.

39. Stempel, 37.

40. See "Mel Brooks: 'I'm an EGOT'; I Don't Need Anymore," May 20, 2013, accessed October 24, 2020, https://www.wbur.org/npr/182609040/mel-brooks-i-m-an-egot-so-i-don-t-need-any-more?ft=3&f=182609040. See also "Mel Brooks: Timeline: 2000 Years of Mel Brooks," February 1, 2013, http://www.pbs.org/wnet/americanmasters/episodes/mel-brooks/timeline-2000-years-of-mel-brooks/2593/.

41. Kisseloff, *The Box*, 312.

42. Ted Sennett, *Your Show of Shows*, rev. ed. (New York: Applause Theater & Cinema Books, 2002), 48.

43. For literature on the fool who "though imbecile . . . is expected to say profound things" (Empson, 178), see William Empson, "Fool in *Lear*," *The Sewanee Review* (Spring, 1949): 177–214. For more on the Jewish incarnation of the fool "stock figure," see also Solveig Eggerz, "Stock Figures in Jewish Folklore: Universal Yet Uniquely Jewish," *The American Council for Judaism*, Summer 1996, http://www.acjna.org/acjna/articles_detail.aspx?id=72.

44. *The Sid Caesar Collection: The Fan Favorites [The Professor and Other Clowns]* (Beverly Hills, CA: SidVid, LLC, 2001), DVD.

45. *The Sid Caesar Collection*.

46. David Margolick, "The Deep Jewish Roots of Television's Caesar," *Tablet*, February 14, 2014, http://www.tabletmag.com/jewish-arts-and-culture/163060/sid-caesar-show-of-shows.

47. See also Mel Brooks' and Carl Reiner's later comic creation, the Thousand-Year-Old Man routine, born from this bit on *Show*. This shtick offers a joking homage to Western civilization along the lines of Brooks's later film *History of the World Part I* (1981).

48. Parich, Interview of Lucille Kallen.

49. Kallen, "A Comedy Writer Remembers Her Favorite Years."

50. Kallen.

51. Caesar, *Caesar's Hours*, 125.

52. Kallen, "A Comedy Writer Remembers Her Favorite Years."

53. Kallen.

54. Margalit Fox, "Lucille Kallen, 76, Writer for 'Show of Shows,' Dies," *New York Times*, January 21, 1999, http://www.nytimes.com/1999/01/21/arts/lucille-kallen-76-writer-for-show-of-shows-dies.html.

55. *Caesar's Writers*, VHS.

56. Fox, "Lucille Kallen."

57. Kallen, "A Comedy Writer Remembers Her Favorite Years."

58. Kisseloff, *The Box*, 312.

59. Kallen, "A Comedy Writer Remembers Her Favorite Years."

60. Kallen.

61. Kallen.

62. Parrish, *It's Good to Be the King*, 71. See also *Caesar's Writers*, VHS.

63. Kisseloff, *The Box*, 310.

64. Caesar, *Caesar's Hours*, 131.

65. Letter from Mel Tolkin to the WGA Journal, February 17, 1989, Box 2, Folder 3, LKP.

66. Letter from Mel Tolkin.

67. Though certainly all the writers contributed in some respect, Tolkin would correspond with Kallen years later and complain that Carl Reiner took too much credit for the Hickenloopers: "He . . . [took] more credit for writing that Show than he should have. Like, the ideas for the domestic sketches were based also on Carl and Estelle." See Letter from Tolkin, January 19, 1987, Box 2, Folder 3, LKP.

68. Parich, Interview of Lucille Kallen. According to Kallen: "The humor sprang from our own lives. Everybody was married. . . . Brooks was married the last. But that's where we got our material. I, maybe more than anybody else, felt secure in writing about people doing ordinary things, because my humor worked in that context. . . . We latched onto the things that everybody experiences."

69. Arnold Mann, "Mel Tolkin: Still Learning from Life," *Emmy Magazine* 7, no. 1 (Jan/Feb 1985). Box 6, Folder 45, Tamiment Playhouse Records, New York University.

70. Parich, Interview of Lucille Kallen. All of the writers on *Show* attested to the "universality" of their comedy, though by "universal," what they meant was a mass appeal directed toward a middle-class viewer who could afford a television and was attuned to both high and low cultural references. Kallen's description makes that more clear than other accounts.

71. Elaine Tyler May, *Homeward Bound: American Families in the Cold War Era*, 20th Anniversary Edition (New York: Basic Books, 1990), 86.

72. Kisseloff, *The Box*, 309.

73. Parich, Interview of Lucille Kallen. According to Kallen: "The humor sprang from our own lives. . . . I, maybe more than anybody else, felt secure in writing about people doing ordinary things, because my humor worked in that context. . . . We latched onto the things that everybody experiences."

74. Parich.

75. Full episodes of *Your Show of Shows* are rare, but they can be pieced together through DVD compilations, museums like the Paley Center, and online archives. See "SID CAESAR: Chinese Food [THE HICKENLOOPERS]," YouTube, accessed January 31, 2020, http://www.youtube.com,/watch?v=kwx NiXMFCdE. This sketch can also be found in a 1976 rebroadcast compilation held at the Paley Center, Catalog ID T83:0360, Paley Center for Media, New York City.

76. From *The Sid Caesar Collection: The Fan Favorites [Love and Laughter]* (Beverly Hills, CA: SidVid, LLC., 2001), DVD.

77. Parich, Interview of Lucille Kallen.

78. "The Clock" sketch was broadcast on September 15, 1953. See *The Sid Caesar Collection: The Magic of Live TV* (Beverly Hills, CA: SidVid LLC, 2000), DVD.

79. Henri Bergson, "Laughter," in *Comedy*, ed. Wylie Sypher (Baltimore: Johns Hopkins University Press, 1956), 84, 73, 71.

80. See this reading of *I Love Lucy* in the book's introduction.

81. "Interview with Mel Brooks," *Sid Caesar Collection: Inside the Writers' Room* (Beverly Hills, CA: SidVid, LLC, 2000), DVD.

82. Fox, "Lucille Kallen."

83. Lucille Kallen, "Memo to Whoever Is Concerned," Box 40, Folder 4, LKP. While the memo is not dated, it is filed in the "Other Writings, 1969–1986" section of her papers, meaning she likely wrote this long after *Your Show of Shows*, her career in television over or close to its conclusion.

84. Parich, Interview of Lucille Kallen. Kallen would speak of how Caesar, as the star and a creative force in his own right, was both a "generator" and a "contributor" to the show's comedy.

85. Kisseloff, *The Box*, 309–10. See also the 1980 personal correspondence with Coca in Box 1, Folder 9, LKP.

86. Parich, Interview of Lucille Kallen.

87. Adir, "Imogene Coca," 93.

88. See Lauren Berlant, *The Female Complaint: The Unfinished Business of Sentimentality in American Culture* (Durham, NC: Duke University Press, 2008).

89. "Saturday Night Revue: *Your Show of Shows*," March 25, 1950. Paley Center for Media, New York City.

90. Katherine Parkin, "Campbell's Soup and the Long Shelf Life of Traditional Gender Roles," in *Kitchen Culture in America*, edited by Sherrie A. Inness (Philadelphia: University of Pennsylvania Press, 2000), 52.

91. See May, *Homeward Bound*, where she argues that the "containment" of women to homemaking duties was part of the larger "containment" project of Cold War America (see introduction).

92. Philip Young, "The Mother of Us All: Pocahontas Reconsidered," *Kenyon Review* 24, no. 3 (Summer 1962): 415.

93. Young, 415.

94. Elizabeth M. Matelski, *Reducing Bodies: Mass Culture and the Female Figure in Postwar America* (New York: Routledge, 2017), 1.

95. Ronie-Richele Garcia-Johnson, "Imogene Coca," in *Notable Hispanic American Women*, ed. Diane Telgen and Jim Kamp (Detroit: Gale Research Inc., 1993), 102. See also Parich, Interview of Lucille Kallen.

96. See Sid Caesar Papers, Manuscript Division, Library of Congress, Washington, D.C. In the Library of Congress version (entitled "Best Dressed Woman," January 6, 1951, Box 3, Folder 8, SCP). This sketch may be adapted from Tamiment sketches "The Well-Dressed Woman" or "Glamour," solo numbers for Coca. For the 1949 Tamiment Playhouse season, the revues were written collaboratively by Tolkin, Kallen, and Liebman (see "Playbills 1949," Tamiment Playhouse Records; TAM 107; Box 1; Folder 11; Tamiment Library/Robert F. Wagner Labor Archives). See also "Best Dressed Woman [script]," Box 561, Folder 7, NBC Papers, Wisconsin Historical Society at the University of Wisconsin Madison, hereafter UWM.

97. Sennett, *Your Show of Shows*, 67.

98. See Judith Butler, *Gender Trouble* (New York: Routledge, 2007). See also Mary Ann Doane, "Film and the Masquerade: Theorizing the Female Spectator," *Screen* 23, nos. 3–4 (1982): 74–88.

99. Sennett, *Your Show of Shows*, 66–67.

100. "*Your Show of Shows* (PROGRAM #6, EXCERPT)(TV)," April 1, 1950, Paley Center Media.

101. Roland Barthes, "Striptease," in *Mythologies*, trans. Richard Howard and Annette Lavers (New York: Hill and Wang, 2012), 167.

102. Barthes, 167.

103. Barthes, 165.

104. *Your Show of Shows* script (December 30, 1950), Box 3, SCP. "Yours, Only Yours" is similar to Tolkin's musical sketch, "Mon Amour Americaine," in which Coca is instructed to play the vamp in the vein of Marlene Dietrich in *The Blue Angel*. See "Mon Amour Americaine: Coca Single," *Your Show of Shows* #24 (November 19, 1950), Box 3, SCP.

105. Pete Barnum, "Subject: Imogene Coca," May 21, 1954, Box 380, Folder 26, NBC Papers, UWM.

106. Kisseloff, *The Box*, 315.

107. "*The Imogene Coca Show* (TV)," February 5, 1955, Paley Center, New York City, NY.

108. Jessamyn Neuhaus, "Women and Cooking in Marital Sex Manuals," in *Kitchen Culture in America*, ed. Sherrie A. Inness (Philadelphia: University of Pennsylvania Press, 2000), 107.

109. Lucille Kallen, Max Wilk, and Ernest Kinoy, Script dated [1954?], "The Imogene Coca Show" folder, NBC Papers, UWM.

110. Adir, "Imogene Coca," 105.

111. Parrish, *It's Good to Be the King*, 96.

112. Kisseloff, *The Box*, 315.

113. Adir, "Imogene Coca," 105.

114. See the network memos 1954–55, Box 380, Folder 26, NBC Papers, UWM. See also Kisseloff, *The Box*, 314.

115. Kisseloff, *The Box*, 310–311.

116. See Parrish, *It's Good to Be the King*, 48. Brooks acknowledges his youthful arrogance in *Caesar's Writers* and admits that *Your Show of Shows* producer Max Liebman hated him for good reasons. See also Parich, Interview of Lucille Kallen.

117. Lynn Peril, *Swimming in the Steno Pool: A Retro Guide to Making It in the Office* (New York: W.W. Norton, 2011), 19.

118. Peril, *Swimming*, 19. See also Parrish, *It's Good to Be the King*, 97. After a mass exodus of talent from *The Imogene Coca Show*, including Kallen, Brooks became the show's head writer. Brooks's biographer Patrick McGilligan writes that Brooks "couldn't save the show, not with his lateness and absences and impractical suggestions," adding, "He was neither comfortable nor adept at writing for women" (121, 143). See Patrick McGilligan, *Funny Man: Mel Brooks* (New York: Harper, 2019).

119. "Letter from Mel Tolkin (January 19, 1987)."

120. Kisseloff, *The Box*, 310.

121. Glenn Collins, "Mother Lode of TV Comedy Is Found in Forgotten Closet," *New York Times*, November 14, 2000, accessed October 24, 2020, http://www.nytimes.com/2000/11/14/nyregion/mother-lode-of-tv-comedy-is -found-in-forgotten-closet.html?pagewanted=all.

122. Walter Winchell, "Talk of the Town," *Cincinnati Enquirer* November 14, 1955, 8.

123. "The Imogene Coca Show, June 18, 1955," Box 380, Folder 26, NBC Papers, UWM.

CHAPTER 3. BERG, LYNCH, AND THE "SMALL SITUATION"

1. Robert Kleiner, "Robert Q. for Human Humor," *Times* (Cumberland, MD), June 27, 1953, Scrapbook, Package 3, Peg Lynch papers, Coll 066, Special Collections & University Archives, University of Oregon Libraries, Eugene, Oregon, hereafter referred to as PLP.

2. Lauren Bratslavsky has similarly described *The Goldbergs* as a companion to *Ethel and Albert* in her presentation, "Recovered Visual Records and Expanded Histories: How *Ethel and Albert* Broadens Sitcom History," Society of Cinema and Media Studies Annual Conference, March 28, 2015.

3. Berg's *The Goldbergs* played on both radio and television in 1949, while Lynch's *Ethel and Albert* seems to have moved from radio to television. See Thomas Doherty, *Cold War, Cool Medium: Television, McCarthyism, and American Culture* (New York: Columbia University Press, 2003), 39.

4. Donna Halper, "Speaking for Themselves: How Radio Brought Women into the Public Sphere," in *Radio Cultures: The Sound Medium in American Life*, ed. Michael C. Keith (New York: Peter Lang, 2008), 91.

5. *Star Dust* (WAAT) radio interview with Gertrude Berg, hosted by Jay Stanley, May 26, 1940, Box 51, Gertrude Berg Papers, Special Collections Research Center, Syracuse University Libraries, Syracuse, NY, hereafter referred to as GBP.

6. Miranda J. Banks, "*I Love Lucy*: The Writer-Producer," in *How to Watch Television* (New York: New York University Press, 2013), 244–252.

7. Banks, 245.

8. Cary O'Dell, "Gertrude Berg," in *Women Pioneers in Television* (Jefferson, NC: McFarland & Company, 1997), 45.

9. See Margaret McManus, "Up Before Sunrise, in Bed by 8 p.m. That's Peg Lynch," *Boston Sunday Globe*, June 12, 1955, 75.

10. Vincent Brook, "The Americanization of Molly: How Mid-Fifties TV Homogenized *The Goldbergs* (and Got 'Berg-larized' in the Process)," *Cinema Journal* 38, no. 4 (Summer 1999), 45.

11. Bruce Weber, "Peg Lynch, Writer and Star of Early Situation Comedy, Dies at 98," *New York Times*, July 27, 2015. See also "*Ethel and Albert* C.V." Scrapbook, Package 3, PLP.

12. "*Ethel and Albert* C.V.," Scrapbook, PLP.

13. Weber, "Peg Lynch, Writer and Star."

14. Gertrude Berg, with Cheney Berg, *Molly and Me* (New York: McGraw-Hill Book Company, Inc., 1961), 160–161. See also Cary O'Dell, "*The Gold-*

bergs: Sammy Goes into the Army," Library of Congress: National Registry (2013), accessed October 26, 2020, https://www.loc.gov/static/programs/national -recording-preservation-board/documents/goldbergs.pdf.

15. Berg, *Molly and Me*, 160–161.

16. Berg, 154.

17. Berg, 155.

18. For more on Gertrude Berg and the assimilation politics of *The Gold-bergs*, see Brook, "The Americanization of Molly," 45.

19. O'Dell, "Gertrude Berg," 44.

20. Glenn D. Smith Jr., *"Something on My Own": Gertrude Berg and American Broadcasting, 1929–1956* (Syracuse, NY: Syracuse University Press, 2007), 7.

21. Michele Hilmes, *Radio Voices: American Broadcasting, 1922–1952* (Minneapolis: University of Minnesota Press, 1997), 271.

22. This point will be discussed further in chapter 4 on soap opera writer Irna Phillips.

23. For more on how sponsors impacted television narrative and form, see James Hay's "Rereading Early Television Advertising: When Wasn't the Ad the Story?," *Journal of Film and Video* 41, no. 1 (Spring, 1989): 4–20.

24. See Lynn Spigel, *Make Room for TV: Television and the Family Ideal in Postwar America* (Chicago: University of Chicago Press, 1992). See also Cynthia B. Meyers, "The Problems with Sponsorship in US Broadcasting, 1930s–1950s: Perspectives from the Advertising Industry," *Historical Journal of Film, Radio and Television* 31, no. 3 (September 2011): 355–372.

25. "September 5, 1949," *The Ultimate Goldbergs* (Los Angeles, CA: Shout Factory, 2011), DVD.

26. For more on this, see Spigel, *Make Room*, and Susan Murray, *Hitch Your Antennae to the Stars: Early Television and Broadcast Stardom* (New York: Routledge, 1999). See also Berg, *Molly and Me*: "Molly, when I first began to work with her, was an amalgam of my mother and my grandmother Czerny" (166). Finally, see George Lipsitz, "The Meaning of Memory: Family, Class, and Ethnicity in Early Network Television," in *Time Passages: Collective Memory and American Popular Culture* (Minneapolis: University of Minnesota Press, 1990, 39–75.

27. Spigel, *Make Room*, 9.

28. Spigel, 169. The italics are Spigel's.

29. Spigel, 169.

30. Hilmes, *Radio Voices*, 20.

31. "Housewives See Selves Reflected on TV," *News of Radio and Television*, May 6, 1954, Scrapbook, PLP.

32. "No Pencil by the Telephone" and "Free Tickets to a Movie Premiere," *Ethel and Albert* kinescopes, PLP.

33. Lynn Spigel, "Installing the Television Set," in *Private Screenings: Television and the Female Consumer*, edited by Lynn Spigel and Denise Mann (Minneapolis: University of Minnesota Press, 1992), 20, 9.

34. Spigel, 14.

35. See more on gendering the television writer in chapter 1.

36. Paddy Chayefsky, "Marty" (1953): Shooting Script (Alexandria, VA: Alexander Street Press, 2006), e-book, https://search.alexanderstreet.com/preview/work/bibliographic_entity%7Cbibliographic_details%7C3068174#search/marty; Peg Lynch, "Dutch Treat," in *Ethel and Albert Comedies* (New York: Samuel French, Inc., 1955).

37. Tom Stempel, *Storytellers to the Nation: A History of American Television Writing* (Syracuse, NY: Syracuse University Press, 1996), 49.

38. Kleiner, "Robert Q. for Human Humor."

39. See *Person to Person* (CBS, 1953–1961), June 4, 1954. See also Gertrude Berg, "Why I Hate the Term 'Soap Opera,'" *Everywoman's Magazine*, February 1945, 28–31. See also McManus, "Up Before Sunrise," and Kay Gardella, "TV: What's On? Peg Lynch in Focus . . . ," *New York Daily News*, February 2, 1954, 43.

40. "August 29, 1949 [episode]," *The Ultimate Goldbergs*, DVD.

41. Gertrude Berg, "TV and Molly," *Variety*, July 27, 1949, 46.

42. Banks, "*I Love Lucy*," 49.

43. O'Dell, "Gertrude Berg," 45.

44. Lipsitz, "The Meaning of Memory," 41.

45. "Lynch, Peg," *Current Biography: Who's News and Why* 17, no. 2 (February 1956), 34, "Biographical Material," PLP.

46. Morris Freedman, "From the American Scene: The Real Molly Goldberg," *Commentary*, April 1956, https://www.commentarymagazine.com/articles/morris-freedman/from-the-american-scene-the-real-molly-goldberg/.

47. As Halper writes, "Being a woman [in radio] was not seen as a detriment to stardom, nor was beauty a requirement the way it was for the movies or the stage." See Donna Halper, *Invisible Stars: A Social History of Women in Broadcasting* (Armonk, NY: M.E. Sharpe, 2001), 85.

48. Mary Desjardins, *Recycling Stars: Female Film Stardom in the Age of Television and Radio* (Durham, NC: Duke University Press, 2015), 28.

49. Murray, *Hitch Your Antennae*, 161.

50. Denise Mann, "The Spectacularization of Everyday Life: Recycling Hollywood Stars and Fans in Early Television Variety Shows," in *Private Screenings: Television and the Female Consumer*, edited by Lynn Spigel and Denise Mann (Minneapolis: University of Minnesota Press, 1992), 55.

51. For more on movie stars as gods, see Edgar Morin, *The Stars*, translated by Richard Howard (Minneapolis: University of Minnesota Press, 2005).

52. "Ethel is Jealous of Hildy," *Ethel and Albert* kinescope, PLP.

53. See Mary Ann Doane, "Film and the Masquerade: Theorizing the Female Spectator," *Screen* 23, nos. 3–4 (1982): 74–88.

54. "*The Goldbergs*, August 14, 1953," Box 128, Folder 3, Steven H. Scheuer Collection of Television Program Scripts, Yale Collection of American Literature, Beinecke Rare Book and Manuscript Library, hereafter SSC.

55. Elizabeth M. Matelski, *Reducing Bodies: Mass Culture and the Female Figure in Postwar America* (New York: Routledge, 2017), 79.

56. See *The Goldbergs* episode "The Milk Farm" (August 19, 1956).

57. Smith, "*Something on My Own*," 39.

58. Smith, 38.

59. Smith, 73.

60. Smith, 53.

61. "August 29, 1949 [episode]," *The Ultimate Goldbergs*, DVD.

62. "September 25, 1953 [episode] of *The Goldbergs*," Box 65, Folder 2, SSC.

63. See "TV Academy Presents Top Oscars to Alan Young and Molly Berg," *Boxoffice*, January 27, 1951, 39.

64. Val Adams, "The Lady of *Ethel and Albert*," *New York Times*, May 14, 1950, Scrapbook, PLP.

65. O'Dell, "Gertrude Berg," 46.

66. "Lynch, Peg," *Current Biography*, 35.

67. Ben Birnbaum, "Anything but Average," *Tablet*, January 18, 2008. For more on Jews and Hollywood blacklist, see Joseph Litvak, *The Un-Americans: Jews, the Blacklist, and Stoolpigeon Culture* (Durham, NC: Duke University Press, 2009).

68. See more on Jewishness in early television in chapter 1.

69. "Fixing Up the Den for Albert," *Ethel and Albert* kinescope, PLP.

70. Reginald Rose, "How Not to Write a TV Play," *Variety*, July 27, 1955.

71. James L. Baughman, *Same Time, Same Station: Creating American Television, 1948–1961* (Baltimore: Johns Hopkins University Press, 2007), 34.

72. Radio stations bought up and owned the television networks; film studios were prevented from buying television stations because of the anti-trust Paramount decision/FCC Freeze from 1948–1952. See William Boddy, *Fifties Television* (Urbana: University of Illinois Press, 1990) and Christopher Anderson, *Hollywood TV: The Studio System in the Fifties* (Austin: University of Texas Press, 1994).

73. Stempel, *Storytellers to the Nation*, 25.

74. "Walter Hart Resigns FTP; 'Shambles' and 'Miracle' Highlight His Letter," *Variety*, August 18, 1937, 78.

75. Walter Hart, "Proposals for the FTP," *New York Times*, September 19, 1937, 175.

76. "Walter Hart Dies; TV Producer was 67," *New York Times*, August 2, 1973, 38.

77. Erik Barnouw, *Tube of Plenty: The Evolution of American Television*, 2nd edition (New York: Oxford University Press, 1990), 160.

78. Walter Hart, "Directing for TV," *Theatre Arts*, February 1, 1951, 51–52.

79. Dorothy Manners, "Chatter in Hollywood," *Fort Worth Star-Telegram*, August 20, 1950, 31. See also Wayne Oliver, "Ethel and Albert Begin New True-to-Life Series Tonight," *Asbury Park* (NJ) *Press*, June 20, 1955, 8.

80. Walter Ames, "Hollywood Bowl Is Scene of Horace Heidt Show; Director Uses TV Techniques on Film," *Los Angeles Times*, September 17, 1950, 60.

81. Spigel, "Installing the Television Set," 25.

82. For more on the postwar "apartment plot," see Pamela Robertson Wojcik, *The Apartment Plot: Urban Living in American Film and Popular Culture, 1945–1975* (Durham, NC: Duke University Press, 2010).

83. Spigel, "Installing the Television Set," 23.

84. Spigel, 25.

85. Spigel, 28.

86. Spigel, *Make Room*, 97. See also Margaret Marsh, "Suburban Men and Masculine Domesticity, 1870–1915," *American Quarterly* 40 (June 1988), 165–186.

87. "The Corner of Your Eye," *Ethel and Albert* kinescope, PLP.

88. Chan, "Television Review: *Ethel and Albert*," *Variety*, April 29, 1953, 33. See also Jack Gould, "Television: Civilized Domestic Fun: *Ethel and Albert* Are Back, and in Form," *New York Times*, June 21, 1955, 63.

89. Chan, "*Ethel and Albert*." See also "Molly," *Look*, February 27, 1951, 90-1, Box 54, Folder "Look," GBP.

90. "Women's Club Buys a New Clubhouse," *Ethel and Albert* kinescope, PLP.

91. Bratslavsky, "Recovered Visual Records."

92. "Lynch, Peg," *Current Biography*, 35.

93. Weber, "Peg Lynch, Writer and Star."

94. See Jon Kraszewski, *The New Entrepreneurs: An Institutional History of Television Anthology Writers* (Middletown, CT: Wesleyan University Press, 2010), Kindle.

95. *The Buick-Berle Show*, February 23, 1954, VA14297, UCLA Film & Television Archive, Research & Study Center.

96. "FAQ: Rod Serling Memorial Foundation," accessed May 14, 2016, http://www.rodserling.com/FAQ.htm.

97. "*Ethel and Albert* CV," Scrapbook, PLP. See also "Back to Radio and Beyond," Comedy of the Commonplace: The Sitcom Genius of Peg Lynch, University of Oregon, accessed August 28, 2020, https://expo.uoregon.edu/spotlight/peg-lynch/feature/back-to-radio-and-beyond.

98. Hal Boyle, "Women Love Mrs. Berg," *Kentucky New Era*, March 15, 1950, 2.

99. Diana Gibbings, "Re: Peg Lynch, Writer and Actress," *New York Times*, June 2, 1946, quoted in "Lynch, Peg," *Current Biography*, 34.

100. Bratslavsky, "Recovered Visual Records."

CHAPTER 4. "WHAT GIRL SHOULDN'T"

1. Letter to Sam Gale (March 20, 1947), Box 62, Irna Phillips Papers, Wisconsin Historical Society, hereafter IPP.

2. Cary O'Dell, "Irna Phillips," in *Women Pioneers in Television* (Jefferson, NC: McFarland & Company), 1997, 187.

3. For more on how Phillips worked to write sponsor-friendly scripts for radio, see Ellen Seiter, "'To Teach and to Sell': Irna Phillips and Her Sponsors, 1930–1954," *Journal of Film and Video* 41, no. 1 (Spring 1989): 21–35. Seiter describes Phillips as "forceful in protecting her own reputation and conformist in her acquiescence to the sponsors' demands and limitations" (27).

4. Michael Z. Newman and Elana Levine, *Legitimating Television: Media Convergence and Cultural Status* (New York: Routledge, 2012), 38.

5. Seiter, "'To Teach and to Sell,'" 21. See also Seiter, 33: "Phillips' representation of the audience typified a third alternative, the 'uplift approach,' combined with a sentimental, reverential view of the role of women in the family and the importance of maintaining women in the home."

6. Seiter, 39.

7. Seiter, 25.

8. Elana Levine, *Her Stories: Daytime Soap Opera & U.S. Television History* (Durham, NC: Duke University Press, 2020), 22, 57.

9. "Deaths: Queen of Soap Operas Miss Irna Phillips, 72," *Miami Herald*, December 30, 1973, 6-B.

10. Ien Ang, *Watching Dallas: Soap Opera and the Melodramatic Imagination* (New York: Routledge, 1996), 122–23.

11. The complicated generic identity of Studs' Place is discussed in Andrew Daglas, "Studs' Place offers a little-seen angle on a medium and an icon," *This Was Television*, September 11, 2012, https://thiswastv.com/2012/09/11/studs-place-offers-a-little-seen-angle-on-a-medium-and-an-icon/.

12. Tania Modleski, *Loving with a Vengeance: Mass-Produced Fantasies for Women*, 2nd ed. (New York: Routledge, 2008), 80.

13. Levine, *Her Stories*, 57.

14. Levine, 45.

15. Robert C. Allen, *Speaking of Soap Operas* (Chapel Hill: University of North Carolina Press, 1985), 11.

16. James Thurber, "Soapland," *The Beast in Me and Other Animals* (Mattituck, NY: Aeonian Press, 1973), 191.

17. Robert J. Landry, "Save Your Quips, the Soap Opera May Rise Again," *Variety*, January 21, 1959, 78.

18. Landry, 78.

19. Dwight MacDonald, "A Theory of Mass Culture," *Diogenes* 3 (Summer 1953), 12.

20. Michelle Hilmes, "*Radio Voices: American Broadcasting, 1922–1952* (Minneapolis: University of Minnesota Press, 1997), 131, 151.

21. Marsha Cassidy, *What Women Watched: Daytime Television in the 1950s* (Austin: University of Texas Press, 2005), 2.

22. Thurber, "Soapland," 192.

23. Bruce Hutchinson, "Dreadful Morning," *The Ottawa Citizen*, July 9, 1952, 30.

24. Allen, *Speaking*, 26.

25. Marilyn Lavin, "Creating Consumers in the 1930s: Irna Phillips and the Radio Soap Opera," *Journal of Consumer Research* 22, no. 1 (June 1995), 85.

26. Allen, *Speaking*, 21–22.

27. Ann Douglas, *The Feminization of American Culture* (New York: Knopf, 1977), 10.

28. Andreas Huyssen, "Mass Culture as Woman: Modernism's Other," in *Studies in Entertainment: Critical Approaches to Mass Culture*, ed. Tania Modleski (Bloomington: Indiana University Press, 1986), 194.

29. Huyssen, "Mass Culture as Woman, 189.

30. Huyssen, 196.

31. See Shelley Stamp, *Movie-Struck Girls: Women and Motion Picture Culture after the Nickelodeon* (Princeton, NJ: Princeton University Press, 2000).

32. This is explored further in previous chapters through the discussion of Lauren Berlant and her formulation of the "female complaint." See Berlant, *The Female Complaint* (Durham, NC: Duke University Press, 2008).

33. See Elaine Tyler May, *Homeward Bound: American Families in the Cold War Era,* 20th Anniversary Edition (New York: Basic Books, 1990).

34. Roel van den Oever, *Mama's Boy: Momism and Homophobia in Postwar Culture* (New York: Palgrave Macmillan, 2012), 1, 22. According to van den Oever, Edward A. Streck, Ferdinand Lundberg, Marynia F. Farnham, Erik H. Erikson, and Vincent T. Lathbury wrote works that responded to or expounded on Wylie's *Generation of Vipers.*

35. van den Oever, 22.

36. Cassidy, *What Women Watched,* 159.

37. Cassidy, 162, 182.

38. Cassidy, 167.

39. *The Guiding Light* (3/25/53), *Classic TV Soaps: 6 Sudsy DVDs* (The Nostalgia Merchant, 2008), DVD.

40. Allen, *Speaking,* 15-16.

41. "Chi Soapie Flacking Lathers 400 GFWC FemConvention Reps," *Billboard,* June 26, 1946, 10.

42. "Chi Soapie," 10.

43. Thurber, "Soapland," 213.

44. Thurber, 199–200. As Robert Allen writes that within "discourse[s] less critical of the broadcasting industry the manipulator/manipulated image of the relationship between the soap opera and its audience is transformed into its 'positive' inverse: teacher/student. Soap operas serve as a sort of remedial ethics and civics less for the socially retarded" (Allen, *Speaking,* 26).

45. Levine writes that "Phillips knew how to create stories and characters, but she also required Felton's directorial skill to invent the daily TV soap" (Levine, *Her Stories,* 23).

46. O'Dell, "Irna Phillips," 27.

47. Hilmes, *Radio Voices,* 156. This was also true of Gertrude Berg and Peg Lynch (chapter 3), who came from radio.

48. Thurber, "Soapland," 199.

49. Ray Wilson, "Irna Phillips as Big Business," *Variety,* May 29, 1940, 26.

50. Cassidy, *What Women Watched,* 63.

51. Wilson, "Irna Phillips"; see also Thurber, "Soapland," 197.

52. Peter Wyden, "Madam Soap Opera," *Saturday Evening Post,* June 25, 1960.

53. "Irna Phillips' Ghost Writers," *Variety,* August 5, 1942, 40.

54. "Irna Phillips Tests Her Video Ideas on Radio Studio Audience," *Billboard,* July 29, 1944, 12.

55. "Irna Phillips Tests," 12, See also Levine, *Her Stories,* 23: "Phillips . . . craft[ed] television by attending to both narrative effectiveness and audience expectations."

56. "Irna Phillips Tests."

57. Dan Goldberg, "She Knows Her P.'s & G.'s," *Variety,* May 29, 1940, 26.

58. O'Dell, "Irna Phillips," 181, 182.

59. O'Dell, 182.

60. O'Dell, 188.

61. Allison J. Waldman, "70 Years of *Guiding Light*: Keeping a Bright 'Light' Shining," *TV Week,* January 22, 2007, accessed October 22, 2020, https://www.tvweek.com/in-depth/2007/01/70-years-of-guiding-light-keep/.

62. Wilson, "Irna Phillips."

63. "All My Worlds," Box 12, IPP.

64. "Irna Phillips: Mother of the Soap Opera," Old Radio Shows, February 11, 2011, accessed January 30, 2020, http://www.oldradioshows.org/2011/02/irna-phillips-mother-of-the-soap-opera/.

65. Lynn Liccardo, "Irna Phillips," *Harvard Magazine*, January–February 2013, https://harvardmagazine.com/2013/01/vita-irna-phillips.

66. Scrapbook, Box 11, IPP.

67. Rich Samuels, "Chicago School of Television," *Encyclopedia of Chicago*, accessed January 30, 2020, http://www.encyclopedia.chicagohistory.org/pages/266.html.

68. Joel Sternberg, "Chicago School of Television," in *Encyclopedia of Television*, 2nd ed., ed. Horace Newcomb (New York: Routledge, 2013), 501–2.

69. Daniel Berger and Steve Jajkowski (eds.), *Chicago Television* (Charleston, SC: Arcadia Publishing, 2010), 64.

70. John Crosby, "'Authentics' Still Rule in Chicago TV," *Oakland Tribune*, September 15, 1953. See also Marilynn Preston, "Chicago TV—The Old and Future," *Chicago Tribune*, July 31, 1961.

71. Berger and Jajkowski, *Chicago Television*, 63.

72. Studs Terkel, "Chi's TV Imagination vs. Radio City Panjandrums," *Variety*, May 27, 1953, 34.

73. Thurber, "Soapland," 192–93.

74. Thurber, 192.

75. Thurber, 193.

76. Raymond A. Jones, "Chi's Got the Talent," *Variety*, May 27, 1953, 34.

77. "Chicago TV Loss," *Broadcasting, Telecasting*, December 3, 1951, 75.

78. "Hawkins Falls—October 23 1950s—Soap Operas Full Episodes," YouTube, accessed May 1, 2019, https://www.youtube.com/watch?v=FxWpZAD9oqA. Hugh Downs was, for part of the run, the narrator for *Hawkins Falls*.

79. Norman Felton, "The Daytime Serial on Television (2/20/49)," Box 54, IPP.

80. Letter from Ted Mills, Box 54, IPP.

81. Letter from Ted Mills.

82. Goldberg, "She Knows . . ."

83. "Television: No East-Bound Edict Snarls Chi TV Plans," *Variety*, March 2, 1949, 29. See also Chi Dimont [*sic*] as TV Origination Center," *Billboard*, March 12, 1949, 17.

84. "Chi TVers Eye Housewife Biz," *Variety*, February 2, 1950, 28.

85. "Television: No East-Bound Edict."

86. Whet Moser, "RIP Agnes Nixon, the Legendary Creator of *One Life to Live* and *All My Children*," *Chicago Magazine*, September 29, 2016, http://www.chicagomag.com/arts-culture/September-2016/Agnes-Nixon/.

87. Lynn Spigel, *Make Room for TV: Television and the Family Ideal in Postwar America* (Chicago: University of Chicago Press, 1992), 78.

88. "Irna Phillips' Tele Soaper in Mon. Bow," *Variety*, 26 January 1949, 34.

89. "Irna Phillips' Tele Soaper," 34.

90. *These Are My Children*, episode #7, Box 54, IPP.

91. "TV 'Soap Opera,'" *Broadcasting, Telecasting*, February 7, 1949, 57.

92. Jose, "These Are My Children [Television Reviews]," *Variety*, February 9, 1949, 34.

93. Ang, *Watching Dallas*, 52.

94. Norman Felton [interview]," *Television Academy Foundation: The Interviews*, conducted by Lee Goldberg, November 12, 1997, accessed October 27, 2020, https://interviews.televisionacademy.com/shows/these-are-my-children.

95. Box 54, Folder 8, IPP.

96. Lavin, "Creating Consumers in the 1930s," 85–86.

97. Jason Loviglio, "Reading Judy and Jane in the Archive," *Journal of Radio & Audio Media* 23, no. 2 (2016), 308. See also Neil Verma, "Radio's Oblong Blur: On the Corwinesque in the Critical Ear," in *Anatomy of Sound: Norman Corwin and Media Authorship*, eds. J. Smith and N. Verma (Oakland: University of California Press, 2016), 37–38.

98. Norman Felton [interview], *Television Academy Foundation: The Interviews*. See also *These Are My Children*, episode #1, Box 54, IPP.

99. Martha Nochimson, *No End to Her: Soap Opera and the Female Subject* (Berkeley: University of California Press, 1992), 170–71.

100. Ang, *Watching Dallas*, 59, 60.

101. Levine, *Her Stories*, 44.

102. Levine, 55.

103. Goldberg, "She Knows . . ."

104. *These Are My Children*, episode #2, Box 54, IPP.

105. This anxious son–Jewish mother dynamic takes comic shape in the 1977 film *Annie Hall*, in which Alvy's mother responds to his anxiety about the universe expanding with: "You're here in Brooklyn! Brooklyn's not expanding!" Unlike writer-director Woody Allen, Phillips rarely jokes around, and, in her worldview, it is the men, not the women, who are being ridiculous.

106. Seiter, "'To Teach and to Sell,'" 31.

107. *These Are My Children*, episode #2, Box 54, IPP.

108. Seiter, "'To Teach and to Sell,'" 23.

109. van der Oever, *Mama's Boy*, 13.

110. *These Are My Children*, episode #1, Box 54, IPP.

111. Levine, *Her Stories*, 23–24.

112. Levine, 79.

113. Carol Lopate, "Daytime Television: You'll Never Want to Leave Home," *Radical America* 2 (1977), 51.

114. *These Are My Children*, episode #3, Box 54, IPP.

115. Modleski, *Loving*, 80.

116. Julia McCarthy, "Irna Phillips Scripts Single Woman's Woes," *Sunday News*, January 19, 1941, C28.

117. *These Are My Children*, episode #1, Box 54, IPP.

118. *These Are My Children*, episode #1, Box 54, IPP.

119. Levine, *Her Stories*, 52.

120. Gilbert Seldes, *The Great Audience* (Whitefish, MT: Literary Licensing, 2012), 116–17.

121. *These Are My Children*, episode #1, Box 54, IPP.

122. Levine, *Her Stories*, 30.

123. *These Are My Children*, episode #3, Box 54, IPP.

124. Levine, *Her Stories*, 73.

125. Letter from Felton to Phillips (January 10, 1949), Box 54, IPP.

126. Levine, in *Her Stories*, contests Richard Allen's claim that Phillips resisted making the jump to television: "Allen discusses the transition briefly in *Speaking of Soap Operas* and suggests the radio serial creator Irna Phillips was dubious about moving serials to TV, an argument that discounts Phillips' substantive efforts as a TV pioneer and the ways that the TV soap developed its long-standing form in the later 1950s and early 1960s" (20–21). See also Allen, *Speaking*, 122–25.

127. See "Guiding Light 1-25-07 The 70th Anniversary Episode Part 1," YouTube, accessed January 30, 2020, https://www.youtube.com/watch?v= xzPor_xfv2c. See also "Guiding Light 1-25-07 The 70th Anniversary Episode Part 3," YouTube, accessed January 30, 2020, https://www.youtube.com/watch ?v=8TOkeUirPA4&t=77s.

128. "Guiding Light 1-25-07 The 70th Anniversary Episode Part 1."

129. Nochimson, *No End to Her*, 197.

130. Ang, *Watching Dallas*, 74.

131. Modleski, *Loving*, 105.

132. Modleski, 82.

133. Modleski, 98. Madeleine Edmondson and David Rounds, *From Mary Noble to Mary Hartman: The Complete Soap Opera Book* (New York: Stein & Day, 1976), 112.

134. Seiter, "'To Teach and to Sell,'" 27.

135. Levine, *Her Stories*, 34.

CHAPTER 5. "KNOWING ALL THE PLOTS"

1. "*Studio One* Video History: Loring Mandel, interviewed by Franklin Heller," October 5, 1987, Paley Center for Media, New York, NY, hereafter PCM. If rumor is to be believed, Britton was the one to impress or, some say, to liquor up over lunch. See also Jeff Kisseloff, *The Box: An Oral History of Television, 1920–1961* (New York: Viking, 1995), 245.

2. "*Studio One* Video History: Bette Stein Chichon interviewed by Loring Mandel," June 8, 1987, PCM.

3. See Tom Stempel, *Storytellers to the Nation: A History of American Television Writing* (Syracuse, NY: Syracuse University Press, 1996), 51.

4. "Patterns," in *The Golden Age of Television*, directed by Fielder Cook (1955; New York: Criterion Collection, 2009), DVD. Originally broadcast on January 12, 1955 on NBC.

5. Rod Serling was also mentored by Dorothy Hechtlinger; see also J. E. Smyth, *Nobody's Girl Friday: The Women Who Ran Hollywood* (New York: Oxford University Press, 2018).

6. Miranda J. Banks, *Writers: A History of American Screenwriters and Their Guild* (New Brunswick: Rutgers University Press, 2015), 145.

7. Smyth, *Nobody's Girl Friday*, 69.

8. Banks, *Writers*, 14.

9. Margery Davies, *Woman's Place Is at the Typewriter: Office Work and Office Workers, 1870–1930* (Philadelphia: Temple University Press, 1984), 130. See also Lynn Peril, *Swimming in the Steno Pool: A Retro Guide to Making It in the Office* (New York: W.W. Norton & Company, 2011).

10. Jane M. Gaines, *Pink-Slipped: What Happened to Women in the Silent Film Industry?* (Urbana: University of Illinois Press, 2018), 22.

11. Al Jean et al., "Writing for Episodic TV: From Freelance to Showrunner," Writers Guild of America, 2004, accessed June 19, 2018, http://dumbstoryideas .com/media/WGA_WritingForTV.pdf.

12. Jean et al., 5.

13. Erin Hill, *Never Done: A History of Women's Work in Media Production* (New Brunswick, NJ: Rutgers University Press, 2016), 175.

14. Peter Martin, "Pictures: ABC's Script Editor Answers 'Story Dearth,'" *Variety*, November 7, 1951, 124.

15. Vincent Tilsley, "The Quarter: Style in Drama: The Role of Script Editor," *Contrast*, July 1, 1964, 226.

16. Hill, *Never Done*, 171.

17. The Television Writers' Association (TWA), now defunct, was supplanted by the Writers' Guild of America in 1954. See Michelle Hilmes, "Never Ending Story: Authorship, Seriality, and the Radio Writers Guild," in *A Companion to Media Authorship*, ed. Jonathan Gray and Derek Johnson (Oxford: Wiley-Blackwell, 2013), 195. Since 1999, story analysts, formerly of the Story Analysts Union, have been represented by the International Alliance of Theatrical Stage Employees (IATSE), while story editors are represented by the Writers' Guild of America. See Rona Edwards and Monika Skerbelis, *I Liked It, Didn't Love It: Screenplay Development from the Inside Out* (Beverly Hills, CA: Edwards Skerbelis Entertainment, 2016), 22.

18. Christine Gledhill and Julia Knight, "Introduction," in *Doing Women's Film History: Reframing Cinemas, Past and Present* (Urbana: University of Illinois Press, 2015), 8.

19. E-mail correspondence with Erin Hill, June 11, 2018.

20. See Helen Christene Hoerle and Florence B. Saltzburg, *The Girl and the Job* (New York: Henry Holt and Company, 1919), 146. A 1919 professional guide, *The Girl and the Job* argued that "the feminine viewpoint is most necessary [in a scenario department]. Filmmaker Alice Guy Blaché declared women the "authority on the emotions," while screenwriter Clara Beranger wrote that women comprised the majority of the film-going public and that "women writers know better what pleases their sisters than men for has it not been true since time immemorial that men never understood women but the baby girl just beginning to toddle knows men?" See Alice Blaché, "Woman's Place in Photoplay Production (1914)," in *The Red Velvet Seat*, ed. Antonia Lant and Ingrid Perez (New York: Verso, 2006), 657. See also Clara Beranger, "Feminine Sphere in the Field of Movies Is Large Indeed (1919): Interview with Clara Beranger," in Lant and Perez, *Red Velvet Seat*, 654.

21. June Mathis, "The Feminine Mind in Picture Making," in Lant and Perez, *Red Velvet Seat*, 664.

22. For more on "talkies" and the advent of sound cinema in Hollywood, see Donald Crafton, *The Talkies: American Cinema's Transition to Sound, 1926–1931* (Berkeley: University of California Press, 1997).

23. Idwal Jones, "The Muse in Hollywood," *New York Times*, December 27, 1936, 4.

24. Hill, *Never Done*, 47. For more on "creative labor," see also Liz Clarke, "'No Accident of Good Fortune': Autobiographies and Personal Memoirs as Historical Documents in Screenwriting History," *Feminist Media Histories* 2, no. 1 (2016), 47.

25. Christopher Anderson, *Hollywood TV: The Studio System in the Fifties* (Austin: University of Texas Press, 1994), 5.

26. Anderson, 13.

27. David Waterman, *Hollywood's Road to Riches* (Cambridge, MA: Harvard University Press, 2005), 39.

28. "Three Quit CBS Story Department," *Billboard*, September 5, 1953, 6.

29. "3 Leave CBS-TV Story Dept," *Broadcasting, Telecasting*, August 31, 1953, 71. See also "CBS-TV Story Dept.'s Wholesale Walkout," *Variety*, September 2, 1953, 25.

30. "CBS-TV Story," *Variety,* September 2, 1953. Heinemann is called "head" of the story department in this article rather than script editor.

31. Gaines, *Pink-Slipped*, 189.

32. John F. Carr, *H. Beam Piper: A Biography* (Jefferson, NC: McFarland Publishing, 2014). The final note was bad news indeed: "Janet Wood has been sacked at Avon—another of those publishing-house revolutions" (180). She died in 1971, at the age of sixty-six. According to an obituary in the *Daily News* (New York), Janet (Wood) Carse was the widow of writer and "merchant mariner" Robert Carse, but earlier notices suggest she was in the process of divorcing or, at least, was formally separated from Carse. (Throughout, she seemed to have worked professionally under her maiden name.) In their divorce report, in 1934, Wood Carse alleged cruelty against her husband. See "Janet W. Carse," *Daily News*, March 24, 1971, 284. See also "Carse Divorce Report Accepted," *Hartford Courant*, March 3, 1934, 20.

33. Michel Foucault, "The Lives of Infamous Men," in *Power, Truth, Strategy* (Sydney: Feral Publications, 1979), 79–80.

34. "Antidote to Agents," *Variety,* December 11, 1940, 7.

35. For more on the rise of agents in 1950s Hollywood, see Denise Mann's *Hollywood Independents: The Postwar Talent Takeover* (Minneapolis: University of Minnesota Press, 2008). See also Tom Kemper, *Hidden Talent: The Emergence of Hollywood Agents* (Berkeley: University of California Press, 2010).

36. One *Variety* article also suggests that the advent of a British tax caused "all companies . . . [to] retrench . . . on coverage of stories and plays. See "Col Folds Story Depts. in New York, London," *Variety*, December 3, 1947, 6.

37. Edward Jay Epstein, *The Big Picture: Money and Power in Hollywood* (New York: Random House, Inc., 2006), 280.

38. Smyth, *Nobody's Girl Friday*, 12.

39. "Economy Axe Hits Story Depts. Hard," *Variety*, September 17, 1947, 5.

40. "Col Folds," *Variety*, December 3, 1947.

41. Henry Klinger, "Today's Story Editor Buys to Please World," *Variety*, January 9, 1957.

42. "Fates and Fortunes: Deaths," *Broadcasting*, March 29, 1971, 110.

43. "Hollyw'd Duo to Head New Series for Y-R," *Billboard*, September 2, 1950, 5.

44. "Quick Takes," *Billboard*, November 22, 1952: 11. See also "Briefs from the Lot," *Variety*, April 7, 1954, 16.

45. Donovan Pedelty, "Crawford Flares Up Again," *Picturegoer*, April 16, 1955, 13. See also "Studio Personnelities: Scripters," *Boxoffice*, August 8, 1953, 36.

46. "'You're Only as Good as Your Story Editor'—Good Ones Are Hard to Find," *Variety*, September 5, 1962.

47. Hill, *Never Done*, 172.

48. See Theatre Guild Archive. Yale Collection of American Literature, Beinecke Rare Book and Manuscript Library; see also "Lois Jacoby," IMDb, accessed May 14, 2016, http://www.imdb.com/name/nm1097476/. According to a syndicated column by Louella O. Parsons, Lois Jacoby moved to Hollywood in the fall of 1943, alongside Lawrence Langner and his wife, Armina Marshall, to run the Theatre Guild's "new motion picture producing unit . . . represented by the Myron Zelznick office." See Louella O. Parsons, "Greer Garson Due for Another Smash as Mrs. Parkinson," *Courier-Post* (Camden, NJ), November 24, 1943. Jacoby's correspondence in the Theater Guild Archive papers runs from 1943 to 1946.

49. Stephen Battaglio, *David Susskind: A Televised Life* (New York: St. Martin's Press, 2010), 50. The "A Tale of Two Cities" of *The DuPont Show of the Month* (CBS, 1957–1961) aired on March 27, 1958, with the "adapted by" screenwriting credit going to Michael Dyne. The "Ethan Frome" episode, also on *DuPont*, aired on February 18, 1960, and Gellen and Babbin shared the "adapted by" credit.

50. "Audrey Gellen Maas Dies at Forty; Producer, Adapter of TV Plays," *New York Times*, July 3, 1975.

51. "Jacqueline Babbin" (profile), She Made It, accessed May 14, 2016, http://www.shemadeit.org/meet/biography.aspx?m=86. See also Jon Thurber, "Jacqueline Babbin, 80; TV Writer, Editor and Producer," *Los Angeles Times*, October 12, 2001, http://articles.latimes.com/2001/oct/12/local/me-56319.

52. "Tele Follow-Up Comment," *Variety*, December 30, 1953, 28. See also "Fella Phillips," IMDb, accessed May 14, 2016, http://www.imdb.com/name/nm3747645/.

53. "Network People," *Broadcasting*, December 5, 1955, 107.

54. *Climax!* Show Bible, Martin Manulis Collection, Writers Guild Foundation Archive, WGF.

55. "'Climax' Lays Down Policy: 'No Messages, Just Entertainment,'" *Variety*, July 4, 1956, 20.

56. For more on postwar "domestic containment," see Elaine Tyler May, *Homeward Bound: American Families in the Cold War Era*, 20th Anniversary edition (New York: Basic Books, 1990). This teleplay is discussed at length in the opening of chapter 5.

57. See, among others, the work of Molly Schneider on the American anthology drama and the work of Rod Serling. See also Rick Worland, "Sign-Posts Up Ahead: *The Twilight Zone, The Outer Limits*, and TV Political Fantasy 1959–1965," *Science Fiction Studies* 23, no. 1 (March 1996): 103–122.

58. "Network People," *Broadcasting*. There was a DuMont program of the same name that ran from 1949–1950, but, based on the date of this published item, this seems to refer to the CBS series.

59. Maria Little, "'Topaze' coverage," *Climax!* Show Bible, Martin Manulis Collection, WGF.

60. Miriam Geiger, "'No Stone Unturned'/'Melodrama Coverage,'" *Playhouse 90*, Martin Manulis Collection, WGF.

61. Sonia Chernus, "'Pale Horse, Pale Rider' coverage," *Climax!* Show Bible, Martin Manulis Collection, WGF.

62. "Alice Young Edits 'Mason,'" *Variety*, April 30, 1958, 28.

63. See "Maria Little" IMDb, accessed May 14, 2016, http://www.imdb.com/name/nm0514623/; "Miriam Geiger," IMDb, accessed May 14, 2016, http://www.imdb.com/name/nm1602035/; "Sonia Chernus," IMDb, accessed May 14, 2016, http://www.imdb.com/name/nm0155963/.

64. See Arthur W. Eddy, "Short Shots from New York Studios," *Film Daily*, August 29, 1929, 10. See also "Obituaries: Dorothy Hechtlinger," *Variety*, June 6, 1979, 93. In the years between her time at Paramount and at Twentieth Century Fox, she served as the secretary to Columbia's Gilbert Miller. See "Times Square Chatter: Hollywood," *Variety*, February 21, 1933, 60.

65. "The Women Who Run the Men," *Variety*, October 7, 1942, 15.

66. "The Women Who Run the Men," 15.

67. "Miss Hechtlinger Leaves," *Variety*, July 14, 1943, 27.

68. Finding Aid, Theatre Guild *United States Steel Hour* Records, *T-Mss 1975-006. Billy Rose Theatre Division, The New York Public Library for the Performing Arts.

69. *Ross Reports—Television Index*, January 1, 1956, 17.

70. Glenn Fowler, "Armina Marshall is Dead at 96," *New York Times*, July 22, 1991, 24. Marshall is described as "part American Indian."

71. Tim Hollis, *Ain't That a Knee-Slapper: Rural Comedy in the Twentieth Century* (Jackson: University Press of Mississippi, 2008).

72. Smyth, *Nobody's Girl Friday*, 69.

73. "Letter from Hechtlinger," Box 1022, Folder 12757, Theatre Guild Archive. Yale Collection of American Literature, Beinecke Rare Book and Manuscript Library.

74. "Letter from Hechtlinger."

75. Madelyn Pugh Davis with Bob Carroll Jr., *Laughing with Lucy: My Life with America's Leading Lady of Comedy* (Cincinnati, OH: Clerisy Press, 2007), 110–111.

76. Eileen Kowalski, "Peggy Chantler Dick," *Variety*, November 26, 2001.

77. Smyth, *Nobody's Girl Friday*, 69.

78. See Hal Humphrey, "Have We Seen TV's 'Good Old Days'?" *Miami Herald*, April 14, 1960, 3-B.

79. Correspondence with J. E. Smyth, June 19, 2018; see also Smyth, *Nobody's Girl Friday*, 69.

CHAPTER 6. "A GIRL'S GOTTA LIVE"

1. "Sorry, Wrong Number," VA10738, UCLA Film & Television Archive, Research & Study Center. The "anthology drama" in a postwar broadcasting context refers to a radio or television series in which each episode has a new set of characters and its own discrete plot. In a contemporary context, television critics often refer to a show in which each *season* has its own storyline and focus as an "anthology drama," one such example being Ryan Murphy's *American Horror Story* (FX, 2011–ongoing.)

2. Helen Wheatley, *Gothic Television* (Manchester: Manchester University Press, 2006), 107.

3. This ending is the same in the 1948 film of *Sorry, Wrong Number*. In the development of the television suspense aesthetic, CBS's *Suspense* (1949–1964) and NBC's *Lights Out* (1949–1952), which both began as radio programs, borrowed from their "radiophonic" tradition "through the deployment of low-budget sound effects and minimal orchestration" (Wheatley, 125).

4. The radio play of "Sorry, Wrong Number," featuring Agnes Moorehead as Leona, broadcast on *Suspense* (CBS Radio, 1940–1962) on May 25, 1943.

5. Matthew Solomon, "Adapting 'Radio's Perfect Script': 'Sorry, Wrong Number' and *Sorry, Wrong Number*," *Quarterly Review of Film & Video* 16, no. 1 (1997), 29.

6. The concluding or summarizing remarks on this report read as follows: "Male TV viewers are relatively stronger on Westerns than females, though Westerns are second choice with women. The reverse is true with Mystery & Detective plays. Women like serious plays about family life twice as much as men do. (Female viewers don't like sports.)" Box 1026, Folder 12816, Theatre Guild Archive. Yale Collection of American Literature, Beinecke Rare Book and Manuscript Library.

7. Jeff Kisseloff, *The Box: An Oral History of Television, 1920–1961* (New York: Viking, 1995), 229–30. Doris Frankel, whose papers are held at the New York Public Library, wrote for such programs as *The Guiding Light* (CBS, 1952–2009), *Suspense* (CBS, 1949–1954), and *Playhouse 90* (CBS, 1956–1960), among many others. Doris Halman wrote for *Lights Out* (NBC, 1946–1952) and *Armstrong Circle Theatre* (NBC, CBS, 1950–1963), while Phyllis Coe adapted stories and wrote original teleplays for *Lights Out* and *The Clock* (NBC, ABC 1949–1952). See the Internet Movie Database (IMDb.com) for these credits and others.

8. Jan Olsson, *Hitchcock à la Carte* (Durham, NC: Duke University Press, 2015), 143.

9. Thomas M. Leitch, "The Outer Circle: Hitchcock on Television," in *Alfred Hitchcock: Centenary Essays* (London: BFI, 1999), 60. "Frequent series writer" Robert Bloch ("The Changing Heart," "The Gloating Place") described Hitchcock in these terms.

10. Mary Ann Doane, "The 'Woman's Film': Possession and Address," in *Home Is Where the Heart Is: Studies in Melodrama and the Woman's Film*, ed. Christine Gledhill (London: BFI Books, 1987), 284.

11. For more on the placement and the place of television in the postwar American home, see Lynn Spigel, *Make Room for TV: Television and the Family Ideal in Postwar America* (Chicago: University of Chicago Press, 1992).

12. Sianne Ngai, *Ugly Feelings* (Cambridge, MA: Harvard University Press, 2005), 299.

13. Tania Modleski, "Suspicion: Collusion and Resistance in the Work of Hitchcock's Female Collaborators," *A Companion to Alfred Hitchcock*, ed. Thomas Leitch and Leland Poague (Malden, MA: Wiley-Blackwell, 2011), 180.

14. Bruce Eder, "Ethel Lina White: Full Biography," *New York Times*, 2010, http://www.nytimes.com/movies/person/311782/Ethel-Lina-White/biography. This link is no longer available online. Throughout the first half of the twentieth century, Ethel Lina White wrote novels and suspense books, such as *The Wishbone* (1927), *Sinister Light* (1931), *The First Time He Died* (1935), and *Wax* (1935).

15. John McCarty and Brian Kelleher, *Alfred Hitchcock Presents: An Illustrated Guide to the Ten-Year Television Career of the Master of Suspense* (New York: St. Martin's Press, 1985), 17.

16. McCarty and Kelleher, 17.

17. Hitchcock's move from short stories to the adaptation of novels and novellas was a move that one reporter suggested "may hurt the television sales of short stories . . . [a] market . . . [that] has already been curtailed in recent years by the increasing use of non-fiction in magazines." See Murray Schumach, "'Hitch' Courts the Novelists," *Atlanta Constitution*, October 22, 1962, 18A. As Hitchcock explains to this reporter: "It is much easier . . . to prune a novel and reshape it for a full hour show than it is to build up a short story to that length in the limited time available"; the work of such novelists as Rebecca West and Margaret Millar were purchased for the Hour. For more on Hitchcock and Elsom, see Olsson, *Hitchcock à la Carte*, 71. For more on Hessler, see Leitch, "The Outer Circle," 60.

18. Cynthia Lowry, "Crime Pays This Nice Young Gentlewoman," *Toledo Blade*, June 11, 1960, Sec. 4, 1.

19. Tania Modleski, *Loving with a Vengeance: Mass-Produced Fantasies for Women*, 2nd ed. (New York: Routledge, 2008), 10, 51–52.

20. Modleski, 11.

21. Modleski, 11.

22. Livia Tenzer and Jean Casella, "Publisher's Foreword: Women Write Pulp," in *Bunny Lake Is Missing*, by Evelyn Piper (New York: Feminist Press, 2004), vii. Note: Evelyn Piper was the pen name for author Merriam Modell. A film version of the novel directed by Otto Preminger was released in 1965.

23. "You Can't Trust a Man," *Alfred Hitchcock Presents* (NBC, May 9, 1961).

24. Sarah Weinman, *Troubled Daughters, Twisted Wives: Stories from the Trailblazers of Domestic Suspense* (New York: Penguin, 2013), 139.

25. Mary Ann Doane, "The 'Women's Film': Possession and Address," in *Home Is Where the Heart Is: Studies in Melodrama and the Woman's Film*, ed. Christine Gledhill (London: BFI Books, 1987), 291.

26. Modleski, "Suspicion," 164.

27. Modleski, 164.

28. Solomon, "Adapting," 23, 24.

29. Maria LaPlace, "Producing and Consuming the Woman's Film: Discursive Struggle in *Now, Voyager*," in *Home Is Where the Heart Is: Studies in Melodrama and the Woman's Film*, ed. Christine Gledhill (London: BFI Books, 1987), 139.

30. LaPlace, 139.

31. Regina Christiane Lange, "Positioning Gina Kaus: A Transnational Career from Vienna Novelist and Playwright to Hollywood Scriptwriter," PhD diss., University of Iowa, 2012, 65, 69.

32. "The Legacy," *Alfred Hitchcock Presents*, May 27, 1956, written by Gina Kaus.

33. Robert J. Landry, "Mags Must Pitch Entertainment," *Variety*, November 2, 1955, 7.

34. Christina Lane, *Phantom Lady: Hollywood Producer Joan Harrison, The Forgotten Woman Behind Hitchcock* (Chicago: Chicago Review Press, 2020), 247.

35. *Alfred Hitchcock Mystery Magazine* seems to be the same thing as *Alfred Hitchcock's Suspense Magazine*, though the literature on this title change is nonexistent. See Linda Landrigan (ed), "Introduction," in *Alfred Hitchcock's Mystery Magazine Presents Fifty Years of Crime and Suspense* (New York: Pegasus Books, 2006), xii.

36. "People Who Read and Write," *New York Times*, February 9, 1947, BR8. Fletcher's cowriter on the 1948 novel version is Allan Ullman.

37. "Radio-Television: Merchandising as Pubrelations, Promotion Tool: Benson Formula," *Variety*, July 20, 1960, 41. See also Campbell, "Film Buys Hypo Mag Story Swing."

38. McCarty and Kelleher, *Alfred Hitchcock Presents*, 14–15; Lane, *Phantom Lady*, 247.

39. Lane, *Phantom Lady*, 244.

40. Lane, 248.

41. Lane, 248, 258.

42. Martin Grams and Patrik Wikstrom, *The Alfred Hitchcock Presents Companion* (Whiteford, MD: OTR Publishing, 2001), 37.

43. Grams and Wikstrom, 27.

44. Thierry Méranger, "Norman Lloyd présente: entretien avec Norman Lloyd," *Cahiers du Cinéma* 702 (2014), 82. See also Lane, *Phantom Lady*, 249.

45. Lane, *Phantom Lady*, 8.

46. Lane, 251. Specifically, Lane points out how "Harrison's earlier collaborations with Hitchcock informed her solo work in the 1940s, the "perverse textures and pathological violence [of *Jamaica Inn* (1939)] speak[ing] directly to Harrison's preoccupation with what lies hidden beneath romantic, marital, and familial relationships," her efforts on *Rebecca* (1940) "g[iving] her practical

experience in thinking about how sets and props could reveal character," and her job on *Foreign Correspondent* (1940) being "to maintain continuity of vision and voice" (84, 95, 106).

47. Lane, 105, 106.

48. Lane, 142.

49. Bob Thomas, "Joan Harrison Seeks No Favors as Producer," *Miami Post*, June 1, 1946, 15.

50. Lane, *Phantom Lady*, 252, 253.

51. Bob Thomas, "Joan Harrison Making Good in a Man's World," *Daytona Beach Morning Journal*, May 20, 1963, 15.

52. McCarty and Kelleher, *Alfred Hitchcock Presents*, 34.

53. Grams and Wikstrom, *Alfred Hitchcock Presents Companion*, 34.

54. Moira Finnie, "Joan Harrison: In Hitch's Shadow," *Movie Morlocks: Powered by TCM*, posted March 18, 2009, http://moviemorlocks.com/2009/03/18/joan-harrison-the-phantom-lady/.

55. Myrna Oliver, "Joan Harrison, 83; Producer, Writer for Alfred Hitchcock," *Los Angeles Times*, August 24, 1994.

56. Gilbert Millstein, "Harrison Horror Story," *New York Times*, July 21, 1957, in Tim Snelson, *Phantom Ladies: Hollywood Horror and the Home Front* (New Brunswick, NJ: Rutgers University Press, 2015), 196.

57. Hedda Hopper, "Hedda Hopper in Hollywood: An Exception to the Rule."

58. Finnie, "Joan Harrison."

59. Olsson, *Hitchcock à la Carte*, 193.

60. Stéphane Delorme, Mathieu Macheret, Florence Maillard, and Stéphane du Mesnildot, "Alfred Hitchcock en dix episodes," *Cahiers du Cinéma* no. 702 (2014), 78. Translated by the author.

61. See Méranger, "Norman Lloyd," 82; this is discussed further in Olsson, *Hitchcock à la Carte.*

62. Olsson, *Hitchcock à la Carte*, 194–95. Correspondence held at the Dahl Museum and Story Centre.

63. See Lane, *Phantom Lady*: "Less than a month after ["Lamb to the Slaughter"] aired, Hitchcock's *Vertigo*, in which Bel Geddes plays main character Scottie Ferguson's best friend (and ex-fiancée), premiered. . . . One effect of this dynamic was to create the sense that Hitchcock's films and his television series—despite the fact that, in the series' ten-year run, he personally directed only 18 of the 359 episodes—had an almost seamless relationship" (261).

64. Delorme et al., "Alfred Hitchcock en dix episodes," 77.

65. Richard C. Allen, *Hitchcock's Romantic Irony* (New York: Columbia University Press, 2007), 140.

66. Ann Waldron, "Charlotte Armstrong," *Journal of Popular Culture* 5, no. 2 (Fall 1971), 441.

67. Waldron, 445.

68. Amanda Cockrell, e-mail to author, February 13, 2013.

69. Amanda Cockrell, e-mail to author, August 31, 2015.

70. Cockrell, August 31, 2015.

71. See "The Rose Garden," *Alfred Hitchcock Presents: Season 2*, directed by Francis Cockrell (Universal City, CA: Universal Home Entertainment, 2006), DVD.

72. Weinman, *Troubled Daughters*, 267; e-mail correspondence with Amanda Cockrell, February 13, 2013.

73. "Letter from Benjamin, April 26, 1956," Box 45, Folder 56, Charlotte Armstrong Collection, Howard Gotlieb Archival Research Center, Boston University, hereafter CAC.

74. "Letter from Carol Brandt, June 30, 1956," Box 45, Folder 56, CAC.

75. "Letter from Charlotte Armstrong, April 30, 1956," Box 45, Folder 56, CAC.

76. Rick Cypert, *The Virtue of Suspense: The Life and Works of Charlotte Armstrong* (Selinsgrove, PA: Susquehanna University Press, 2008), 76.

77. Doane, "Woman's Film," 285.

78. Modleski, *Loving*, 57.

79. Allen, *Hitchcock*, 93.

80. Shelley Cobb, "Adaptation, Fidelity, and Gendered Discourses," *Adaptation* 4, no. 2 (2011), 29.

81. Cobb, 32.

82. Cobb, 30.

83. Cobb, 35–36.

84. Cobb, 29.

85. John Collier, "Wet Saturday," *New Yorker*, July 16, 1938, 15.

86. "Wet Saturday," *Alfred Hitchcock Presents: Season 2*, directed by Alfred Hitchcock (Universal City, CA: Universal Home Entertainment, 2006), DVD.

87. John Cheever, "The Five-Forty-Eight," *New Yorker*, April 10, 1954, http://www.newyorker.com/magazine/1954/04/10/the-five-forty-eight.

88. *The Apartment*, directed by Billy Wilder (1960; Los Angeles: United Artists, 20th Century Fox, 2001), DVD.

89. Olsson, *Hitchcock à la Carte*, 175–76.

90. Olsson, 181.

91. Olsson, 8, 121.

92. Olsson, 101.

93. Christina Lane concurs: "While Joan guaranteed the show's 'Hitchcock' quotient, she also provided a Harrison touch, playing a crucial historical role in importing film noir into television" (Lane, *Phantom Lady*, 251).

94. "The Cake Baker," *The Alcoa Hour*, DVD6848, UCLA Film & Television Archive, Research & Study Center. The Shaws contributed a single original teleplay to *Alfred Hitchcock Presents*, titled "The Pearl Necklace" (May 2, 1961).

CONCLUSION

1. *30 Rock*, "Rosemary's Baby" (NBC, October 25, 2007).

2. The program, started in 2005, has since changed its name to Women@Paley. See "The Museum of Television and Radio Launches SHE MADE IT Initiative," December 1, 2005, https://www.paleycenter.org/press-release-she-made-it-2005-launch. See also "Welcome to . . . Women@Paley," https://www.paleycenter.org/the-paley-center-for-media-ted-tedwomen.

3. A. O. Scott, "Carrie Fisher: A Princess, a Rebel and a Brave Comic Voice," *New York Times*, December 27, 2016.

4. A longer discussion of Diamond's persona can be found in the book's introduction.

5. For more on the character of Laura Petrie and the figure of the content stay-at-home performer-partner, see Annie Berke, "Laura Petrie and Performance as Wifely Duty," *Flow: A Critical Forum on Media and Culture*, February 19, 2017.

6. See *The Dick Van Dyke Show*, "Where You Been, Fassbinder?" (NBC, March 14, 1962), where Sally is alone on her birthday; *The Dick Van Dyke*, "Dear Sally Rogers" (NBC, February 23, 1966), in which Sally puts out a call for a husband on national television.

7. Elahe Izadi, "Your Favorite TV Show Probably Owes a Debt to Mary Tyler Moore," *Washington Post*, January 26, 2017.

8. *A Face in the Crowd*, directed by Elia Kazan (1957; New York: Warner Brothers, 2005), DVD.

9. Giuliana Muscio, "Clara, Ouida, Beulah, et al.: Women Screenwriters in American Silent Cinema," in *Reclaiming the Archive: Feminism and Film History*, ed. Vicki Callahan (Detroit: Wayne State University Press), 289.

10. Valerie J. Nelson, "Agnes Nixon Dies at 93; Creator of *One Life to Live*, and *All My Children*," *Los Angeles Times*, September 28, 2016, https://www.latimes.com/local/obituaries/la-me-agnes-nixon-snap-story.html.

11. Miranda J. Banks, *The Writers: A History of American Screenwriters and Their Guild* (New Brunswick: Rutgers University Press, 2015), 138, 140.

12. See Lynn Spigel, "White Flight," in *Welcome to the Dreamhouse: Popular Media and Postwar Suburbs* (Durham, NC: Duke University Press, 2001).

13. Nina C. Liebman, *Living Room Lectures: The Fifties Family in Film and Television* (Austin: University of Texas Press, 1995), 86.

14. Liebman, 72.

15. Liebman, 55.

16. See Susan Douglas, *Where the Girls Are: Growing Up Female with the Mass Media* (New York: Times Books, 1995).

17. Sherwood Schwartz, "Why I Want to be a Television Writer" *Variety*, January 6, 1960, 92.

18. Madelyn Pugh Davis, with Bob Carroll Jr., *Laughing with Lucy: My Life with America's Leading Lady of Comedy* (Cincinnati, OH: Clerisy Press, 207), 115.

19. Ella Taylor, *Prime-Time Families: Television Culture in Post-War America* (Berkeley: University of California Press, 1991), 36.

20. Taylor, 39.

21. Liebman, *Living Room Lectures*, 25.

22. Taylor, *Prime-Time Families*, 39.

23. Michael Z. Newman and Elana Levine, *Legitimating Television: Media Convergence and Cultural Status* (New York: Routledge, 2012), 55.

24. Liam Stack, "D.C. Fontana, First Female *Star Trek* Writer, Dies at 80," *New York Times*, December 3, 2019.

25. See Jennifer Keishin Armstrong, *Mary and Lou and Rhoda and Ted: And All the Brilliant Minds Who Made "The Mary Tyler Moore Show" a Classic*

(New York: Simon & Schuster, 2013). See also Herbie Pilato, *Twitch upon a Star: The Bewitched Life of Elizabeth Montgomery* (Lanham, MD: E Trade Publishing, 2012). See also "Press Release: The Museum of Television & Radio Launches SHE MADE IT Initiative," December 1, 2015, accessed October 17, 2020, https://www.paleycenter.org/press-releases/press-release-she-made-it-2005-launch/.

26. "Lucille Kallen," IMDb, accessed May 14, 2016, http://www.imdb.com/name/nm0435974/. See also Finding Aid, LKP.

27. See Finding Aid for Lucille Kallen Papers, LKP.

28. Lucille Kallen, *Out There, Somewhere!* (New York: The Macmillan Company, 1964), 97.

29. Interview of Lucille Kallen by Sunny Parich, Archive of American Television, April 25, 1998, Ardsley, NY, https://interviews.televisionacademy.com/interviews/lucille-kallen#interview-clips.

30. Allan Wallach, "The Show Behind *Your Show of Shows*," *New York Newsday*, November 22, 1993, Box 2, Folder 9, LKP. See also Parich, Interview of Lucille Kallen.

31. "Lucille Fletcher," *The Economist*, September 14, 2000, https://www.economist.com/obituary/2000/09/14/lucille-fletcher.

32. Lauren Bratslavsky, "Recovered Visual Records and Expanded Histories: How *Ethel and Albert* Broadens Sitcom History," Society of Cinema and Media Studies Annual Conference, March 28, 2015.

33. Correspondence with Astrid King, May 2, 2016. See also John Waring, "Becket's Peg Lynch Returns to Radio with Updated *Ethel and Albert* Series," Scrapbook, PLP.

34. Bruce Weber, "Peg Lynch, Writer and Star of Early Situation Comedy, Dies at 98," *New York Times*, July 27, 2015.

35. Various *Mrs. G. Goes to College* scripts can be found in Boxes 50 and 51, GBP. One of the pilot's original titles is "The Freshman" (Box 50).

36. Glenn D. Smith, *"Something on My Own": Gertrude Berg and American Broadcasting, 1929–1956* (Syracuse, NY: Syracuse University Press, 2007), 213.

37. Alex McNeil, *Total Television: The Comprehensive Guide to Programming*, 4th ed. (New York: Penguin, 1996), 1147.

38. Troy Brownfield, "How the Queen of Soaps Created a Television Dynasty," *Saturday Evening Post*, January 31, 2019, https://www.saturdayeveningpost.com/2019/01/how-the-queen-of-soaps-created-a-television-dynasty/.

39. See "Helen Nielsen," IMDb.

40. See Charlotte Armstrong Collection, Howard Gotlieb Archival Research Center, Boston University. The finding aid for this collection is available at: http://archives.bu.edu/collections/collection?id=121563.

41. Christina Lane, *Phantom Lady: Hollywood Producer Joan Harrison, The Forgotten Woman Behind Hitchcock* (Chicago: Chicago Review Press, 2020), 272.

42. Lane, 275.

43. Murray Schumach, "Woman Produces a Mystery Series; Joan Harrison Says 'Polite Murders' Are TV Mainstay of *Hitchcock Presents*," *New York Times*, November 1, 1960.

44. As just one of many examples, see Julie D'Acci's *Defining Women: Television and the Case of Cagney and Lacey* (Chapel Hill: University of North Carolina Press, 1994).

45. Shonda Rhimes, *Year of Yes: How to Dance It Out, Stand in the Sun, and Be Your Own Person* (New York: Simon & Schuster, 2015), Kindle, Loc 977.

46. Rhimes, Loc 54.

47. See "Once Haunted Still: Meet the Filmmakers," September 16, 2019, https://blackfilmcenterarchive.wordpress.com/2019/09/16/once-haunted-still -meet-the-filmmakers-september-18-7pm-in-wells-048-iulmia-screening-room/.

48. Rhimes, *Year of Yes*, Loc 62.

49. Claire Perkins and Michele Schreiber, "Independent Women: From Film to Television," *Feminist Media Histories* 19.7 (2019), 920. See also Sarah Banet-Weiss, *Empowered: Popular Feminism and Popular Misogyny* (Durham, NC: Duke University Press, 2018), 10.

50. Rebecca Lewis, "*Friends* Writers Shared 'Sordid Sex Stories for Inspiration and Joked about Joey Becoming a Rapist,'" *Metro* (UK), November 5, 2018, https://metro.co.uk/2018/11/05/friends-writers-shared-sordid-sex-stories -for-inspiration-and-joked-about-joey-becoming-a-rapist-8105575/?ito= cbshare.

51. See chapter 1.

52. Lewis, "*Friends* Writers."

53. Linda Bloodworth Thomason, "*Designing Women* Creator Goes Public with Les Moonves War: Not All Harassment Is Sexual (Guest Column)," *Hollywood Reporter*, September 12, 2018, https://www.hollywoodreporter .com/news/designing-women-creator-les-moonves-not-all-harassment-is-sexual -1142448.

54. Thomason.

55. "The Beauty Contest," *Designing Women*, October 6, 1986.

56. Jessica Bennett and Jesse Ellison, "Behind *Good Girls Revolt*: The *Newsweek* Lawsuit That Paved the Way for Women Writers," *Daily Beast*, July 14, 2017, https://www.thedailybeast.com/behind-the-good-girls-revolt-the -newsweek-lawsuit-that-paved-the-way-for-women-writers.

57. Elahe Izadi, "Roy Price canceled *Good Girls Revolt*. For the show's stars, it's 'horribly meta,'" *Washington Post*, October 24, 2017, https://www .washingtonpost.com/news/arts-and-entertainment/wp/2017/10/24/roy-price -canceled-good-girls-revolt-for-the-shows-stars-its-horribly-meta/.

58. Bryn Elise Sandberg and Lesley Goldberg, "*Good Girls Revolt* Creator Slams Amazon over Cancellation: 'They Run Some People Out,'" *Hollywood Reporter*, December 7, 2016, https://www.hollywoodreporter.com/live-feed /good-girls-revolt-creator-slams-amazon-cancellation-they-run-some-people -953552. In keeping with themes of female solidarity and coordinated struggle, Calvo has since moved on to co-showrun HBO Max's *The Dune: The Sisterhood*, described by *Deadline* to be the *Dune* "universe through the eyes of a mysterious order of women: the Bene Gesserit . . . [as they] expertly weave through the feudal politics and intrigue of The Imperium" (see Denise Petski, "Dana Calvo to Co-run *Dune: The Sisterhood* under New Overall Deal with Legendary TV Studios," *Deadline*, July 23, 2019, https://deadline.com/2019

/07/dana-calvo-to-co-run-dune-the-sisterhood-under-new-overall-deal-with-legendary-tv-studios-1202651452/. See Elizabeth Alsop's work on "contemporary television's evocation of sororal rhetoric and themes" (1027) in "Sorority Flow: The Rhetoric of Sisterhood in Post-Network Television," *Feminist Media Studies* 19, no. 7 (2019), 1027.

59. Sandberg and Goldberg, "*Good Girls Revolt* Creator Slams Amazon."

60. Brit Marling, "Harvey Weinstein and the Economics of Consent," *The Atlantic*, October 23, 2017, https://www.theatlantic.com/entertainment/archive/2017/10/harvey-weinstein-and-the-economics-of-consent/543618/.

61. Joe Utichi, "Lisa Kudrow and Michael Patrick King Discuss *The Comeback*'s 9-Year Break and Season 3: The Show Has 'Its Own Timeframe,'" *Deadline*, June 22, 2015, https://deadline.com/2015/06/lisa-kudrow-michael-patrick-king-interview-the-comeback-1201451562/.

62. Utichi.

63. For more on this in the context of studio Hollywood, see Thomas Schatz, *The Genius of the System: Hollywood Filmmaking in the Studio Era* (Austin: University of Texas Press, 1988).

64. This term is developed in Roland Barthes, "Myth Today," in *Mythologies*, trans. Richard Howard and Annette Lavers (New York: Hill and Wang, 2012).

65. Credit to Jane Gaines.

66. Aisha Harris, "Same Old Script," *Slate*, October 18, 2015, http://www.slate.com/articles/arts/culturebox/2015/10/diversity_in_the_tv_writers_room_writers_and_showrunners_of_color_lag_far.html.

67. "Women's Committee Statistics Report," November 7, 1974, WGF.

68. Kate Fortmueller, "Time's Up (Again?): Transforming Hollywood's Industrial Culture," *Media Industries* 6, no. 2 (2019), 7–8.

69. Fortmueller, 10.

70. "Women on the Job" brochure, Box 16, Folder 5 (Publications Part 3), American Women in Radio and Television Records, University of Maryland Archival Collections.

71. Thomas Schatz, "Film Studies, Cultural Studies, and Media Industries Studies," *Media Industries* 1, no. 1 (2014), 42.

72. Caldwell, *Production Culture*, 7.

73. Maya Montañez Smukler, *Liberating Hollywood: Women Directors and the Feminist Reform of 1970s American Cinema* (New Brunswick, NJ: Rutgers University Press, 2018).

Bibliography

ARCHIVES
Individual archival items are cited in endnotes.

American Women in Radio and Television Records
University of Maryland Archival Collections
College Park, MD

Billy Rose Theater Division
New York Public Library
New York, NY

Charlotte Armstrong Collection
Howard Gotlieb Research Center
Boston University
Boston, MA

Gertrude Berg Papers
Syracuse University Special Collections Research Center
Syracuse University
Syracuse, NY

Irna Phillips Papers
Wisconsin Historical Society Archives
University of Wisconsin–Madison
Madison, WI

Paley Center for Media
New York, NY

Peg Lynch Papers
University of Oregon Special Collections and University Archives
University of Oregon
Eugene, OR

Sid Caesar Papers
Manuscript Division
Library of Congress
Washington, D.C.

Tamiment Library/Robert F. Wagner Labor Archives
Elmer Holmes Bobst Library
New York University
New York, NY

Theatre Guild Archive
Yale Collection of American Literature
Beinecke Rare Book & Manuscript Library
Yale University
New Haven, CT

Television Academy Foundation Interviews
Archive of American Television
Ardsley, NY

UCLA Film & Television Archive
Special Collections
University of California, Los Angeles
Los Angeles, CA

Writers' Guild Foundation, Archive
Writers' Guild of America, West
Los Angeles, LA

BOOKS AND JOURNAL ARTICLES

Adir, Karen. "Imogene Coca." In *The Great Clowns of American Television*, 89–107. Jefferson, NC: McFarland & Company, Inc., 1988.
Allen, Richard. *Hitchcock's Romantic Irony*. New York: Columbia University Press, 2007.
Allen, Robert C. *Speaking of Soap Operas*. Chapel Hill: University of North Carolina Press, 1985.
Alsop, Elizabeth. "Sorority Flow: The Rhetoric of Sisterhood in Post-network Television." *Feminist Media Studies* 19, no. 7 (2019), 1026–1042.

Anderson, Christopher. *Hollywood TV: The Studio System in the Fifties*. Austin: University of Texas Press, 1994.

Ang, Ien. *Watching Dallas: Soap Opera and the Melodramatic Imagination*. New York: Routledge, 1996.

Armstrong, Jennifer Keishin. *Mary and Lou and Rhoda and Ted: And All the Brilliant Minds Who Made "The Mary Tyler Moore Show" a Classic*. New York: Simon & Schuster, 2013.

Banet-Weiss, Sarah. *Empowered: Popular Feminism and Popular Misogyny*. Durham, NC: Duke University Press, 2018.

Banks, Miranda J. "*I Love Lucy*: The Writer-Producer." In *How to Watch Television*, 244–252. New York: New York University Press, 2013.

———. *The Writers: A History of American Screenwriters and Their Guild*. New Brunswick: Rutgers University Press, 2015.

Barlow, William. *Voice Over: The Making of Black Radio*. Philadelphia: Temple University Press, 1999.

Barnouw, Erik. *Tube of Plenty: The Evolution of American Television*, 2nd edition. New York: Oxford University Press, 1990.

Barthes, Roland. "Striptease." In *Mythologies*, translated by Richard Howard and Annette Lavers, 165–168. New York: Hill and Wang, 2012.

Basinger, Jeanine. *A Woman's View: How Hollywood Spoke to Women, 1930–1960*. New York: Alfred A. Knopf, 1993.

Battaglio, Stephen. *David Susskind: A Televised Life*. New York: St. Martin's Press, 2010.

Baughman, James L. *Same Time, Same Station: Creating American Television, 1948–1961*. Baltimore: Johns Hopkins University Press, 2007.

Beranger, Clara. "Feminine Sphere in the Field of Movies Is Large Indeed: Interview with Clara Beranger (1919)." In *The Red Velvet Seat*, edited by Antonia Lant and Ingrid Perez. New York: Verso, 2006.

Berg, Gertrude, with Cheney Berg. *Molly and Me: The Memoirs of Gertrude Berg*. New York: McGraw-Hill, 1961.

Berger, Daniel, and Steve Jajkowski (eds), *Chicago Television*. Charleston, SC: Arcadia Publishing, 2010.

Bergson, Henri. "Laughter," in *Comedy*, edited by Wylie Sypher, 61–190. Baltimore: Johns Hopkins University Press, 1956.

Berke, Annie. "Laura Petrie and Performance as Wifely Duty." *Flow: A Critical Forum on Media and Culture*. February 19, 2017.

Berlant, Lauren. *The Female Complaint*. Durham, NC: Duke University Press, 2008.

Blaché, Alice. "Woman's Place in Photoplay Production (1914)." In *The Red Velvet Seat*, edited by Antonia Lant and Ingrid Perez, 662–665. New York: Verso, 2006.

Boddy, William. *Fifties Television*. Urbana, IL: University of Illinois Press, 1990.

Bradley, Patricia. *Maintaining Separate Spheres: The Career of Margaret Cousins*. Paper presented at the Annual Meeting of the Association for Education in Journalism and Mass Communication, Memphis, 1985.

Bratslavsky, Lauren. "Recovered Visual Records and Expanded Histories: How 'Ethel and Albert' Broadens Sitcom History." Society of Cinema and Media Studies Annual Conference, March 28, 2015.

Brook, Vincent. "The Americanization of Molly: How Mid-Fifties TV Homogenized *The Goldbergs* (And Got 'Berg-larized' in the Process." *Cinema Journal*, 38, no. 4 (Summer, 1999): 45–67.

Brower, Jordan, and Josh Glick. "The Art and Craft of the Screen: Louis Reeves Harrison and the Moving Picture World." *Historical Journal of Film, Radio and Television* 33, no. 4 (2013): 533–551.

Butler, Judith. *Gender Trouble*. New York: Routledge, 2007.

Caesar, Sid. *Caesar's Hours: My Life in Comedy, with Love and Laughter*. New York: Public Affairs, 2003.

Caldwell, John Thornton. *Production Culture: Industrial Reflexivity and Critical Practice in Film and Television*. Durham, NC: Duke University Press, 2008.

Carr, John F. *H. Beam Piper: A Biography*. Jefferson, NC: McFarland Publishing, 2014.

Cassidy, Martha. *What Women Watched: Daytime Television in the 1950s*. Austin: University of Texas Press, 2005.

Clarke, Liz. "'No Accident of Good Fortune': Autobiographies and Personal Memoirs as Historical Documents in Screenwriting History." *Feminist Media Histories* 2, no. 1 (2016): 45–60.

Cobb, Shelley. "Adaptation, Fidelity, and Gendered Discourses." *Adaptation* 4, no. 2 (2011): 28–37.

Cohen, Lizabeth. *A Consumer's Republic: The Politics of Mass Consumption in Postwar America*. New York: Vintage, 2008.

Coontz, Stephanie. *A Strange Stirring: "The Feminine Mystique" and American Women at the Dawn of the 1960s*. New York: Basic Books, 2011.

Cooper, Mark Garrett. *Universal Women: Filmmaking and Institutional Change in Early Hollywood*. Urbana: University of Illinois Press, 2010.

Crafton, Donald. *The Talkies: American Cinema's Transition to Sound, 1926–1931*. Berkeley: University of California Press, 1997.

Cypert, Rick. *The Virtue of Suspense: The Life and Works of Charlotte Armstrong*. Selinsgrove, PA: Susquehanna University Press, 2008.

D'Acci, Julie. *Defining Women: Television and the Case of Cagney and Lacey*. Chapel Hill: University of North Carolina Press, 1994.

Davies, Margery. *Woman's Place Is at the Typewriter: Office Work and Office Workers, 1870–1930*. Philadelphia: Temple University Press, 1984.

Davis, Madelyn Pugh, with Bob Carroll Jr., *Laughing with Lucy: My Life with America's Leading Lady of Comedy*. Cincinnati, OH: Clerisy Press, 2007.

Delorme, Stéphane, Mathieu Macheret, Florence Maillard, and Stéphane du Mesnildot, "Alfred Hitchcock en dix episodes." *Cahiers du Cinéma* no. 702 (2014): 76–78.

Desjardins, Mary. *Recycling Stars: Female Film Stardom in the Age of Television and Radio*. Durham, NC: Duke University Press, 2015.

Dhoest, Alexander. "Breaking Boundaries in Television Historiography: Historical Research and the Television Archive, University of Reading, 9 January 2004." *Screen* 45, no. 3 (Autumn, 2004): 245–249.

Doane, Mary Ann. "Film and the Masquerade: Theorizing the Female Spectator." *Screen* 23, nos. 3–4 (1982): 74–88.

―――. "The 'Woman's Film': Possession and Address." In *Home Is Where the Heart Is: Studies in Melodrama and the Woman's Film*, edited by Christine Gledhill, 283–298. London: BFI Books, 1987.

Doherty, Thomas. *Cold War, Cool Medium: Television, McCarthyism, and American Culture*. New York: Columbia University Press, 2003.

Douglas, Ann. *The Feminization of American Culture*. New York: Knopf, 1977.

Douglas, Susan. *Where the Girls Are: Growing Up Female with the Mass Media*. New York: Times Books, 1995.

Dow, Bonnie. *Prime-Time Feminism: Television, Media Culture and the Women's Movement since 1970*. Philadelphia: University of Pennsylvania Press, 1996.

Edmondson, Madeleine, and David Rounds. *From Mary Noble to Mary Hartman: The Complete Soap Opera Book*. New York: Stein & Day, 1976.

Edwards, Rona. *I Liked It, Didn't Love It: Screenplay Development from the Inside Out*. Beverly Hills, CA: Edwards Skerbelis Entertainment, 2016.

Eggerz, Solveig. "Stock Figures in Jewish Folklore: Universal Yet Uniquely Jewish." *The American Council for Judaism*, Summer 1996.

Ehrenreich, Barbara. *The Hearts of Men: American Dreams and the Flight from Commitment*. New York: Anchor Books, 1983.

Empson, William. "Fool in *Lear*." *The Sewanee Review* (Spring, 1949): 177–214.

Endrijonas, Erika. "Processed Foods from Scratch: Cooking for a Family in the 1950s." In *Kitchen Culture in America*, edited by Sherrie A. Inness, 157–173. Philadelphia: University of Pennsylvania Press, 2000.

Epstein, Edward Jay. *The Big Picture: Money and Power in Hollywood*. New York: Random House, Inc., 2006.

Farber, David, and Beth Bailey, et al. *The Columbia Guide to America in the 1960s*. New York: Columbia University Press, 2001.

Finnie, Moira. "Joan Harrison: In Hitch's Shadow." *Movie Morlocks: Powered by TCM*, posted March 18, 2009, http://moviemorlocks.com/2009/03/18/joan-harrison-the-phantom-lady/.

Fiske, John. "Television: Polysemy and Popularity." *Critical Studies in Mass Communication* 3.4 (December 1986): 391–408.

Fortmueller, Kate. "Time's Up (Again?): Transforming Hollywood's Industrial Culture." *Media Industries* 6, no. 2 (2019), 1–16.

Foucault, Michel. "The Lives of Infamous Men." In *Power, Truth, Strategy*, 76–91. Sydney: Feral Publications, 1979.

Friedan, Betty. *The Feminine Mystique*. New York: W.W. Norton & Company, 1997.

Gaines, Jane. "Of Cabbages and Authors." In *Feminist Reader in Early Cinema*, edited by Jennifer M. Bean and Diane Negra, 88–118. Durham, NC: Duke University Press, 2002.

―――. *Pink-Slipped: What Happened to Women in the Silent Film Industry?* Urbana: University of Illinois Press, 2018.

Garcia-Johnson, Ronie-Richele. "Imogene Coca." In *Notable Hispanic American Women*, edited by Diane Telgen and Jim Kamp, 101–103. Detroit: Gale Research Inc., 1993.

Gledhill, Christine, and Julia Knight (eds), "Introduction." In *Doing Women's Film History: Reframing Cinemas, Past and Future*, 1–12. Urbana: University of Illinois Press, 2015.

Grams, Martin, and Patrik Wikstrom. *The Alfred Hitchcock Presents Companion*. Whiteford, MD: OTR Publishing, 2001.

Hall, Stuart. "Encoding/Decoding." In *Culture, Media, Language*, edited by Stuart Hall, Dorothy Hobson, Andrew Love, and Paul Willis, 128–138. London: Hutchinson, 1980.

Halper, Donna. *Invisible Stars: A Social History of Women in Broadcasting*. Armonk, NY: M.E. Sharpe, 2001.

———. "Speaking for Themselves: How Radio Brought Women into the Public Sphere." In *Radio Cultures: The Sound Medium in American Life*, edited by Michael C. Keith, 77–93. New York: Peter Lang, 2008.

Hastie, Amelie. *Cupboards of Curiosity: Women, Recollection, and Film History*. Durham, NC: Duke University Press, 2007.

Havens, Timothy, Amanda D. Lotz, and Serra Tinic. "Critical Media Industry Studies: A Research Approach." *Communication, Culture & Critique* 2 (2009): 234–253.

Hawes, William. *Filmed Television Drama, 1952–1958*. Jefferson, NC: McFarland & Company, Inc. 2002.

Hay, James. "Rereading Early Television Advertising: When Wasn't the Ad the Story?" *Journal of Film and Video* 41, no. 1 (Spring 1989): 4–20.

Henderson, Felicia D. "The Culture Behind Closed Doors: Issues of Gender and Race in the Writers' Room." *Cinema Journal* 50, no. 2 (Winter 2011): 145–152.

Hennefeld, Maggie. *Specters of Slapstick and Silent Film Comediennes*. New York: Columbia University Press, 2018.

Hill, Erin. *Never Done: A History of Women's Work in Media Production*. New Brunswick, NJ: Rutgers University Press, 2016.

Hilmes, Michele. "Never Ending Story: Authorship, Seriality, and the Radio Writers Guild." In *A Companion to Media Authorship*, edited by Jonathan Gray and Derek Johnson, 181–199. Oxford: Wiley-Blackwell, 2013.

———. *Radio Voices: American Broadcasting, 1922–1952*. Minneapolis: University of Minnesota Press, 1997.

Hoberek, Andrew. *The Twilight of the Middle Class: Post-World War II American Fiction and White-Collar Work*. Princeton, NJ: Princeton University Press, 2005.

Hoerle, Helen Christene, and Florence B. Saltzburg. *The Girl and the Job*. New York: Henry Holt and Company, 1919.

Hollis, Tim. *Ain't That a Knee-Slapper: Rural Comedy in the Twentieth Century*. Jackson: University Press of Mississippi, 2008.

Horowitz, Daniel. *Betty Friedan and the Making of "The Feminine Mystique."* Amherst: University of Massachusetts Press, 1998.

Huyssen, Andreas. "Mass Culture as Woman: Modernism's Other." In *Studies in Entertainment: Critical Approaches to Mass Culture*, edited by Tania Modleski, 188–208. Bloomington: Indiana University Press, 1986.

Irvin, Richard. *George Burns Television Productions, The Series and Pilots, 1950–1981*. Jefferson, NC: McFarland & Company, 2014.

Jacoby, Lois. "The New York Market." In *TV and Screenwriting*, edited by Lola Goelet Yoakem. Berkeley: University of California Press, 1958.

Kallen, Lucille. *Out There, Somewhere!* New York: The Macmillan Company, 1964.

Kanfer, Stefan. *Ball of Fire: The Tumultuous Life and Comic Art of Lucille Ball*. London: Faber, 2003.

Kemper, Tom. *Hidden Talent: The Emergence of Hollywood Agents*. Berkeley: University of California Press, 2010.

Kisseloff, Jeff. *The Box: An Oral History of Television, 1920–1961*. New York: Viking, 1995.

Kraszewski, Jon. *The New Entrepreneurs: An Institutional History of Television Anthology Writers*. Middletown, CT: Wesleyan University Press, 2010. Kindle.

Lafferty, William. "A Note on Alternative Sources of Television Programming," In *Private Screenings: Television and the Female Consumer*, edited by Lynn Spigel and Denise Mann, 273–276. Minneapolis: University of Minnesota Press, 1992.

Landrigan, Linda (ed). "Introduction." In *Alfred Hitchcock's Mystery Magazine Presents Fifty Years of Crime and Suspense*. New York: Pegasus Books, 2006.

Lane, Christina. *Phantom Lady: Hollywood Producer Joan Harrison, The Forgotten Woman Behind Hitchcock*. Chicago: Chicago Review Press, 2020.

Lange, Regina Christiane. "Positioning Gina Kaus: A Transnational Career from Vienna Novelist and Playwright to Hollywood Scriptwriter." PhD diss. University of Iowa, 2012.

LaPlace, Maria. "Producing and Consuming the Woman's Film: Discursive Struggle in *Now, Voyager*." In *Home Is Where the Heart Is: Studies in Melodrama and the Woman's Film*, edited by Christine Gledhill, 138–166. London: BFI Books, 1987.

Lavin, Marilyn. "Creating Consumers in the 1930s: Irna Phillips and the Radio Soap Opera." *Journal of Consumer Research* 22, no. 1 (June 1995): 75–89.

Leitch, Thomas M. "The Outer Circle: Hitchcock on Television." In *Alfred Hitchcock: Centenary Essays*, 59–71. London: BFI, 1999.

Levine, Elana. *Her Stories: Daytime Soap Opera and US Television History*. Durham, NC: Duke University Press, 2020.

Liebman, Nina C. *Living Room Lectures: The Fifties Family in Film and Television*. Austin: University of Texas Press, 1995.

Lipsitz, George. "The Meaning of Memory: Family, Class, and Ethnicity in Early Network Television." In *Time Passages: Collective Memory and American Popular Culture*, 39–75. Minneapolis: University of Minnesota Press, 1990.

Litvak, Joseph. *The Un-Americans: Jews, the Blacklist, and Stoolpigeon Culture*. Durham, NC: Duke University Press, 2009.

LoMonaco, Martha Schmoyer. *Every Day a Broadway Revue*. New York: Greenwood Press, 1992.

Lopate, Carol. "Daytime Television: You'll Never Want to Leave Home." *Radical America* 2 (1977), 33–51.

Loviglio, Jason. "Reading Judy and Jane in the Archive." *Journal of Radio & Audio Media* 23, no. 2 (2016), 306–322.

MacDonald, Dwight. "A Theory of Mass Culture." *Diogenes* 3 (Summer 1953): 10–17.

Mann, Denise. *Hollywood Independents: The Postwar Talent Takeover.* Minneapolis: University of Minnesota Press, 2008.

———. "The Spectacularization of Everyday Life: Recycling Hollywood Stars and Fans in Early Television Variety Shows." In *Private Screenings: Television and the Female Consumer,* edited by Lynn Spigel and Denise Mann, 41–69. Minneapolis: University of Minnesota Press, 1992.

Marsh, Margaret. "Suburban Men and Masculine Domesticity, 1870–1915." *American Quarterly* 40 (June 1988): 165–186.

Martin, Catherine. "In Their Own Little Corner: The Gendered Sidelining of NBC's Information Department." *Journal of Radio & Audio Media* 26, no. 1 (2019): 88–103.

Matelski, Elizabeth M. *Reducing Bodies: Mass Culture and the Female Figure in Postwar America.* New York: Routledge, 2017.

Mathis, June. "The Feminine Mind in Picture Making." In *Red Velvet Seat,* edited by Antonia Lant and Ingrid Perez, 663–665. New York: Verso, 2006.

May, Elaine Tyler. *Homeward Bound: American Families in the Cold War Era.* 20th Anniversary Edition. New York: Basic Books, 1990.

McCarthy, Anna. *The Citizen Machine: Governing by Television in 1950s America.* New York: The New Press, 2010.

McCarty, John, and Brian Kelleher. *Alfred Hitchcock Presents: An Illustrated Guide to the Ten-Year Television Career of the Master of Suspense.* New York: St. Martin's Press, 1985.

McCracken, Allison. "Scary Women and Scarred Men: *Suspense,* Gender Trouble, and Postwar Change, 1942–1950." In *Radio Reader: Essays in the Cultural History of Radio,* edited by Michele Hilmes and Jason Loviglio, 183–207. New York: Routledge, 2002.

McGilligan, Patrick. *Funny Man: Mel Brooks.* New York: Harper, 2019.

McHugh, Kathleen Anne. *American Domesticity: From How-To Manual to Hollywood Melodrama.* New York: Oxford University Press, 1999.

McNeil, Alex. *Total Television: The Comprehensive Guide to Programming,* 4th ed. New York: Penguin, 1996.

Mellencamp, Patricia. "Situation Comedy, Feminism, and Freud: Discourses of Gracie and Lucy." In *Studies in Entertainment: Critical Approaches to Mass Culture,* ed. Tania Modleski, 80–95. Bloomington: Indiana University Press, 1986.

Méranger, Thierry. "Norman Lloyd présente: Entretien avec Norman Lloyd." *Cahiers du Cinéma,* no. 702 (2014): 81–83.

Meyerowitz, Joanne. "Introduction." In *Not June Cleaver: Women and Gender in Postwar America, 1945–1960,* 1–16. Philadelphia: Temple University Press, 1994.

Meyers, Cynthia B. "The Problems with Sponsorship in US Broadcasting, 1930s–1950s: Perspectives from the Advertising Industry." *Historical Journal of Film, Radio and Television* 31, no. 3 (September 2011): 355–372.

Miller, Quinlan. *Camp TV: Trans Gender Queer Sitcom History.* Durham, NC: Duke University Press, 2019.

Modleski, Tania. *Loving with a Vengeance: Mass-Produced Fantasies for Women,* 2nd ed. New York: Routledge, 2008.

———. "Suspicion: Collusion and Resistance in the Work of Hitchcock's Female Collaborators." In *Blackwell Reference Online: A Companion to Alfred Hitchcock,* edited by Thomas Leitch and Leland Poague, 162–180. Malden, MA: Wiley-Blackwell, 2011.

Morin, Edgar. *The Stars.* Translated by Richard Howard. Minneapolis: University of Minnesota Press, 2005.

Morey, Anne. "Elinor Glyn as Hollywood Labourer." *Film History: An International Journal* 18, no. 2 (2006): 110–118.

———. "'Have You the Power?' The Palmer Photoplay Corporation and the Film Viewer/Author in the 1920s." *Film History* 9, no. 3 (1997), 300–319.

———. "Would You Be Ashamed to Let Them See What You Have Written? The Gendering of Photoplaywrights, 1913–1923." *Tulsa Studies in Women's Literature* 17, no. 1 (Spring, 1998): 83–99.

Morreale, Joanne. *The Donna Reed Show.* Detroit: Wayne State University Press, 2012.

Mulvey, Laura. "Visual Pleasure and Narrative Cinema," *Screen* 16.3 (Autumn 1975), 6–18.

Murray, Susan. "Ethnic Masculinity and Early Television's Video Star." *Cinema Journal* 42, no. 1 (Fall 2002): 97–119.

———. *Hitch Your Antennae to the Stars: Early Television and Broadcast Stardom.* New York: Routledge, 1999.

Muscio, Giuliana. "Clara, Ouida, Beulah, et al.: Women Screenwriters in American Silent Cinema." In *Reclaiming the Archive: Feminism and Film History,* edited by Vicki Callahan, 289–308. Detroit: Wayne State University Press, 2010.

Neuhaus, Jessmyn. "Women and Cooking in Marital Sex Manuals." In *Kitchen Culture in America,* ed. Sherrie A. Inness, 95–117. Philadelphia: University of Pennsylvania Press, 2000.

Neuwirth, Allan. *They'll Never Put That on the Air.* New York: Allworth Press, 2006.

Newcomb, Horace, and Paul M. Hirsch. "Television as a Cultural Forum." In *Television: The Critical View,* 6th ed., edited by Horace Newcomb, 561–573. New York: Oxford University Press, 2000.

Newman, Michael Z., and Elana Levine. *Legitimating Television: Media Convergence and Cultural Status.* New York: Routledge, 2012.

Ngai, Sianne. *Our Aesthetic Categories: Zany, Cute, Interesting.* Cambridge, MA: Harvard University Press, 2012.

———. *Ugly Feelings.* Cambridge, MA: Harvard University Press, 2005.

Nochimson, Martha. *No End to Her: Soap Opera and the Female Subject.* Berkeley: University of California Press, 1992.

O'Dell, Cary. "Kinescope." In *The Encyclopedia of Television,* 2nd ed, edited by Horace Newcomb, 1263–1264. New York: Routledge, 2013.

———. *Women Pioneers in Television.* Jefferson, NC: McFarland & Company, 1997.

Olsson, Jan. *Hitchcock à la Carte*. Durham, NC: Duke University Press, 2015.

Parkin, Katherine. "Campbell's Soup and the Long Shelf Life of Traditional Gender Roles." In *Kitchen Culture in America*, edited by Sherrie A. Inness, 51–67. Philadelphia: University of Pennsylvania Press, 2000.

Parrish, James Robert. *It's Good to Be the King*. Hoboken, NJ: John Wiley & Sons, Inc., 2008.

Patterson, James T. *Grand Expectations: The United States, 1945–1974*. New York: Oxford University Press, 1996.

Peril, Lynn. *College Girls: Bluestockings, Sex Kittens, and Coeds, Then and Now*. New York: W.W. Norton, 2006.

———. *Swimming in the Steno Pool: A Retro Guide to Making It in the Office*. New York: W.W. Norton, 2011.

Perkins, Claire, and Michele Schreiber. "Independent Women: From Film to Television." *Feminist Media Histories* 19.7 (2019), 919–927.

Pondillo, Bob. "Racial Discourse and Censorship on NBC-TV." *Journal of Popular Film and Television* 33, no. 2 (2005): 102–114.

Press, Joy. *Stealing the Show: How Women Are Revolutionizing Television*. New York: Atria Books, 2018.

Rhimes, Shonda. *Year of Yes: How to Dance It Out, Stand in the Sun, and Be Your Own Person*. New York: Simon & Schuster, 2015.

Rowe, Kathleen. *The Unruly Woman: Gender and the Genres of Laughter*. Austin: University of Texas Press, 1995.

Samuel, Lawrence R. *Brought to You By: Postwar Television Advertising and the American Dream*. Austin: University of Texas Press, 2001.

Schatz, Thomas. "Film Studies, Cultural Studies, and Media Industries Studies." *Media Industries* 1, no. 1 (2014): 39–43.

———. *The Genius of the System: Hollywood Filmmaking in the Studio Era*. Austin: University of Texas Press, 1988.

Sekula, Allan. "The Body and the Archive." *October* 39 (Winter 1986): 3–64.

Seiter, Ellen. "'To Teach and to Sell': Irna Phillips and Her Sponsors, 1930–1954." *Journal of Film and Video* 41, no. 1 (Spring 1989): 21–35.

Seldes, Gilbert. *The Great Audience*. Whitefish, MT: Literary Licensing, 2012.

Sennett, Ted. *Your Show of Shows*. Revised edition. New York: Applause Books, 2002.

Smith, Glenn D. Jr. *"Something on My Own": Gertrude Berg and American Broadcasting, 1929–1956*. Syracuse, NY: Syracuse University Press, 2007.

Smukler, Maya Montañez. *Liberating Hollywood: Women Directors and the Feminist Reform of 1970s American Cinema*. New Brunswick, NJ: Rutgers University Press, 2018.

Smyth, J. E. *Nobody's Girl Friday: The Women Who Ran Hollywood*. New York: Oxford University Press, 2018.

Snelson, Tim. *Phantom Ladies: Hollywood Horror and the Home Front*. New Brunswick, NJ: Rutgers University Press, 2015.

Solomon, Matthew. "Adapting 'Radio's Perfect Script': 'Sorry, Wrong Number' and *Sorry, Wrong Number*." *Quarterly Review of Film & Video* 16, no. 1 (1997): 23–40.

Spigel, Lynn. "From Domestic Space to Outer Space: The 1960s Fantastic Family Sitcom." In *Welcome to the Dreamhouse: Popular Media and Postwar Suburbs*, 107–140. Durham, NC: Duke University Press, 2001.

———. "Installing the Television Set." In *Private Screenings: Television and the Female Consumer*, edited by Lynn Spigel and Denise Mann, 3–39. Minneapolis: University of Minnesota Press, 1992.

———. *Make Room for TV: Television and the Family Ideal in Postwar America*. Chicago: University of Chicago Press, 1992.

———. "The Suburban Home Companion: Television and the Neighborhood Ideal in Postwar America." In *Welcome to the Dreamhouse: Popular Media and Postwar Suburbs*, 31–59. Durham, NC: Duke University Press, 2001.

———. "White Flight." In *Welcome to the Dreamhouse: Popular Media and Postwar Suburbs*. Durham, NC: Duke University Press, 2001.

Spigel, Lynn, and Denise Mann, (eds). *Private Screenings: Television and the Female Consumer*. Minneapolis: University of Minneapolis Press, 1992.

Stabile, Carol. *The Broadcast 41: Women and the Anti-Communist Blacklist*. Cambridge, MA: MIT Press, 2018.

Stamp, Shelley. *Lois Weber in Hollywood*. Berkeley: University of California Press, 2018.

———. *Movie-Struck Girls*. Princeton, NJ: Princeton University Press, 2000.

Stempel, Tom. *Storytellers to the Nation: A History of American Television Writing*. Syracuse, NY: Syracuse University Press, 1996.

Sternberg, Joel. "Chicago School of Television." In *Encyclopedia of Television*, 2nd ed., edited by Horace Newcomb. New York: Routledge, 2013.

Taylor, Ella. *Prime-Time Families: Television Culture in Post-War America*. Berkeley: University of California Press, 1991.

Tenzer, Livia, and Jean Casella. "Publisher's Foreword: Women Write Pulp." In *Bunny Lake Is Missing*, by Evelyn Piper. New York: Feminist Press, 2004.

Thurber, James. "Soapland." In *The Beast in Me and Other Animals*. Mattituck, NY: Aeonian Press, 1973.

Tueth, Michael. *Laughter in the Living Room: Television Comedy and the American Home Audience*. New York: Peter Lang, 2005.

Van den Oever, Roel. *Mama's Boy: Momism and Homophobia in Postwar Culture*. New York: Palgrave Macmillan, 2012.

Verma, Neil. "Radio's Oblong Blur: On the Corwinesque in the Critical Ear." In *Anatomy of Sound: Norman Corwin and Media Authorship*, edited by J. Smith and N. Verma, 37–52. Oakland: University of California Press, 2016.

Waldron, Ann. "Charlotte Armstrong." *Journal of Popular Culture* 5, no. 2 (Fall 1971): 435–445.

Waterman, David. *Hollywood's Road to Riches*. Cambridge, MA: Harvard University Press, 2005.

Weinman, Sarah. *Troubled Daughters, Twisted Wives: Stories from the Trailblazers of Domestic Suspense*. New York: Penguin, 2013.

Weiss, Jessica. "She Also Cooks: Gender, Domesticity, and Public Life in Oakland, California, 1957–1959." In *Kitchen Culture in America*, edited by Sherrie A. Inness, 211–226. Philadelphia: University of Pennsylvania Press, 2000.

Weiss, Margaret. *The TV Writer's Guide*. New York: Pellegrini & Cudahy, 1952.

Wheatley, Helen. *Gothic Television*. Manchester, UK: Manchester University Press, 2006.

Wilk, Max. *The Golden Age of Television: Notes from the Survivors*. Chicago: Silver Spring Press, 1999.

Williams, Sonja D. *Word Warrior: Richard Durham, Radio, and Freedom*. Urbana: University of Illinois Press, 2015.

Wojcik, Pamela Robertson. *The Apartment Plot: Urban Living in American Film and Popular Culture, 1945–1975*. Durham, NC: Duke University Press, 2010.

Worland, Rick. "Sign-Posts Up Ahead: *The Twilight Zone, The Outer Limits,* and TV Political Fantasy 1959–1965." *Science Fiction Studies* 23, no. 1 (March 1996): 103–122.

Young, Philip. "The Mother of Us All: Pocahontas Reconsidered." *Kenyon Review* 24, no. 3 (Summer 1962): 391–415.

Index

Founded in 1893,
UNIVERSITY OF CALIFORNIA PRESS
publishes bold, progressive books and journals
on topics in the arts, humanities, social sciences,
and natural sciences—with a focus on social
justice issues—that inspire thought and action
among readers worldwide.

The UC PRESS FOUNDATION
raises funds to uphold the press's vital role
as an independent, nonprofit publisher, and
receives philanthropic support from a wide
range of individuals and institutions—and from
committed readers like you. To learn more, visit
ucpress.edu/supportus.